Diaspora Missiology

Theory, Methodology, and Practice

Enoch Wan

Institute of Diaspora Studies – USA

Copyright © 2011 by IDS-U.S.
Copyright © Second Edition - 2014 by IDS-USA

All rights reserved. No part of this work may be reproduced or transmitted in any form or by any means, electronics or mechanical, including photocopying and recording, without the prior permission of the publisher. The only exceptions are brief quotations in printed reviews.

This book is the first in a series on Diaspora Studies.
Published by the Institute of Diaspora Studies of USA (IDS-USA)
Western Seminary
5511 SE Hawthorne Blvd., Portland, OR 97215, USA.

Diaspora Missiology: Theory, Methodology, and Practice

Enoch Wan, Editor

ISBN: 978-1468117455

For more information on IDS-USA at Western Seminary or Enoch Wan, please visit the following sites:

- www.westernseminary.edu/diaspora
- www.enochwan.com
- www.globalmissiology.org

Scripture for chapter 4 taken from the HOLY BIBLE, NEW INTERNATIONAL VERSION®. Copyright © 1973, 1978, 1984 by International Bible Society. Used by permission of Zondervan Publishing House. All rights reserved.

Scripture for chapter 5 taken from the HOLY BIBLE, NEW AMERICAN STANDARD VERSION®. Copyright © 1960,1962,1963,1968,1971, 1972, 1973,1975,1977,1995 by The Lockman Foundation. Used by permission.

CONTENTS

CONTENTS iii
FIGURES v
PREFACE TO THE SECOND EDITION vii
FORWARD TO THE FIRST EDITION (2011) viii
CONTRIBUTORS xi

PART 1 – ABOUT THIS BOOK

Chapter 1 – Introduction 3

PART 2 – THEORY

Chapter 2 – The Phenomenon of Diaspora 13

Chapter 3 – Theorizing Diaspora 23

Chapter 4 – Exploring the Major Dispersion Terms and Realities in the Bible 35

Chapter 5 – Diaspora Distinctives: The Jewish Diaspora Experience
    in the Old Testament 53

Chapter 6 – Diaspora and Relocation as Divine Impetus for Witness
    in the Early Church 87

PART 3 – METHODOLOGY

Chapter 7 – Managerial Missiology – The Popular Paradigm 111

Chapter 8 – Diaspora Missiology – A Contemporary Paradigm for the 21st Century 123

Chapter 9 – Diaspora Missiology in Progress 136

Chapter 10 – Interdisciplinary Research Methodology for Diaspora Missiology 148

PART 4 – PRACTICE

Chapter 11 – Diachronic Overview of Christian Missions to Diaspora Groups 163

Chapter 12 – Demographic Reality of Diaspora and the Strategy
    of Diaspora Missions 177

Chapter 13 – Relational Paradigm for Practicing Diaspora Missions in the
    21st Century.. 191

Chapter 14 – Diaspora Missions, Strategic Stewardship and
    Strategic Partnership.. 199

Chapter 15 – Case Study 1: Diaspora Jews.. 205

Chapter 16 – Case Study 2: Missiological Implications of Chinese Christians
    in Diaspora... 229

Chapter 17 – Case Study 3: Missions among the Urban Muslim Diaspora
    in the West 247

Chapter 18 – Case Study 4: Reflections of a Church Planter among Diaspora Groups
    in Metro-Chicago: Pursuing Cruciformity in Diaspora Missions 259

Chapter 19 – Case Study 5: Diaspora Missions in Minnesota: Local Actions
    with Global Implications 285

PART 5 – CONCLUSION

Chapter 20 – Conclusion 311

Epilogue.. 315
Bibliography 317
Resources 349
Selected Publications & Presentations on "Diaspora Missiology"
    by Enoch Wan 359

FIGURES

Figure 1.1 – Diaspora Ministry and Missions in DMP 8

Figure 2.1 – Patterns of Human Migration 17

Figure 2.2 – The Evolution of Global Bilateral Migration 1960-2000 17

Figure 2.3 – Numbers of International Migrants by Origin and Destination, 1990-2013 18

Figure 3.1 – "Intervening Obstacles" in Everett S. Lee's Model 26

Figure 3.2 – Chain Migration and Network 28

Figure 5.1 – Old Testament Trajectory of Israel's Experience of Diaspora 56

Figure 5.2 – Abraham: Diaspora Ascriptions and Focus 57

Figure 5.3 – Diaspora Characteristics of the Hebrews in Egypt and Babylon 64

Figure 5.4 – Factors Contributing to the Revitalization of Natal Identity among the Jewish Diaspora in Babylon and Persia 79

Figure 7.1 – Managerial Missiology Paradigm (MMP) 113

Figure 8.1 – Four Dimensions of Diaspora Missiology 124

Figure 8.2 – "Managerial" & "Diaspora" Paradigms Compared 128

Figure 8.3 – The concept and practice of "*with*" approach 133

Figure 10.1 – Migration Theories across Disciplines 154

Figure 10.2 – Interdisciplinary Research Methodology - "Missions *to* the Diaspora" 155

Figure 10.3 – Interdisciplinary Research Methodology for "Missions *through* the Diaspora" 156

Figure 10.4 – Interdisciplinary Research Methodology for "Missions *by and beyond* the Diaspora" 157

Figure 10.5 Interdisciplinary Research Methodology for "Missions *with* the Diaspora" 158

Figure 11.1 – – Scattering (Dispersion) in the Old Testament 164

Figure 11.2 – Gathering (Calling) in the Old Testament 164

Figure 11.3 – Scattering (Dispersion) in the New Testament 165

Figure 11.4 – Gathering (Calling, Covenant, Ecclesiology) in the New Testament ... 165

Figure 11.5 – History of Humaity in Lineal Progression 172

Figure 11.6 – Gathering and Scattering: Cyclical Development 173

Figure 12.1 – Religious composition of international migrants 181

Figure 12.1 – Opportunity: Working with the Diaspora 183

Figure 12.2 – "Missions to the Diaspora"   as "Mission at Our Doorstep" (Wan 2007a:7) 186

Figure 13.1 – Hiebert's "Critical Realism" vis-a-vis   Wan's "Relational Realism" (Wan 2006:2) 194

Figure 13.2 – Relational Paradigm: Synthesizing Diaspora Missiology & Diaspora Missions 197

Figure 14.1 – Partnership in light of the Trinity 200

Figure 15.1 – Demographics of the Jewish Diaspora 210

Figure 18.1 – Major biblicalMotifs of Diaspora Missions Theology 266

Figure 18.2 – Self-Assessment Questions 282

Figure 18.3 – Evaluating Cruciformity 283

PREFACE TO THE SECOND EDITION

Since the release of the first edition in 2011, there has been growing interest in diaspora missiology - an emerging topic of missiological inquiry. The purposes of issuing this second edition are two-fold: to incorporate feedbacks to the first edition and to update the content with pertinent information for readers and researchers. There are substantial revisions to Part 2 and Part 3 and alterations to Part 4.

A major change in Part 2 and Part 3 is as follows: what was labeled "traditional missiology" in the first edition has been replaced by "managerial missiology & practice." Instead of comparing and contrasting dichotomistically "traditional missiology" with "diaspora missiology" in the first edition; the characteristics of "diaspora missiology" are described in the second edition as an updated strategy due to the demographic reality of diaspora and the geo-dynamic shift of global Christianity in the 21st century. The change came as a result of the most recent offering of the course "diaspora missiology"[2] at Western Seminary (April 29-May 3, 2013). Moreover, the strategy of "missions *with* the diaspora" has been added to become the fourth element in diaspora strategy. More explanation and further elaboration will be found in Part 2 and Part 3.

In this revised edition, case studies in Part 4 have been reduced from eight to five. The reason is that each of the three case studies removed from the 1st edition has been expanded to become a monograph in the IDS-USA Series as listed below:
- 2013 on Ghanaian diaspora -- *Scattered Africans Keep Coming*. Yaw Attah Edu-Bekoe and Enoch Wan. (Spring 2013)
- 2014 on Vietnamese diaspora -- *Mobilizing Vietnamese Diaspora for the Kingdom*. Enoch Wan and Thanh Trung Le (Spring 2014)
- 2014 on Sri Lankan diaspora – *Wandering Jews and Scattered Sri Lankans: Understanding Sri Lankan Diaspora in the GCC Region Through the Lens of OT Jewish Diaspora.* Enoch Wan and Ted Rebush (Spring 2014)

FORWARD TO THE FIRST EDITION (2011)

Michael Pocock, D.Miss.
Senior Professor Emeritus, Adjunct Professor, Dallas Theological Seminary

Diaspora Missiology is a first in evangelical circles. Secular authors have chronicled the phenomenon of global migration. An entire issue of *Missiology*, (xxxi, Jan. 2003) was devoted to migration, and Dr. Wan and Michael Pocock (2009) have edited a work on *Missions from the Majority World* (2009) but Enoch Wan has been in the vanguard of what today we may call "the diaspora missions movement." He is well known through his leadership of the Evangelical Missiological Society, and similar study and professional groups in North America and Asia. He is himself a product and participant of the Chinese *diaspora*, an experience involving both the positive and negative polarities of this phenomenon. He has participated, inspired and written extensively for consultations on the missional implications of the accelerated and expanding movement of peoples across the globe. *Diaspora* missions have become the focus of significant gatherings since the Lausanne consultation at Pattaya, 2004: Edmonton, Alberta, in 2006, and at Lausanne, Cape Town 2010. Enoch Wan has been a major contributor to all of these gatherings.

In 2006, I spent a week with Enoch at the Overseas Missionary Study Center in New Haven, CT. Both of us were on sabbatical. I realized that what I was researching as "Migratory Missions," was the same as Enoch's devoted interest in "Diaspora Missiology," the present focus of this volume. The latter term has become the accepted term for the interdisciplinary study of the missionary implications of this incredibly significant movement of peoples. *Diaspora Missiology* is the first full-length exposition of the discipline. It represents exactly what missiology is all about, the integration of insights from the social studies with the biblical and theological foundations behind the practice of mission. It serves as a corrective to managerial missiology, pointing the way to a missiology more suited to the contemporary global reality.

Enoch Wan is the editor of *Diaspora Missiology*, which is intended to be the first of three volumes on the issue. In addition to serving as editor, Enoch is the author of ten chapters, with extremely well researched and written studies of the *diasporic* movement of the peoples in extra-biblical contexts. Narry Santos explains the biblical terms relating to *diaspora* in Old and New Testaments. Ted Rubesh, veteran church planter and professor based in Sri Lanka, expounds on diaspora movements in the Old Testament; Craig Ott in the New

Testament. The conclusion of all three is inescapable: God is orchestrating both the movement of Israel and the Church to bring his people and his blessing to the peoples of the world. God does this either through placing his people into the context of unreached peoples or to draw hitherto unreached peoples into the orbit of God's people, Israel and the Church. This was the very point made by the Apostle Paul in his Areopagus speech (Acts 17), and which Joseph had made centuries earlier in his address to his brothers in Egypt (Gen. 45:4-9).

Diaspora Missiology is divided into three major divisions: Theory, Methodology, and Practice. The last division contains twelve chapters. Eight are case studies of ministry by Majority World writers covering ministry in *diaspora* movements to and from Asia, the Middle East, Latin America, Africa, Europe, and North America.

The point of this work is to lay a basis for and show how *diaspora* missiology differs from managerial missiology. It sets the stage for further focus on the ways ministry in the context of particular ethnic or regional movements will require an approach to missions that differs from traditional mission practice and preparation. The present and future reality of accelerated human movement through international business, labor, study, and as refugees from persecution and instability means that we are truly now engaging in missions without borders.

The vastly increased missionary potential and engagement of churches in what Philip Jenkins has termed "the Global South" (Jenkins, 2006) can probably only be fully realized through appropriate biblical, spiritual and intercultural preparation. The Filipino reality treated by Lius Pantoja, Jr., Sadiri Joy Tira, and Enoch Wan (Eds.) in *Scattered: The International Filipino Diaspora Movement* (2004) was followed up by a practical manual for evangelical Filipinos planning on overseas employment entitled *Worker to Witness: Becoming an Overseas Filipino Worker* (Manzano and Solina, 2007). These works, coupled with *Diaspora Missiology* show the necessity of networking, encouraging, and giving pastoral care to Christian workers within the various *diasporas*. This is the only way to maximize the presence of so many Christians among the international labor force. In 2011 this movement involves some 215 million people, including more than 80% of the peoples present in the Gulf States of the Middle East. About 10 million Filipinos live or work outside their country and millions from other countries have migrated within their own countries or abroad in search of employment. Those who take overseas employment leave behind families with one or both parents absent and children cared for by grandparents, aunts and uncles, all of whom need a new kind of pastoral care.

In addition to the theoretical and methodological components of *Diaspora Missiology*, the case studies make a valuable contribution. The Jewish *diaspora*, a reality since the inter-testamental period, remains a globally challenging phenomenon, addressed by Tuvya Zaretski.

The global Chinese *diaspora*, also a reality in North America, is an eye-opener from Kim-Kong Chan. Moussa Bongoyok explains the Muslim *diaspora* and Yaw Attah Edu-Bekoe the presence of Ghanaians in the U.S. and Than Trung Le shows how Vietnamese are faring in North American communities and Geoff Hart the massive Hispanic presence and possibilities in this country. Cody Lorence and Randy Mitchell explain local church ministries in Illinois and Minnesota, proving that ministry today can be nothing less than "glocal" in nature.

Diaspora Missiology is a great text for what must surely be new courses in seminaries and institutions preparing workers not simply for *foreign* missions, but global ministry in the contemporary reality where multicultural and multi-faith communities are the rule in both urban and rural communities world-wide. Missiologists, mission trainers, and anyone seriously committed to understanding and engaging the global phenomenon of relocating people needs this book. I salute Enoch Wan for the contribution he is making, not only in this volume, but through his Institute for Diaspora Mission Studies at Western Theological Seminary and constant encouragement of fellow missiologists.

Works cited:

Lius Pantoja, Jr., Sadiri Joy Tira, and Enoch Wan, Eds. (2004), *Scattered: The Filipino Global Presence.* Manila, Philippines: LifeChange Publications. http://www.fin-online.org

Jenkins, Philip. (2006) *The New Faces of Christianity: Believing the Bible in the Global South.* New York: Oxford University Press.

Manzano, Jojo and Joy C. Solina. (2007) *Worker To Witness: Becoming an Overseas Filipino Worker.* Makati City, Philippines: Church Strengthening Ministries. www.csm-publishing.org

Wan, Enoch and Michael Pocock, (Eds.) *Missions from the Majority World: Progress, Challenges and Case Studies.* (2009) No. 17, Series of the Evangelical Missiological Society. Pasadena: William. Carey Library.

CONTRIBUTORS

Moussa Bongoyok
President and CEO, Francophone University of International Development; faculty member, Biola University, California. He was born in Cameroon and holds a Ph.D. in Intercultural Studies from Fuller Theological Seminary.

Randy G Mitchell
International Director, OWM (One World Missions). He has served as pastor and missionary for the last 22 years. As the international Director of OWM he works with churches and church networks in the US and around the world to train, mobilize, and equip leaders for missions in over 40 nations.

Ted Rubesh
Professor, Colombo Theological Seminary and Sri Lanka Bible College. He is a D.Miss. candidate at Western Seminary completing a dissertation on Sri Lankan diaspora.

Cody C. Lorance
Senior Pastor and Church Planting Leader, Trinity International Baptist Mission (Carol Stream, IL). He is currently serving with the Chicago Metro Baptist Association in the Chicago metro area among diaspora peoples

Craig Ott
Associate Professor of Mission and Intercultural Studies, Trinity Evangelical Divinity School (Deerfield, USA); co-author of *Encountering Theology of Mission* and *Global Church Planting*.

Narry F. Santos
Church planter, Toronto, Canada; author of *Slave of all, the paradox of authority and servanthood in the Gospel of Mark*; co-author of "A Missio-Relational Reading of Mark," *Occasional Bulletin*: Volume 24, #2 - Spring, 2011.

Tuvya Zaretsky
President, International Coordinating Committee of the Lausanne Consultation on Jewish Evangelism; Director, Staff Training and Development and Board Chair, Jews for Jesus in Israel; Director, MA - Jewish Evangelism Program at Western Seminary. He graduated with a D.Miss. dissertation on diaspora Jews.

Part 1
ABOUT THIS BOOK

Please read this part before proceeding to other chapters.

Chapter 1

Introduction

Enoch Wan

Background

The movement of people spatially at the scale unprecedented in human history is a global phenomenon of the 21st century. Among peoples on the move are those who take up residence away from their places of origin, the *"diaspora,"*[1] and they are the focus of this study. People who move temporarily from their places of origin within a country (e.g., students for academic pursuit, migrant workers from rural areas to urban centers for employment, travelers or tourists, airline crew members, internally displaced persons) and people who go abroad temporarily (e.g. student, diplomat, embassy staff, military personnel) are not the primary focus of this study, for they belong to the category of "quasi-diaspora."

This book is an interdisciplinary study on the 21st century demographic reality that resulted in the development of "diaspora missiology" as an emerging missiological paradigm which subsequently brought about the practice of "diaspora missions" as a contemporary mission strategy. It is an introductory study on the theory, methodology, and practice of "diaspora missiology."

The changing landscape of the 21st century, namely, the global phenomena of large-scale diaspora and Christendom's shifting center of gravity, requires serious reflections on the missiological conceptualizations and strategies for Christian missions. Unprecedented diaspora phenomena in human history take place in China and India. Reaching the large influx of diaspora in urban centers

---

[1]"Diaspora" is different from "migration," according to Brah (1996), Cohen (1997b) and Zhang (2011) in that members of a diaspora share a certain collective consciousness of group distinctiveness and memory of homeland, and social solidarity in a new/host country. "Migration" refers to people moving within the political (state) boundary. "Emigration" is leaving one's native country (going beyond its boundary), similar to "immigration," with the difference that "immigration" is viewed from the perspective of the country of origin. boundary), similar to "immigration," with the difference that "immigration" is viewed from the perspective of the country of origin.

in China, India and elswehre with the gospel require strategic thinking missiologically. In the first 10 years of this century China's cities grew by 200 million due to internal migration, and the government forecasted that a further 250 million rural people will migrate to the cities by 2030. The growth of urban centers in China indicates large scale internal migration of country folks leaving their homeland.

India, with its 20,000 to 40,000 Indian missionaries is probably the second largest missionary sending country in the world. Yet this fact seems to elude Western missiological statisticians who do not count these indigenous missionaries as "real" missionaries because most of them work within the geo-political territory of India. Today, many Christians are still clinging to the traditional definition of a "missionary" as someone sent from his homeland to serve abroad. Another example is the case of the "Filipino Kingdom workers " – contract workers who serve the Kingdom cause in foreign lands. They could be seafarers on board ocean liners or domestic helpers in affluent homes of countries abroad.

The ministries of these Christians, Indians and Filipinos included, for the Kingdom do not fit the stereotype of "missionary service" in traditional sense.[2] Although most of them work in linguistic and socio-cultural contexts different from their own, and although these "Kingdom workers " are engaged in cross-cultural gospel outreach, traditionally they have never been considered "missionaries" or "mission workers" by researchers and statisticians   in missiology.

It is academically irresponsible to exclude this major segment of Christianity from worldwide evangelism, and it is elitist not to recognize these groups as a powerful force for the Kingdom of God. It is equally faulty strategically to expect the Great Commission to be accomplished by efforts of traditional full-time vocational missionaries only.

Thus, this book is an attempt to rectify the deficiencies of stereotyping in Western popular approach in missiology and to respond to the demographic reality of the 21st century. In this book, diaspora ministry and diaspora missions are proposed to be a corrective to the "managerial missiology" that is popular and trendy in the west.

Purposes of the Book

The reality of two global trends (i.e. demographic reality of diaspora and the shifted center of Christian church) in the 21st century require a different missiological paradigm from which new mission strategies and action plans can be developed. This book is a progress report of my journey in search for a

---

[2] See definition below and discussion in Chapter 7.

INTRODUCTION

responsible way to respond missiologically to the new reality of the 21st century by way of:

1. providing a description of the two global demographic trends of the 21st century: the phenomenon of large scale diaspora, and the shifting of Christendom's center of gravity from the west to the rest and from the northern hemisphere to the south (see Part 2);

2. suggesting an interdisciplinary approach for understanding the complexity of the phenomenon of diaspora and to propose "diaspora missiology" as an alternative to the popular managerial missiology (see Part 3);

3. proposing the practice of "diaspora missiology" and "diaspora missions" (see case studies in Part 4).

In this revised edition, a new chapter (Chapter 7) is added introducing "managerial missiology paradigm" (hereafter referred to as "MMP"). Then MMP is compared with "diaspora missiology paradigm" (hereafter is referred to as "DMP") followed by a critique (Chapter 8).

It is important to point out that the author does not categorically deny the vailidity and viability of using statistics and strategy in Christian ministry and mission practices. For DMP emerged from the two global trends (i.e. diaspora phenomenon and epic shift of Christian center) that is both statistical and strategic in nature; but not "managerially statistical and strategic." The reason of devoting four chapters (i.e. Chapters 8, 12, 13, 14) proposing "why" and explaining "how" relational approach for the practice of DMP is to counter the dehumanizing and secularized ways of misusing statistics and strategy. The several case studies clearly show a strong emphasis on "relaltional approach" to rectify problems caused by embracing and practing MMP. Statistics and strategy can be employed by godly servants (vertically) led and empowered by the Triune God and guided by His holy Word to serve others (horizontally) within the context of godly and loving relational networks.

Definition of Key Terms

In this book, the following key terms are being used as defined below:

Diaspora Ministry — serving the diaspora in the name of Jesus Christ and for His sake in these two ways: (1) ministering to the diaspora, i.e., serving the diaspora, and (2) ministering through the diaspora, i.e., mobilizing the diaspora to serve others.

Diaspora Missiology Paradigm (DMP) — a missiological framework for understanding and participating in God's redemptive mission among diaspora groups.[3]

Diaspora Missions — Christians' participation in God's redemptive mission to evangelize their kinsmen on the move, and through them to reach out to natives in their homelands and beyond.[4] There are four types of diaspora missions (see Figure 1.1)[5]:

1. **Missions *to* the Diaspora** — reaching the diaspora groups in forms of Evangelism or pre-evangelistic social services, then disciple them to become worshipping communities and congregations.
2. **Missions *through* the Diaspora** — diaspora Christians reaching out to their kinsmen through networks of friendship and kinship in host countries, their homelands, and abroad.
3. **Missions *by* and *beyond* the Diaspora** — motivating and mobilizing diaspora Christians for cross-cultural missions to other ethnic groups in their host countries, homelands, and abroad.
4. **Missions *wth* the Diaspora** — mobilizing non-diasporic Christians individually and institutionally to partner with diasporic groups and congregations.

Managerial Missiology Pardigm (MMP) – the framework of engaging in the academic study of missiology by uncritically adopting the secular management paradigm and proposing the practice of Christian mission accordingly.

Managerial Mission Practice - ways and means of practicing Christian mission in the same manner of secular management in business that might be "biblical" and secularly contextual; but definitely not "scriptural."[6]

Migration – the crossing of the boundary of a political or

---

[3] See "The Seoul Declaration on Diaspora Missiology," accessed March 25, 2010; available at http://www.lausanne.org/documents/seoul-declaration-on-diaspora-missiology.html.
[4] Enoch Wan, "Global People and Diaspora Missiology," presentation at Plenary session,Tokyo 2010-Global Mission Consultation, Tokyo, Japan, May 13, 2010.
[5] Adapted from Enoch Wan, "Research Methodology for Diaspora Missiology and Diaspora Missions," presentation at Regional EMS Conference, North Central, Trinity Evangelical Divinity School, Deerfield, IL., February 26, 2011.
[6] Enoch Wan, "A critique of Charles Kkraft's use/misuse of communication and social sciences in iblical interpretation and missiological formulation,"
http://ojs.globalmissiology.org/index.php/english/article/viewFile/120/346 Accessed Dec 20, 2013.

administrative unit for a certain minimum period of time. It includes the movement of refugees, displaced persons, uprooted people as well economic migrants. **International migration** is "people moving for carious reasons to a country other than that of their usual residence, for a period of at least twelve months"[7]

Migrant – There is no universally accepted definition for the term "migrant," whereas "**long-term migrant**" (according to UN) is defined as "a person who moves to a country other than that of his or her usual residence for a period of at least a year (12 months), so that the country of destination effectively becomes his or her new country of usual residence."[8]

Ministry — rendering service to people in the name of Jesus Christ and for His sake.

Mission — Christians (individuals) and the Church (institutional) continuing on and carrying out the *missio Dei* of the Triune God ("mission") at both individual and institutional levels spiritually (saving soul) and socially (ushering in *shalom*) for redemption, reconciliation, and transformation ("missions").[9]

Missions — ways and means of accomplishing "the mission" which has been entrusted by the Triune God to the Church and Christians (Wan 2003b:1).[10]

Missiology — the systematic and academic study of missions in the fulfillment of God's mission.

Missiological Research Methodology — the systematic, and interdisciplinary manner of conducting research in missiological studies (Wan 2003b:1).

---

[7] Recommendations on Statistics of International Migration, Statistical Papers Series M, No. 58, Rev. 1, United Nations, New York, 1998 http://unstats.un.org/unsd/publication/SeriesM/SeriesM_58rev1e.pdf Accessed Dec. 20, 2013.
[8] "Glossary of Statistical Terms," OECD. http://stats.oecd.org/glossary/detail.asp?ID=1562 Accessed Dec. 20, 2013.
[9] Enoch Wan, "'Mission' and 'Missio Dei': Response to Charles Van Engen's 'Mission Defined and Described'," in *MissionShift: Global Mission Issues in the Third Millennium*, ed. David J. Hesselgrave and Ed Stetzer (Nashville: B & H Publishing Group, Nashville, 2010d), 41-50.
[10] Enoch Wan, "Rethinking Missiological Research Methodology: Exploring a New Direction," *Global Missiology*, October 2003b; available at www.GlobalMissiology.org.

Figure 1.1 Diaspora Ministry and Missions in DMP

DIASPORA MISSIOLOGY		DIASPORA MINISTRY			
	Type	ministering **to** the diaspora		ministering **along** the diaspora	
	Means	the Great Commandment as pre-evangelistic and holistic		the Great Commission – imperative and inclusive	
	Recipient	focusing on diaspora: serving the diaspora by ministering - social and spiritual dimensions		focusing beyond diaspora: mobilizing diaspora Christians to serve other diaspora people or non-diaspora	
		DIASPORA MISSIONS			
	Type	missions **to** the diaspora	missions **through** the diaspora	missions **by** & **beyond** the diaspora	missions **with** the diaspora
	Means	motivate & mobilize diaspora individuals & congregations to partner with others: the Great Commission, i.e. evangelistic outreach, discipleship, church planting and global missions			
	Recipient	focusing on diaspora		focusing beyond diaspora	
		members of diaspora community	kinsmen in homeland & elsewhere; not cross-culturally	cross-culturally to other ethnic groups in host society and beyond	partnership between diaspora and others in Kingdom ministry

Strategic Stewardship — the wise use of God-endowed resources and God-given opportunities to His glory and for Kingdom extension.[11]

Strategic Partnership — partnering for the wise use of God-endowed resources and God-given opportunities to His glory and for Kingdom extension.

Organization of the Book

This book is organized into five parts: introduction, theoretical formulation, methodological exploration, ministerial practice illustrated

---

[11] Enoch Wan, "Rethinking Missiology in the Context of the 21st Century: Global Demographic Trends and Diaspora Missiology," *Great Commission Research Journal*, Volume 2, Issue 1 (Summer 2010c).

by five case studies,[12] and conclusion. The book begins with phenomenological descriptions and theorizing of diaspora, and concludes with proposing DMP that is a corrective to MMP which is popular and trendy in the West.

Parts 1 and 2 deal with the complexity of the phenomenon of diaspora, such as multiple causes, varied patterns, and ministerial implications. The study of this phenomenon requires a new approach – DMP, an interdisciplinary methodological study that includes biblical foundation, theological formulation, and ministerial application.

In Part 1, a description of the phenomenon of diaspora (Chapter 2), is followed by a discussion on theorizing diaspora (Chapter 3). The contributors of Chapters 4, 5, and 6 trace the diaspora history of the Hebrew people and the early church, and portray the characteristics and impacts of these diasporas as a whole. In Chapters 4 and 5, the Hebrew people's diaspora is seen as a prototype for the studies of other diaspora groups in the eight case studies of Part 4. Thus, the case of diaspora Jews (Chapter 15) precedes all other case studies in Part 4.

Issues of methodological nature are covered in Part 3. It begins with the introduction of MMP as a popular paradigm in the west in Chapter 7. DMP is introduced in Chapter 8 as a contemporary paradigm for the 21st century with four variations in approach, i.e. ***to, through, by/beyond*** and ***with***. Chapter 9 is a progress report of the development and implementation of DMP. Although "interdisciplinary research" (descriptive of what entails) has been distinguished from "integrative approach" (complementarily synthetic) in earlier studies,[13] in this book only "interdisciplinary research" is introduced as the methodology for the study of diaspora missiology in Chapter 10.

Part 4 begins with a diachronic overview of Christian missions to diaspora groups in Chapter 11 and demographic reality of diaspora in Chapter 12, followed by five case studies ranging from group-specific (Chapters 15, 16), and state-specific (Chapter 17,18 - urban, 19 - rural). These case studies are informative of DMP in action. They provide insightful understanding of the two types of "diaspora ministries" and four types of "diaspora missions" as diagramatically listed in Figure 1.1.

---

[12] For references in "case study," see Robert E. Stake, *The Art of Case Study Research*. (Thousand Oaks: Sage, 1995); Robert K. Yin, *Case Study Research: Design and Methods*. (Thousand Oaks: Sage, 1994).

[13] See the two articles below for details:
- Enoch Wan, "Rethinking Missiological Research Methodology: Exploring a New Direction" in *Global Missiology* (October 2003b). Available at www.GlobalMissiology.org.
- Enoch Wan, "The Paradigm and Pressing Issues of Inter-disciplinary Research Methodology," *Global Missiology* (January 2005a). Available at www.GlobalMissiology. org.

This book is an introductory study on the emerging DMP. It is written with seminarians and practitioners in mind. It is also intended to be a guide for those engaging in "diaspora missions." Researchers interested in further studies on the subject may find useful information in the footnotes, bibliography and references listed at the end of the book. It is hoped that case studies in Part 4 will serve as an inspiration to practitioners as they engage in diaspora missions locally and globally.

Part 2
THEORY

This section includes a descriptoin of the phenomenon of diaspora, a discussion on "theorizing diaspora," and an introduction to "diaspora missiology" as an alternative paradigm of missiological conceptualization in response to the phenomenon of diaspora in the 21st century.

Chapter 2

The Phenomenon of Diaspora

Enoch Wan

Introduction

Many forces ushered in socio-cultural changes as we entered the 21st century - globalization, post-modern orientation, pluralist religiosity, etc. This chapter describes two global demographic trends of the 21st century, beginning with the phenomenon of large scale diaspora and followed by the shifting of Christendom's center of gravity from the west to the rest and from the northern hemisphere to the southern hemisphere.

The Phenomenon of Diaspora as a Demographic Trend of the 21st Century

Demographically people often moved spatially due to famine, war, and political and religious oppressions. Since the last century, the number of people moving on large scales and at high rates has increased significantly. Consequently, this brought about an unprecedented number of diasporas. Historically the word *diaspora* was used to refer to the population of Jews exiled from Israel in 607 BC under the Babylonians, and from Judea in 70 AD under the Roman Empire. The term was later used to reference the Assyrian two-way "mass deportation policy of conquered populations" to deny future territorial claims on their part (Galil and Weinfeld 2000:96-97).

Etymologically, the term "*diaspora*" is a derivation from the Greek word "*diaspeirein*" which means "to scatter about" (disperse– from, *dia*– about, across + *speirein* – to scatter).[14] The term is found in Deuteronomy 28:25 in the

---

[14] Accessed August 20, 2011; available at
http://www.etymonline.com/index.php?search=dKiaspora+ &searchmode=none.

Septuagint, but was assimilated broadly into English by the mid-1950s in reference to significant numbers of long-term expatriates.[15]

In the 20th century, diaspora at global scale have occurred as listed in the the following facts:[16]

1. Ethnic cleansing and genocide, e.g., Armenian, Assyrian, and Greek genocides of 1915-1918; Rwandan genocide in 1994; and diaspora of Tamils in the 1980s;

2. Colonization of Korea in 1910 and the creation of Manchukuo by the Japanese in 1937-1945, creating millions of Chinese diaspora in southeast Asia and more than 100,000 Koreans crossing the Amur River into Eastern Russia;

3. Ethnically directed persecution, oppression, and genocide such as Armenians, Assyrians, and Greeks who were forced out of Anatolia by the Ottoman Turks during the Armenian, Assyrian, and Greek genocides of 1915-1918;

4. Political conflicts in countries such as Nicaraguans, Salvadorans, Guatemalans, Hondurans, Costa Ricans, and Panamanians in Central America;

5. Military and dictatorial rule causing thousands of Chilean and Uruguayan refugees to flee from South America to Europe during periods of military rule in the 1970s and 1980s;

6. Afghan diaspora as a result of the former Soviet Union's 1979 invasion, creating over 6 million refugees, one of the largest refugee populations in contemporary history;

7. Iranian diaspora caused by the 1979 Iranian Revolution following the fall of the Shah;

8. Jewish diaspora in Europe caused by Nazi Germany, and the Palestinian diaspora created as a result of Israel's re-establishment as a country state in 1948, and again in 1967 during the Arab-Israeli War.

In the 21st century, people continue to move away from their homelands and scatter around the world with increased frequency and complexity. These

---

[15] For use of the term "diaspora" in reference to long-term expatriates in significant numbers, see http://www.worldbusinesslive.com/research/article/648273/the-worlds-successful-diasporas; http://web.worldbank.org/WBSITE/EXTERNAL/WBI/WBIPROGRAMS/KFDLP/0contentMDK:20692386~pagePK:64156158~piPK:64152884~theSitePK:46119800.html; accessed August 20, 2011.

[16] Adapted from a personal report by Amador Remigio at LCWE Diaspora Consultation 2006.

people constitute the "diasporas" and some demographic facts are listed below, indicative of such trend:[17]

1. The size and significance of diasporas have increased in the 21st century. Approximately 3.2% of the global population lives in countries other than their places of birth[18] because of urbanization, international migration, and displacement by war and famine. According to a recent UN report, diaspora population was 175 million in year 2000, 192 million in year 2005, and 154 in 1990 and the total sum of international migrants will hit as many as 405 million by 2050.[19] Figure 2.1 below shows the global pattern by direction and scale diagrammatically.

2. "If the world's 214 million international migrants were counted as one nation, they would constitute the fifth most populous country on the globe, just behind Indonesia and ahead of Brazil."[20]

3. Migrant populations have increased globally, and are moving "from south to north, and from east to west"[21] towards seven of the world's wealthiest countries. These countries have less than 16% of the total world population; yet 33% of the world's migrant population is found there.[22] See Figure 2.2 and Figure 2.3 below.

4. In the early 1990s there were about 17 million internally displaced people, 30 million "regular" migrants, and another 30 million migrants with an "irregular" status. The combined total of 97 million persons represents a doubling of the global migrant population in the space of five years.

---

[17] For details, see Enoch Wan & Sidiria Joy Tira, "Diaspora Missiology and Missions in the Context of the 21st Century," *Torch Trinity Journal*, May 30, 2010, Volume 13, No.1, 46-60. Also in *Global Missiology*, October 2010; available at www.GlobalMissiology.org.
[18] David Lundy, *Borderless Church: Shaping the Church for the 21st Century* (UK: Authentic, 2005), xiv.
[19] For the UN report, see http://esa.un.org/unmigration/wallchart2013.htm (Accessed Dec. 20, 2013)
[20] "Faith on the Move – The Religious Affiliation of International Migrants," Pew Research Religion & Public Life Project. http://www.pewforum.org/2012/03/08/religious-migration-exec/ accessed Dec. 20, 2013.
[21] Leonore Loeb Adler and Uwe P. Gielen, eds. *Migration: Immigration and emigration in international perspective* (Westport, CT: 2003), 16.
[22] For further discussions, see Daniele Joly, ed. *International Migration in the New Millennium: Global movement and settlement* (London: Ashgate, 2004); SOPEMI, "Trends in international migration: Continuous Reporting System on Migration," OECD (www.SourceOECD.org); Myron Weiner and Michael S. Teitelbaum, *Political demography, demographic engineering* (New York: Berghahn, 2001).

5. According to statistics, almost one in every 35 people in the world is a migrant. This includes migrant workers, international students, and refugees.[23]

6. Diaspora movements have increased temporally and spatially in scale and scope. The major flow in recent years, according to Kapu and Mchale (2005),[24] is rural to urban migration within two developing countries - China and India. The second largest wave of diaspora is found within developing countries, from the poorer to the more affluent. And the third wave is from developing to developed countries.

7. On global migration and the phenomenon of diaspora as observed by Kapur and McHale (2005): "analyze four key channels through which international skilled migration affects developing countries through the concepts of prospect, absence, diaspora, and return."[25]

8. Globalization and migration:
"A globalizing world brings greater interaction among countries, regions, and institutions. Increasing and intensified labor migration is an important component of the globalization process, as some people migrate from city to city or emigrate from their home country to work in another country." [26]

---

[23] The BBC News Online looks at the numbers of people migrating, where they are going and some of the implications of migration: "Over the past 15 years, the number of people crossing borders in search of a better life has been rising steadily. At the start of the 21st Century, one in every 35 people is an international migrant. If they all lived in the same place, it would be the world's fifth-largest country." Accessed September 20, 2011; available at
http://news.bbc.co.uk/2/shared/spl/hi/world/04/migration/html/migration_boom.stm.
Also, according to the International Federation of Red Cross and Red Crescent Societies: "Migrants make up three per cent of the global population, meaning approximately one in 35 people in the world is a migrant," accessed Setember 20, 2011; available at http://ifrc.org/en/what-we-do/migration.
[24] Devesh Kapur and John McHale, *The Global Migration of Talent: What Does it Mean for Developing Countries?* Center For Global Development. Washington D.C., 2001. Accessed August 20, 2011; available at http://ucatlas.cisr.ucsc.edu/blog/?p=46.
[25] Devesh Kapur and John McHale (2005): *The Global Migration of Talent: What Does it Mean for Developing Countries?* Center For Global Development. Washington D.C. Accessed August 20, 2011; available at http://ucatlas.cisr.ucsc.edu/blog/?p=46._
[26] "Migration Conceptual Framework: Why do people move to work in another place or country?"AAG Center for Global Geography Education.
http://cgge.aag.org/Migration1e/ConceptualFramework_Jan10/ConceptualFramework_Jan10_print.html Accessed Dec. 20, 2013.

THEORIZING DIASPORA

Figure 2.1 - Patterns of Human Migration[27]

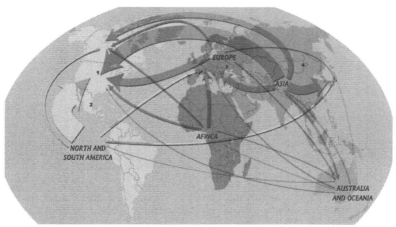

Note: The larger the arrow, the more migrants, or people on the move, from the continent named.

Figure 2.2 - The evolution of global bilateral migration 1960-2000. [28]

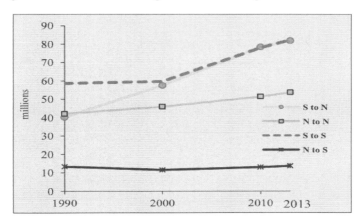

---

[27] "Migration: The Human Journey" – National Geography Action! http://www.nationalgeographic.com/xpeditions/activities/09/gapacket05.pdf Accessed Dec. 20, 2013

[28] "International migration: 2013: Migrants by origin and destination," UN Dept. of Economic and Social Afairs, Population Divisin, No. 2013/3, Sept. 2013. http://filipspagnoli.wordpress.com/stats-on-human-rights/statistics-on-xenophobia-immigration-and-asylum/statistics-on-migration/ Accessed Dec. 20, 2013.

17

Figure 2.3 - Numbers of international migrants by origin and destination, 1990-2013. [29]

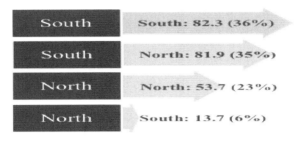

From the demographic descriptions of the phenomenon of diaspora, the following missiological implications are drawn and will be discussed in detail in Part 3 and Part 4.

9. A missiological paradigm different from Western popular approach in missiology is needed to cope with the new demographic reality of large scale and intensified diaspora movement of people in the 21st century. Therefore, diaspora missiology is proposed in Chapter 7.

10. Diaspora people, being on the move, are more receptive to spiritual matter such as spiritual conversion and involvement in global missions. Thus they are to be motivated and mobilized for the Great Commission as explained in Chapter 10 and illustrated in case studies in Part 4.

11. Diaspora people have been, and will increasingly be, the primary vehicle of missions in this century. They have helped in revitalizing Christianity in countries of the post-Christian west (Wan, 2011a). More discussion on strategy related to diaspora missions/ministry will be found in Chapter 10.

12. The Church should actively engage in these tasks: (a) to impart a missional sense to believers who are on the move; (b) to equip and mobilize the diaspora Christians (Chapter 10); (c) to provide pastoral care for family members of the diaspora who stay behind in the home country; (d) to partner with related organizations in building networks for outreach to the diaspora, (e) to nurture the

---

[29] "International migration: 2013: Migrants by origin and destination," UN Dept. of Economic and Social Afairs, Population Divisin, No. 2013/3, Sept. 2013.
http://filipspagnoli.wordpress.com/stats-on-human-rights/statistics-on-xenophobia-immigration-and-asylum/statistics-on-migration/ Accessed Dec. 20, 2013.

spiritual growth of the diaspora for outreach ministry in host countries and beyond. (See Chapters 10 & 12).

13. Recent phenomena of social media (Twitter, Face Book, etc.) powered by new technology of communication enabled people to be connected in real time yet without personal interaction.[30] In contemporary society, there is a lack of "relational reality" in Western society socio-culturally thus relational paradigm is proposed in Chapter 11.

14. The large influx of diaspora from southern hemisphere into industrial countries in the west, including high percentage of Christians and immigrants from Muslim and Hindu backgrounds has positive factors of revitalizing the Christian community in post-Christian west and creating new opportunities to reach the previously "unreached people group" in the neighborhood of Christian churches in the west. (See discussion in Chapter 10).

15. The decline in Western Christian churches has greatly reduced their resources in personnel and finance and decreased their global impact in Christian missions. Conversely, churches in the majority world, such as the churches in South Korea, are on the rise in their involvement in global missions. Thus, the Western churches should practice "strategic stewardship," and engage in "strategic partnership" with the growing churches of the majority world as proposed in Chapter 12.

Shifting of the Center of Gravity in the Christian World[31]

In the last few decades, statistical data about the state of Christianity globally have consistently shown its decline in the west and the rise in the southern hemeisphere.[32] Before the turn of the century, Scotish missiologist Andrew Walls in 1984 oberved that there was a "massive southward

---

[30] "A Warm, but Empty Voice? Reflections on Face-to-Face Interactions," Blog post *by Enoch Wan* at Evangel-Vision:
http://www.evangel-vision.com/2013/12/a-warm-but-empty-voice-reflections-on.html Accessed Dec. 2, 2013
[31] This section is based on an earlier work of Enoch Wan, "Global People and Diaspora Missiology: From Edinburgh 2010 to Tokyo 2010," in *Handbook of Global Mission: Consultation, Celebration*, 2010a, 92-106.
[32] See Bryant L. Myers, *The New Context of World Mission* (MARC, 1996); Patrick Johnstone, Robin Johnstone and Jason Mandryk, *Operation World*, 6th edition. Paternoster Lifestyle, 2001; *World Christian Encyclopedia: A comparative survey of churches and religions in the modern world* (2nd edit.), David B. Barrett, George T. Kurian, Todd M. Johnson, Oxford University Press, 2001.

shift of the center of gravity of the Christian world"[33] that set the new balance in terms of quantitative and the qualitative strength/growth between the west and the rest at global scale.

In 1986, Swiss missiologist Walbert Buhlman employed a millanial-schema to credit the Eastern Church (orthodox Church) and the Western Church (within the Roman Empire) for leadership in Christianity globally for the first two millennium respectively then made the following observation regarding contemporary Christianity:

> "Now the Third Millennium will evidently stand under the leadership fo the Third Church, the Southern church. I am convinced that the most important drives and inspirations for the whole church in the future will come from the Third Church."[34]

Peruvian missiologist Samuel E. Escobor in 2003 in *The New Global Mission: The Gospel from Everywhere to Everyone* adopts Walbert Buhlman's expression to discuss "the shift of Christianity to the South" and supports his point from his peronal experience and observation then called for "mission from below."[35] (Escobor 2003:15-20)

In *The Next Christendom: The Coming of Global Christianity*, Philip Jenkins defines "Christian" in a broad and "emic" perspective:[36] "A Christian is someone who describes himself or herself as a Christian" (Jenkins 2001:88). He observes that Christianity is increasingly moving to the southern hemisphere toward its place of origin (Jenkins 2001:14) and that the center of gravity of the Christian world has shifted from Europe and the United States to the southern hemisphere due to factors such as secularization of Christianity in the west and liberalization of churches and countries in eastern Europe. The fact that there are now nearly 50 million Protestant believers and more than 400 million Catholics in South America (Jenkins 2001:57) illustrates such demographic shift.

Jenkins concludes that Christianity is growing at a phenomenal rate in the southern hemisphere as well as in China, thus altering the global outlook of Christendom (Jenkins 2001:81-85; 94-105). By the year 2050, only one Christian in five will be non-Latino and "white." The center of gravity of the Christian world will then be shifted firmly to the southern hemisphere.

For centuries, Christian churches in the west have been weakened by internal secularization. External forces such as the rise of various non-Christian and anti-Christian religions (New Age Movement, Satanism, etc.) have also turned many historically Christian and missionary-sending countries into

---

[33] Andrew Walls, "Culture and Coherence in Christian History," *Evangelical Review of Theology*, 9, no. 3, 1984:215.
[34] Walbert Buhlman, *The Church of the Future.* (Orbis) 1986:6.
[35] Samuel E. Escobor, *The New Global Missio: The Gospel from Everywhere to Everyone.* InterVasity Press 2003.
[36] An "emic perspective" is an insider's view, in contrast to "etic perspective" being an outsider's. See Kenneth Pike, *Talk, Thought, and Thing: The Emic Road Toward Conscious Knowledge* (Dallas: Summer Institute of Linguistics, 1993), 16.

mission fields. A role reversal of sending and receiving is taking place between the traditional Christian west and the majority world (see "reverse missions" in Chapter 12 and Chapter 14).

Summary

This chapter provides descriptions of two global demographic trends of the 21st century and derived missiological implications. These descriptions lead to a basic understanding of the complex and multifaceted diaspora phenomenon for further discussions on theory and methodology in subsequent chapters in this book.

Chapter 3

Theorizing Diaspora

Enoch Wan

Introduction

The phenomenon of diaspora has attracted the attention of government officials and researchers in fields such as sociology, anthropology, government policy, and international migration for multiple reasons. As a result, various attempts to theorize diaspora can be found in recent publications as selectively reviewed in this chapter after an introduction to foundational understanding.

There are two types of migration in terms of **"spatial movement":** international migration (two types: forced and voluntary) and internal migration (i.e. movement of people within the country with three patterns (i.e. rural-urban, urban-suburban, and from metropolitan to non-metropolitan regions).

There is **"temporal element"** in migration and in terms of process, there are three types of migration, according to Global Migration Group:[37]

1. Forced Migration
   Forced migration is a general term to describe a migratory movement in which an element of coercion exists, including threats to life and livelihood, arising from natural or man-made causes, such as movements of refugees and internally displaced persons as well as people displaced by political instability, conflict, natural or environmental disasters, chemical or nuclear disasters, famine, or development projects.
2. Transit Migration
   Transit migration refers to the regular or irregular movement of a person through any state on any journey to the state of employment

---

[37] "International Migration and Human Rights: Challenges and Opportunities on the Threshold of the 60th Anniversary of the Universal Declaration of Human Rights," Global Migration Group. http://www.globalmigrationgroup.org/uploads/documents/Int_Migration_Human_Rights.pdf Accessed Dec. 20, 2013.

or from the state of employment to the state of origin or the state of habitual residence.
3. Return Migration
Return migration refers to the "movement of a person returning to his/her country of origin or habitual residence usually after spending at least one year in another country. This return may or may not be voluntary. Return migration includes voluntary repatriation."

Theoretical Development

Classical approach

Robin Cohen provides a basic conceptualization for the initial discussion of diaspora theory. He sees diaspora communities as a group of people:

> Settled outside of their natal (or imagined natal) territories, acknowledge that "the old country"– a notion often buried deep in language, religion, custom or folklore—always has some claim on their loyalty and emotions. That claim may be strong or weak, or boldly or meekly articulated in a given circumstance or historical period, but a member's adherence to a diasporic community is demonstrated by an acceptance of an inescapable link with their past migration history and a sense of co-ethnicity with others of a similar background (Cohen 1997:ix).[38]

One key reference on the subject is *Theorizing Diaspora: A Reader*.[39] The authors provide a review of key theories on diaspora in three ways:

> …reiterate different theories about national community and diaspora, but revisit some of the crucial theoretical writings on diaspora and nation, inquiring why diaspora has become such an important category of critical analysis in the social sciences literature, and the humanities (Braziel and Mannur 2003:3-4).

True to its title, the authors made contributions in different ways of theorizing diaspora. Unfortunately, the collection lacks balance due to its special bend on "black Atlantic" diaspora, in spite of the wide variety of literature on diaspora that could have been included. However, the following quotation is highly informative on theorizing diaspora:

---

[38] Cohen, Robin. *Global Diasporas: An Introduction.* Seattle, WA: University of Washington Press, 1997.
[39] Jana Evans Braziel and AnitaMannur, eds. *Theorizing Diaspora: A Reader* (Malden, MA: Blackwell Publishing Ltd., 2003).

THEORIZING DIASPORA

"The term 'diaspora' has been increasingly used by anthropologists, literary theorists, and cultural critics to describe the mass migrations and displacements of the second half of the twentieth century, particularly in reference to independence movements in formerly colonized areas, waves of refugees fleeing war-torn states, and fluxes of economic migration in the post-World War II era. *Diaspora, diasporic,* and *diaspora-ization*...Are contested terms, the meanings and multiple referents of which are currently being theorized and debated." (Braziel and Mannur 2003:4).

Another helpful publication is Michelle Reis' article "Theorizing Diaspora: Perspectives on 'Classical' and 'Contemporary' Diaspora."[40] Contrary to "classical diaspora" literature in which the term "diaspora" refers exclusively to the Jews and Jewish diaspora as the "archetype," Reis in this study expands "the classification of three principal broad historical waves of Jewish Diaspora" through "historicizing of diasporization" for "an empirical discussion of the three major historical waves that influenced the diasporic process throughout the world." He categorizes the three waves as follows:

1. the Classical Period of ancient Jewish and ancient Greek diaspora;
2. the Modern Period of slavery and colonization, further subdivided into three major phases: (1) the expansion of European capital (1500–1814), (2) the Industrial Revolution (1815–1914), and (3) the Interwar Period (1914–1945);
3. the Contemporary or Late-modern Period from immediately after World War II to the present day, specifying the case of the Hispanics in the United States as one key example.

Vijay Mishra (1996) and Susanah Lily L. Mendoza (2002) also offer group-specific theorizing, i.e. diaspora on Indian diaspora and Filipino diaspora respectively.[41] The classic theory of push-pull migration is built on the conceptualization of the bipolar pattern of "origin" and "destination." In *A Theory of Migration,* Everett S. Lee (1996) proposes the concept of "intervening obstacles" (or opportunities) as diagrammatically shown below:[42]

---

[40] Michele Reis, "Theorizing Diaspora: Perspectives on 'Classical' and 'Contemporary' Diaspora," *International Migration* Volume 42, Issue 2 (June 2004): 41-60.
[41] Vijay Mishra, "The diasporic imaginary: Theorizing the Indian diaspora" in *Textual Practice* Volume 10, Issue 3 (1996): 421-447.
 Susanah Lily L. Mendoza. *Between the homeland and the diaspora: the politics of theorizing Filipino* (New York: Routledge, 2002).
[42] Everett S. Lee. "A Theory of Migration,' *Demography,* Vol. 3, No. 1. (1966), pp. 47-57

Figure 3.1 – "Intervening Obstacles" in Everett S. Lee's Model[43]

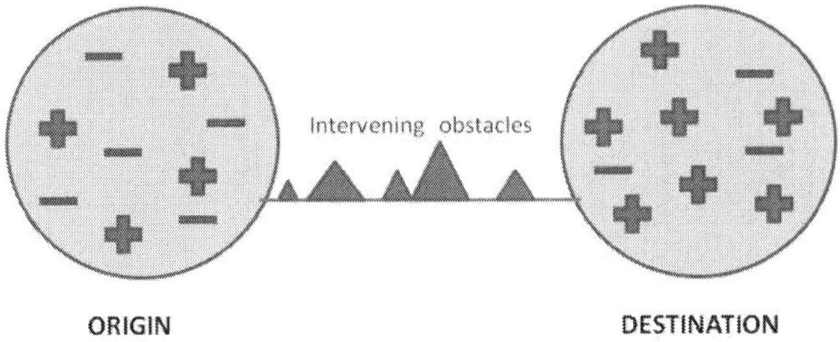

ORIGIN   DESTINATION

NOTE: Intervening obstacles include spatial and socio-cultural distances, restrictive immigration laws, etc. and positive (+) and negative (-) signs in both locations are contributing factors to migration.

Traditionally, the focus of classical push-pull theory of migration is based on an individual's choice of economic nature (i.e. single-factor and rationalistic); whereas contemporary studies include multi-factor and socio-cultural dimensions at both individual level (e.g. gender, age, marital status, educational and skill levels, entrepreneurship, proprietorship, etc.) and institution level (e.g. roles of family/household, intermediate agent, government policy, transnational corporation, etc.) (Muniz et al. 2006; Brettell and Hollifield 2008)[44]

For example, James Rubenstein understands diaspora movements as diverse in their methods, reasons, purposes, desires and hopes. International migrants do not follow one pattern but there are many economic, cultural, and environmental "push" and "pull" factors in place as people emigrate and immigrate often fleeing harsh conditions in view of better quality of life, safety, or education and work, either voluntarily or involuntarily.[45]

---

[43] "Migration Conceptual Framework: Why do people move to work in another place or country?" AAG Center for Global Geography Education http://www.aag.org/cs/cgge/modules Accessed Dec. 20, 2013.
[44] Collaboration of seven US and Latin American researchers, Osaldo Muniz et al., AAG Panel on US and Latin America. Collaboration in Georgraphic Research and Education, Race, Ethnicity, and Place Conference, Texas State University, San Marcos, 1-4 Nov. 2006.
http://www.aag.org/galleries/project-programs-files/US_and_Latin_American_Collaboration.pdf Accessed Dec. 20, 2013. Caroline Brettell and James Frank Hollifield Migration Theory: Talking Across Disciplines. Routledge, 2000
[45] James M. Rubenstein, *An Introduction to Human Geography: The Cultural Landscape* 9th Ed. (Upper Saddle River: Prentice Hall, 2008), 82-85.

Neoclassical model of migration

"Migration selectivity" is a neoclassical model of migration based on the concept of "spatial inequality" (i.e. real income differentials) of the two locations (poorer place of origin → richer destination) to account for movement of people and to explain migration pattern, e.g. the study on education by Ravi Kanbura and Hillel Rapoport[46] (2003) and on labor by Jorge A. Bustamante, Guillermina Jasso, J. Edward Taylor & Paz Trigueros Legarreta (1998).[47] Migrant's selectivity (or "differentiation") such as age, class, gender, marital status, etc. has much bearing on attitudinal difference that manifested in behavioral variations. (Todaro 1969, Harris and Todaro 1970, White and Woods 1980). A typical scenario is that young single migrants tend to be more mobile for migration than their older and married counterpart. Related to migrant selectivity is "chain migration"[48] (Fawcett 1989, Banerjee 1983, Shah & Menon 1999, Kevin R. Cox 1972), as shown in the diagram below.

---

[46] Ravi Kanbura and Hillel Rapoport, "Migration Selectivity and The Evolution of Spatial Inequality," September 2003. http://www.arts.cornell.edu/poverty/kanbur/KanRap.pdf Accessed Dec. 20, 2013.

[47] Jorge A. Bustamante, Guillermina Jasso, J. Edward Taylor & Paz Trigueros Legarreta, "The Selectivity of International Labor Migration and Characteristics of Mexico-to-U.S. Migrants: Theoretical Considerations," USCIR - Binational Research Papers http://www.utexas.edu/lbj/uscir/binpap-v.html Accessed Dec. 20, 2013. *"Characteristics of Migrants: Mexicans in the United States,"* Jorge A. Bustamante, Guillermina Jasso, J.Edward Taylor and Paz Trigueros Legarreta
http://www.utexas.edu/lbj/uscir/binpapers/v1-2bustamante.pdf Accessed Dec. 2013.

[48] James T. Fawcett, "Networks, Linkages, and Migration Systems," *International Migration Review.* Vol. 23, No. 3 Special Silver Anniversary Issue: International Migration an Assessment for the 90's (Autumn, 1989), pp. 671-680. Published by: The Center for Migration Studies of New York, Inc.
Biswajit Banerjee, "Social Networks in the Migration Process: Empirical Evidence on Chain Migration in India," *The Journal of Developing Areas*, Vol. 17, No. 2 (Jan., 1983), pp. 185-196. College of Business, Tennessee State University. Nasra M. Shah & Indu Menon, "Chain Migration Through the Social Network: Experience of Labour Migrants in Kuwait," *International Migration,* Volume 37, Issue 2, pages 361–382, June 1999. International Organization for Migration. Kevin R. Cox, Man, Location, and *Behavior: An Introduction to Human Geography.* NY: Wiley. 1972

Figure 3.2 - Chain Migration and Network

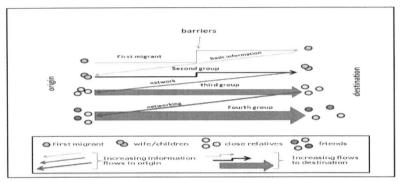

NOTE: kinsmen and friends tend to follow the initiate move of first migrants from the same community of homeland, i.e. homeward information helps to remove "obstacles" (in Lee's model of Figure 3.1 above) to facilitate outflow of migrant to destination.

Diaspora theorists are exploring many new directions, pushing beyond the *who, what,* and *how* questions (though there is certainly plenty of room for further examining those questions) and examining the questions of *to what extent, to what impact,* and *to what end* (future trends). Mahalingam observes that diasporas serve as political liaisons and "soft power" brokers between sending and receiving countries. He notes that the Chinese and Jewish diasporas in Europe and North America have favorable influenced economic and foreign policy as it regards China and Israel respectively. Optimistically, he looks to the 25 million Indians dispersed through 136 countries to influence Indian interests abroad, though he bemoans the slow response by the Indian government to utilize this force.[49] Other studies consider the impact diasporas have on democracy and brain drain in their home and host nations.[50]

Development in theorizing the identity aspect of diaspora is enhanced by the volume *Transnational Migration and Human Security: The Migration-Development-Security Nexus* edited by Thanh-Dam Truong and Des

---

[49] Mahalingam M, *India's Diaspora Policy and Foreign Policy: an Overview*, Global Research Forum on Diaspora and Transformation, http://grfdt.com/PublicationDetails.aspx?Type=Articles&TabId=30 Accessed 12/31/2013. Similarly, *Pioneers East: The Early American Experience in the Middle East*, details the ways in which American missionaries—certainly a diaspora in a nontraditional sense—influenced United States foreign policy by serving as conduits of information in an age when the United States did not have direct (colonial) influence in the Middle East. David Finnie, *Pioneers East: The Early American Experience in the Middle East*, Harvard Middle Eastern Studies, no 13. Cambridge: Harvard University Press, 1967.

[50] Çaglar Özden and Maurice Schiff, *International Migration, Remittances, & the Brain Drain*, (New York: Palgrave and Macmillan, 2006), Devesh Kapur, *Diaspora Development and Democracy*, (New York: Oxford University Press, 2010), and Gabriel Sheffer, *Diaspora Politics: At Home Abroad*, (Cambridge: Cambridge University, 2003) are just a few samples of these ideas.

Gasper.[51] They suggest that "within their various levels, social fields contain institutions, organizations, and experiences that generate categories of identity that are ascribed to or chosen by individuals or groups." The authors describe the fluidity of diaspora identity in this way:

> "Individuals can be embedded in a social field but not identify with any label or cultural politics associated with that field. Because they live within a social field, they have the potential to act or identify with it at any particular time, though not all choose to do so" (Truong and Gasper 2011:4).

Diaspora and Transnational Network

Nina Glick (1995) and several researchers look at the diaspora phenomenon from an anthropological perspective and provide unique contributions in theorizing diaspora: "Contemporary immigrants cannot be characterized as the 'uprooted.' Many of them are transmigrants, becoming firmly rooted in their new country but maintaining multiple linkages to their homeland."[52]

Peggy Levitt's study[53] on transmigration of diaspora offers a similar perspective on "multiple linkages," foregoing the methodological nationalism and broaden beyond the traditional nation-state framework in diaspora study.

A breakthrough in theorizing diaspora is found in *New Approaches to Migration? Transnational Communities and the Transformation of Home*, edited by Nadje Sadig Al-Ali and Khalid Koser.[54] The contributors present a "transnational perspective" that views

> "international migrants not as anomalies, but rather as representative of an increasingly globalized world who "found it possible to have multiple localities and arguably also multiple identities. As a result, family and kinship ties have moved from a largely local to a global scale…the development of new identities among migrants, who are anchored (socially, culturally and physically) neither in their place of origin nor in their place of destination" (Al-Ali and Koser 2002:3-4)."

Many more diverse views and theories have emerged since the launch of the journal *Diaspora: A Journal of Transnational Studies* by the University of

---

[51] Thanh-Dam Truong and Des Gasper, eds. *Transnational Migration and Human Security-the migration-development-security nexus* (Springer: Berlin & Heidelberg, 2011).
[52] Nina Glick, Schiller, Linda Basch and Cristina Szanton Blanc, "From Immigrant to Transmigrant: Theorizing Transnational Migration," *Anthropological Quarterly* Vol. 68, No. 1 (January 1995): 48-63.
[53] Peggy Levitt, "Transnational Migrants: When "Home" Means More Than One Country" in *Migration Information Source*, Migration Policy Institute, accessed August 20, 2011; available at http://www.migrationinformation.org/feature/display.cfm?ID=261._
[54] Nadje Al-Ali and Khalid Koser, eds. *New Approaches to Migration? Transnational Communities and the Transformation of Home* (New York: Rouledge, 2002).

Toronto (Canada) in 1991 and the special issue[55] on diaspora by Duke University since spring 2010.

Schiller, Basch and Blanc theorize that the traditional notions of the immigrant, a person who relocates and assimilates, needs to be replaced with the concept of transnationalism.[56] This idea adds a fascet to diaspora theory highlighting those who move back and forth between their country of origin and their other home, i.e. return migration. In addition to "rural to urban" internal migration, there is "back-to-the-land movement," i.e. urban to rural areas for better quality of life (without traffic congestion, air and noise pollution). (Jacob 1996, 1997; Halfacree 2007)[57]

The application of "network theory" to the study of migration has proven to be meaningful and fruitful, e.g. Banerjee (1983), Brettell 2000, Vertovec 2002.[58] The validity of such approach is clearly stated below:

> "Networks connect migrants across time and space. Once begun, migration flows often become self-sustaining, reflecting the establishment of networks of information, assistance and obligations which develop between migrants in the host society and friends and relatives in the sending area. These networks link populations in origin and receiving countries and ensure that movements are not necessarily limited in time, unidirectional or permanent." (Boyd 1989:641)[59]

Network perspective provides a new approach to the old issue of "brain drain" as proven by the two studies:

- Meyer, J-B. and M. Brown (1999) 'Scientific diasporas: A new approach to the brain drain,' Paris: UNESCO-MOST Discussion Paper No. 41 (www.unesco.org/most/meyer.htm)

---

[55] *Boundary 2: An International Journal of Literature and Culture*, Duke University, 37(1) (Spring 2010).

[56] Linda Basch, Nina Glick Schiller, and Cristina Szanton Blanc. *Nations Unbound.- Transnational Projects, Postcolonial Predicaments, and Deterritorialized Nation-States*. (Langhorne, Pa, 1994). Quoted in: R. Stephen Warner; Judith G. Wittner. *Gatherings In Diaspora: Religious Communities and the New Immigration* (Kindle Location 182). Kindle Edition 1998.

[57] Jacob, J.R. and Todaro, M.P. "The North American back-to-the-land movement," *Community Development Journal.* 31:241-249, 1970. Jacob J., *New Pioneers: The Back-to-land Movement and the Search for a Sustainable Future.* University Park: Pennsylvania State University Press. Halfacree, K. Back-to-the-land in the twenty-first-century: Making connections with rurality. *Tijdschrift voor Economische en Sociatle Geografie* 98(1):3-8, 2007.

[58] Banerjee B, "Social networks in the migration process: empirical evidence on chain migration in India," *The Journal of Developing Areas,* Vol. 17, No. 2, Jan., 1983. Brettell, C.B. (2000) 'Theorizingmigration in anthropology: The social construction of networks, identities, communities and globalscapes,' in Migration Theory, C.B. Brettell and J.F. Hollifield (eds.), London: Routledge, pp. 97-135. Steven Vertovec, "Transnational Networks and Skilled Labour Migration," Paper presented at the conference: Ladenburger Diskurs "Migration" Gottlieb Daimler- und Karl Benz-Stiftung, Ladenburg, 14-15 February 2002.

[59] Boyd, M. (1989) 'Family and personal networks in international migration: Recent developments and new agendas,' *International Migration Review* 23(3): 638-70.

- Meyer, J-B. (2001) 'Network approach versus brain drain: Lessons from the diaspora,' *International Migration* 39: 91-108

It is interesting to note that Meyer and Brown (1999) have identified at least 41 formal knowledge networks linking 30 countries to their skilled diaspora abroad in several types:

"student/scholarly networks, local association of skilled expatriates, expert pool assistance through TOKTEN, and intellectual/scientific diaspora networks. Just as such networks exist to 'tap the diaspora' for home country development, they can also be utilized for skilled labour recruitment and movement outside of the homeland." (Steven Vertovec 2002:8)

Unlike the migrants of earlier generation, the phenomena of "connectivity" and "transnationalism" are possible and prominent due to more efficient and lower cost in communication and transportation at the turn of the century:

"Newer, cheaper, and more efficient modes of communication and transportation allow migrants to maintain transnationally their home-based relationships and interests. Today, globally 'stretched' patterns of activity affect a variety of migrants' social relations (including friendship, kinship and status hierarchies), modes of economic exchange, processes political mobilization, practices of cultural reproduction (including religious practices, institutions like marriage, images and symbols affecting group identity) forms of information transfer, and nature of professional association." (Steven Vertovec 2002:4)[60]

The Phenomenon of Diaspora with Significant Missiological Implications

Advance communication technology enables people stay connected regardless of spatial distance and improved transportation system accelerates the movement of people at large scale and at reduced time. More affordable and accessible media for communication and more economical and efficient mode of transportation facilitate a closer tie between globalized market economy and transnational work force. These multi facets of 21st century reality have multiple

---

[60] Vertovec's paper and the extensive listing of intellectual diaspora organizations/networks identified by Meyer and Brown are available:
http://www.transcomm.ox.ac.uk/working%20papers/WPTC-02-02%20Vertovec.pdf Accessed Dec. 20, 2013.
Steven Vertovec, "Transnational Networks and Skilled Labour Migration," Paper presented at the conference: Ladenburger Diskurs "Migration" Gottlieb Daimler- und Karl Benz-Stiftung, Ladenburg, 14-15 February 2002.

implications for research on the phenomenon of diaspora with significant missiological implications as covered in Part 3 and Part 4:

In diaspora study, temporal-spatial factors are vitally important yet both have been significantly impacted by advanced technology in communication and transportation in the 21st century. For example, in Figure 3.1, increased flow of information and affordable transportation minimize (and even remove) "obstacle" between locations (i.e. origin and destination) in migration.

Spatial inequality in economy and opportunity between origin and destination generates powerful forces for influx of migrants who seek greener pasture, better living condition and more opportunity in distant land.

Technological advancement in social media and mode of transportation is impactful on reducing temporal-spatial gaps and removing barriers for diaspora. They are helpful in the understanding of the dynamics of homeward flow of information and export of migrants to destination (see Figure 3.2).

These factors also enable diaspora to become "transnational" with real

time news from homeland (communication) and on-gong contact (connectivity) with those who stay behind. They can also live within the context of "double culture" simultaneously; not bi-cultural in the assimilation model but "liminal."

The above factors, along with the forces of globalization, generate

powerful forces that led to the global movement of diaspora from southern hemisphere to the northern hemisphere (the "industrial west" though Japan and Australia are not geographically north or west).

In this 21st century reality with lesser temporal-spatial rigidity/boundary/modality, there is the cultural fluidity (luminality), fusion of ethnic identity (even hybridity) and transnational linkage (connectivity) among diaspora both personally and socially, at individual and institutional levels. See Chapter 10 for definition and discussions of the following terms: temporal-spatial rigidity/boundary/modality, connectivity, hybridity, luminality.

In the 21st century, people are highly mobile and better connected virtually via social media but are starving for real relationship. Thus the study of network and the practice of personal/relational approach are essential and effective.

Summary

In the last few decades, the phenomenon of diaspora has increased in scale and intensity thus attracting attention of researchers and practitioners. Consequently, many have theorized diaspora with fruitful outcomes. Christian missiologists and ministerial practitioners cannot afford to be uninformed by findings of non-Christian researchers and scholars. Instead, they should be responsive to the challenge of the phenomenon of diaspora and take hold of opportunities presented by the massive movement of people in contemporary society.

Chapter 4

Exploring the Major Dispersion Terms and Realities in the Bible

Narry F. Santos

Introduction

The concept of Jewish scattering or dispersion is evident throughout the Bible. From the time of the Old Testament, the Jews have been dispersed out of Palestine. As used in this paper, the expression "Jewish dispersion" refers to the scattering of Jews outside their homeland. It is also the technical name for all the nations outside of Palestine where Jewish people had come to live (Moo 2000:50).

In a general and expanded way, the Jewish dispersion began with the deportations by the Assyrians (722 B.C.) and Babylon (597 B.C.), and later spread throughout the Roman Empire to Egypt, Asia Minor, Greece, and Italy. The focus of this study will be on the Jews living outside of Palestine (Brown 1967: 55) throughout the known world during the biblicalperiod.

This chapter fulfills three purposes. First, it seeks to survey all the Hebrew words of the Old Testament and all the Greek words of the New Testament that reveal the concept of scattering or dispersing of the Jewish people. Second, it explores dispersion realities during biblicaltimes (e.g., synagogues, proselytes, God-fearers). Third, in light of the first two purposes, this paper aims to list some insights on the impact of the Jewish dispersion on Christianity and its missions mandate.

Biblical Terms for the Concept of Scattering

The study of biblicalscattering begins with an investigation of the major terms used in the Old and New Testaments on the concept of dispersion. This section inspects all the occurrences of the seven Hebrew roots that communicate dispersion in the Old Testament. In addition, this section discusses the two Greek cognate words on dispersion in the New Testament.

Hebrew Root Words on the Old Testament Concept of Dispersion

The concept of dispersion or scattering in the Old Testament is contained in seven root words with different contexts and uses. Such a variety of words in Hebrew shows that there is no fixed or technical word for the concept of dispersion. The seven root words that communicate different aspects of the concept of scattering are: (1) *gola* (exiles)/*gala* (remove)/*galut* (captivity), (2) *zara* (spread, winnow), (3) *nadah* (banish), (4) *napas* (scatter), (5) *pus* (disperse), (6) *pazar* (scatter abroad), and (7) *parad* (separate).

Gola (Exiles)/Gala (Remove)/Galut (Captivity)

The Hebrew word *gola*, which occurs 41 times in the Old Testament,[61] can mean captivity, captive, those carried away, or removing. It is a feminine noun that refers to anyone carried away captive or to captivity itself. Most of the references to captivity apply to the Babylonian captivity of Judah resulting from Judah's sinful disobedience.

Related to the noun *gola* is the verb *gala*, which occurs 187 times.[62] In its transitive sense (which is found in the Qal, Niphal, Piel, Pual, and Hithpael stems), *galah* means "to uncover" (occurring 112 times in the Hebrew and 7 times in the Aramaic). In its intransitive sense (which is found in the Qal, Hiphil, and Hophal stems), it means "to go into exile, to remove, to depart," and occurs 75 times in the Hebrew and twice in the Aramaic). *Galah* is remotely related to the Ugaritic verb of motion *gly*, "to leave" or "to arrive at," and to the Arabic *gala*, "to emigrate."

The basic meaning of the intransitive *gala* appears in Ezekiel, where the prophet receives the command to "go forth," and in the lament of Phineas's grieving wife: "The glory of Israel is departed." Similarly, this meaning is found in Isaiah's words of lament: "The mirth of the land is gone" (Isaiah 24:11) and in

---

[61] The 41 occurrences of *gola* are found in the prophets (e.g., Jeremiah, Ezekiel, Amos, Nahum, Zechariah) and Kings, Chronicles, Ezra, Nehemiah, and Esther.
[62] Of the 187 instances of *gala*, 50 are in the Qal, 32 in the Niphil, 56 in the Piel, 38 in the Hiphil, 7 in the Hophal, 2 in the Pual, and 2 in the Hitpael.

Zophar's description of the fate of the wicked: "The increase of his house shall depart" (Job 20:28).

The prophets, especially Amos and Jeremiah,[63] prominently announce the judgment on Israel of being led or carried away into exile. In some passages, the Lord is designated as the one who leads Israel into captivity (Jeremiah 29:4, 7, 14; Ezekiel 39:28; Amos 5:27; Lamentations 4:22; 1 Chronicles 5:41). At one time, His activity of judging the nation is identified clearly with a political event: ". . . the Lord by the hand of Nebuchadnezzar" (1 Chronicles 5:41).

The Lord's judgment to lead Israel out of the land into exile functions as a major contrast to his carrying out his promises to give the people the land as a gift at the beginning of their history as a nation. Similarly, his repeated promises to them in giving the land contrasts sharply with his repeated warnings through the prophets to lead them out of the land. Thus, *gala* may have become a specialized term later in the nation's history to mean "to be taken into exile," when deportations of whole population groups as a means of conquest entered into Israel's history (Jenni and Westermann 1997:316).

In addition to *gala* and *gola*, the Hebrew word *galut* adds value to the concept of scattering. *Galut* means "captivity, captive, or carried away captive." The 15 references to the feminine noun *galut* point to a group of captives (Isaiah 20:4, 45:13; Jeremiah 24:5, 28:4), or to a period of captivity, variously specified as the captivity of Jehoiachin (2 Kings 25:27; Ezekiel 1:2) or our captivity (Ezekiel 33:21, 40:1). Almost all of the occurrences refer to the exile of Judah in Babylon.

Zara (Spread, Winnow)

Aside from *gola/gala/galut*, the Hebrew root *zara*, which occurs 38 times in the Old Testament, contributes to the concept of dispersion the ideas of fanning, casting away, and winnowing. The basic thought behind the verb *zara* is to stir up the air to produce a scattering and spreading effect. In its verbal forms, *zara* indicates the acts of scattering or dispersion for purification or chastisement.

As grain is cleansed of chaff by using a fan to blow it away, God's people need purifying and chastening too. Thus the Lord is said to metaphorically "fan" his people (Jeremiah 15:7), with the result of them being scattered as chaff to various distant places. Moses warned Israel that this would happen if they forsook the covenant (Leviticus 26:33). Jeremiah (49:32) and Zechariah (1:19; 2:2) also referred to Israel's dispersion by the Gentile foreign invaders. They were to suffer the consequences of their disobedience and unfaithfulness to God.

---

[63] The prophetic passages that talk of Israel's judgment in being led into captivity are Amos 1:5; 5:5, 27; 6:7; 7:11, 17 and Jeremiah 13:19, 20:4, 22:12, 27:20; cf. Lamentations 1:3.

Nadah (Banish)

So far, we have seen that *gola/galah/galut* refer to captivity or exile and that *zara* refers to being spread or winnowed (with a view to purification or chastisement in relation to Israel). The next Hebrew word on dispersion is *nadah*, which occurs 55 times in the Old Testament, meaning "to impel, drive away, or banish." The root basically refers to the action of forcibly driving or pushing something away.

The basic meaning of *nadah* emerges in Deuteronomy 19:5 and 20:19, where it represents the swinging action of an ax (i.e., impelling something away from oneself). David also used this forceful figure when he spoke of the disaster Absalom intended to bring upon him (2 Samuel 15:14). The root *nadah* also pictures the force of wind blowing away a swarm of locusts (Joel 2:20), and the intensity of driving a flock of sheep away (Deuteronomy 22:1) through lions (Jeremiah 50:17), men (Isaiah 13:14), or inept shepherds (Ezekiel 34:4).

Moreover, the Hebrew root is used of God, the great shepherd, who will disown and dispel the flock if they follow false under-shepherds (Deuteronomy 30:17). The flock of God's people will be driven away from his presence into the thick darkness of captivity (Isaiah 8:22) in foreign lands, where they will be mocked (Jeremiah 24:9), eat unclean bread (Ezekiel 4:13), prefer death and will eventually die (Jeremiah 8:3).

However, in contexts where *nadah* appears, God promises not only that he will refine them, but also that he will not completely destroy them (Jeremiah 46:28). He will also return his purified flock to the green fields of the Promised Land (Ezekiel 34:16). God will gather and tend his flock, punish their former oppressors (Jeremiah 46:28), establish his own people forever in his grace (Zephaniah 3:19), and extend his grace beyond the physical descendants (Isaiah 56:8).

Napas (Scatter)

In addition to *gola/galah/galut*, *zarah*, and *nadah*, the fourth Hebrew root on dispersion is *nadas*, which means "to break, dash, beat in pieces, overspread, and scatter." It occurs in only three instances (Genesis 9:19; 1 Samuel 13:11; Isaiah 33:3), where the idea of scattering involves the act of shattering or breaking into pieces. When the concept of being broken up happens, then the scattering also occurs.

Pus (Disperse)

The fifth Hebrew root on scattering is *pus*, which occurs 66 times in the Old Testament.[64] It basically means to disperse or scatter. This word is first used in Scripture to describe the scattering of the families of the Canaanites (Genesis 10:18). It happens on the heels of the Tower of Babel incident (Genesis 11), in which the builders of the tower did not want to be scattered abroad upon the earth. However, the Lord made scattering inevitable by destroying their language.

Three categories repeatedly serve as the subject or object of *pus*, namely: (1) scattering of armies, either the enemy's (Numbers 10:35) or Israel's own (1 Samuel 11:11); (2) scattering of sheep (Ezekiel 34:5-6; Jeremiah 23:1) inadvertently, or through some external threat or the absence of a shepherd; and (3) scattering of Israel, which is sometimes likened to scattered sheep (1 Kings 22:17). When the clause "I/He/the Lord scatters Israel" occurs, it is confined to the prophetic books, either as a reference to past scattering (Ezekiel 20:23) or as a threat of future scattering (Ezekiel 22:15). Thus, it is not the Assyrians or Babylonians who scatter the people of God. They are simply instruments of scattering. God himself is the "scatterer."

Pazar (Scatter Abroad)

The first five Hebrew roots reveal different aspects of the Old Testament concept of scattering: (1) *gola/galah/galut* show captivity, (2) *zarah* highlights spreading or winnowing, (3) *nadah* stresses the idea of banishment, (4) *napas* emphasizes scattering, and (5) *pus* surfaces the idea of dispersing. The sixth Hebrew root, *pazar*, occurs ten times in the Old Testament (half of which are found in the Psaltery).[65] It basically means "to scatter abroad, give freely." *Pazar* is also related to the Hebrew root *bazar*, which means "to distribute, to scatter."

Parad (Separate)

The seventh and last Hebrew root related to scattering is *parad*, which appears 26 times in the Old Testament. The basic meaning of *parad* is to divide or separate. There are four categories in the use of this word: (1) separation of a river into tributaries (Genesis 2:10), (2) separation of the wings of a bird (Ezekiel 1:11), (3) separation of friends on an amiable basis (Genesis 13:9), and (4) dispersal of peoples (Genesis 10:5). In Proverbs, *parad* has the nuance of driving

---

[64] The 64 occurrences of *pus* are broken down as follows: 12 times in the Qal, 15 times in the Hiphal, 37 times in the Hiphil. This Hebrew root is used most often in the prophets (37 times, with 18 of them in Ezekiel and 10 in Jeremiah).

[65] The ten occurrences of *pazar* are found in Esther 3:8; Psalm 53:5, 89:10, 112:9, 141:7, 147:16; Proverbs 11:24; Jeremiah 3:13, 50:17; Joel 3:2.

a wedge between solid friendships, thus dividing and separating friends through discord (Proverbs 16:28; cf. 18:1, 18).

In summary, there is no single, fixed, or technical Hebrew root for the concept of scattering or dispersion. Seven Hebrew words express different aspects of the concept. Of these seven roots, the words *gola/gala/galut* probably communicate more the process of "leading away," "deportation," or "exile." They may have become technical terms for exile or banishment after the destruction of Jerusalem and loss of the Palestinian homeland (Schmidt 1962:99).

Regarding Israel's captivity and scattering, God is the one who does the scattering, using foreign nations as instruments of the dispersion. Yet God will not allow the scattering to be permanent. He will cause the people's return, after refinement and chastisement of the whole nation.

Greek Words in the New Testament for the Concept of Dispersion

Besides investigating the major Hebrew roots on the Old Testament concept of scattering, it is important to check out the Greek words on the same concept in the New Testament. Two Greek words convey this concept of dispersion; namely: *diaspora* (scattered) and *diaspeiro* (to scatter). These two New Testament words add depth to the Old Testament understanding of dispersion.

Diaspora (Scattered)

The Greek word *diaspora,* a verbal substantive, is commonly translated as "scattered." It occurs only thrice in the New Testament. These are:

1. "The Jews said to one another, 'Where does this man intend to go that we cannot find him? Will he go where our people live scattered among the Greeks, and teach the Greeks?'" (John 7:35);

2. "James, a servant of God and of the Lord Jesus Christ, To the twelve tribes scattered among the nations: Greetings" (James 1:1); and

3. "Peter, an apostle of Jesus Christ, To God's elect, strangers in the world, scattered throughout Pontus, Galatia, Cappadocia, Asia and Bithynia" (1 Peter 1:1).

In John 7:35, the Jews in Palestine raise the questions, "Where does this man intend to go that we cannot find him? Will he go where our people live *scattered* among the Greeks, and teach the Greeks?" Their questions reveal a lack of comprehension of Jesus' comment, "You will look for me, but you will not find me; and where I am, you cannot come" (John 7:34).

EXPLORING THE MAJOR DISPERSION TERMS AND REALITIES IN THE BIBLE

In these questions by the Jews, the word *diaspora* ("scattered") is used as a reference to the Jewish minority in the midst of other religions, in this case the Greek-speaking environment (Sänger 1990:311). The "Greeks" are a general reference to Gentiles, whom Jews would normally call Greeks (cf. Col. 3:11).

In James 1:1, James greets "the twelve tribes *scattered* among the nations" in his salutation. The mention of the "twelve tribes" can either refer to the literal twelve tribes of the nation of Israel or to the figurative "twelve tribes," as a reference to the true people of God (thus broadening the Jewish roots to include the church of James' day).

Although the figurative sense of Christians (both Jews and Gentiles) may be the possible reference to "the twelve tribes *scattered* among the nations," it seems better to take the scholarly consensus[66] that the expression refers to the Jewish Christians, who were scattered across the Roman empire. The following references to Jewish institutions and practices contribute to the conclusion of a Jewish audience:

1. the believers whom James addressed met in a "synagogue" (James 2:2);
2. the believers shared the assumption that monotheism is a foundational belief (James 2:19);
3. the people believed that the law was central to God's dealings with his people (James 1:21, 24-25; 2:8-13; 4:11-12); and
4. the people understood the Old Testament imagery of the marriage relationship to indicate the nature of the relationship between God and his people (James 4:4).

In 1 Peter 1:1, Peter describes his audience as "God's elect, strangers in the world, *scattered* throughout Pontus, Galatia, Cappadocia, Asia and Bithynia." Like James' use, the Petrine *diaspora* refers to the scattered communities outside Palestine.

Particularly, Peter lists the Jewish Christians who lived in the Gentile regions of "Pontus, Galatia, Cappadocia, Asia and Bithynia." These localities refer to the northwest quadrant of Asia Minor bordering the Black Sea (Davids 1990:7), an area which Luke reports Paul was not allowed to evangelize.[67] In addition to a Jewish Christian audience, Paul addresses the Gentile Christians (1

---

[66] Dibelius simply specifies the addressees as the *diaspora* Jewish Christian church and thus not Palestinian (Dibelius 1976: 47). Other scholars even venture to name the provenance of the letter. Moffat locates the work in Egypt, due to its alleged wisdom affinities (Moffatt 1928). Reicke and Laws see similarities between the epistle to Hermas and alleged Roman flavor, such that they argue for a Roman provenance (Reicke 1964, 6 and Laws 1980, 22-26). Ropes places James in Caesarea of Palestine-Syria (Ropes 1916, 49; cf. Davids 1982, 28-34).

[67] In Acts 16:6-10, Luke narrated that Paul established churches in the southern area of Galatia. Of course, Paul did so later in the Western province of Asia.

Peter 1:14,18; 2:9-10, 25; 3:6; 4:3-4). He even applies categories to them that relate to Jews.[68]

Thus, Peter's use of *diaspora* can include the "communities of people living outside their native land, which are not Jerusalem or Palestine but the heavenly city" (Davids 1990:46). These scattered communities were to view their lives on earth as temporary (thus, as aliens, sojourners, pilgrims, and foreigners who belonged to heaven).

Diaspeiro (Scatter)

Aside from the three occurrences of the word *diaspora* found in John 7:35, James 1:1, and 1 Peter 1:1, it is important to discuss the verb form of *diaspora*, which is *diaspeiro*. Only three instances of this verb appear in the New Testament. These three instances occur in the following verses (all found in the Book of Acts:

1. "On that day a great persecution broke out against the church at Jerusalem, and all except the apostles were scattered throughout Judea and Samaria" (Acts 8:1b);

2. "Those who had been scattered preached the word wherever they went" (Acts 8:4); and

3. "Now those who had been scattered by the persecution in connection with Stephen traveled as far as Phoenicia, Cyprus and Antioch, telling the message only to Jews" (Acts 11:19).

In all three cases, *diaspeiro* relates to the scattering of the Christians of Hellenistic Jewish origin, Greek-speaking Jewish Christians from the *diaspora*, into areas with a non-Jewish majority (Acts 11:19), but also in the area around Jerusalem and toward Samaria (Acts 8:1). The unique contribution of these verses in the use of *diaspeiro* is that those who were scattered served an essential purpose in the expansion of early Christianity or to missions (Acts 8:4-8, 40; 11:19-21).

Use of Dispersion in the Septuagint

Besides the Hebrew and Greek words for dispersion in the Old and New Testaments, the use of the word *diaspora* in the LXX (Septuagint) can shed light on progressive use of the term over time. In the Greek translation of the Hebrew

---

[68] For example, Peter described the Gentile Christians (i.e., who were "once not a people" and now are "the people of God" [2:10a]) as "a chosen people, a royal priesthood, a holy nation, a people belonging to God" (which are descriptions given earlier for Israel).

Old Testament (i.e., LXX or Septuagint, including the Apocrypha), the technical term *diaspora* is found in 12 passages: Deuteronomy 28:25; 30:4; Nehemiah 1:9; Psalm 146:2; Isaiah 49:6; Jeremiah 13:14; 15:7; 34:17; Daniel 12:2; Judith 5:19; 2 Maccabees 1:27; and Psalm of Solomon 8:34. They generally refer to the "dispersion of the Jews among the Gentiles" or "the Jews as thus scattered" (Schmidt 1962:99).

The term *diaspora* is used in the LXX for the exile of the scattered people of God among the Gentiles (Deuteronomy 28:25; 30:4; Psalm 146:2; Isaiah 49:6; Jeremiah 15:7; 34:17; 2 Maccabees 1:27; Judith 5:19). Moreover, *diaspora* can refer to both the dispersion and the totality of the dispersed (Isaiah 49:6; Psalm 146:2; 2 Maccabees 1:27; Psalm of Solomon 8:34). However, in the LXX the three cognate Hebrew words *gola/gala/galut* are always rendered in the Greek with words other than *diaspora*.[69]

Dispersion Realities in the Bible

The study of the major Hebrew and Greek words on dispersion reveals the understanding and usage of the concept throughout the Bible. In addition, a quick survey of some key passages or instances in the Bible delineated the dispersion realities of the Jewish people in both the Old and New Testaments.

Dispersion Realities in the Old Testament

It is difficult to ascertain how early the voluntary dispersion of the Jewish people to non-Palestinian communities began. However, there is a hint of an established Jewish colony in Damascus during the reign of King Ahab. Ben-Hadad said to the king, "I will return the cities my father took from your father. You may set up your own market areas in Damascus, as my father did in Samaria" (1 Kings 20:34). Possibly, similar alliances of Kings David and Solomon with Phoenicia would have created more similar colonies there.

However, the conquests of the Assyrian kings introduced the new dimension of dispersion. Assyria forced the transplantation of segments of the Jewish population to other parts of the empire. In the eighth century BC, Tiglath-pileser III carried many Israelites captive to Assyria (2 Kings 15:29), and Sargon transported 27,290 Hebrews from Samaria and settled them in Mesopotamia and Media (2 Kings 17:6).

Then the more thorough dispersion began with the Babylonian exile. King Nebuchadnezzar transplanted to Babylonia the choicest of the Judean population (2 Kings 24:12-16; 25:11; Jeremiah 52:15). Probably 50,000 were

---

[69] The Greek words αιχμαλωσια, αποικια, αποικισμος, μετοικεσια, ανδ παροικια, are associated with the three Hebrew words *gola/gala/galut*.

transported, and Jewish communities were formed in Babylonia, as in Tel-Abib (Ezekiel 3:15) and Casiphia (Ezra 8:17). Here the Jewish religion was maintained; prophets like Ezekiel and priests like Ezra sprang up; the old laws were studied and worked over; the Pentateuch was elaborated.

Many Jews decided to remain in Babylonia, despite Cyrus's permission for the Jews to return to their land (2 Chronicles 36:22-23; Ezra 1:1-4). From this center, Jews radiated to many parts of the East (Nehemiah 1:1ff; Tobit 1:9-22; Isaiah 11:11). Thus, the Jews reached Media, Persia, Cappadocia, Armenia, and the Black Sea.

In 608 BC, Necho took King Jehoahaz and probably others to Egypt. In this general period, colonies of Jews lived in Egyptian cities of Memphis, Migdol, Tahpanhes, and Pathros in Egypt (Jeremiah 44:1). Recently discovered papyri prove the existence of a large Jewish colony and a Jewish temple at the First Cataract in the fifth century BC.[70]

Dispersion Realities in the New Testament

Having looked at the Old Testament realities of the Jewish dispersion, it is time to examine dispersion realities in the New Testament. These are quite evident in the events or passages that show the Jewish scattering, and in the presence of synagogues, proselytes, and God-fearers in the historical books of the New Testament, particularly the Acts of the Apostles.

Dispersion Realities during the New Testament Period

After his capture of Jerusalem in 63 BC, Pompey carried off hundreds of Jews to Rome, where they were sold as slaves. But in the middle of the second century BC, the Roman Senate was anxious to extend protection to the Jews. The Senate had a circular letter in favor of the Jews written to the kings of Egypt, Syria, Pergamum, Cappadocia, and Parthia, and to a number of Mediterranean provinces, cities, and islands where Jews were presumably present (1 Maccabees 15:15ff).

Thus, it is no surprise to read that at the Feast of Pentecost in Jerusalem, there were present after Jesus' ascension "Parthians, Medes and Elamites; residents of Mesopotamia, Judea and Cappadocia, Pontus and Asia, Phrygia and Pamphylia, Egypt and the parts of Libya near Cyrene; visitors from Rome (both Jews and converts to Judaism); Cretans and Arabs" (Acts 2:9-11). This account of the Pentecost crowd demonstrates that the spread of the dispersion

---

[70] Other Jews seem to have followed Alexander the Great to Egypt (Jos. *BJ* II. xviii. 8; *c. Apion* ii. 4). Many others migrated to Egypt under the Ptolemys (*Ant.* xii. i. 1, ii. 1 ff). Philo estimated the number of Jews in Egypt in the reign of Caligula (38-41 AD) at a million.

was not confined to the Roman empire. It was also prominent in the Persian sphere of influence.

These dispersion communities visited Jerusalem and made pilgrimages for the three great national feasts of Israel as they were able (Acts 2:5ff; 8:27), and often had closer ties with the mother-country. They even paid the half-shekel tax for upkeep and services in the Temple and maintained contact with each other and with Jerusalem (Acts 28:21ff). Moreover, they gave voluntary submission to the national polity and decrees of the great Sanhedrin. Thus, despite their distance, these dispersion communities were loyal to the religion of the homeland.

Dispersion Reality through the Synagogues

However, the dispersion communities were situated in different cultural settings, and they formed their own synagogues (like the "Synagogue of the Freedmen"[71] in Acts 6:9). The synagogues were places of assembly used by Jewish communities primarily for public worship and instruction, or for assembly purpose.

The Greek derivation of the term *sunagogei* indicates a gathering, void of any religious connotation. But with the first century AD, the term *sunagogei* appeared in Jewish sources (like Philo and Josephus) and especially in the New Testament more and more in the sense of a "place of assembly" (cf. Grabbe 1988:401-410) and a "house of worship and instruction"[72] (cf. Kee 1990:1-24).

Although the origin of the synagogue cannot be certainly recovered, a dominant theory has been proposed. The beginning of the synagogue could have been during the Babylonian exile, with its consolidation in Palestine as a result of Ezra's work. In the sixteenth century, Carolus Sigonius, an expert in the field of political institutions of the Greeks and Romans, described this dominant view:

> I would surmise that synagogues were first erected in the Babylonian exile for the purpose that those who have been deprived of the Temple of Jerusalem, where they used to pray and teach, would have a certain place similar to the temple, in which they could assemble and perform

---

[71] The "freedmen" refers to a group of Jews originally from Italy who had settled in Jerusalem and had their own synagogue. Philo (*Legatio ad Gaium* 23.155) tells of Jews who lived across the Tiber in Rome, "most of whom were emancipated Roman citizens," originally captives brought to Italy.
[72] Aside from *sunagogei*, another Greek name for the place of Jewish worship is *proseuchei*, "prayer." It is used metonymically in the sense of "house of prayer." The two terms *sunagogei* and *proseuchei* probably originated from different cultural centers. The term *proseuchei* seems to have been adopted by the Hellenistic Jews of Egypt and spread to Greece, Asia Minor, and Rome. It is sometimes used as a technical term for a place where Jews gathered to pray (cf. 3 Maccabees 7:20). On the other hand, *sunagogei* reflects the Palestinian scene.

> the same kind of service. The same, I think, did the other Jews in the dispersion, be it in Asia or in Egypt or in Europe. It was for this reason that the custom of synagogues was first established in the provinces where there was no temple. After the return from Babylon and the restoration of the temple of Jerusalem, the Jews still retained the well-established institution of the synagogue, namely, so that while the residents of the city of Jerusalem attended the reading of the Law in the temple, all those coming to the city from the provinces attended the reading of the Law in their respective synagogues (quoted in Hastings 1989: 478-479).

Thus, reading from the Scriptures and exposition of the Law constituted the focal point in sabbatical gatherings, which gave the synagogues the character of an educational institution. But it has long been recognized that synagogues were not confined to religious worship. They fulfilled some secular and semi-secular functions such as funeral services (*Tosef. Meg.* III), political gatherings (*Life* LIV), meeting places for public announcements (*Lev. Rabbah* 6.2), inns for itinerant travelers (*P.T. Ber.* 5d),[73] and law courts for administering justice. In the New Testament, synagogues are even found in juxtaposition to magistrates (Luke 12:11).

Paul saw the strategic role that synagogues played in the missionary expansion of God's word. Luke's Acts of the Apostles is full of the narrative motif of depicting Paul, along with his missionary cohorts, evangelizing diaspora Jews first. When he arrived at a new place, his first stopover was a diaspora synagogue.

This pattern in Paul's activity is seen in the synagogue of Damascus (Acts 9:20). It is repeated in Pisidian Antioch (Acts 13:14), Iconium (Acts 14:1), Philippi (Acts 16:13), Thessalonica (Acts 17:1-2), Berea (Acts 17:10), Athens (17:17), Corinth (Acts 18:4-6), and Ephesus (Acts 18:19; 19:8). Even though he declared in Pisidian Antioch that he would "now turn to the Gentiles" (Acts 13:46) due to the Jews' rejection, Paul still continued to address fellow Jews first in synagogues (Acts 18:4-6, 19; 19:8).

Paul saw himself as Christ's chosen instrument to carry the Lord's name "before the Gentiles and their kings and before the people of Israel" (Acts 9:15). Although he spoke of his conversion on the road to Damascus as the place where he received the call to preach Christ among the Gentiles (Galatians 1:16), and although he called himself "an apostle of the Gentiles" (Romans 11:13), Paul nevertheless thought himself obligated to all human beings:

> "To the Jews I became like a Jew, to win the Jews. To those under the law I became like one under the law (though I myself am not under the law), so

---

[73] A Tannaitic ruling forbids eating, drinking, and sleeping in the synagogue (*T.B. Meg.* 28a-b). However, most scholars take the term *synagogue* in this context in its larger sense of comprising the precinct, which contained a special guest room.

as to win those under the law. To those not having the law I became like one not having the law I became lone one not having the law (though I am not free from God's law but am under Christ's law), so as to win those not having the law" (1 Corinthians 9:20-21).

Thus, in Paul's missionary journeys, Luke depicts Paul as continuing to enter the synagogues of the Jews.

Dispersion Realities through Proselytes and God-fearers

Both proselytes and God-fearers are found in the New Testament. They were influenced toward Judaism because of the efforts of the diaspora Jews. In the Acts of the Apostles, Paul encounters and addresses these two groups that show the dispersion realities of that period.

At Pentecost, the different peoples gathered in Jerusalem were described as "both Jews and converts to Judaism" (Acts 2:11). The term "converts to Judaism" comes from the Greek noun *proselytos*, which literally means "one who has come over" (Fitzmyer 1998:243) or "to turn around" (Neusner and Green 1999:133). It is used in this passage in a technical sense, as a "convert" to Judaism, one who has submitted to circumcision and has been won over by Jewish missionary efforts among Gentiles (cf. Matthew 23:15).

In a less technical sense, *proselytos* occurs in the LXX as the translation of the Hebrew term *ger*, which refers to a "resident alien" (Exodus 22:21; Ezekiel 14:7). Although some rabbis vehemently opposed accepting converts (claiming that they were the source of the troubles that often plagued the Jews), many other rabbis favored accepting converts into the community, describing Abraham as the first Jew to seek converts and teaching that all Jews should follow his lead by attempting to win over Gentiles to the worship of Yahweh.

However, some restrictions or theoretical distinctions were maintained. Apparently, converts could not marry into a priestly family, especially into the high priest's clan. Several sages believed that converts could not own a parcel of Israel's land, and some held that they could not address Yahweh as "the God of our ancestors" in public worship.

If men submitted to circumcision, sojourners could participate in some rituals. In Exodus 12:48, the instruction is clear: "An alien living among you who wants to celebrate the Lord's Passover must have all the males in his household circumcised; then he may take part like one born in the land. No uncircumcised male may eat of it." In addition, Esther 8:17 is the first textual example of conversion to a new belief system, as opposed to ethnic affiliation: "And many people of other nationalities became Jews (i.e., *mityehudim*, "declared themselves Jews").

Conversion to Judaism was not an uncommon phenomenon in antiquity, as attested by sources as diverse as Juvenal, Josephus, Joseph and Asenath, and early Christian documents.[74] Jewish rituals of conversion included circumcision for males, donation of money to the Temple, and eventually ritual immersion.

Besides the proselytes or converts, Paul also talked about another group of Gentiles who were influenced by diaspora Jews. This second group is known as the "God-fearers." In Acts 10:2, Paul described Cornelius, the Roman centurion, as devout and God-fearing. The Greek expression for "God-fearing" is *phoboumenos ton theon* (literally, "fearing God"). It is a quasi-technical phrase that occurs again in Acts 10:22, 35; 13:16, 26 and undoubtedly reflects the Septuagintal expression *hoi phoboumenoi ton Kyrion* ("fearing the Lord") — seen in Psalm 115:11; 118:4; and 135:20 as a reference to Jews.

But more often, the term "God-fearers" is taken as the equivalent of the more Hellenistic *sebomenos ton theon*, "worshiping God" or "God-worshiper" (Acts 13:50; 16:14; 17:4, 17; 18:7; cf. 18:13; 19:27). As quasi-technical phrases, both seem to have been used to denote "God-fearers" who were non-Jews sympathetic to Judaism, and who did not submit to circumcision or observe the Torah in its entirety, but who did agree with the ethical monotheism of the Jews and attended their synagogue services (cf. Wilcox 1981:102-22). In other words, "God-fearers" is a quasi-technical term for Gentile sympathizers who followed many Jewish practices without becoming full converts (especially males, for whom circumcision would have been a difficult step to take).

Dispersion Realities in Extra-Biblical Literature

Besides biblical literature and dispersion realities through the synagogues, proselytes, and God-fearers, a number of extra-biblical sources picture the period of the Jewish dispersion.[75] Probably few major cities or regions lacked a community of resident Jews.[76]

Evidence of Jewish settlements or communities were found in Nehardea, Nisibis (Josephus *Ant.* 18.9.1 §§311-312), Seleucia (Josephus *Ant.* 18.9.8-9 §§372-379), Antioch (Josephus *Ant.* 12.3.1 §119),[77] Lydia and Phrygia in Asia

---

[74] According to Josephus, John Hyrcanus I converted the Idumeans; Aristobolus I, the Itureans; and Alexander Janneus, Pella. Among the more famous Jewish converts or proselytes are the Ammonite Achior (Judith), the royal house of Adiabene, Flavius Clemens (Vespasian's nephew), Fulvia (the wife of senator Saturninus), and Nicolaus, the Deacon (Acts 6:5).

[75] A sampling of these extra-biblical sources are as follows: Artapanus; Aristobulus, Demetrius; *Joseph and Aseneth*; Josephus; *Epistle of Aristeas*; Philo; Pseudo-Philo; *Pseudo-Phocylides*; some of the *Sibylline Oracles*; *Testament of Abraham* and Wisdom of Solomon. Other sources include some papyri and inscriptions, six excavated *diaspora* synagogues, and texts from non-Jewish authors who wrote their perceptions on Jews and Judaism.

[76] Instances that support the statement that probably few major cities or regions were without a community of resident Jews are as follows: Philo *Leg. Gai* 214, 281-83; *Flacc.* 45-46; *Vit. Mos.* 2.232; Josephus *Ant.* 14.7.2 §115; *J.W.* 7.3.3 §43; 1 Macc. 15:23-24; *Sib. Or.* 3:271-272; Acts 2:9-11.

[77] The Jewish community in Antioch, which was the largest in Syria, probably began in the third century B.C.

Minor (Josephus *Ant*. 12.3.4 §§147-153),[78] the kingdom of Bosporus,[79] Egypt,[80] Teuchira, Apollonia, Ptolemais, and Latin-speaking North Africa (Trebilco 2000:284), Macedonia, Greece, Thessaly, Boetia, Aetolia, Attica, Argos, Corinth, most of the Peloponnese and the islands of Euboea and Crete (Philo *Leg. Gai.* 281-282), and Rome.[81]

By the end of the first century B.C., Philo could claim that "Jews dwelling in Alexandria and Egypt from the Libyan slope to the borders of Aethiopia do not fall short of a million" and that "no single country can contain the Jews because of their multitude" (Philo *Flacc*. 43, 45). Although Philo's figures are not reliable, there is no doubt that the Jewish population did grow fast (Collins 2000:5).

Evidence seems to indicate that the total Jewish population of the *diaspora* considerably exceeded the Jewish population in Palestine (Tcherikover 1970:292-295), and that diaspora Jews constituted a group of significant size. Scholars often suggest that five to six million Jews were living in the *diaspora* during the first century, but such figures can be only speculative.

What was the economic situation of the diaspora Jews? While the general impression from the papyri "is that of a hard-working people earning its living by tenacious labor," there were many who prospered, and no branch of economic life was closed to them (Tcherikover and Fuks 1957-1964:19; Applebaum 1976:701-727).

Specifically, Jews of the diaspora were soldiers, land-owning farmers, agricultural laborers, shepherds, artisans, manual workers, traders, merchants, bankers, government officials, and slaves (Trebilco 2000:286). In some Roman writers, Jewish poverty was a byword (Juvenal *Sat*. 3.14-16; 6.542-547). However, there were also some very wealthy Jews. Thus, diaspora Jews were found in almost all socio-economic strata of that period.

So far, the first major section of this paper has surveyed the different Hebrew and Greek words in the Old And New Testaments respectively, and in extra-biblical literature during the biblicalperiod. In the second major section, this chapter looks at dispersion realities during biblicaltimes, especially those that reveal the influence of diaspora Jews through the synagogues, proselytes, and God-fearers. In the third and last section, this paper will provide insights on the Jewish dispersion in relation to Christianity and its missionary mandate.

---

[78] Between 221 and 205 B.C., Antiochus III transferred 2,000 Jewish families from Mesopotamia and Babylonia to Lydia and Phrygia as military settlers. This provides unambiguous evidence of Jewish communities in Asia Minor.

[79] Jews lived in at least three towns in the kingdom of Bosporus. A Jewish inscription from Gorgippia dated 41 A.D. refers to the manumission of a female slave in a synagogue (Levinskaya 1996:227-246). The author spends a whole appendix on the inscriptions from the Bosporan kingdom.

[80] The Jewish communities in Egypt were the largest. At the time of the Babylonian conquest, some Jews fled to Egypt (Jer. 43:6-7, 44:1, 46:14). Aramaic papyri of the 5th century B.C. give evidence of a Jewish military colony at Elephantine, a colony that included a Jewish temple.

[81] A significant number of Jews lived in Rome. Josephus recorded that Pompey brought a number of Jews to Rome as prisoners of war in 63 B.C. (Josephus *Ant*. 14.4.4-5 §§70-71, 79). He also wrote that 8,000 Roman Jews supported an embassy from Judea (Josephus *Ant*. 17.11.1 §300).

Insights on the Impact of the Jewish Dispersion

Movements of individuals (e.g., Abram to the Promised Land; Joseph to Egypt; Ruth with Naomi to Israel) and groups (e.g., Jacob and his household to Egypt; Moses and the Israelites out of Egypt and toward the wilderness experience) appear early in the Old Testament. Various reasons existed for voluntary migration, but the reason for more widespread and expanded forced migration was the series of conquests by foreign nations.

The Jewish dispersion was mainly triggered by conquests of the Assyrian,[82] Babylonian,[83] and Roman (specifically, Pompey)[84] empires. The harsh realities of conquest would have severely wounded the pride of God's chosen people. They reminded the Jews of the outworking of God's severe judgment through scattering; thus, emphasizing pain and curse. In addition, the Jews would have been ridiculed and derided (cf. Psalm 79:4, 10) by the enemies of God, because of their exile.

However, despite the pain and consequences of conquest and their eventual dispersion, the Jewish people learned valuable lessons throughout their national experiences. These experiences were also used providentially by God to impact more people worldwide in relation to Christianity and its missionary mandate.

Four lessons of lasting value to the Jewish nation can be learned from the scattering of its people: (1) God's orchestration and control of the Jewish dispersion; (2) the hope and reality of the people's regathering after the scattering; (3) Israel's role as a witness to all nations in the midst of its dispersion; and (4) sovereign preparation for the advent of Christ and the spread of Christianity.

---

[82] After the death of Solomon (931 B.C.), the kingdom was divided into two, Israel consisting of the northern tribes with important shrines at Dan and Bethel and the capital subsequently set at Samaria. Judah consisted of the southern tribes of Judah and Benjamin, with Jerusalem as the capital. The Northern Kingdom of Israel came to an end in the 8th century B.C., when Samaria fell to the Assyrians in 722. The Assyrians took large numbers of the population captive and replaced them with immigrants. Cf. 2 Kings 15–17.

[83] In the 6th century B.C., the Southern Kingdom of Judah fell to the invading Babylonians, who then dominated the Middle East. Jerusalem fell in 597 and was deported in 581 B.C. Large deportations of the population followed. After the fall of Babylon to Cyrus of Persia (539-530 B.C.), Jews were encouraged to return from exile (although a significant number stayed). However, the monarchy was not restored. Cf. 2 Kings 23-25 (cf. 2 Chronicles 36).

[84] Pompey took hundreds of Jews to Rome as prisoners of war (Trebilco, "Diaspora Judaism," in Craig A. Evans and Stanley E. Porter, eds. *Dictionary of New Testament Background* (Downers Grove, IL: InterVarsity, 2000), 280-296).

God's Orchestration and Control of the Dispersion

God warned the people through Moses that if they forsook his covenant with them (Leviticus 26:33; Jeremiah 49:32; Zechariah 1:19; 2:2), they would be dispersed by foreign Gentile invaders. The Scriptures also make it clear that the foreign invaders were merely instruments of the dispersion. God was often referred to as the orchestrator of the dispersion, the controller of its scope and intensity.

The prophets consistently echoed God's message of judgment to those who refused to changed their ways—the flock of God's people will be driven away from his presence into the thick darkness of captivity (Isaiah 8:22) and into foreign lands where they will be mocked (Jeremiah 24:9). They will eat unclean bread (Ezekiel 4:13), prefer death, and will eventually die (Jeremiah 8:3). Again, God was presented as the source of the dispersion, the purpose of which was for the people's purification, discipline, and chastisement (Jeremiah 29:4, 7, 14; Ezekiel 39:28; Amos 5:27; Lamentations 4:22; 1 Chronicles 5:41). God wanted to keep for Himself a holy nation.

Hope of Regathering after the Scattering

The first lesson for the nation is God's full control of the Jewish dispersion for the purpose of purification. However, the second lesson brings a message of hope. He will not chastise them forever. His process of refining them will not lead to their destruction (Jeremiah 46:28). He will bring them back to the land that he promised to them (Ezekiel 34:16).

As their good shepherd, He will gather and tend His flock, punish their enemies (Jeremiah 46:28), establish His own people under his care (Zephaniah 3:19), and extend his grace beyond what they deserve (Isaiah 56:8). Just as He is in charge of the scattering of the people, so is he also in full control of their regathering. He brings the lost heart of the people back to Himself.

Israel's Role as Witness to the Nations

While the Jewish nation was dispersed, it served as a witness to the nations. Its witness, especially throughout the Roman world, was to be a light for monotheism, and a testimony for the value of Scriptures and the messianic hopes. It was due to the strange and unique influence of Judaism and circulation of the glowing visions of Israel's prophets among the nations that so widespread an expectation existed (mentioned by Tacitus, Suetonius, and Josephus) that from Judea would arise a ruler whose dominion would be over all.

Preparation for Christ's Advent and the Spread of Christianity

It is now believed that Virgil's conception of a Better Age which was to be inaugurated by the birth of a child was derived from Isaiah's prophecies. Not only did the Jewish dispersion prepare the way for Christ, the world's redeemer in the fullness of time, but when he had come, suffered, died, risen, and ascended, it furnished a valuable vehicle for the proclamation of the gospel.

Wherever the apostles and the early preachers traveled with the good news, they found Jewish communities to whom they offered first the gift of salvation. The synagogues became convenient locations for the effective ministry of Paul and his colleagues. It was in the synagogue where they first sought an audience in the cities they visited. The presence of proselytes and God-fearers in these synagogues and cities showed the influence and impact of Judaism through the Jewish dispersion.

Thus, God has used the Jewish dispersion to draw forth the understanding of God's sovereign hand in scattering and regathering his people, in using them to be a witness to the nations despite Israel's chastisement, and in preparing the way for the coming of Christ and the spread of Christianity.

Even to this day, the preservation of the "dispersed of Israel" is one of the marvels of God's providential government of the world, proving the truth of his word through Amos: "For I will give the command, and I will shake the house of Israel among all the nations as grain is shaken in a sieve, and not a pebble will reach the ground" (Amos 9:9).

Summary

In this chapter, a survey had been conducted to cover all the Hebrew words of the Old Testament and all the Greek words of the New Testament that reveal the concept of scattering or dispersing of the Jewish people. Dispersion realities during biblicaltimes, e.g. synagogues, proselytes, God-fearers, had been explored. Gleaned from the survey and dispersion realities are insights on the impact of the Jewish dispersion on Christianity and its missions mandate. Thus a biblicalfoundation is in place for the study of other diasporic groups in the many case studies of Part 4.

Chapter 5

Diaspora Distinctives: The Jewish Diaspora Experience in the Old Testament

Ted Rubesh

Introduction

This chapter is an attempt to view the experience of the Jewish people in the Old Testament through a diasporic lens, and to relate those experiences to the growing phenomenon of global diaspora today. Bound by the parameters of the Hebrew Bible,[85] it will seek to elicit the salient characteristics and dynamics of the Jewish diaspora experience, and to suggest in preliminary form how those experiences serve as progenitors and reference points for understanding the dynamics of the larger diaspora experience emerging across the globe today.

The study begins by briefly discussing the relationship of the Jewish diaspora to diaspora studies in general.[86] It then examines the very root of this ancient community's diaspora experience in the person of its patriarch and "founding father," Abraham himself. This is followed by an attempt to describe and analyze the two seminal diaspora experiences that emerge from Jewish

---

[85] All Scripture quotations in this chapter are taken from the New American Standard Version.
[86] While considerable debate exists about the precise meaning and content of the word *diaspora* as it is currently used, this paper follows Robin Cohen's lead in describing *diasporas* as communities with shared identities such as "language, religion, custom or folklore" that "have settled outside their natal (or imagined natal) territories" and that maintain some sort of loyalty and emotional links with "the old country." See Robin Cohen, *Global Diasporas: An Introduction* (Seattle: University of Washington Press, 1997a), ix. *Diaspora* is in fact a word found in the Greek translation of the Bible, and derives from the verb "to sow" and the preposition "over"; that is, to sow over a wide area, or "to scatter." See Cohen 1997a:2.

history of the Old Testament: the experience of the Hebrew[87] diaspora at the beginning of Israel's national history during the time of its captivity in Egypt, and the experience of the Jewish diaspora in Babylon and Persia at the end of the Old Testament era.[88]

The Global Diaspora and Its Relation to the Jewish Diaspora Experience

The study of diaspora, like the study of many other great movements in history, often begins by building on an archetype or progenitor. Such an archetype provides a model or a foundational reference point from which comparisons and similarities to other diasporas can be drawn. Clearly, the study of the modern global diaspora phenomena takes its cue from the diaspora experience of the ancient Jewish community. Its roots and early history, traced in the Hebrew Bible, provide a formative model for diaspora study, demonstrating significant features of the diaspora experience both globally and historically.[89] The idea of building modern global diaspora studies on an ancient Jewish base is not new. As Cohen says, "… it is impossible to understand the notions of diaspora without first coming to grips with some central aspects of the Jewish experience" (Cohen 1997:2). He goes on to add, "All scholars of diaspora recognize that the Jewish tradition is at the heart of any definition of the concept" (Cohen 1997:21). Boyarin goes so far as to say that "Diaspora … may be the most important contribution that Judaism has to make to the world …."[90]

This is scarcely surprising. Until recently, with the exception of its more theological use in the New Testament, the very word 'diaspora' was used with

---

[87] Without discussing the etymology or the various nuances of the terms "Jewish," "Israelite" and "Hebrew," these terms and their cognates are used interchangeably unless specifically noted otherwise.

[88] For the Old Testament narratives that deal with these diasporic experiences, several assumptions will shape the discussion. It will be assumed for my purposes that the Old Testament is not simply a valuable theological document, but that it is also historically reliable. As such this paper assumes that the biblical record of Israel's experiences both in Egypt and in Babylon/Persia are viable and credible, and that data emerging from the relevant texts (such as numbers of years, numbers of people, major players and key events) are to be taken seriously in understanding the historical context of the diasporic experience. See Lester L. Grabbe, *Ancient Israel* (New York: T&T Clark, 2007) ; Robert B. Coote, *Early Israel: A New Horizon* (Minneapolis: Fortress, 1990) for classic minimalist approaches to the issue of the historicity of the Old Testament narratives.

[89] This is not to say that the parameters of modern diaspora study are limited to a Jewish model. The study of global diasporas will obviously often transcend and supersede the Jewish diasporic tradition.

[90] Daniel and Jonathon Boyarin, "Generation and the Ground of Diaspora" in *Theorizing Diaspora: A Reader*, eds. Jana E Braziel and Anita Mannur (Malden MA: Blackwell Publishing, 2003), 110.

DIASPORA DISTINCTIVES: THE JEWISH DIASPORA EXPERIENCE IN THE OLD TESTAMENT

almost exclusive reference to the Jewish diaspora.[91] To speak of one was essentially to speak of the other.[92] This of course has radically changed in recent years. The diaspora landscape today encompasses a truly global breadth, the word itself being a cipher for scattered communities of many different ethnicities around the world. Yet there is no denying its initial Jewish ambience. The simple fact is that the Jewish experience of diaspora has framed the diaspora discussion and continues to significantly pervade it. Furthermore, it is one of the earliest known and certainly one of the earliest to be documented in written form, as articulated in the Old Testament. For all these reasons it takes a seminal place in diaspora studies.[93]

Scholarly study of the Jewish diaspora typically begins with the exile of the Jewish community at the time of Nebuchadnezzar of Babylon in the latter part of the sixth century B.C. (Cohen 1997:3). This, however, fails to take into consideration the considerable diaspora import of the nation's initial experience in Egypt at the beginning of its national narrative.[94] It also tends to bypass the roots of the community's diaspora experience at the time of the patriarchs, particularly in the person of its "founding father," Abraham himself. The trajectory of the Jewish diaspora experience in the Old Testament in its entirety thus unfolds around three primary sources rather than one: the Jewish diaspora experience in Babylon/Persia at the end of the Old Testament narrative, the Jewish diaspora experience in Egypt at the commencement of its national history, and Jewish diaspora antecedents that preceded these and first emerged in the patriarchal era (Figure 5.1).

---

[91] See Narry F. Santos, "Diaspora in the New Testament and Its Impact on Christian Mission," *Torch Trinity Journal* 13.1 (2010) for a discussion of the New Testament usage of the word *diaspora*.

[92] In the Greek translation of the Old Testament (the LXX), the technical term diaspora is found in a dozen passages generally referring to the "dispersion of the Jews among the Gentiles" or "the Jews as thus scattered." See Narry F. Santos, p. 6. While the specific term has limited employment in the Old Testament text, the fact is that the concept of diaspora and the complex of ideas, events and cognate terms that cluster around it are significantly represented in the Old Testament and make "diaspora" a major theme in the Hebrew Bible.

[93] See also James Clifford,"Diasporas," *Current Anthropology* 9 (3) (1994): 303;
B. Kirshenblatt-Gimblett, "Spaces of Dispersal," *Cultural Anthropology* 9 (3) (1994): 340; J. Boyarin, "Powers of Diaspora." Paper presented to a panel on diaspora at the International Congress of the Historical Sciences, Montreal, 1995.

[94] This narrative is found in the last chapters of the book of Genesis and the early chapters of the book of Exodus.

Figure 5.1 Old Testament Trajectory
of Israel's Experience of Diaspora

1. Jewish diaspora antecedents in the patriarchal era
   Israel's transition from Canaan to Egypt
2. The Jewish diaspora experience in Egypt
   Israel's national narrative in the Land
3. The Jewish diaspora experience in
   Babylonia and Persia

Jewish Diaspora Antecedents in the Patriarchal Era

In Genesis 1–11 we are given a sweeping biblical vision of the trajectory of human history from the creation of the universe to the global dispersion of humankind at the Tower of Babel (Genesis 11). Genesis 10, commonly known as the Table of Nations, traces the immediate descendants of the three sons of Noah, who become the forbears of the world's developing dispersement of nations in embryonic form.[95] From this multinational perspective, the writer of Genesis suddenly constricts his focus in Genesis 12 to the experience of one man and his wife. The diaspora macro-narrative of human history is reduced to the diaspora micro-narrative of a single couple, Abraham and Sarah. It is in them that the Jewish diaspora experience finds its roots. Looked at from this perspective, what does the story of Abraham contribute to the discussion of Jewish diaspora?

Patriarchal Diaspora Descriptives

In the Old Testament books of Genesis and Deuteronomy, two interesting descriptives attach themselves to Israel's patriarchs, each one lending itself to helpful diaspora associations. In Genesis 14:13, Abraham is given the ascription "Abram the Hebrew." In Deuteronomy 26:5, his grandson Jacob is described as a "wandering Aramean." As Jacob clearly inherited his Aramean identity and his wandering lifestyle from his grandfather, we will allow this ascription to be

---

[95] In a broad sense, one could well argue that the impetus for diaspora finds its ultimate biblical origins in God's commands to both Adam and Eve and to Noah and his extended family to "Be fruitful and multiply, and fill the earth" (Gen.1:28; 9:1), as well as to God's sovereign interference in proactively instigating global human dispersion at the time of the tower of Babel (Gen. 11:1-7). For further discussion of this, see Ted Rubesh, "Foundations for the Nations: The Nations in Genesis 1-12," in *A Cultured Faith*, eds. Prabo Mihindukulasuriya, Ivor Poobalan (Colombo: CTS Publishing, 2011), 37.

used here as a helpful cipher for Abraham himself, and as an expression of the diaspora elements of his story (see Figure 5.2).

Figure 5.2 Abraham: Diaspora Ascriptions and Focus

BIBLICAL REFERENCE	ASCRIPTION	FOCUS
Deuteronomy 26:5	Abram (Jacob) – "a wandering Aramean"	Diaspora Ethos and Disposition
Genesis 14:13	Abram – "the Hebrew"	Diaspora Ascriptions and Associations

A Diaspora Ethos: Abram the "Wandering Aramean"

It is nothing but intriguing that the national history of Israel in the Old Testament, bracketed as it is by two major diaspora experiences, should find its catalyst in the personal history of a roving Aramean named Abram.[96] When the reader is first introduced to him in Genesis 11, Abram and his extended family are settled Semitic citizens of the ancient Sumerian city of Ur. However, settledness in this cosmopolitan urban center turns to uprootedness when Abram experiences a divine encounter and is asked to "go forth from (his) country, and from (his) relatives and from (his) father's house" to "a land" which his God would show to him (Gen. 12:1).[97]

In this command, the harbingers of a much broader diaspora experience lie close to the surface. Trans-migration from the natal land, and trans-location into an alien one, together with all of the uncertainties, risks and adjustments inherent in such a move, are recognizable diaspora themes. These were clearly the lot of Abram and his family. His little band eventually finds itself encamped in distant Palestine, vulnerable aliens in a world of indigenous Canaanites and an Amorite population who had recently migrated from northwest Mesopotamia and settled in the central hill country.[98] Armed with little more than the hope of a divine promise to bless him and make him a great nation, Abram (now Abraham) exchanges his former

---

[96] Aram was the Hebrew term for what we know as Mesopotamia, and the general area from which Abram originally came. Thus *Aram-naharaim*, Aram of the Two Rivers (referring to the Tigris and Euphrates), is also often called *Paddan-Aram* in the Genesis narratives (Gen. 25:20, 28:1-7, 31:18).

[97] While Abram's uprooting involved a lengthy sojourn in the city of Haran, it is clear from Acts 7:2-3 that the initial process began in the city of Ur.

[98] Eugene Merrill, *Kingdom of Priests: A History of Old Testament Israel*, (Grand Rapids: Baker Books, 1996), 29. See also Keith Schoville, "Canaanites and Amorites," in *Peoples of the Old Testament World*, eds. Hoerth, Mattinly, Yamauchi (Grand Rapids: Baker Books, 1994), 166.

sedentary lifestyle in urban Ur for that of a semi-nomadic wanderer. Living in tents, he and his growing clan move gingerly as newcomers through the length and breadth of the land. Little wonder that the "wandering Aramean" ascription readily affixes itself to Abraham and his progeny.

All the while, like many diasporas that will follow him, Abraham and his immediate descendants refrain from thorough social and cultural integration with their host neighbors, stubbornly maintaining their unique ethno-religious identity[99] and proactively preserving filial relations with kinfolk back in the Mesopotamian natal land.[100] And thus to the end, while he and his clan are far from being a nation that can lay claim to diaspora credentials, Abraham projects an ethos of diaspora that casts a catalytic shadow into a diaspora future. It is an ethos that he will pass on to his grandsons who will eventually provide the tribal foundation for the promised nation to come. It is also an ethos that will come to be one of the most enduring characteristics of Jewish experience. As Davies puts it:

> Exile has been the distinctive characteristic of Jewish life … Certain historical facts are fundamental. The Land of Israel was not the birthplace of the Jewish people, which did not emerge there (as most peoples have on their own soil). On the contrary, it had to enter its own Land from without; there is a sense in which Israel was born in exile. Abraham had to leave his own land to go to the Promised Land.[101]

In short, the Jewish nation is birthed from the start in a diaspora ethos. Abraham's experience almost seems to function as a midwife for a far greater experience of diaspora that was in fact to characterize much of the Jewish nation's Old Testament history. Many years later the men and women of Israel and Judah would still be confessing, "I am a stranger with you, a sojourner, as all my fathers were" (Psalm 39:12). An enduring ethos of diaspora is echoed in such statements.

This is significant, for while the concept of a promised land has always been fundamental in Jewish thought, it is evident that core Jewish identity has never been at the mercy of the vagaries of an actual physical hegemony over land. The record of Jewish history from the time of the destruction of Jerusalem

---

[99] Abraham's unambiguous refusal to accept the proffered gifts and rewards of the grateful King of Sodom following his victory over the marauding kings of the east (Genesis 14:1-24) is a clear indication of his reticence to move beyond the Habiru ethos for the convenience of moving into mainstream Canaanite culture. The pressure on the patriarchs to do so is also clearly seen in the story of the massacre at Shechem (Genesis 34) when Jacob and his clan are urged by the local Canaanite community to intermarry with them, and to live, trade and acquire property in the land (34:10).
[100] The account of the effort to which Abraham went to seek a wife for his son from amongst his own people is an example of this (Genesis 24). The accounts of Esau and then of Jacob's son Judah taking wives from the local Canaanite population is an example of the difficulty the Abrahamic clan faced in maintaining this distinctiveness (Genesis 26:34-35, 38:2ff).
[101] William D. Davies, *The Territorial Dimension of Judaism* (Minneapolis: Fortress Press, 1991), 63.

under the Romans in 70 A.D. is ample evidence of this. For most of the last 2,000 years in fact, Jewish history has been diaspora history. Surely the roots of such diaspora tenacity can be traced to Abraham, the "wandering Aramean," whose legacy of faith and identity bequeathed a vibrant diaspora ethos that enabled his descendants, the "sons of Abraham," the "children of Israel," to survive … and thrive … through many difficult and scattered years to come.

Diaspora Ascriptions: "Abram the Hebrew"

The ethos of diaspora that emerges from the Abrahamic narratives is underlined and heightened by a second descriptive that attaches itself to the patriarch's name. Not only is Abraham a "wandering Aramean"; he is also Abraham "the Hebrew."

It is in Genesis 14:13 that the Bible first makes use of the word Hebrew. At the outset it seems clear that the word is an ethnic designation that finds its etymological origin in the name of Eber, the ancestor of Abram (Gen. 10:2, 25).[102] Thus Abram and the extended clan he came from were "Hebrews" inasmuch as they were ethnic descendants of Eber their forefather.

However, the term "Hebrew" (or "the Hebrews") clearly took on wider social associations as the story of the Jewish nation developed. A major reason for this was the presence in the ancient near east of a group of people known variously as the "*apiru*," "*hapiru*" or "*habiru*," an ascription strikingly similar to the term Hebrew, and one which virtually all scholars agree shares at least some measure of association with it. The impact and spread of the *habiru* clans extended from the Hittite kingdoms in the north to the Egyptian empire in the south, and is extensively attested to in numerous ancient near eastern texts (Bright 1981: 94-95).

The question of course is who these *habiru* were, and in what way they may have been associated with the Hebrews of the Old Testament narratives.[103] The consensus of scholarly opinion thus far is that the *habiru* were in fact not an ethnic group but a marginal social stratum or class who tended to live in bands or clans on

---

[102] John Bright, A *History of Israel*, (Philadelphia, Westminster Press, 1981), 94. See also Eugene Merrill, 38.
[103] For a fuller discussion of the relationship between the two terms, see Moshe Greenberg, *The Hab/piru* (New Haven: American Oriental Society, 1955). See also Nadav Na'aman, "Habiru and Hebrews: The Transfer of a Social Term to the Literary Sphere," *Journal of Near Eastern Studies* 45, (1986): 278-85; also Julius Lewy, "Origin and Significance of the biblical term 'Hebrew'," in *Hebrew Union College Annual XXIV* (1957):1-13. More recently see Robert Wolfe, "From Habiru to Hebrews: The Roots of the Jewish Tradition" in *New English Review*, October 2009; accessed 27 May 2010; Available at http://www.newenglishreview.org/custpage.cfm/frm/48464/sec_id/48464.

the edges of society, and were generally to be found in a broad swath of societies and nations around the ancient near east.[104]

The term apparently denoted a class of people without citizenship, who lived on the fringes of the existing social structure, without roots or fixed place in it. At times pursuing a pastoral existence, living either peacefully or by raiding, and, as occasion offered, they settled in the towns (Bright 1981:95).

As such, the *habiru* are sometimes described negatively as bandits, mercenaries, or runaway slaves. More kindly, they might be known as rootless refugees or itinerant wanderers with scant local ethnic affiliations. Negatively or positively, they were seen as a class of people who tended to live outside the mainstream of settled society.

As perennial outsiders the *habiru* undoubtedly shared many of the traits that have characterized diasporas throughout history. Vulnerable, stateless and often landless, they, like Abraham and his descendants, carried with them a distinctive diaspora ethos. Like him, they were a people apart, seeking to survive by fair means or foul, in an often dangerous world.

It should come as no surprise, then, that many scholars have long suspected some kind of connection between the ancient Hebrews and the *habiru* who were coincident with them. Certainly the diaspora ethos of the patriarchs described above, as well as the diaspora experiences of the Hebrews later on in Egypt, both bear marked similarities to the lifestyle of *habiru* bands; so close in fact that many are tempted to simply identify the two groups as one and the same. However, a simple equating of the two is not tenable. The *habiru* ascription is repeatedly attested to in ancient records in far broader periods of time and in more far-flung places than the Hebrews could ever have occupied. The *habiru* were a socio-economic class that was represented by many different languages and ethnicities in many different places (Wolfe 2009). On the other hand, the Hebrews were by definition a contained and well-defined ethnic group, the physical descendants of Eber and Abraham (c. Gen. 10:21; 11:10-26).

However, while one cannot say that the *habiru* were necessarily all Hebrews, it can well be argued that the Hebrews, particularly in their formative years, were generally looked on by outsiders as being *habiru*. In other words, it is likely that the Hebrews were seen by others as one particular expression of the larger *habiru* phenomenon. The two ascriptions are so phonetically similar that it is not difficult to imagine that over time a considerable merging in the understanding and use of the terms developed, and that the term "Hebrew" gradually took on some of the more disparaging associations that came with the *habiru* "package."[105]

---

[104] Michael B. Rowton, "Dimorphic Structure and the Problem of the ʾapirû-ʿibrîm," in *Journal of Near Eastern Studies* Vol. 35 no. 1 (January 1976): 17.

[105] Rowton convincingly demonstrates the dynamic change and interchange of the meanings and content of many ethno-socio ascriptions in history. He argues that some terms initially used as social descriptions evolved into ethnic ascriptions and vice versa. Thus he posits that the term *"habiru,"*

DIASPORA DISTINCTIVES: THE JEWISH DIASPORA EXPERIENCE IN THE OLD TESTAMENT

It is interesting to note that in the Old Testament's initial ascription of the term "Hebrew" to Abraham in Genesis 14:13, the context is that of Abraham's mustering of 318 "trained men" (v.14) for a unilateral armed action. This, together with his migratory lifestyle and apparent reticence to join "mainstream" Canaanite society, would clearly have been in concert with the image of the quasi-independent roving mercenary that was part of the *habiru* ethos, undoubtedly solidifying his perceived image as a local *habiru* chieftain.

The negative associations that typically came with the *habiru* ascription are never more evident than in the numerous references to the *habiru* found in a large collection of clay tablets discovered at Tell el-Amarna in Egypt toward the end of the 19th century. Many of these tablets consist of letters written during the 14th century BC and sent to the Pharaoh in Egypt from various Egyptian puppet rulers in Canaan. The "Amarna correspondence" as it is called is filled with complaints about troublesome *habiru*, who are accused of leading a rebellion against Egyptian rule in Canaan, and plundering the cities of local rulers who came under the nominal authority of Pharaoh (Wolf 2009). If one allows the relevant chronological data of the Old Testament narratives to be taken seriously, it is possible that at least some of the *habiru* mentioned in the Amarna tablets can be identified with the Hebrew conquerors of Canaan under Joshua.[106] If this is the case, it is not difficult to imagine that to battered Canaanite communities the two groups were perceived as one and the same. As Merrill says, "To the Canaanites ... *'apiru* were Hebrews and Hebrews were *'apiru* (Merrill 1996:102).

From this perspective, it is interesting to note the way in which the word "Hebrew" is used in the Old Testament. The first observation is that the word itself is surprisingly seldom used, appearing only 33 times in the Hebrew Bible as a whole (Wolfe 2009). Moreover, when it is employed, it is very rarely used by the Hebrews to describe themselves, the term "Israelites" or "children of Israel" clearly being their preferred self-designation. Rather, it is generally found in the Bible as an epithet on the lips of non-Hebrews in reference to ethnic Israelites, and frequently in a disparaging sense.[107] Nadav Na'aman points out that the use of the term 'Hebrew' is especially prevalent "in the stories of the book of Exodus, in which it is applied to Israelites who were enslaved and exploited by the Egyptians for hard labor" (Na'aman 1986:270). The fact that Egyptian history of the same period also makes frequent reference to the presence of *habiru* slave labor lends weight to the idea that the two terms,

---

initially a socio-economic ascription, took on ethnic connotations that eventually produced the ethnonym "Hebrew." See Rowton 1976, 13-20.

[106] Merrill 1996,102. Merrill's discussion places the date of Joshua's conquest of Canaan squarely in the period of the Amarna correspondence. See pages 100–108 for his very helpful perspective on the issue.

[107] Rowton 1976:18. See Genesis 39:14, 17; Exodus 2:6; Exodus 21:2 and 1 Samuel 4:6, 9.

phonetically so similar, may frequently have been confused or purposely merged as an expression of disparagement by those hostile to the Hebrews.[108] This may well explain the seeming Hebrew reticence in using the term to describe themselves.[109] Thus, while the two ascriptions do not appear to be etymologically related, a sociological link, pregnant with historical associations seems eminently plausible. The *habiru*, like the Hebrews, were forged in a diaspora milieu. As noted above, they shared many of the same kinds of struggles and challenges diasporas have experienced throughout history.

Thus to the diaspora ethos that "wandering" Abraham bequeathed the incipient Hebrew people, the *habiru* loaned the diaspora associations, positive and negative, that came with the *habiru* name and lifestyle. It was an association that apparently did not die easily. In the mid 8th century BC, some 17 centuries after the time of Abraham, we are introduced to another wandering descendent of the patriarch, this time a runaway Israelite prophet named Jonah. Caught "on the run," at sea in a life-threatening storm, far from the shores of his natal land, he faces a bobbing raft of suspicious interrogators and fellow travelers. Anxious to determine if Jonah is the cause of their predicament, they demand, "Tell us now … what is your occupation? And where do you come from? What is your country? From what people are you?" (Jonah 1:8)

Significantly, Jonah does not answer by laying claim to a specifically Israelite pedigree. Rather he replies, "I am a **Hebrew** (emphasis mine), and I fear the LORD God of heaven who made the sea and the dry land" (1:9). And with this rather unusual and atypical self-designation Jonah identifies himself with the diaspora ethos, ascriptions and associations … not to mention the diaspora faith … that are his inheritance as a son of Abraham. It is an identity he shares with multitudes of his fellow Israelites, past, present and future, whose history in the Old Testament would be bracketed by major national diaspora experiences in both Egypt and Babylon.

It is intriguing that Jonah's diaspora inheritance is one that he shares not only with his Hebrew ancestors and descendants, but with other scattered and far-flung diasporas around the world throughout history. The diaspora legacy that Father Abraham, the 'wandering Aramean' left to his Hebrew descendants became in fact part of a bequest that has shaped the larger phenomenon of diaspora to this day. While every diaspora springs from its own unique complex of historical ethno-social circumstances, there is no denying that the legacy of Abraham and his scattered Jewish descendants left their mark on the notion or the conception of "diaspora." As pointed out in the introduction, the Jewish tradition is at the heart of any understanding of the concept of diaspora.

---

[108] James Hoffmeir, *Israel in Egypt: The Evidence for the Authenticity of the Exodus Tradition* (New York: Oxford University Press, 1996), 113, 115 for strong evidence of Semitic presence, and specifically habiru presence in Egypt during this time.

[109] The *habiru* nuances that attached themselves to the term "Hebrew" apparently faded in later Jewish history, as "Hebrew" / "the Hebrews" gradually became a generalized expression for the people of Israel.

What this means is that while the Jewish diaspora may not have lent specifically historical roots to other diasporas, it has surely lent its ethos to many of them. This is evident in the way the language, symbols and stories that have congealed around the Jewish experience through the years, particularly as expressed in the Old Testament, have often been pressed into service by subsequent diasporas from vastly different origins and eras. Struggling to find metaphors and inspiration to express their own experience of scattering, they have often found a wellspring of resources in the diaspora ethos inherited from the children of Abraham.

Perhaps no example in history is clearer than that of the African and Caribbean diasporas. Growing out of the horrific experiences of the trans-Atlantic slave trade of the 17th and 18th centuries, the cultures of these diasporas easily found in the Jewish experience, motifs and themes that deeply reflected their own (Cohen 1997: 31-32). For instance, the lyrics of the negro spirituals that peppered the early black American experience dipped constantly into Jewish diaspora roots, using Old Testament language of redemption and making symbolic references to "Zion," "Canaan," "Egypt," "the promised land," and "crossing over the River Jordan." "I am a poor wayfaring stranger," sang one plaintive piece, with words that could have come from Father Abraham himself.

In his discussion of the Afro-Caribbean diaspora, Cohen makes frequent reference to the cross-identification of elements of the Jewish diaspora with movements such as Jamaican Rastafarianism and "Ethiopianism (Cohen 1997: 38-39, 147). More recently, one needs to go no further than many of the speeches made by Martin Luther King Jr. at the height of the American civil rights movement to find a harvest of such associations. Clearly the vision King had for the scattered African-American community found its roots in the vision of hope Moses had had for the wandering Hebrew diaspora in his charge. It was a vision that ultimately traced its pedigree to the covenant promises given to a wandering Aramean named Abraham and to the tenacity of the diaspora ethos he left in his wake. That ethos continues to color and give expression to the world of diaspora today.

The Jewish Diaspora Experience in Egypt

As mentioned above, studies of the Jewish diaspora usually take the exile from Jerusalem at the time of Nebuchadnezzar as their starting point. I have suggested that as an identifiable community, the Jewish experience of diaspora congeals around two seminal diaspora events: the early period of the Hebrew captivity in Egypt, as well as the later period of exile in Babylon and Persia at the end of the Old Testament narrative.[110] The two experiences—Egyptian and Babylonian-Persian, one at each end of the Old Testament story—serve to "bookend" the Jewish national narrative that unfolds between them.

In surveying the characteristics of the Old Testament Jewish diaspora, it will be helpful then to describe and compare the two experiences, Egyptian and Babylonian/Persian. The initial Egyptian experience will be analyzed in terms of seven salient diaspora characteristics that emerge from the story. This will be followed by a discussion of the later diaspora experience in Babylon/Persia, noting two supplemental diaspora characteristics of the latter period (Figure 5.3).

Figure 5.3 Diaspora Characteristics of the Hebrews in Egypt and Babylon

DIASPORIC CHARACTERISTICS	REFLECTED IN EGYPT	REFLECTED IN BABYLON / PERSIA
The Foundation of an Incipient National Identity	Patriarchal Affinities	National and Historical Affinities
The Impetus of a Corporate Crisis	Famine	Defeat; exile
The Influence of Powerful Advocacy	Joseph; Moses	Daniel; Esther
The Legacy of Negative Historical Associations	Hyksos	Realpolitik; rebellion; international intrigue
The Experience of Marginalization and Exploitation	Bondage	Banishment; exile
The Inheritance of Shared Diaspora Memory	Proactive, documentary preservation	Prophetic documentation; Feast of Purim
The Abiding Historical and Theological Links to Natal Land	Covenant promises and hope	Covenant promises and prophetic hope
Supplemental Babylonian Diaspora. The Characteristics of Healthy Diaspora/Host Interaction	N/A	Jewish Babylonians
The Revitalization of Natal Identity	N/A	Babylonian Jews

---

[110] In an attempt to draw up a definitive list of elements that define a diaspora, Cohen's first limitation is that a diaspora is a community that has experienced "dispersal from an original homeland ... to *two or more* foreign regions" (see Cohen 1997a, 26; italics mine). In this case, the Hebrew community in Egypt at the time would not constitute a true diaspora. However, given the Jewish community's enduring cohesive uniqueness, its sense of alienship in Egypt, and its strong sense of natal land, there is no doubt in my mind that it qualifies as a genuine expression of the diaspora experience.

Diaspora Distinctives

Seven elements of diaspora significance emerge from Israel's experience in Egypt that appear well reflected in the larger diaspora experience today.

The Foundation of an Incipient National Identity

Diasporas are by definition groups of people who share a number of affinities with each other.[111] Scattered people are not necessarily a diaspora unless they perceive themselves to be at least marginally bound to each other by such affinities. Thus all true diasporas have their roots in at least an incipient shared identity, whether that is linguistic, religious or ethnic. As Cohen reminds us, "the idea of a shared origin … is a common feature of diasporas," and "acts to 'root' a diaspora consciousness and give it legitimacy" (Cohen 1997:184). The nascent Hebrew nation at the time of the Old Testament patriarchs brought together an affinity of shared origin. For the primitive nation, the term "Father Abraham" was more than just metaphorical. It was quite literal.

Additionally, they saw themselves as distinct from the larger socio-cultural milieu of Canaan. Eschewing the pan-Canaanite pantheons of their neighbors, they uniquely worshipped Yahweh as the "most High God," and perceived themselves as the inheritors of a divine plan that gave them a shared trajectory into the future. These affinities were to provide a strong glue that would bind them together and keep them distinct as a people through the initial diaspora experience in Egypt, … an experience that arguably lasted for over four centuries![112] It is conceivable that without them, the Hebrew diaspora would simply have evaporated in Egypt in the course of time.

The durability of any diaspora will clearly be in proportion to its ability to maintain the kind of affinities that have kept the Hebrew diaspora viable. Where intermarriage and cultural assimilation are major factors in the settling of a scattered community abroad, its unique identity can easily dissipate into the majority culture and eventually disappear. Where diaspora affinities are preserved, however, the diaspora "essence" like that of the Hebrews in ancient Egypt is sustained and preserved.

---

[111] See footnotes in the Introduction section.

[112] Considerable scholarly debate exists concerning the length of the Israelite sojourn in Egypt. If it is acknowledged as historical at all, the period is generally seen as lasting from just over two centuries (c. Bright 1981,78, 110ff.) to just over four centuries. My position gives maximum weight to the biblical data, and assumes a period of four-plus centuries. See Eugene Merrill 75-78, for a robust summary of the evidence of a long sojourn.

The Impetus of a Corporate Crisis

The impetus that produces the diaspora phenomenon will have many different sources. Cohen alludes to this by proposing a typology of "victim, labor, trade, imperial and cultural diasporas," each representing a different conglomerate of motivating factors producing a particular kind of diaspora (Cohen 1997:x).

The Genesis narrative makes clear the motivation behind the Hebrew venture into Egypt from Canaan. A severe famine of seven years had ravaged the eastern Mediterranean world. In a day bereft of global emergency relief efforts, such famines could spell the end for small vulnerable people groups, especially those living outside the complex of the majority society as did the Hebrews in Canaan. Simple survival dictated a move to Egypt where the foresight of government planning had stockpiled enough food supplies to weather the storm.[113] In the process, the incipient Jewish nation in Canaan became a vulnerable Jewish diaspora in Egypt, or to put it in Cohen's typology, a "victim diaspora."

Entering Egypt as refugees, the Hebrew community was at the mercy of the good or ill will of its hosts. All the insecurities, questions and fears known to victim diasporas throughout history were theirs. Like all such diasporas, they were defenseless and easy targets for the unscrupulous. The diaspora descendants of the Hebrews in ancient Egypt continue to populate our planet. The impetus of crisis—be it war or natural catastrophe— continues to provide, as it did for the Hebrews, the thrust for the formation of diaspora communities around the world to this day.

The Influence of Powerful Advocacy

Fortunately for the Hebrew community in ancient Egypt, vulnerability and weakness were balanced at least twice by the considerable intervention and support of two powerful advocates. The biblical narrative introduces us to two major players whose roles in the Jewish diaspora experience at the time were pivotal. The first was Joseph, whose advocacy served the community at the time of their arrival in Egypt. The second was Moses, whose advocacy engineered their departure from the land some four centuries later.

It is interesting to note that both men rose and addressed the needs of the Hebrew diaspora in hours of its greatest vulnerability. The key to such a diaspora's survival will often rest in the hands of those who pursue their advocacy. Such was Joseph. Ironically, a member and a blood relative of the Hebrew clan himself,

---

[113] Note James K. Hoffmeir's comment that the "epigraphic and archaeological data clearly demonstrates that Egypt was frequented by the peoples of the Levant, especially as a result of climatic problems that resulted in drought ... from the end of the Old Kingdom ... through the Second Intermediate Period ..." (Hoffmeir 1996, 68).

DIASPORA DISTINCTIVES: THE JEWISH DIASPORA EXPERIENCE IN THE OLD TESTAMENT

Joseph had risen by an amazing complex of circumstances to the post of prime minister under the pharaoh of Egypt.[114] The narrative leaves us no doubt as to the breadth of influence he wielded across the land (c. Genesis 41:40ff).

Thus when Joseph's "poor relatives" showed up in Egypt, they had the inestimable advantage of having an advocate, a blood relative no less, serving in the host nation's second-most powerful public office. With Joseph's influence, the transition from settled community in Canaan to diaspora community in Egypt was made infinitely easier. Joseph immediately sees to the needs of his kith and kin. Through his influence the Hebrew clan was settled in the well-watered land of Goshen, a region ideally suited for their pastoral livelihoods and sufficiently removed from major Egyptian centers to avoid exacerbating cultural frictions between the two groups.[115] It is clear that the purposeful segregation of the Hebrew clan from mainstream Egyptian society in these early days played a large part in the ability of the diaspora to maintain its socio-cultural and religious distinctives. The community therefore fact thrived and multiplied (Exodus 1:7). What is clear is that this surely could not have happened without the timely and discerning advocacy of Joseph.

As the Hebrew sojourn in Egypt drew to a close centuries later, it was the towering figure of Moses who stepped into the role of advocate. Like Joseph, Moses was himself a Hebrew by birth. Through an amazing series of events he was taken into the Egyptian court and raised as an adopted member of the royal family.[116] Like Joseph, he took on the role of advocate for his natal people, using his royal connections with the court to challenge the iron grip the Egyptians now held over the Hebrew diaspora. Eventually it was Moses who won their release, becoming in the process the "fulcrum-figure in Jewish history, the hinge around which it all turns."[117]

---

[114] Considerable debate exists about the identity of the pharaoh(s) under whom Joseph served. In my view, the most likely candidates would be Sesostris II, Ammenemes II, and Sesostris III of ancient Egypt's 12th dynasty, who reigned from approximately 1971 to 1843 B.C. See Merrill, *Kingdom of Priests*, 50. See also James R. Battenfield, "A Consideration of the Identity of the Pharaoh of Genesis 47" in *JETS* 15, (1972):77-85.

[115] The biblical record in Genesis takes pains to underline the fact that the pastoral occupations providing the prime means of livelihood for the Hebrews were anathema in Egyptian society. Potential cultural frictions between the two groups were then most easily avoided by settling the Hebrews far from the centers of Egyptian society.

[116] While the account of Moses's adoption and rearing in the Egyptian court is generally dismissed by minimalist scholars as the stuff of legend, the fact is that the practice of rearing foreign princes and princesses in Egyptian nurseries dedicated to purposes of training imperial civil leadership has clear attestation in the period of Egypt's New Kingdom. Thus Hoffmeier says, "The picture of Moses in Exodus 2 being taken to the court by a princess where he was reared and educated is quite consistent with the emerging information about the *dedicated nurseries* (italics mine) in the New Kingdom, the only period for which there is evidence of foreigners being included in this royal institution." Hoffmeier 1996:143, 224.

[117] Paul Johnson, *A History of the Jews* (New York: Harper and Row Publishers, 1987), 27.

The details of Moses' story are well known and need not be rehearsed here. Suffice it to say that a vital key to the health and viability of the Hebrew diaspora in Egypt lay in the availability and the power of advocacy to represent its needs. It will be noted later on that the Jewish experience of diaspora at the end of the Old Testament era benefited similarly from the influence of powerful advocates. What is clear is that advocacy is a key ingredient in diaspora issues both yesterday and today, and is increasingly being recognized in governmental structures as an important dynamic in the process of diaspora engagement.[118] Wherever diasporas have appeared, their ability to cope and often to thrive has been in large part due to those who carry influence and weight in the corridors of power, and are willing to use these advantages to serve as advocates for scattered peoples in difficult times.

The Legacy of Negative Historical Associations

When a particular diaspora begins to take root in a host nation, it brings with it a package of associations and linkages that are often unintentional, and can be detrimental to its role as a minority within the mainstream culture. This is nothing new. The Hebrew diaspora in Egypt likewise faced a surfeit of negative associations.

A brief sketch of some of the major currents of Egyptian history at the time will be helpful. The periods of Egypt's Middle and New Kingdoms[119] are separated by an intermediate period of about 150 years, during which an aggressive group of Semitic peoples collectively known as the Hyksos invaded and ruled much of Egypt.[120] The Hyksos dominance of Egypt was deeply resented, and with the eventual emergence of a powerful new native Egyptian pharaoh named Amosis in 1570 BC, the hated interlopers were finally driven out. Amosis then became the founder of ancient Egypt's 18th dynasty, and with him the Egyptian nation experienced rebirth and renewal in the establishment of the New Kingdom (Merrill 1996:54-55).

The salient point here is the shared Semitic backgrounds of the Hyksos invaders and the Hebrew diaspora, both of whom arguably made Egypt their home for limited but overlapping periods of time (Hoffmeier 1996:68). Semitic culture was in many ways vastly different to that of Egypt. The inherent

---

[118] "Diaspora Engagement: Remittances and Beyond," in U.S.AID, *Global Partnerships*, accessed 23 June 2010; available at http://www.usaid.gov/our_work/global_partnerships/gda/remittances.html.
[119] The Middle Kingdom encompassed Dynasties 11 and 12 and is dated roughly from 2040 to 1786 BC. (see Bright 1981:51.) The New Kingdom encompassed the 18th and 19th Dynasties and is dated from 1570 to 1223 BC. See Merrill 1996:49-50, 58-59.
[120] Bright 1981, 59-61. Also Van Seters, *The Hyksos*, (New Haven: Yale University Press, 1966) , 194-195. See also S. David Sperling, "Hyksos," in *Encyclopaedia Judaica*, 2008, Jewish Virtual Library, accessed 7 October 2001; avaible at
http://www.jewishvirtuallibrary.org/jsource/judaica/ejud_0002_0009_0_09361.html.

tensions between the two cultures can be clearly seen in the latter part of the Joseph narratives in Genesis, where differences of language, vocation and personal grooming are specifically mentioned (Genesis 42:23; 43:32; 46:34).[121] As pointed out above, Joseph's wisdom took these ethno-cultural differences seriously when allocating land in Goshen to his immigrating kinfolk.

It is probably safe to say that during the period of Hyksos dominance in Egypt, the resident Hebrew diaspora experienced relative good will under the governance of their fellow Semites. If this is so, it is reasonable to assume that with the ejection of the Hyksos and the re-emergence of native Egyptian power in the New Kingdom, the remaining resident Hebrew diaspora paid a heavy price for their Semitic heritage. Burdened not only by the negative associations that likely came with being perceived as *habiru*, they would now have faced hostility by virtue of their ethnic proximity to the Hyksos. This in fact is exactly what the biblical record seems to imply. The first chapters of Exodus describe a process of increasing estrangement in the relationship between the Hebrew population and their native Egyptian hosts. We are told in Exodus 1:8 that "there arose a king who knew not Joseph," and that it was under his rule that the relationship between the Hebrews and the Egyptians began to deteriorate.[122] The narrative clearly highlights Egyptian concerns that the Hebrew population was growing in numbers and could become a dangerous "fifth column" threatening Egyptian security (Exodus 1:9-10). If the narrative is read in the context of an Egyptian reaction to the now displaced Hyksos, it is not difficult to imagine the ethnically related Hebrews who remained after the Hyksos withdrawal bearing the brunt of that reaction (Hoffmeir 1996:122).

The experience of the Hebrews in Egypt is not unlike that of many diasporas that have followed similar paths. Already tainted by perceived linkages with the marginal *habiru*, the negative association of the Hebrews with the ousted Hyksos clearly multiplied their woes. This phenomenon could find many parallels in today's world. What is apparent is the tendency for certain kinds of diaspora populations to unintentionally carry with them negative associations and perceptions that can cause them to live under a cloud of suspicion and hostility in a host nation.

---

[121] For a brief discussion on the interface between Egyptian and Semitic culture of the time see K.A. Kitchen, "Egypt, Egyptians," in *Dictionary of the Old Testament: Pentateuch*, 209.

[122] While it is impossible to make definitive statements about precisely which pharaoh the narrative has in mind, I believe there are cogent arguments that it could in fact have been Amosis himself. As the one responsible for driving out the Hyksos and as founder of a restored native Egyptian kingdom, it is not difficult to see why he may have adopted a strenuous anti-Hebrew policy (c. Merrill 1996 58-59).

The Experience of Marginalization and Exploitation

The Hebrew experience in Egypt did not end with negative associations and accusation. Estrangement slowly led to outright hostility and exploitation. As a means of keeping the growing Hebrews in check, Egyptian authorities reduced them to slave labor and set them to work in the construction of public works projects.[123] When this failed to contain their growing numbers, a policy of male infanticide was put into place with the obvious intention that Hebrew women would be forced to marry into the local Egyptian population and thus achieve a de facto assimilation (Exodus 1:15-22).

While the final Egyptian measures were extreme by today's standards, the preceding measures were not. Physical and economic exploitation such as the Hebrews experienced in Egypt is easily attested to in the growing world of the diaspora today.

Whether they are underpaid Mexican migrant workers in the United States or sexually exploited Filipina housemaids in the Middle East, physical abuse and political and economic exploitation have often been hallmarks of the diaspora experience. The Hebrew diaspora in Egypt may have been among the first in history to experience such treatment, but they certainly were not the last.

The Inheritance of Shared Diaspora Memory

Cohen's introduction to the subject of global diasporas seeks to modify earlier attempts by Safran to delineate a set of features that give a measured definition to the term diaspora.[124] Among his modifications of Safran's characterization of diasporas, he includes the corporate experience of a single formative and catalytic event. To quote Cohen:

> Dispersal from an original centre is often accompanied by the memory of a single traumatic event that provides the folk memory of the great historic injustice that binds the group together (Cohen 1997:23).

This implies that part of what binds a scattered group together is the corporate memory of a shared negative experience. Cohen limits this to a "single traumatic event." However, the Hebrew experience in Egypt would suggest that the binding power of a negative experience can be much broader than a single event. While their initial transition from settled community to diaspora community was brought on by a famine that was traumatic enough, it

---

[123] Hoffmeier 1996, 115. Hoffmeier convincingly demonstrates that the specific characterizations of forced labor found in the Exodus narrative reflect Egyptian practice of the time, and are amply attested to in Egyptian textual evidence. See Hoffmeier, 112-116.

[124] See W. Safran, "Diasporas in modern societies: Myths of Homeland and Return," *Diaspora* (1991,10):83-99.

was in fact the lengthy experience of shared misery and exploitation over many years that fixed itself particularly in the collective memory. In short, several centuries of abuse and ill-treatment were never forgotten.

Significantly, neither were these experiences simply preserved in an informal folk memory. According to Gerhard Von Raad, the collective diaspora memories were safeguarded in Israel's cultic confessions.[125] Her diaspora roots were to be rehearsed and remembered.[126] Further, the Exodus narrative itself attests to a documentary recording of the events, and not simply an oral tradition. It is interesting that the legal code which eventually emerged as Israel's "constitution" specifically enjoined the Israelites of later days not to forget that they had once been "aliens in the land of Egypt" (Leviticus 19:34) and "slaves to Pharaoh in Egypt" (Deuteronomy 6:21). Once the Hebrews were permanently settled in Canaan, the Levitical code concerning the Hebrew management of debt and personal property frequently based its appeal on remembering the fact that the Hebrews had been "brought out from the land of Egypt" (c. Leviticus 25:36, 38, 42, 55).[127] The memory of having been an exploited diaspora was to be rehearsed and never forgotten. Thus the binding impact of the experience served not only to fuse together the future generations of Jews who inherited its memory, but significantly influenced the ideals behind many of Old Testament Israel's economic and social laws.

Of particular interest in the case of the Hebrew experience in Egypt is the specifically stated purpose for what might seem to be an unnecessarily morbid rehearsal of the past. The repeated call to remember the painful diaspora past clearly had in mind a constructive and positivist future. The shared memory was not to serve as a nursery to foster feelings of bitterness or revenge, but as a motivation for the ethical and just treatment of the alien communities the Hebrews were one day to find living as minorities in their own midst (c. Exodus 22:21; 23:9; Deuteronomy 15:15). As Wright says:

> The treatment of aliens within their own *(Hebrew)* society ... was to be marked with compassion, born of the memory of Egypt where it had been denied to themselves (Wright 1992:179 italics mine).

In this regard, Wolfe draws attention to an amazing Deuteronomic injunction that in the context of its day can only be described as revolutionary:

> You shall not hand over to his master a slave who has escaped from his master to you. He shall live with you in your midst, in the place

---

[125] Gerhard von Rad, *The Problem of the Hexateuch and Other Essays* (London: Oliver and Boyd, 1966), 1-78.
[126] See Deuteronomy 26:5-8.
[127] Chris Wright, *Living as the People of God: The Relevance of Old Testament Ethics* (Leicester, England: Intervarsity Press, 1992), 83.

which he shall choose in one of your towns where it pleases him; you shall not mistreat him (Deuteronomy 23:15-16).

"Would the authors of the Torah have promulgated such an injunction," he argues, "unless they were themselves in actual fact descended, at least in part, from fugitive slaves? I doubt it" (Wolfe 2009). Thus the collective memory of the diaspora experience, while extremely negative in its essence, had the potential to shape positive and constructive outcomes in the future nation of Israel.

The power of a shared corporate memory, perhaps especially when it is painful, is arguably a common diaspora feature mirrored in the unfolding history of the diaspora experience. The shared inheritance of painful memories from the distant past is not easily swept under the rug. It is in fact often rehearsed, reinforced and bequeathed to passing generations in both formal and informal ways, and these memories serve as a glue that binds the community together. In addition, such memories can motivate negative or positivist responses in the subsequent history of a particular diaspora. Sadly, far too often the negative is the default reaction. However, the Hebrew experience lets us know that when a diaspora community is proactive (at least ideally), good things can come from painful memories.

The Abiding Historical and Theological Links to Natal Land

The account of the Jewish experience in Egypt suggests yet one more element characteristic to many diasporas. Students of the diaspora phenomenon such as Cohen and Safran inevitably include in their lists of pan-diaspora features a "collective memory and myth about the homeland, including its location, history and achievements," and

> an idealization of the putative ancestral home and a collective commitment to its maintenance, restoration, safety and prosperity, even to its creation (Cohen 1997:26).

Put simply, all diasporas acknowledge the idea of "the old country," the conception of a linkage, actual or perceived, to a natal land that lays some claim on the community's loyalty and emotions. Perhaps no diaspora in history so clearly demonstrates this as does the Jewish diaspora. The association of the Jewish people with the "promised land" of Canaan is not only the engine behind the modern Zionist movement and the creation of the state of Israel, it is an association that traces itself back to the very origins of the Hebrews as an identifiable community. Indeed, the relationship between the Hebrew community and the "promised land" is deeply embedded and inextricably intertwined in the foundational covenant formula that began with the patriarch Abraham and was often repeated to his son Isaac and his grandson Jacob. Eventually it is Jacob, renamed 'Israel,' who lends his name as an eponym not only for the nation of Israel, but for the very land itself.

DIASPORA DISTINCTIVES: THE JEWISH DIASPORA EXPERIENCE IN THE OLD TESTAMENT

The linkage of covenant community to the covenant land was then incorporated into and expanded on in the legal code that emerged in the time of Moses. When Moses appears at the tail end of the Egyptian diaspora period, centuries after the time of the original patriarchs, his entrance on the scene is attended with references to "the God of your father, the God of Abraham, the God of Isaac, and the God of Jacob" (Exodus 3:6). This is followed immediately with a divine promise to Moses and his people of the gift of the land of Canaan (3:8), a clear reiteration of the original land promises given to the patriarchs. Moses together with Aaron then relates to the gathered Israelite elders "all the words which the LORD had spoken to Moses" (4:30), promises that clearly include a continuing relationship to the natal "promised land." It is apparent that these promises were neither new nor unknown to Moses ... or to the leaders of the Hebrew diaspora community in Egypt. Throughout the centuries of abuse and exploitation, the promise of a land given initially to their forefathers served to bind the community together and maintain their cohesion as a diaspora. A strong sense of autochthony persisted,[128] and though the glowing sense of natal land must surely have burned low at times, it is also clear that the collective memory had never forgotten its landed roots. Bound by those roots from the past, the Hebrew diaspora kept the glow alive.

And so it is today. What was and is true of the Jewish community continues to be true for many diaspora communities around the world today. Whether they are Lebanese in Australia or Armenians in California, the shared sense of autochthony and natal land continues to play an important role in shaping the self-perceptions of scattered communities abroad. It is a characteristic of the diaspora experience that is fraught with socio-geopolitical understanding, and no serious study of diaspora can avoid it. The claims and counter-claims to natal land are part of the diaspora landscape, a landscape often tragically transformed into vicious battlegrounds, and must be taken seriously in addressing the problems and challenges faced by emerging diasporas today.

One further point must be made in understanding the link between the Hebrew diaspora community and their natal land. While they nurtured their historical links to the land as descendants of the patriarchs, it is also evident that they anticipated restored links to that land in the time to come. The Jewish people saw their relationship to the land as part of a trajectory that would eventually take them into the future. From their perspective, their link to the land was not just a passing chapter in the larger unfolding human story. It was part of their future story. In fact, it was larger than that! For the Jews, it was a centerpiece in Yahweh's unfolding universal story. The land-bond was not built simply on historical links to the patriarchs of the past, but on a theological

---

[128] Autochthony is the sense whereby residents of a country or region claim superior rights over others based on some alleged historical status as "sons of the soil."

understanding of the promises of the future. The Hebrew diaspora's return to Canaan was endowed with a sense of mission "from on high." The bottom line of the Abrahamic covenant underscored the fact that their existence as a community in the "promised land" was not only ordained of God, but in order that through them "all the families of the earth will be blessed" (Genesis 12:3). While this global focus was later often conveniently forgotten, the hope and anticipation engendered by a sense of playing a key role in a much larger cosmic drama must surely have had a powerful effect on a struggling diaspora. They might be mere slaves in the eyes of the Egyptians, but to those with the eyes of faith, they were nothing less than God's "chosen people."

Perhaps few things can bind a scattered and exploited people together more powerfully than a sense of the divine. Religion and faith can define a people as much as ethnicity, history or language, especially if some kind of positivist future is factored into the worldview. This the Hebrews had in the promises their God had given to their fathers, and it stood them in good stead through many a dark year. Linked not only by the commonalities of the past but also by a corporate faith in the future, they survived as a community and continue to be part of the world's social tapestry and landscape to this day. Whatever form it may take, hope for the future will always be a vital ingredient in the vibrancy, energy, and strength of a diaspora community. "Without a vision the people perish," says the wise man in Proverbs 29:18 (KJV). For the diaspora communities of the world today, that adage is perhaps particularly true.

The Jewish Diaspora Experience in Babylon and Persia

Following their dramatic exit from Egypt recorded in the book of Exodus, the Hebrew diaspora eventually settled in Canaan. For the next one thousand years, the Jewish nation rooted and established itself in the land, eventually maturing into a recognizable monarchy. With the advent of Solomon's son Rehoboam, the Israelite kingdom was tragically split into two with the secession of ten of the original twelve tribes. The political map now comprised of two sibling nations, the ten seceding tribes making up the Northern Kingdom of Israel, and the tribes of Judah and Benjamin making up the Southern Kingdom of Judah, centered around the Davidic capital of Jerusalem. In a world shaped by voracious imperialistic appetites, the viability of the two small Jewish kingdoms was inevitably threatened, challenged, and brought to the brink of extinction. In 722 B.C. the northern kingdom was decimated by an Assyrian juggernaut, and its population forcibly marched off to the hinterlands of the Assyrian empire (Bright 1981:275; Merrill 1996:398). Some 130 years later in 586 B.C., it was the turn of the southern kingdom to see its glorious temple and its capital in Jerusalem destroyed by the surging Chaldeans, its population dragged off in chains to Babylon (Merrill 1996:453).

DIASPORA DISTINCTIVES: THE JEWISH DIASPORA EXPERIENCE IN THE OLD TESTAMENT

The exiled populations of the northern kingdom were largely assimilated to their (enforced) host cultures, and eventually lost their identity as a unique and discernible people. However, the trajectory of the Jewish population of the Southern Kingdom of Judah was significantly different from that of their northern brethren. With the destruction of Jerusalem, the Judean kingdom ceased to exist. Jewish life and identity now largely rested in the hands of the diaspora transplanted in the heart of the Babylonian empire (Bright 1981: 453). Here, unlike their deported northern tribal kin a century or more earlier, the Judean diaspora grew and flourished. Over the course of the next several hundred years they staged what was in fact nothing less than a most remarkable comeback, multiplying in numbers and influence across the ancient near east and the Mediterranean world. Indeed, such was the increase that it is estimated that by the time of Christ, 7% of the Roman-dominated Mediterranean world was said to have been Jewish.[129] Hedlund, quoting Harnack, concludes that the total Jewish population at this time amounted to around four and one-half million at the beginning of the Christian era—one million each in Syria, Egypt, and Palestine, plus one and a half million in Asia Minor, Europe, and Africa (Hedlund 1997:155).

Whatever the precise details, it is clear that the Jewish diaspora in Babylon laid the foundations for a diaspora identity that would eventually grow in reach and impact far beyond its initial size. The question of interest is of course how this happened. In particular, what were the distinctive characteristics of the Jewish diaspora in Babylon that gave them the impetus to so energetically flourish and grow?

Comparison to the Egyptian Hebrew Diaspora

An initial perusal of the Jewish diaspora in Babylon immediately yields a number of interesting comparisons to the earlier Hebrew diaspora in Egypt. It would not be difficult to find at least a measure of each of the seven characteristics of the Egyptian period duplicated in the Babylonian experience. The importance of an incipient national identity mentioned earlier, or the impetus of a corporate crisis, or the experience of marginalization and exploitation under the Egyptians, all find similar echoes in the experience of the exiled Jewish community as it scrabbled to set up a new life in the dominating social milieu of Babylon.

Perhaps the clearest parallel between the two diaspora experiences is in the matter of advocacy. The narratives of Daniel, Esther and Nehemiah, like those of Joseph and Moses of old, underline again the important, if not life-saving

---

[129] Roger Hedlund, *God and the Nations* (Delhi: ISPCK, 1997), 155.

roles that well-placed advocates can play in the experience of vulnerable and threatened diaspora communities. Without them, a diaspora community often remains a people without a voice. With them, it has a powerful platform from which to air its concerns and problems. Advocacy, it would seem, is a vital and important ingredient in the health and development of a diaspora.

Diaspora Distinctives of the Babylonian/Persian Exile

Two unique diaspora characteristics emerge uniquely from the period of Israel's Babylonian exile (See Figure 5.3). As with the Egyptian captivity, these emerge from the narratives surrounding the time, and find ready parallels in many subsequent diaspora experiences in history.

The Credibility of Healthy Diaspora-Host Interaction

Much of what is written on the subject of diaspora today tends to focus on the difficulties and challenges faced by vulnerable diasporas in unsympathetic or antagonistic host contexts. Perhaps more needs to be said about the positive and proactive integration of diasporas into their host cultures. It is here that the experience of the exiled Jewish community in Babylon lends a constructive and helpful model.

Tragic as the loss of Jerusalem and its temple were to the Jewish community, the exiled diaspora's response to Babylonian overlordship was never one of disengagement and detachment. To the contrary, both the biblical and secular records of the time include plenty of evidence that the Jewish exiles wasted little time in becoming part of the fabric of the empire.[130] This was in fact the instruction of no less powerful a voice than the prophet Jeremiah. He had warned of Jerusalem's impending destruction for years, and then had been an eyewitness to it. Nevertheless, once the inevitable had taken place, he urged a spirit of accommodation. To those exiles who may have been embittered by the experience, and to those who no doubt dreamed of a quick return home, Jeremiah gave instructions to settle, raise families and seek the welfare of their host nation (see Jeremiah 29:5-7). The prophet's message to this diaspora could not have been clearer. Constructive long-term engagement with the host culture was to be the pattern. The ancient covenantal dictum that they had been called to be a blessing to the nations was to be as true for them as a diaspora as it was for them as a settled nation.

No doubt the pace for this was set early on with the education and advancement of young Daniel and his associates in preparation for a lifetime of civil service in the Babylonian administration. Advancing to some of the highest

---

[130] Richard De Ridder, *Discipling the Nations* (Baker Book House, Grand Rapids, 1971), 66.

levels of public office, Daniel served successive administrations (and indeed a change of empire) with faithfulness, skill and integrity. With his example (and no doubt his aid and encouragement) the Jewish exiles seem to have followed suit. Biblical evidence, corroborated by occasional Babylonian records, testifies to a community that, by and large adjusted remarkably well (Merrill 1996:471). Cuneiform records of the time reveal Jewish names on Babylonian military rolls and business transactions.[131]

There can be little doubt that the artisans and craftsmen brought over from Jerusalem were well employed in Babylon's many building projects.[132] The capacity of this transplanted community to settle and flourish can be surmised from the fact that when given the opportunity to return to the natal land under Ezra many years later, the majority elected to stay in Babylon where life was undoubtedly more amenable (Merrill 1996:473). It would appear that the exiled Jewish community, while initially "weeping by the rivers of Babylon" (Psalm 137:1), were in fact "reaping by the rivers of Babylon" in relatively short order.

Thus in many areas of public life the Jewish diaspora community, while retaining its Jewish identity, became Jewish Babylonians, contributing positively to the life and shalom of the city as Jeremiah had challenged them to do. By the time of Esther a hundred years later, Jewish communities had spread to every province of the then incumbent Persian empire (Esther 3:8; 8:9), underlining the increasingly pervasive presence of a Jewish diaspora community that had learned not only how to survive, but also how to prosper in alien contexts.

Perhaps one of the most common stereotypes of diaspora communities is that they tend to be insular, detached, and defensive in relationship to the majority host culture. While this may often be true, it is not necessarily a default stance. The Jewish experience in Babylon and in the Persian empire that followed it demonstrates that a diaspora community can work proactively and constructively within a host culture, engaging it in positive ways that do not compromise its essential identity. Surely the subsequent history of the Jewish diaspora, fraught though it is with imposed horrors of the ghetto and the holocaust, is a tribute to the ability of a diaspora community to contribute to and deeply enrich the life of a host culture.

---

[131] Ricciotti cites the records of one Jewish commercial firm ("Murashu & Sons Bank") having dealings with Persians, Medes, Arameans and others in international trade. See G. Ricciotti, *History of Israel* (II, 1958), 63.

[132] Ely Emanuel Pilchik, *Judaism Outside the Holy Land: The Early Period* (New York: Block Publishing Col, 1964), 106.

The Revitalization of Natal Identity

The Jewish exiles in Babylon became Jewish Babylonians, proactively engaging in the socio-cultural milieu of their day. And yet, as we have pointed out above, they never divested themselves of their Jewish distinctiveness. While becoming Jewish Babylonians, they never lost their identity as Babylonian Jews. If they had done so, the diaspora would likely have gone the way of their northern Israelite kinfolk before them, and in the process been lost to history. This did not happen, in large part due to a revitalized appreciation of their Jewish identity, faith and heritage. Over the next few centuries, Babylon in fact became a major center of Jewish revival and revitalization.

It is estimated that by the time of Christ, Babylon alone had a Jewish population numbering 1,000,000 or more.[133] This is a remarkable achievement in light of the fact that the initial influx of Jews into Babylon at the time of the exile likely numbered no more than 36,000 to 48,000 men, women, and children.[134] It speaks of a communal vibrancy fed by a resurgence of Jewish identity. The simple fact is that while the formal "exile" was short in that it lasted only seventy years, as Paul Johnson puts it, "its creative force was overwhelming (Johnson 1987: 83). It was here that the institution of the synagogue first developed and flourished. It was here that Jewish scholars and scribes developed a Babylonian Talmud and a Masoretic school that produced a network of invaluable biblical texts and manuscripts (Pilchik 1964:103ff; Merrill 1996:481-482). In short, Babylonian centers of Judaism rivaled all others for eras to come.

The resurgence of the Jewish diaspora was remarkable, all the more so as Jewish identity had for hundreds of years been centered on a physical relationship to Jerusalem, and in particular its glorious Solomonic temple. With the destruction of both it is amazing that the diaspora community retained its faith, uniqueness, and self-perception at all, and indeed fostered its growth. However, the fact remains that it did. As De Ridder says, "… Israel threw off the vestment of her statehood together with her kingdom with remarkable ease and without apparent internal crisis" (Johnson 1987: 83). Speaking of the vibrancy of later expressions of diaspora Judaism, Davies says:

> It was its ability to detach loyalty from "place," while nonetheless retaining "place" in its memory, that enabled Pharisaism to transcend the loss of its land (Davies 1992:103).

---

[133] S.W. Baron, *A Social and Religious History of the Jews*, I (New York: Columbia University, 1937), 132; S. Grayzel, *A History of the Jews* (Philadelphia: Jewish Publication Society of America, 1968), 138; F.A. Norwood, *Strangers and Exiles: A History of Religious Refugees* (New York: Abingdon Press, 1969), 141.
[134] Jewish Encyclopedia, *The Babylonian Captivity*, 2002; [on-line]; accessed June 4, 2010; available at http://www.bible-history.com/map_babylonian_captivity/map_of_the_deportation_of_judah_jewish_encyclopedia.html.

The Jewish community it seems, displayed a remarkable propensity to adapt quite comfortably to its new surroundings. By Esther's time a hundred years later, Jewish communities had scattered over the length and breadth of the Persian empire, remaining a distinct and discernible identity wherever they settled (Esther 3:8). For better or for worse, the Jewish diaspora retained its core identity, being distinct enough that in any of the 127 provinces of the Persian empire, it could be recognized and marked out (Esther 3:13).

This dissociation of the Jewish diaspora from a physical political hegemony over a natal space is, according to Boyarin, a "lesson" that the Jewish experience of diaspora has to teach the diaspora milieu today, namely that "... peoples and land are not naturally and organically connected," and that "it is possible for a people to maintain its distinctive culture, its difference, without controlling land ...." (Boyarin 2003:110). The relevance of this concept to the claims and counterclaims of any number of modern competing diaspora return movements is easily discerned. At the very least we can agree that the "divorce" between the Jewish diaspora and its natal land, whether temporary or permanent, did not sound the diaspora's death knell, but in fact, as we shall see, played a significant role in revitalizing its sense of natal identity.

However, the question remains: how did the Jewish diaspora in the environs of Babylon and beyond not only survive but thrive? Five factors arise from the biblical record that may help to explain how this happened (Figure 5.4).

Figure 5.4 Factors Contributing to the Revitalization of Natal Identity among the Jewish Diaspora in Babylon and Persia

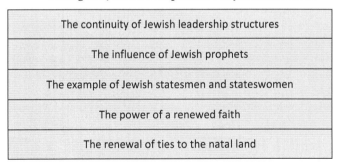

The Continuity of Jewish Leadership Structures

The fall of Jerusalem was of course a massive blow to Jewish national aspirations. Jewish identity had for many years coalesced around Jerusalem, the sacred capital of God's chosen people, and its glorious temple as the dwelling place of Yahweh. The inviolability of both was accepted almost as an article of faith (Davies 1992:56). Yahweh's unconditional promises of a never-ending

Davidic dynasty and His choice of Zion as its earthly locus were the dogma on which state and cult were founded (Bright 1981:347). Nebuchadnezzar's battering rams, however, made short work of such theology. With Jerusalem's destruction, inviolability was shown to be a house of cards as the central structures of Jewish identity were reduced to rubble.

The smoking rubble of Jerusalem, however, did not necessarily lead to an amorphous Jewish rabble in Babylon. To the contrary, right from the start there was a measure of continuity in the leadership and administrative structures the Babylonians allowed the Jewish community to retain. As long as the internal organization of the diaspora community was strong enough to resist the influences of an alien environment, Jewish identity could be maintained (De Ridder 1971:76). It is interesting for instance to note that Jeremiah's letter to the community exiled in Babylon is addressed to "the rest of the elders of the exile, the priests, the prophets and all the people whom Nebuchadnezzar had taken into exile from Jerusalem to Babylon" (Jeremiah 29:1). Clues like these suggest that many of the leadership structures that had organized and administered life in Jerusalem were still to some degree functioning among the diaspora community in Babylon.

Most interesting of all is the suggestion that even a semblance of the Jewish monarchy was to some degree retained. While Jehoiachin, the next to last king of independent Judah, had been marched off to Babylon together with his family in the second deportation, we are told that the Babylonian king eventually released him, put him on a royal stipend and afforded him royal recognition (2 Kings 25:27-30). In Babylonian tablets he is referred to as "King of Judah," and it is apparent that the Jewish community in Babylon continued to look on him as the rightful Judean king, in opposition to his uncle Zedekiah who had replaced him on the Judean throne in Jerusalem's final years.[135] Implied in all of this is the clear sense that the institution of the Judean monarchy found some sort of expression among the diaspora community in Babylon.

Thus one of the reasons for the relative health and stability of the Jewish diaspora can be traced to the existence, operation, and continuity of familiar Jewish institutions of leadership that provided a semblance of structure and stability for a community seeking to find its feet in a strange land.

The Influence of Jewish Prophets

Certainly a great deal of credit for the Jewish diaspora's viability can be laid at the feet of some of the most powerful voices of the Hebrew prophetic institution. It is interesting that the tone of the prophetic message both before and during the final fall of Jerusalem was generally very critical of a nation that

---

[135] Merrill 1996:452; see also William Albright, "King Jehoiachin in Exile," *The Biblical Archaeologist Reader*, ed. David Noel Freedman and G. Ernest Wright (Garden City, N.Y.: Doubleday, 1961), vol.1, 106-107.

had largely abandoned any genuine adherence to the covenant law of Moses. However, once the destruction of Jerusalem was complete and the bulk of the Jewish population were exiles in a strange land, the tone of the prophetic message often changed dramatically. The latter parts of both Isaiah's and Jeremiah's prophecies drip with hope for the future of God's chosen people. While these men were not physically on the scene in Babylon, their words were, and they carried weight, reminding the diaspora of their shared historical roots and of their future calling and purpose as God's covenant people. As Bright says, "… their affirmation … of the ultimate triumph of Yahweh's redemptive purpose provided men with a hope to which they could cling" (Bright 1981:349).

In addition, there were prophets like Ezekiel and Daniel, men who lived and ministered among the diaspora themselves, but whose visions of the future encouraged an exiled people not to lose hope in God's plans for them in the years to come. To a discouraged and dispossessed people, the words of the prophets imported what is probably one of the most essential ingredients for the viability and health of any true diaspora … a sense of shared hope for the future.

Examples of Jewish Statesmen and Stateswomen

If the message of Jewish prophets inspired hope, the example of courageous Jewish statesmen and women serving in the public realm inspired admiration. Find a diaspora that has survived and flourished through thick and thin, and one will likely find a hero. Whether mythical or factual, such a figure tends to provide a catalytic model that embodies the best and purest ideals of the identity that a dislocated people is struggling to keep alive. Certainly this could be said of the Jewish diaspora at the time of the exile. The iconic stories that emerge—Daniel and the lions' den, Shadrach, Meshech, Abednego and the fiery furnace, Queen Esther risking her life before the Persian king for her people—are stories that were guaranteed to build a sense of ethnic and national pride. The life and testimony of one such person could be more powerful than a thousand words, for in them the abstract ideals of the prophets were put into flesh and blood. Such people gave to the diaspora living examples of loyal citizens of the empire who carried weight in high places, who in the same breath were unapologetically Jewish. What is sure is that as their stories are told and retold, the cohesiveness of a scattered people is strengthened and the shared associations revitalize and invigorate the community.

The Power of Renewed Faith

Another primary reason for the growth and flowering of the Jewish diaspora in the beginning years of the exile was the fundamental renewal of the faith they had inherited from the patriarchs and covenantal law of Moses. Throughout much, if not most, of Israel's history as an independent nation, fidelity to the covenant with Yahweh had been seriously compromised. Indeed, according to the prophets, this was the very reason Yahweh had forsaken Jerusalem and His sacred dwelling place in the temple, allowing His covenant people to be driven from the land by the invading Babylonians.

The hiatus in Babylon however, was never meant to be final. Its purpose was to be disciplinary and redemptive. Its ultimate goal had always been to turn the people's hearts back to their God in repentance. The remarkable thing is that to some degree this seems to be what happened. In their initial years as a vulnerable diaspora, they rediscovered a fresh faith in God and His covenant law. Evidence for this is found in the fact that the Jews at this time became what one might call the first truly monotheistic people. Further evidence lies in the missionary efforts of the Jewish diaspora as they continued to spread throughout the near east and the Mediterranean world. De Ridder and Hedlund document the passion and energy of Jewish mission during the period between the Old and the New Testaments, and ascribe much of the astounding multiplication of Jewish populations at the time to this missionary activity. Quoting Harnack, Hedlund says:

> It is utterly impossible to explain the large total of Jews in the Diaspora by the mere fact of the fertility of Jewish families. We must assume ... that a very large number of pagans ... trooped over to the religion of Yahweh (Hedlund 1997:155).

What significance does this have from a diaspora perspective? Simply that at the outset of the Babylonian exile, we are introduced to a people whose faith and spiritual distinctives are on very thin ice. Yet before much time has passed, they become a group with a singular religious focus and a passion to spread that focus wherever they go. A renewed sense of spiritual calling and purpose gripped their hearts and put a disparate broken people on a fast track to rejuvenation. As mentioned earlier, few things will bind a people together more tightly than a shared sense of the divine flowing in their midst. That sense flowed in the Babylonian Jewish diaspora, and bound them together in a unity that nothing else could match.

The Renewal and Revitalization of Ties to the Natal Land

As the final years of the exile came to a close, the vast bulk of the Jewish world were living outside the bounds of the "promised land." Diaspora was now in fact the predominant expression of Jewish life. Interestingly, however, the last chapter of the Old Testament narrative was not a diaspora story. Though it was in fact a minority story, it was one in which the locus was once again the promised land.

With the ebb and flow of history having swept Cyrus and his Persians into imperial ascendancy, the scattered Jewish diaspora was given a remarkable opportunity to return to its natal land.[136] In the first year of his reign in Babylon (538 B.C.), Cyrus issued a decree mandating the re-establishment of the Jewish community and religion in Palestine (Bright 1981:361). Over roughly the next one hundred years, the biblical narrative indicates that several waves of Jewish exiles took advantage of this opportunity to return to the land of their fathers.[137] Under the leadership of men such as Zerubbabel, Ezra, Nehemiah, Haggai, and Zechariah, the returnees were able to restore a semblance of Jewish life and religious practice in Jerusalem and its environs. From this reseeding of the natal land eventually grew the million-strong Jewish community that populated Palestine by the time of Christ.

Two observations immediately arise in regard to the relationship of the "return movement" and the diaspora that remained at large in the Persian empire. The first is that only a very small percentage of the Jewish diaspora actually returned to their native land (Merrill 1996:493). This, as noted above, was no doubt due to the fact that life the empire had brought the diaspora afforded them a fair measure of settled comfort. Life in the natal land, on the other hand, had little to offer but the exhausting struggles of rebuilding on the ruins of a bygone era. Thus a return to the natal land simply did not generate widespread enthusiasm among the Jewish diaspora.

However, this did not mean there was a radical "disconnect" between the diaspora and its sense of natal land. Quite the contrary! Whether one chose to return or to stay, no Jew could ever deny his or her natal links to the land. "By the rivers of Babylon," the captive exiles had sung, "there we sat down and wept, when we remembered Zion" (Psalm 137:1). "If I forget you, O Jerusalem," they continued, "may my right hand forget her skill. May my tongue cling to the roof of my mouth if I do not remember you, if I do not exalt Jerusalem above my chief joy" (137:5-6).

Some seventy years later, the exiled Daniel, who most likely died without ever setting eyes again on the Jerusalem of his youth, had not forgotten! Despite threats to his life, his orientation to his natal land was expressed by physically

---

[136] While the opportunity to return was indeed remarkable, it was not unique. The policy of return was in fact part of a broader Persian policy authorizing all captive peoples in Babylonia to return to their places of origin.

[137] The biblical books of Ezra and Nehemiah give passing descriptions of these returns. The post-exilic prophets Haggai, Zechariah, and Malachi give additional background regarding the struggles the returnees faced upon return.

facing Jerusalem three times a day in prayer. Clearly, neither the threat of death nor long years in exile had dimmed his attachment to Jerusalem as his true spiritual home.

Sometime later, noting that the seventy-year exile prophesied by Jeremiah was close to completion (9:2), Daniel was stirred into a majestic prayer of confession on behalf of his people. In it he makes reference to "the land," "Jerusalem," "the inhabitants of Jerusalem," "Your holy mountain," "Your city Jerusalem," "Your desolate sanctuary," "the holy mountain of God" … ten times in eighteen verses (9:3-20). Clearly you could "take the boy out of Jerusalem," but you could never "take Jerusalem out of the boy!" After a lifetime among the exiled diaspora in Babylon, the natal land and its spiritual associations remained the focus of his heart.

There can be no doubt that Daniel's attitude to his natal land was to some degree reflective of the attitude of the rest of the diaspora to their homeland. While it is true that the numbers of returnees to Palestine were small, the fact remains that between the leadership of men like Zerubbabel and Sheshbazaar, over 50,000 exiles did indeed make the journey back to Palestine and rebuilt their lives on the ruins of Jerusalem and its environs. The vast majority of these returnees would have been Jewish exiles who had been born and raised in the diaspora and had likely never set eyes on the land of their forefathers. Yet they returned! A deeply held sense of shared natal roots energized them into a radical and corporate return to a homeland most of them would actually only be seeing for the first time.

Not only were the numbers of returnees not insignificant, they were indicative of a much larger diaspora community that would have been necessary to support and finance such a venture. Indeed, Ezra makes clear that financial support for the first wave of returnees under Zerubbabel came not only from the king's treasuries, but also from the pockets of the diaspora (Ezra 1:6). Clearly the vision of the natal land generated a momentum that continued in the years to come. In 458 B.C., some eighty years after the first return, Ezra led a second return to Palestine (Bright 1981:361). Though much smaller in size, it is indicative of a continued interest within the Jewish diaspora in matters relating to Palestine. Roughly thirteen years later in 445 B.C., it was the turn of Nehemiah to make his way to Jerusalem. The impetus that pushed him sprang from the same deep sense of identification with natal land that had so moved Daniel, Ezra and countless others (Nehemiah 1:1-4). Once again there seems to be a strong thread of deep emotive identification with the natal land that neither time nor distance could remove.

The interplay between the Jewish diaspora and natal land described above reveals two dynamics that are worth pausing to note. The first is that the deep attachment of the Jewish diaspora to the concept of a natal land was a value that bound the scattered community together. This is underlined by the distinction many diaspora Jews made between "exile" and simple "dispersion." In the mind of the Jewish diaspora, these terms were not necessarily synonymous. The

DIASPORA DISTINCTIVES: THE JEWISH DIASPORA EXPERIENCE IN THE OLD TESTAMENT

Jews did not perceive themselves as simply a people in dispersion. They were a people in exile. As Davies says,

> Jews outside Palestine conceived of their existence not simply as a dispersion [that?] meant that, wherever they were, they were still bound symbolically, theologically as well as historically, to their home base, to Eretz Israel: they were not simply scattered. The Diaspora maintained the notion of its existence as *(an)* exile (Davies 1992:80, italics mine).

Thus to a people who perceived themselves as a nation in "exile," the land remained a viable, emotive and living issue. There was a fundamental orientation to the natal land that bound the dispersed men and women of Israel together. Shared linkage to a natal land is an affinity that continues to bind diasporas of all shapes and sizes together today. And the emotions and feelings that are generated in the hearts of scattered people who dream of ancient homelands find their diaspora ancestors in the scattered Jewish communities of the Bible.

A second diaspora dynamic arises from the association of the global Jewish family in biblical history with its natal land. It is noteworthy that the renewal and revitalization of Jewish life *in* the land came from the Jewish diaspora *outside* the land. It is clear from the accounts in Ezra, Nehemiah and the post-exilic prophets that, left to itself, the replanted Jewish community struggled to maintain its covenant uniqueness as the people of God. Spirits quickly flagged, and social and religious compromise rapidly became a viable *modus operandi*. It was from the heart of the *diaspora* that the challenge to covenant faithfulness in the land so often came to the rescue. It was not "insiders" but "outsiders" like Ezra and Nehemiah who brought renewal and recommitment to those who had resettled in the promised land.

Perhaps this is a unique contribution that any diaspora can make to the people and place from which it stems. Perhaps in an age of increasing change and globalization, every nation wedded to its soil needs fresh air and new perspective from without, if it is to survive and thrive.[138] Thus it seems to have been in the Old Testament history of Israel from beginning to end. The impetus for renewal and return had come from men like Ezra and Nehemiah who lived beyond the borders of their natal land and the Jewish community that resided there. The broader perspective from "beyond" gave vitality to their Jewish identity, and in the fresh air of the diaspora they became catalysts for renewal.

---

[138] Illustrative of this point, Robin Cohen says, "Although born in China, Sun Yixian (Sun Yat-sen) developed his political consciousness in Hong Kong and in the Chinese community in Hawaii. His Society for the Revival of China was a crucial instrument in the promotion of a modern Chinese nationalism" (p.185).

Could it be that the best thing that could happen to a nation may be the new life, hope, and direction that its diaspora can bring? The likes of Daniel, Ezra and Nehemiah would surely answer in the affirmative.

Summary

We have sought to understand the Jewish experience in the Old Testament through a diaspora lens. From the narratives of Abraham's life in the book of Genesis, we have traced the diaspora roots and associations that shaped and colored the Jewish experience of diaspora throughout biblicalhistory. From the accounts of the Jewish diaspora experience in Egypt and Babylon/Persia, nine salient characteristics have emerged that lent the diaspora community its cohesiveness and durability.

While these distinctives were experienced in a unique way by the ancient Jews, we have argued that they are applicable to the broader community of diasporas throughout the world and history. In this way, the affinities that blend together to give a diaspora community its identity are perhaps reflected in *trans-diasporic* affinities that give all diasporas a shared unity of identity and experience. Can yesterday's diasporas bequeath an inheritance of wisdom and hope to the diasporas of today? One can only hope the answer will be "yes!" Perhaps the Hebrews in ancient Egypt and the Jews in ancient Babylon and Persia, both finding their roots in a "wandering Aramean" named Abraham, can provide just such a model.

Chapter 6

Diaspora and Relocation as Divine Impetus for Witness in the Early Church

Craig Ott

Introduction

Migration is a phenomenon that has accompanied humanity since the expulsion of Adam and Eve from the Garden. Modern day globalization has only accelerated and intensified the movement of peoples. Today about three percent of the world's population live in a country other than where they were born. According to a United Nations report:

> Globally, the number of international migrants in 2010 is estimated at 214 million, up from 195 million in 2005. Females account for 49 per cent of the total. Six out of every ten international migrants (128 million) reside today in developed countries, and the majority of those (74 million) originated in developing countries (United Nations 2010:3).

This reality has profound implications on interactions among peoples and their religious beliefs in general, and on Christian mission in particular. Though the extent of human migration has been exponentially intensified by globalization, the opportunities for Christian mission are not new.

Much has been written elsewhere on migration of peoples both in the Bible and in the contemporary world, and diaspora missions has become a much discussed theme in missiology.[139] This discussion will be limited to exploring New Testament examples, primarily from the Book of Acts, of how human

---

[139] For a sampling see Campese and Ciallella. 2003; *Missiology* vol. 31, no. 1 (2003), entire issue; Escobar 2004; Lausanne Occasional Paper 56, 2005; *Zeitschrift für Mission* vol. 31, no. 1-2 (2005), entire issue; Hanciles 2008; Spencer 2008; Cruz 2010; Wan and Tira 2010; *Transformation* vol. 28, no. 1 (2011), entire issue.

migrations and the relocation of people in the first century served as a divine impetus for mission in terms of the cross-cultural spread of the gospel.

We will see that under God's sovereignty such movements of people in the first century created opportunities for the spread of the gospel to the nations. The practical import of this is that we can confidently affirm God's sovereign hand in the movement of peoples today, and we can seek to discover how God may use this for his missional purposes. We act in alignment with the missional trajectory of the New Testament in identifying open doors for the gospel in migration and diaspora today.

God's Sovereignty and the Movement of People

The term diaspora has been variously defined by historians, anthropologists, and theologians. Here it will simply refer to the scattering of a people, who settle for a longer period in a location outside their original homeland. The term "relocation" will refer to movement of individuals or peoples that may not involve permanent resettlement. Throughout history, reasons for relocation and diaspora have been both voluntary and involuntary, caused by war, famine, enslavement, or persecution on the one hand, or by the quest for freedom, economic opportunity, education, or adventure on the other. Movement of people outside their homeland has resulted in both improved lives and impoverished lives.

Behind these reasons God's sovereign hand is at work, and he uses such movement of peoples for his purposes. Scripture affirms of God, "You rule over all the kingdoms of the nations. Power and might are in your hand, and no one can withstand you" (2 Chr 20:6b; cf. 2; Chr 36:22; Jer 27:6; Isa 13:3-5; Eze 29:19, etc.). Natural events such as famine and pestilence are also under the providence of God (2 Sam 24:15; 2 Kg. 8:1; Ex 14:21; Amos 4:10), as are the decisions of political powers, "In the LORD's hand the king's heart is a stream of water that he channels toward all who please him" (Prov 21:1).

God's sovereignty over the movement of peoples has been demonstrated throughout biblical history: for example, in the events surrounding the tower of Babel, Abraham, Joseph, the Babylonian captivity, Daniel, and various famines, plagues and wars that caused migrations among the people of Israel. The English term "diaspora" stems from the Greek, meaning literally "scattering," and is used in both the Septuagint and the New Testament to describe the scattering of God's people. In the Old Testament this was a judgment of Israel for disobedience (e.g., Deut 28:25; 30:4; Neh 1:9; Jer 11:22; Joh 7:35). In the New Testament it describes more the fact of churches existing in various regions (Jas 1:1, 1 Pet 1:1). This sovereign working of God in human history and the movement of peoples we find to be a means of God spreading His glory among all people, and preparing people to receive that message.[140]

At the time of the birth of Christianity, the movement of peoples as individuals and as larger groups was common. The Pax Romana and the Roman roads facilitated international travel and relocation. Merchants moved about to make their living in new locations. According to Eckhard Schnabel, "Caesar Augustus promoted deliberate resettlement policies: they relocated hundreds of thousands of proletarians from Rome, Italic people and veterans, settling them in the provinces" (2004: 639). Some moved into positions of leadership as administrators or as occupying military troops. Others moved in servitude as slaves. How did this movement of people serve to advance the preaching of the Gospel and the early Christian mission?

One important way of seeing the scattering of people as occasion for mission is through the exercise of hospitality and Christian kindness toward those who are new and often vulnerable. This aspect has been thoroughly explored by others (e.g., Pohl 2003), and so that valuable discussion will not be repeated here. Rather, we will examine mission and diaspora in terms of gospel proclamation. Four aspects of diaspora and relocation in relation to mission as witness will be investigated:

- Involuntary scattering of Christians who become bearers of the gospel in new locales.
- Relocation of non-Christians who thereby come into proximity to the gospel
- Diaspora communities that provide an entry point for the gospel
- Diaspora as a preparation for gospel messengers

In each regard the movement of peoples may be viewed as evidence of God's sovereign working in a larger plan for the nations and the spread of the gospel. In this chapter, examples from the Book of Acts will be considered.

Scattered Christians Became Bearers of the Gospel

The Great Commission explicitly mandates "going" to the nations to make disciples (Mt 28:19). The work of the Holy Spirit makes inevitable the disciples crossing geographic, cultural and religious barriers bearing witness to the risen Christ (Acts 1:8). Relocation here does not include the intentional sending of missionaries to the nations (as with Paul and Barnabas in Acts 13), but rather the

---

[140] One of the clearest examples of this in the Old Testament is Daniel and his Hebrew companions; when deported to Babylonia they became witnesses there, resulting in rulers glorifying the God of Israel (Dan 3:28-29, 4:37, 6:26-27).

movement of peoples, usually in larger numbers, at times involuntary and unintentional, but which nevertheless became a missional opportunity.

With perhaps the exception of Peter's visit to Cornelius, one of the more important discoveries that Luke's report in Acts is the emphasis that the Jerusalem Christians, including the apostles, did not mobilize *significantly* to bring the gospel to the nations; until God himself scattered them through persecution. It was neither intentional obedience to the Great Commission nor the inner compulsion of the Holy Spirit, but rather the outward and seemingly human circumstances of persecution that initially brought the early church into cross-cultural missionary motion.

In two very clear instances the scattering of Christians led to missionary witness in the New Testament: the persecution of the Jerusalem Christians, and the expulsion of Jews from Rome.

Persecution and the Scattering of the Jerusalem Christians, Acts 8:1-8; 11:19ff

The persecution described here was unleashed in the wake of Stephen's martyrdom under the accusation that Christians defamed the Temple and the Law (Acts 6:13), and seems to have been directed initially against the Hellenist Christians, though eventually including others (Bammel 1995:358; Bruce 1974: 174; Witherington 1998:278). Various parties in Jerusalem and voices of those such as Gamaliel who called for moderation regarding opposition to Christians (Acts 5:33-39). But after Stephen's martyrdom a "great (or severe) persecution" (διωγμος μεγας) broke out in Jerusalem so severe that "all[141] except the apostles[142] were scattered throughout Judea and Samaria"(Acts 8:2b). The date of this persecution is not certain. It may well have been within a year or two of Jesus' resurrection, although various traditions date it six or seven years after the resurrection. Rainer Riesner's careful discussion of New Testament chronology leans toward the earlier date (1998:59-60, 118-124).

---

[141] "All" in Acts 8:1 is perhaps hyperbolic. The existence of a strong Jewish church in Jerusalem later in Acts seems to speak against literally all Christians being scattered. It may well have been only the Hellenistic believers. The suggestion on the basis of Acts 9:29 that the persecution was carried out primarily by Hellenistic Jews is untenable. Paul arrested Christians on the authority of the highest Jewish leaders (22:4-5).

[142] Why did the apostles remain in Jerusalem, when all others fled? F. F. Bruce writes, "The twelve apostles remained in Jerusalem, partly no doubt because they conceived it to be their duty to stay at their posts, and partly, we may gather, because the popular resentment was directed not so much at them as at the leaders of the Hellenists in the church" (1974, 175). The latter part of this statement is, however, questionable since the apostles were not exempt from persecution and had already been imprisoned (4:1-3, 5:18); indeed their remaining in Jerusalem was more likely an act of courage.

Luke's description of Saul's (Paul's) role evidences the severity of the persecution.[143] By the authority and commission of the chief priests, Paul sought to take both Christian men and women prisoner to Jerusalem to be punished, which included flogging (Acts 8:3; 9:1-2; 22:5, 19; 26:10-12). Others accompanied Paul in the effort (Acts 9:7-8). Not only did the persecution result in the death of Stephen (Acts 7:59), but other Christians were also killed at the hands of Paul (Acts 22:4; 26:10). After Paul's conversion, the Jews sought on two occasions to kill him (Acts 9:23, 29). Later the persecution resumed when Herod had James executed and Peter arrested to please the Jews (Acts12:1-4), and this probably occurred around A.D. 41 or 42 (Riesner 1998:118-124).

Schnabel believes that the scattering of believers meant that "many prominent members of the Jerusalem church, particularly Greek-speaking believers, permanently settled in other regions of the country..." (2004:671). He later remarks that "The fact that they stayed in Samaria is astonishing, given the fact that Samaritans were not friends of the Jews" (2004:681).

The persecution seems to be the first major turning point in fulfilling the words of Acts 1:8. It was unintentional on the part of the disciples, but clearly intentional in the plan of God to reach the nations. Once the persecuted believers were propelled into motion they shared their faith in the Messiah, in a natural way, wherever they landed. God blessed this group of witnesses to plant His church beyond the bounds of Judea. Philip brought the gospel to Samaria (Acts 8:5), and others brought the gospel to Phoenicia, Cypress, and Antioch (Acts11:19). And two phases of the missions resulted from this involuntary scattering.

Proclamation in Samaria through Philip

Philip, a Hellenist leader in the Jerusalem church, brought the gospel to Samaria,[144] fulfilling the third stage of Acts 1:8. The longstanding tension between Judea and Samaria is well known and well documented in scripture and other ancient sources (e.g. John 4:9, 8:48). Josephus portrays Samaritans as non-Jews migrated to the territory of the Northern Kingdom and syncretists who had mixed the Jewish faith with pagan beliefs. V. J. Samkutty writes of Samaritans:

---

[143] Bammel notes, "The data of persecution are merely mentioned in Acts. Hardly any attempt is made to embellish the details and to work out a martyrological history of a hagiographical portrait of nascent Christendom" (Bammel 1995, 361).

[144] "A city in Samaria" (i.e., an indefinite city) is to be preferred over "the city of Samaria" (Schnabel 2004, 676).

Originally, the term was an ethnic designation for the racially mixed and religiously syncretistic northern Palestinian population who had been settled in the territory of Samaria by the Assyrians in the late eighth century BCE. Religiously, these colonists and their descendants were seen by their Judahite neighbors to the south as half-pagan and half-Yahwistic (Samkutty 2006:58).

"From a Jewish point of view, they were outcasts, syncretists, apostates and idolaters, and the legitimacy of their socio-ethnic and religious status was in question" (Samkutty 2006:97). However, some Rabbinic writings consider them equal to Jews.[145] The Samaritans held strictly to the teachings of the Pentateuch alone, rejecting later prophetic writings and Rabbinic interpretations such as the Mishnah and Talmud, thus syncretism may be an inappropriate description.[146] However the religious and ethnic differences between Samaritans and Jews are interpreted, tensions between the two groups were high.

Some Samaritans had come to believe in Jesus through the incident with the woman at Jacob's well (John 4:1-42). Some may also have been baptized by John the Baptizer (Schnabel 2004,647 n.10). But in general the Samaritans had rejected Jesus (Luke 9:51-56). Given this history and these ethnic and religious tensions, it was a bold move for Philip to proclaim the Gospel to them. This marks the witness of the Gospel moving beyond Judea to its near neighbors, who were not only ethnically mixed but also religiously unorthodox. Thus both ethnic and religious barriers were crossed in the Samaritan mission. The fact that Philip proclaimed Jesus as Messiah (Acts 8:5) and that Luke makes no mention of the Samaritans repenting from idolatry indicates that they were not Gentiles, but Samaritan believers in YHWH (Schnabel 2004:677). The result was that many responded with joy to the Gospel message (Acts 8:8), quite different from their earlier response to Jesus. God's favor rested upon the mission to the Samaritans.

After Peter and John had visited the Samaritan believers, encouraged by God's work among them, they "returned to Jerusalem, preaching the gospel in many Samaritan villages" (Acts 8:25). In this way the gospel reached not merely isolated individuals, but people in Samaria as a whole, as a direct result of the Jerusalem persecution. Luke later reports continued growth of the church in Samaria and God's favor upon the movement, "Then the church throughout Judea, Galilee and Samaria enjoyed a time of peace and was strengthened. Living in the fear of the Lord and encouraged by the Holy Spirit, it increased in numbers" (Acts 9:31, cf. 15:3).

---

[145] See the discussion in Samkutty 2006, 79-85 which concludes, "In light of available evidence, it is reasonable to say that Samaritanism as a separate entity is neither Judaism nor a foreign religion" (p. 84).
[146] In this regard some have argued that Judaism and not Samaritan religion is the more syncretistic faith (Dexinger 1998; Williamson and Evans 2000).

In light of Jesus' words in Acts 1:8, the bringing of the gospel to Samaria is of salvation-historical significance, which Luke highlights by the inclusion of this incident.[147] Furthermore, "It is the Samaritan mission, not the Gentile mission, that primarily marks a decisive turning point in the development of the early Church, as the former paves the way for the latter" (Samkutty 2006:220).

But there is a more subtle fruit of the Samaritan mission, which resulted from the persecution. Samkutty suggests that because James and John had desired to call down fire from heaven as judgment on the Samaritans in Luke 9:51-56, the granting of the Spirit was delayed in Samaria so that the apostles would now pray and call down the fire of the Spirit on the Samaritans instead. And their prayers were answered. "The transformation needed to happen not in the Samaritans, but in the Jerusalem based apostles.... Both Peter and John needed to understand that the Samaritans (and the Gentiles) are part of God's plan of salvation and that the apostles should love their neighbors enough to engage in mission to them" (Samkutty 2006:176-177). If this interpretation is correct, it was not so much the command of Jesus as the experienced realities of God's work among the Samaritans and Gentiles that changed the attitudes and missional vision of the apostles. And this was all set in motion by the persecution and scattering of believers.

Philip then moves on toward Gaza and encounters the Ethiopian eunuch, probably also a Gentile God-fearer,[148] who is baptized and then takes the gospel to Africa. The inclusion of an eunuch in the new people of God is also of salvation-historical significance. It representatively marks a reversal of the Mosaic ban of eunuchs from the assembly of the Lord (Deut 23:1) and fulfills the promise of Isaiah 56:1-8. The full inclusion of eunuchs in temple worship turned God's house truly into "a house of prayer for all nations."

Proclamation in Distant Regions

As a result of the persecution, it was other scattered believers who would bring the gospel to the Gentiles and find unprecedented response. Apparently the majority of

---

[147] The gospel has already progressed from Jerusalem to Judea through natural contact with Jerusalem Christians. For example, Acts 5:16 reports, "Crowds gathered also from the towns around Jerusalem, bringing their sick and those tormented by impure spirits, and all of them were healed." Jesus himself had taught in various towns of Galilee (e.g., Mat 11:1) and the disciples had been sent to various towns and villages in Judea (e.g., Lk 10:1, Mat 10:5-6). Lohmeyer (1936) and others have argued that Galilee was virtually Christian prior to Jesus' resurrection.

[148] Bruce writes, "The chamberlain was probably a God-fearing Gentile. ... It is questionable whether a eunuch could have been admitted to the commonwealth of Israel as a full proselyte; at an earlier time eunuchs were excluded from religious privileges in Israel (Deut. 23:1), although Isaiah 56:3ff foreshadows the removal of this ban" (Bruce 1974, 187). Schnabel (Schnabel 2004, 685) argues that if he was not castrated he may have been a proselyte.

scattered Christians were reluctant to preach the gospel to Gentiles. Luke records that they were "spreading the word only among Jews" (Acts 11:19b) even though these regions were largely populated by Gentiles. But a minority of believers "from Cyprus and Cyrene[149] went to Antioch and began to speak to the Greeks also, telling them the good news about the Lord Jesus" (v.20). God grants his approval of this unconventional preaching, "The Lord's hand was with them, and a great number of people believed and turned to the Lord" (v.21). This constitutes the third stage of scattering and fulfillment of Act 1:8.

Antioch was a city that prided itself on its religious toleration (Longenecker 1985:16), as described by Glanville Downey:

> Antioch had shared, with other centers in which Hellenistic religion and philosophy had flourished, the changes characteristic of the Hellenistic age, in which the old religious cults and philosophies were tending to become matters of individual belief, as people sought religious satisfaction for their own problems and aspirations (1963:120).

Antioch was a major commercial and political city, the third largest city in the Roman Empire. Though estimates on the population of Antioch vary wildly,[150] it included perhaps as many as 65,000 Jews; one seventh of the total population, according to Richard Longnecker (1985:14), or one tenth according to Schnabel (2004:784-85). According to Josephus (Wars 7:43-45), in Antioch many Gentiles were attracted as proselytes to Judaism. One of the seven deacons in the Jerusalem church was "Nicolas from Antioch, a convert to Judaism" (Acts 6:5). All of this no doubt made for a receptive environment for the Christian message.

Paul had ministered in Arabia and Cilicia, Peter in the coastal region (Lydda, Sharon and Joppa), and others in Phoenicia and Cypress, but the Antioch church was apparently the first predominantly Gentile church established. This is evident from (1) the fact that other scattered believers preached only to the Jews (Acts 11:19), and (2) the seemingly skeptical reaction of the Jerusalem church sending Barnabas to assess the situation (Acts 11:22). These new believers were neither Jews nor Samaritans, and Luke makes no mention of them even being God-fearers.

Antioch was an ethnically diverse city known for moral laxity, prostitution, and pagan worship. Thus the suspicions of the Jerusalem church are understandable for both theological and moral reasons. It was one thing for individual Gentile God-fearers like Cornelius or even Samaritans to become

---

[149] Cyrene was located in North Africa.
[150] Anywhere from 100,000 to 600,000 inhabitants, though 250,000 seems most likely. Rodney Stark (Stark 1997, 147-162) has calculated that the city would have been more densely populated than modern Bombay, with enormous sanitation problems and health risks in addition to the social chaos of such overcrowded conditions and intense ethnic antagonisms.

Christians, but it was another thing to have an entire church composed largely of uncircumcised Gentile believers. And what would become of their pagan beliefs and lifestyle? How would this impact the expanding messianic community?

Barnabas is commissioned by the Jerusalem church to visit the church in Antioch. "When he arrived and saw what the grace of God had done, he was glad and encouraged them all to remain true to the Lord with all their hearts" (Acts11:22-23). Fortunately God's grace was evident in the lives of the new believers, and Barnabas had eyes to see it. Barnabas not only evaluates the legitimacy of their conversion, he also becomes their teacher, and under his teaching the church continues to grow (v. 24). He then brings Paul to Antioch where Paul teaches a great number of people (v. 25-26), indicating that those who believed continued in the faith.

Three times Luke mentions the large size of the church (Acts 11:21, 24, 26), underscoring the importance of the Antioch church and the magnitude of the breakthrough of the gospel into the Gentile world. It is also here that believers are first called Christians[151] (v.26b), a name probably conferred by outsiders and which may even have been derogatory. But more importantly, the name indicates an emerging identity for the believing community apart from the Jewish community. This was no doubt precipitated by the majority of Gentile believers and the mixed ethnic composition of the church (Witherington1998: 371; Bock 2007:416).

The Gentile believers in Antioch did not need to become full Jewish proselytes as a condition for acceptance in the community of Christ's followers, a decision later confirmed by the Jerusalem Council in Acts 15. Andrew Walls (1997) points out the revolutionary implications of this, "…the abandonment by the early church of the proselyte model of dealing with Gentile converts, well established as it was, guaranteed the future cultural diversity of Christianity; indeed, it built the principle of cultural diversity into Christianity in perpetuity" (1997:148).

It is little surprise that later this church in Antioch sent Paul and Barnabas to bring the gospel to yet more distant, predominantly Gentile regions. Indeed, by Luke's account, Antioch now becomes the geographic focus of attention as "to the ends of the earth" (i.e. the Gentile mission) is taken up by the Acts narrative. Schnabel is justified in his remark that, "The establishment of the church in Antioch was one of the most significant events in the history of the early church" (2004:786).

---

[151] Here the term χριστιανοι adds the ending -ιανοι to χριστος, indicating that the new identity is not ethnic but with the person of Christ. Similar endings were used to indicate followers of Herod and others (Witherington 1998, 371).

Thus persecution and the scattering of the Jerusalem church proved to be the divine impetus for these early breakthroughs.[152] Interestingly, in the case of Antioch, the evangelists to Gentiles are not even Jerusalem believers, but believers from Cyprus and Cyrene (Acts11:20).

It can be fairly said that persecution gave the impetus of mission to the nations in the early church. Both with Peter's vision and the conversion of Cornelius, and with the conversion of large numbers of Gentiles in Antioch, the Jerusalem Christians remained skeptical regarding overt mission to the Gentiles.[153] Once the church was by necessity set in motion, mission was launched and was not to be turned back. Growing consciousness, conviction and confidence of God's desire to save the Gentiles are evident, and further propel the mission of the early church. Acts 1:8 was becoming reality as a result of the involuntary scattering of Christians,

> Taking Acts 8-11 together, one gains the rather clear impression that Luke is presenting a complex picture of the origins of the proclamation of the good news to Gentiles. It was not a mission originated by the leadership of either the Jerusalem or Antioch church but by God through a variety of means... (Witherington1998:369).

Expulsion of Jews from Rome: Priscilla and Aquila, Acts 18:2

In Acts 18:2 we read of Paul in Corinth: "There he met a Jew named Aquila,[154] a native of Pontus,[155] who had recently come from Italy with his wife Priscilla,[156] because Claudius had ordered all Jews to leave Rome." What we have is another example of Christians (Priscilla and Aquila) being scattered from one part of the world to another, resulting in gospel witness in new places.

It is likely that they became Christians while in Rome. We know that visitors from Rome were present at Pentecost (Acts 2:10).[157] Perhaps Priscilla

---

[152] As noted above, the precise dating of Stephen's martyrdom and the ensuing mission to Samaria and eventually Antioch is difficult to determine. Schnabel (Schabel 2004, 51-52, 786) estimates the founding of the church in Antioch between 32 and 35 A.D. But Barnabas does not summon Paul to Antioch until about A.D. 42/43 (ibid., 790; Riesner 1998, 322); thus the founding of the church may be closer to that date.

[153] Acts 11:2 explicitly notes the opposition to Peter by "circumcised believers." After Peter recounts the incident, opponents are convinced, "When they heard this, they had no further objections and praised God, saying, 'So then, even to Gentiles God has granted repentance that leads to life.'" (v.18). The chronological relationship between the conversion of Cornelius and the preaching in Antioch is not clear (see discussion in Witherington 1998, 367).

[154] "Aquila is a Latin name meaning 'eagle.' This and the fact that he had recently lived in Rome suggested to Ramsay that he was a Roman from the Roman province of Pontus" (Witherington 1998, 538).

[155] Pontus was a region on the southern border of the Black Sea, east of Bithynia, at times under Roman rule. It included Jewish settlements.

[156] "Priscilla's name may suggest that she was a freedwoman of a famous Roman matron of the same name" (Witherington 1998, 539).

[157] For other suggestions see Schnabel (2004, 801).

and Aquila heard the gospel from these Jewish pilgrims who had become Christians and returned to Rome. Though originally from Pontus, they had recently come to Corinth from Italy due to an expulsion of Jews by Caesar Claudius who ruled from 41-54 A.D. The date of the expulsion was probably A.D. 49 or 50. A text by Roman historian Suetonius reads, "He banished from Rome all the Jews, who were continually making disturbances at the instigation of one Chrestus" (Claudius 25).[158] It is debated whether the expulsion really included all Jews in Rome, or if only troublemakers were expelled and "all" in Acts 18:2 is hyperbolic.[159] Historian Dio Cassius (60.6.6) writes that the Jews lost the right to assemble under Claudius, which may have been a precursor to the expulsion.[160]

Expulsion of foreigners from Rome was not uncommon. Earlier expulsions of Jews included only leading Jewish propagandists.[161] The religious liberties granted to Jews had limitations and forbade wholesale Jewish propaganda. Thus it may well be that the expulsion of Acts 18:2 was related to controversies over evangelism by Jewish believers in Christ. Indeed, Suetonius' reference to "Chrestus" is probably a mistaken reference to Christ, and the "disturbances" may relate to controversy over teaching in the synagogues that Jesus is the Christ.[162] In this case the Jewish Christians (including Priscilla and Aquila) would have been expelled along with other Jews stirring up conflict.

Whatever the exact nature of Caesar's decree, by necessity Priscilla and Aquila left Rome. The fact that Luke includes this detail points to the expulsion as being the primary if not sole reason for their move to Corinth. Yet it becomes an unforeseen opportunity for witness and ministry. Arriving in Corinth "recently" from Rome (Acts 18:2) in about A.D. 50, they meet the Apostle Paul. Initially they are fellow tentmakers with him and offer him hospitality, perhaps becoming business partners (18:3). But soon they become full mission partners with Paul in the pioneer work in Corinth. They then join the itinerant missionary band accompanying him to Syria and then to Ephesus

---

[158] http://www.fordham.edu/halsall/ancient/suetonius-claudius-worthington.html, accessed on December 12, 2010.

[159] The word "all" (Greek πάντας) is often used hyperbolically in Acts. Tacitus and Josephus do not mention the expulsion, which they surely would have if the expulsion applied to all Jews. Furthermore, between 40,000 and 50,000 Jews may have been living in Rome at the time, also making a total expulsion unlikely (Schnabel 2004, 802). Riesner 1998, 199 also notes that Jews who were Roman citizens would have had to been brought individually before the court.

[160] For more complete discussions of the various documents and interpretations relating to the expulsion of Jews from Rome and its dating, see Lampe 2003,11-16; Levinskaya 1996, 171-182; Riesner 1998, 194-201; Witherington 1998, 539-541.

[161] For example, an expulsion of Jews under Tiberius in A.D. 19 was the result of overzealous proselytizing among native Romans. Dio Cassius (57.18.5) wrote that they were expelled because they "flocked to Rome in great numbers and were converting many of the natives to their ways" (cited in Witherington 1998, 539).

[162] Suetonius wrote many decades after the event. See Witherington 1998, 539-541; Lampe 2003, 12-13; Hoerber 1960.

(Acts 18:18-19). There they become the primary disciples of the great teacher Apollos (Acts 18:24-26) and host a church in their home (1 Cor 16:19).

Later Priscilla and Aquila end up back in Rome, with a church meeting in their home (Rom 16:3-5). Apparently the decree of expulsion had been rescinded or expired when Claudius was no longer emperor in A.D. 54 (Witherington 1998:45; Riesner 1998:200). Paul indicates in his greeting to the Romans, "They risked their lives for me. Not only I but all the churches of the Gentiles are grateful to them" (v. 4). Though Paul is no doubt speaking hyperbolically, the ministry of Priscilla and Aquila had indeed touched many lives beyond Rome, Corinth, and Ephesus.

We can only speculate about what Priscilla and Aquila might have done had they not been forced out of Rome. But because of what happened to them, they became witnesses for Christ and partners of Paul to bring the gospel to unreached places they would not otherwise have gone. God used them in a significant way: as bearers of the gospel, mentors to Apollos, and partners in Paul's missionary team.

Relocated Non-Christians Came into Proximity with the Gospel

We now turn to the other aspect of diaspora—mission through relocation. It involves those who, through relocation, come into proximity with the gospel and in turn become local witnesses as a church is planted among them. Here we examine Cornelius the Roman Centurion and Apollos.

Cornelius, the Roman Centurion, Acts 10:1-11, 18

Although not an example of diaspora in the usual sense, Cornelius presents us with the case of a person who by military service, is relocated far from home when he comes in contact with the gospel. He is described by Luke as "a centurion in what was known as the Italian Regiment" (Acts 10:1). Although little is known specifically about the Italian cohort, it was an auxiliary unit similar to units stationed in Palestine during the time in question.[163] Caesarea was the Roman provincial capital with a considerable Roman presence.

Centurions always had Italian names and "came from the oldest and most deeply Romanized sections of the middle class" (Le Bohec cited in Cotter 2000:

---

[163] We have minimal documentary evidence about this Italian cohort. We know that it was in Syria in A.D. 69, and perhaps earlier. "What we do know is that cohorts such as this one were begun by the enrollment of freedmen in the auxiliary units, and that it *was* auxiliary units which were used in Palestine both before, after, and perhaps even during the reign of Herod Agrippa I (A.D. 41-44)" (Witherington 1998, 346).

281). A soldier in the legionary was normally a freeborn Roman citizen, whereas soldiers of the auxiliary (like the Italian cohort) were not. The name "Cornelius" may well indicate that he was a descendant of one of the ten thousand freed slaves who took on the name of their liberator, the famous Roman general Cornelius Sulla in 82 B.C. (Witherington 1998:346).

Cornelius is also referred to as a "God-fearer." Considerable discussions exist about the exact meaning of the terms "God-fearer" and "God worshipper." They most likely refer to Gentiles who had adopted the monotheistic and ethical standards of the Jews, and perhaps attended the synagogue, but remained uncircumcised and were not full proselytes.[164] Wendy Cotter (2000) explains in detail that as a centurion Cornelius would have been obligated to participate in Roman cultic practices honoring Caesar and to swear oaths. Religion played a major role in Roman military life with the worship and veneration of a variety of deities, genii, spirits (*numina*), and ritual sacrifices and cleansings. Roman historian John Helgeland called Roman military camps a "religious microcosm" (cited in Cotter 2000:286). Given the importance of a centurion being a role model for his soldiers, Cornelius, as a centurion, could hardly have followed the Jewish prohibitions related to pagan worship.

In light of this, there is little wonder that the Jerusalem church opposed to the inclusion of such a person in the Jewish messianic community (Acts 11:2). Indeed, apart from a recurrent dream, Peter would not even have considered entering Cornelius' home. Only the extraordinary story of Peter's and Cornelius's visions and the divine sign of the Holy Spirit falling upon Cornelius would convince the doubters that God accepted believing Gentiles without circumcision or becoming full Jewish proselytes. Darrell Bock points out that Luke uses only Cornelius's first name, which intentionally underlines his Gentile origins. "To the Jewish mind, Cornelius would be a real threat if he were to come to the newly emerging faith. It would make Jews who feared close relations with Gentiles nervous…" (Bock 2007:386-87).

Did Cornelius come into contact with Judaism during his military assignment in Caesarea? We don't know. Probably yes, although there were Jews living throughout the Roman Empire. Roman soldiers informally participated in local religious practices and honored local deities, but Cotter notes that "outside the New Testament there is no ancient evidence of Roman soldiers converting to Judaism or sympathizing with Judaism as 'god-fearers'" (2000:298). Furthermore, Jewish men were not required by Julius Caesar to serve in the Roman army, so there would have been no contact through Jewish soldiers. On the other hand, evidence exists that Roman soldiers stationed in a location for a long period developed relations with the local people. The fact

---

[164] See discussions in Witherington 1998, 341-44 and Schnabel 2004, 129-133.

that centurions received generous pay lends credence to the statement that Cornelius gave generously to those in need (Acts 10:2).

Significantly, Cornelius is perhaps the first Gentile to be welcomed into the church and it happened because he was stationed in Caesarea. Schnabel calls Peter "The first missionary among the Gentiles" (2004:717). Consider for a moment the extreme unlikelihood that a centurion, as described above, would become the follower of a Galilean carpenter-prophet who was condemned and executed as an insurrectionist under Roman authority. Consider also the far-reaching consequences such a decision would bring to a centurion. Yet this is precisely what occurred, emphasizing all the more the supernatural work of the Spirit and the dramatic breakthrough of the gospel, that for the first time an uncircumcised Gentile was welcome into the church.

Apollos, Acts 18:24-28

We read in Acts 18:24, "Meanwhile a Jew named Apollos, a native of Alexandria, came to Ephesus. He was a learned man, with a thorough knowledge of the Scriptures." In Ephesus Apollos joins Paul's itinerate missionary band. We are not told the reason for his migration, but he serves as an example of someone who, as a result of migration, came into contact with the Christian message (like Cornelius) and became part of Paul's missionary team (like Priscilla and Aquila).

Luke identifies Apollos as a well-educated Jew from Alexandria where, according to other sources, there was "the largest and most powerful Jewish settlement in the entire Greek-speaking world" (Pearson 1986:207). Apollos would have been part of the large Hellenistic Jewish community there, and may even have studied under the great Hellenistic Jewish philosopher Philo. Acts 18:25-26 indicates that Apollos had previously been "instructed in the way of the Lord" and "taught about Jesus accurately," although this instruction was incomplete. We can only speculate about where he received this teaching.[165] Jews from Egypt were present at Pentecost (Acts 2:10) and they may have brought the gospel to Alexandria. According to various early traditions, Mark evangelized Alexandria. But we know virtually nothing reliable about the first century Christians in Alexandria.

Ephesus was the largest city in Asia Minor and one of the largest in the Roman Empire with 200,000 to 250,000 residents. According to Josephus a large Jewish community existed in Ephesus, through which Apollos (himself a diaspora Jew) came into contact with Paul's missionary team.

---

[165] "If the 'Western' reading at Acts 18:25 is historically correct, we have a clear reference to the existence of a Christian community in Alexandria at that time, for according to that variant, Apollos 'had been instructed in the word in his home country'" (Pearson 1986, 210). A text from the seventh century *Chronicon Paschale* (PG 92, 521c) counts Apollos among the seventy disciples of Jesus, though this seems unlikely (Schnabel 2004, 860).

What is important for our purposes here is that Apollos comes to full knowledge of the gospel in Ephesus. He soon becomes one of the most gifted teachers of the early Christian mission and travels to Corinth where, "When he arrived, he was a great help to those who by grace had believed. For he vigorously refuted his Jewish opponents in public debate, proving from the Scriptures that Jesus was the Messiah" (Acts18:27b-28).

Diaspora Communities Providing an Entry Point for the Gospel

It is well documented that by the first century Jews had scattered throughout the Roman Empire and established significant communities in the diaspora. Indeed the numbers of Jews living outside Palestine were far greater than those remaining in Palestine.[166] We do not know how many of these were Gentile proselytes. But did the Jewish diaspora and the existence of synagogues throughout the Roman Empire facilitate the spread of the gospel? Rodney Stark (1997) contends so in his sociological analysis of the growth of early Christianity.

Paul always began his preaching in a synagogue when he arrived in a city. Normally he was rejected by the Jewish establishment, which often instigated opposition. This is not entirely surprising, as diaspora communities are often more rigid in their beliefs and practices in an effort to preserve their religious and cultural identity. And this was the case for the first century Jewish diaspora (Levinskaya 1996, 12). Nevertheless, some Jews usually accepted Paul's message (Acts 13:43, 14:1,16:13-15,17:4,18:20), and in Berea many did (Acts 17:11-12).

We have already seen that Gentile God-fearers came into contact with Judaism's monotheism and to some extent worshipped YHWH and observed Jewish morals. These individuals were at times present in the synagogue when Paul preached (Acts 13:16, 17:17) and many of them embraced the gospel (Acts 13:43, 16:14, 17:4). Their contact with Judaism was no doubt an important preparation for their reception of the message.

Taken together, both Jews and God-fearers associated with the synagogue and diaspora Judaism comprised the initial core of the many churches planted by Paul in the predominantly Gentile world. Only after rejection in the synagogue did he turn to the Gentiles, among whom he often found an even more responsive audience (Acts 13:46-49, 18:5-8). Jews and God-fearing believers were likely among the leaders in the new congregations given their

---

[166] Schnabel 2004, 122 estimates in the first century a total of around 8 million Jews, of which only 700,000 to 2.5 million lived in Palestine.

familiarity with the Hebrew scriptures and biblicalethics. Timothy and Apollos are two such examples.

We have more reliable information about the Jewish diaspora community in Rome than elsewhere, and this example is instructive. The earliest reference to a Jewish community in Rome comes from Valerius Maximus, who describes the expulsion of Jews from Rome in 139 B.C. "During the time of Cicero, Jews made up a significant proportion of the Roman population" (Wiefel 1977:87). According to Philo (Embassy to Gaius 155,157) most Jews had been brought to Rome as prisoners of war. Inscriptions seem to indicate the presence of few proselytes in the Roman Jewish community.

Estimates of the Jewish population in Rome during the first century range from 10,000 to 60,000 (see Brändle and Stegemann 1998:120 n.11; Levinskaya 1996:182 n.67). Jewish catacomb inscriptions reveal the existence of at least eleven synagogues in Rome (Levinskaya 1996:182-185). These inscriptions were usually in Greek, indicating the likelihood that it was the language used in the synagogues, the language of Paul's Epistle to the Romans (Wiefel 1977:89-90).

We know that the Christian faith preceded Paul in Rome (Rom 1:11-13) and as evidenced in the faith of Priscilla and Aquila. Writing in the late 50s A.D., Paul states in Romans 15:23 that "for many years" he had hoped to visit the Christians in Rome. All evidence indicates that it was in the Jewish diaspora community that Christianity first gained a foothold in the capital of the Roman Empire. "Since the mission of early Christianity was usually started in synagogues, the existence of a larger Jewish community in Rome offered the necessary precondition for the creation of a new Christian congregation" (Wiefel 1977:89). Wiefel (1977:92) believes that because the synagogues in Rome were autonomously structured with no central Jewish governance, this made the penetration of Christianity among the Jews of Rome easier than in more tightly structured Jewish communities.

Suetonius' aforementioned reference to Jews being expelled from Rome due to disturbances related to "Chrestus" seems to indicate that those involved in the controversy related to Christ were Jews only. Furthermore, Suetonius does not mention *Christianoi* as a distinct community in Rome until later under the Nero regime. This strengthens the view that the Christian community in Rome had its beginnings in the Jewish community. Based upon this and other evidence, Brändle and Stegemann argue that

> "Non-Jews in Rome only came into contact, initially, with 'Christ-faith' if they had already come into contact with Jews, and therefore lived as proselytes or God-fearers in more or less close communication with the Jewish community" (1998:118).

Priscilla and Aquila, as described above, are specific examples of Jews who likely received the message of Christ in Rome. Various Jews in the Roman church are specifically named in Paul's greetings in Romans 16:7,11. By the time of the writing of Romans around A.D. 57, the church in Rome had many, if not a majority of, Gentile believers. Peter Lampe (2003: 69-72) thinks that many of these Gentiles would have previously been God-fearers associated with the synagogues. Paul specifically addresses Gentile Christians in the church there (Rom 1:6; 11:13), and he notes the believers' knowledge of the law (Rom 7:1). Thus not only Jewish but also Gentile believers apparently had exposure to the Torah, pointing again to Jewish origins of the Christian community in Rome. The discussions in Romans 14 regarding dietary observances and Romans 15 regarding God's acceptance of Gentiles also point to probable conflicts between Jewish and Gentile believers in the Roman church.[167]

In summary, the presence of diaspora Jews throughout the Roman Empire provided at least in part a group of people—both Jews and Gentile God-fearers—who were receptive to the gospel. Thus churches were built around a core of believers instructed in the Old Testament and biblicalethics. The church in Rome most likely had its beginnings exclusively within the Jewish diaspora community. This church would eventually become predominantly Gentile, and the strategic launching point for Paul's ministry further westward to Spain and for Christianity to expand to the rest of the Roman Empire.

The Impact of Diaspora in Preparing the Messenger

The Apostle Paul

Of the practical skills that a missionary needs, the most obvious are the ability to adapt to the lifestyle of another culture and the ability to communicate clearly in another language. Ultimately the gospel must be contextualized into thought forms and expressions that are appropriate to the culture while remaining faithful to scripture. Monocultural individuals face a greater challenge in this regard than do bicultural individuals who are at home with more than one culture and who have some experience traversing cultural gaps. Diaspora is one way by which people become bicultural and through which people are prepared for cross-cultural mission. Paul himself, being from Tarsus (Acts 9:11; 21:39; 22:3), is an extraordinary example of a diaspora Jew[168] who, after being

---

[167] Lampe 2003, 80-81 further points out indications in Paul's letter to the Romans of social stratification and diversity within the Roman church. This includes the call for giving alms for the poor (Rom 12:13, 8) anticipated support (Rom 15:24, 28), some paid taxes (Rom 13:6-7). Reciprocity is also a common theme in Romans.

[168] It is not certain how Jews came to settle in Tarsus. "One conjecture is that a number of Jews moved there in the early period of the Seleucid empire. Antiochus III the Great (223-187) settled large colonies

exposed to both Jewish and Greek cultures, was positioned to serve as a bridge for the gospel from the Jewish world to the Gentile world.

As a Jew who had attended synagogue schools and studied at the feet of the great Rabbi Gamaliel in Jerusalem (Acts 22:3), Paul was well versed in the Old Testament scriptures and Jewish theology and law. He was "a Hebrew of Hebrews" (Phil 3:5) and a member of the Pharisee party, indeed "descended from Pharisees" (Acts 23:6). Paul's main point with these biographical comments is to demonstrate his Jewish pedigree, devotion, and orthodoxy. Although it is uncertain whether Paul spent his early years in Tarsus or Jerusalem,[169] Andrie B. Du Toit points out that regardless of when Paul traveled to Jerusalem to study, "Tarsus was Paul's main sociological and cultural home, although he also received his first religious impressions there. Jerusalem was his religious and theological home, although he also socialized there" (2000:401). Schnabel comments,

> If Paul grew up in Tarsus, his educational experience may have resembled that of Philo, his contemporary in Alexandria. The sons of Jewish diaspora families were educated in the following Jewish and Hellenistic institutions: synagogue, elementary school in the synagogue, gymnasiums, ephebeia, public lectures, public library, and private philosophical schools (2004:924).

While Paul's education under Gamaliel in Jerusalem shaped his Jewish thinking, as a Roman citizen and resident of Tarsus he would also have been familiar with Hellenistic culture and thought. The Jews of Tarsus were known to have been tolerant toward Hellenism (Blaiklock 1975:602). Paul was a Roman citizen by birth (Acts16:37-38, 22:25-29) and would have been acquainted with Roman law and the imperial world. His native language was likely Greek, the language of Tarsus and of commerce and government in the eastern empire. This enabled him to communicate with ease throughout the empire, and to formulate the subtleties of theology with clarity and nuance in the Greek language.

Tarsus, capital of the Roman province of Cilicia, had become the Athens of the eastern Mediterranean and home of a Stoic school of philosophy. The Greek geographer Strabo (63/64 B.C. – ca. A.D. 24) compared the quality of philosophy

---

of Jews in Phrygia and Lydia, and Sir William Ramsey conjectured that a group of Jews had been brought to Tarsus by his son Antiochus IV Epiphanes (175-163), the desecrator of the Temple in Jerusalem" (Johnson 1980, 109).

[169] The argument is made by van Unnik (1962) and others (e.g., Johnson 1980:105; Witherington 1998, 668-669) that Paul's statement in Acts 22:3, "I am a Jew, born at Tarsus in Cilicia, but brought up in this city at the feet of Gamaliel, educated according to the strict manner of the law of our fathers…" points to his being brought to Jerusalem while still a child. Others (e.g., Hengel 1991; Roetzel 2009) claim that the evidence is inconclusive and that Paul's excellent command of the Greek language and familiarity with the LXX speak in more favor of his early years being in Tarsus. More recent discoveries have blunted the edge of the debate (Du Toit 2000, 376).

and rhetoric in Tarsus with that of Athens and Alexandria, and names notable philosophers, poets and intellectuals there (Geogr.13.5.13; 14.5.14-15). Although Paul downplays any attempt to use philosophy or persuasive speech to convince his audience (1 Cor 2:1-5), his exposure to such teaching is reflected in his Areopagus speech (Acts 17:22-31). There he employs classical rhetoric and quotes freely from poet-philosophers Epimenides and Aratus (Witherington 1998:518; Charles 1995).[170] Johnson (1980) comments that Paul's oratory style shows noticeable Greek influence:

> But although Paul's style is individual, recent studies prove beyond doubt that Paul knew and used the methods of the Greek orators of his time. Again and again the structure of his letters conforms to models set forth by Quintilian and other ancient rhetoricians. In dealings with his opponents in Second Corinthians he resorts to the types of arguments and emotional appeals that we find in Socrates and in the whole Socratic tradition (1980:111).

Hock (2003) attributes this to the Greco-Roman education Paul received. At the same time, Paul departed from significant aspects of Greco-Roman rhetoric to faithfully communicate the gospel and draw less attention to himself (cf. Schnabel 2008:341-354). Thus he uses different tools to skillfully communicate the God of the Hebrew Bible.

Paul's experience as a diaspora Jew in Tarsus may well have prepared him for engaging an environment of religious pluralism, competing worldviews, and value systems. This skill is seen in his Areopagus speech and his ability to dialogue with both Jewish and Gentile audiences.

It is this Jew of the diaspora, the bicultural Saul/Paul who becomes the great "apostle to the Gentiles" (Rom 11:13). He is the first example of what Paul Hiebert (2006) called "missionary as mediator" in both intercultural communication of the faith and global theologizing. We may forgive E. M. Blaiklock for a touch of overstatement when he writes, "No other man known to history from that time combined these qualities as did Paul of Tarsus. It is difficult to imagine any other place whose whole atmosphere and history could have so effectively produced them in one person" (1975:602). Similarly, Johnson concludes:

> How could Paul have learned to argue as he does, if not in Tarsus? He may not have attended one of the fashionable schools of grammar and rhetoric, but if he lived in the city for some time he must have heard

---

[170] In 1 Corinthians 15:33 Paul quotes Meander's *Thais* in writing "Bad company corrupts good character," though not too much should be made of this quote, since by the first century it had become a popular epigram (Fee 1987, 733, n. 61). Similar maxims might include "Cretians are always liars…" (Titus 1:12) attributed to Epimenides and "Love of money is the root of all evils" (1 Tim 6:10).

its best orators. The Greeks were inveterate talkers and politicians. Paul's dual cultural upbringing and what can only be called native genius prepared him in a unique fashion to be the cosmopolitan apostle to the Gentiles when he was captured by the risen Christ (1980:112).

Calvin J. Roetzel concurs:

> Thus as a young man his feet were firmly planted in two different worlds: the Hellenistic world with its rich cultural heritage, and the world of the people of Israel with its Scriptures, traditions, and law. So firmly comfortable in both was he that he was an ideal person for translating a Gospel that was fundamentally Jewish for the Hellenistic environment of his converts (2009:475).

Much ink has been spilled over questions of Hellenistic influence upon Paul's theology, which need not be recounted here. What concerns us is the basic fact that as a bicultural diaspora Jew, Paul was positioned to communicate the gospel in ways not available to the ordinary Hebrew believers of Judea.

Similar circumstances might also be explored in the personal backgrounds of Apollos or those individuals from Cyprus and Cyrene who launched the gospel mission to the Gentiles in Antioch (Acts11:20). We simply note here that as Jews of the diaspora they were particularly suited for missionary work in the Gentile world.

Implications of the Diaspora in the Book of Acts

God is at work in similar ways today through the movement of peoples in diaspora around the globe.

1. The Christian diaspora today presents unprecedented opportunities for gospel witness. Throughout the history of the church, as Christians moved about the world, they have become witnesses to the risen Christ, established new churches, and reached unreached peoples with the gospel. Modern globalization has only accelerated the movement of peoples and expanded the opportunities for scattered Christian believers to serve as witnesses for Christ. This often occurs in the most unlikely places, as Christians relocate to places like the Muslim world, inaccessible to traditional missionary efforts. It also occurs often with the most unlikely of Christians—untrained Christian workers become powerful witnesses in unlikely places. For example, an estimated 10 million Filipinos, mostly Christians, have relocated to some 193 countries, many in the Arab world. They have become glowing witnesses for Christ in places otherwise impossible to

reach, and training programs have been launched specifically to prepare them for witness as diaspora Christians in difficult places.[171]

2. Today millions of otherwise unreached refugees, students, and business people move around the globe and come into contact with the gospel. Much in the way that Cornelius and Apollos came into contact with the gospel only after leaving their homeland, globalization today has increased the number of people coming into contact with Christians. Millions from communities unreached with the gospel have relocated to communities where Christians can freely share the gospel with them. Evangelistic ministry among international students is one example. Refugees from the civil war in Sudan who relocated to camps in Uganda and Kenya also came to Christ by the thousands there.[172] After the fall of the Iron Curtain, tens of thousands of Russian Jews immigrated to Germany. Many of these have discovered Christ as Messiah, and numerous messianic congregations have been formed.[173] Examples like these could be multiplied many times over.

The internationalization, multiculturalism and ethnic diversity of most urban centers can enhance missionary preparation for cross-cultural ministry. Today's urban centers have become mosaics of ethnic diversity. In schoolyards, neighborhoods, factories, and offices the average citizen rubs shoulders daily with individuals of another culture. Casual contact can deceptively reinforce stereotypes or lead to conflict. But if, like Paul, Christians make an effort to truly understand and appreciate the values, lifestyles and worldview of the ethnically other, this can be the start of developing intercultural sensitivity, understanding and communication skills. Such multicultural environments also provide opportunities to gain firsthand experience in cross-cultural ministry without leaving home. Such experiences also serve as training and preparation for overseas cross-cultural ministries.

---

[171] See Pantoja, Tira and Wan, 2004; Lopez 2006; available at http://conversation.lausanne.org/en/conversations/detail/10523.

[172] Internal reports from ReachGlobal ministry among Sudanese refugees.

[173] Stefanie Pfister's doctoral dissertation revealed that from 1991 to 2006 nearly 226,651 Jews immigrated to Germany. As of 2007 there were some 20 messianic congregations and an additional nineteen small groups of messianic believers regularly meeting in Germany (Pfister 2008, 101-102, 160).

Summary

In this chapter, the incidents in Acts serves as a biblicaland theological foundation is laid for theorizing and strategizing missiologically diaspora movements of people in the 21st century.

We can conclude from this discussion that God in his sovereign authority over the events of history moved peoples and individuals to serve and to advance the gospel. The first concerted cross-cultural mission to Samaria and Antioch resulted from the persecution and scattering of Christians. Four of the most gifted missionaries of the early church—Paul, Priscilla, Aquila, and Apollos—had all been in some way formed or mobilized for mission as a result of relocation or diaspora. The Jewish diaspora communities throughout the Roman Empire became launching points for the formation of new Christian communities that would include Gentiles of various ethnicities.

God is indeed sovereign today, as he was in the first century, continuing to move and prepare people in ways that will advance the progress of the gospel. The church must be alert to these opportunities and must intentionally maximize them for the glory of God and the advancement of his kingdom.

Part 3
METHODOLOGY

In PART THREE, the inter-disciplinary approach, including biblical and theological foundations, is proposed as a methodology for the study of diaspora missiology in order to gain an understanding in the complex phenomenon of diaspora.

Chapter 7

Managerial Missiology – The Popular Paradigm

Enoch Wan

Introduction

In this chapter, we shall introduce the popular "managerial missiology" and "managerial mission practice" in "managerial missiological paradigm," followed by a critique. For the sake of clarity, definition of two key-terms are listed below again (from Chapter 1):

Managerial Missiology Pardigm (MMP) – the framework of engaging in the academic study of missiology by uncritically adopting the secular management paradigm and proposing the practice of Christian mission accordingly.

Managerial Mission Practice - ways and means of practicing Christian mission in the same manner of secular management in business that might be "biblical" and secularly contextual; but definitely not "scriptural."

Popular paradigm of "Managerial Missiology" & "Managerial Mission Practice"

ETYMOLOGY AND DEFINITION

The term "managerial missiology" was coined by Samuel Escobar, according to James Engel.[174] From the perspective of MMP, Christian mission is

---

[174] "Escobar coined the phrase managerial missiology to refer to an unduly pragmatic orientation…" see link below: http://www.rebuildjournal.org/articles/cmsnorcmpgn.html (Accessed Dec. 20, 2013)

an enterprise, therefore, the gospel is a product to be marketed to the target group (or consumers) with measurable goals through carefully crafted strategy. One of the characteristics is the extensive use of marketing and communication technique for the quantifiable success with efficiency. According to the free online *Missions Dictionary*[175]

> **Managerial Missiology.** The belief that missions can be approached like a business problem.   With the right inputs, the thinking goes, the right outcomes can be assured.   Any number of approaches have been haled as the 'key' to world evangelization or to reaching particular groups—everything from contextualization to saturation evangelization. Most while successful up to a point, also have been shown to have limits."

Another definition of "managerial missiology" is found in the *Dictionary of Mission Theology*"[176] as follows:

> "The term managerial missiology refers to a trend within evangelical missiology that emphasizes the management of mission practice. It developed in North America during the last third of the twentieth century. It came from a cluster of institutions connected to the Church Growth school and movements such as AD 2,000 and Beyond. It is an effort to reduce Christian mission to a magaeable enterprise." (Escobar 2007:216)

The major features of "managerial missiology paradgim"(MMP) are listed in Figure 7.1 below.

---

[175] Missions Dictionary of "The Missiology Homepage" managed by Gailyn Van Rheenen, 1997. http://www.missiology.org/?p=24#M (Accessed Dec. 20, 2013)
176 Samuel Escobar, "Managerial missiology" In Dictionary of Mission Theology. John Corrie (ed.) InerVarsity Press 2007:216-218.

Figure 7.1 Managerial Missiology Paradigm (MMP)

ASPECTS	MANAGERIAL MISSIOLOGY
#1 - FOCUS	• marketing approach: commodification of Christianity & consumerism • entrepreneurship: efficiency-oriented • technology: formulaic & methodical, impersonal and no-relational, e.g. target group, operational plan, etc.
#2 - CONCEPTUALI-ZATION	• instrumentalism (functionalism): receptor-oriented, "felt needs" approach • pragmatism: measurable success, outcome-base
#3 - PERSPEC-TIVE	• territorial: Euro-American centric & spatial • binary pattern: sending & receiving, home & foreign mission, local & global, etc.
ORIENTA-TION	• emulating secular business management model • humantistic and operational mentatlity • managerially statistical and strategic

One outstanding feature of the "**focus**" of MMP is the marketing approach. James Engel was one of the leading figures in managerial missiology for he had successfully convinced evangelicals to accept his communication model and **marketing principles** in Christian missions, from his former training and career. He published and co-authored many books in the areas of communication theory, consumer behavior, promotional strategy, proposed the "Engel's Scale," [177] and led missiology in "a major leap onto the secular stage of strategic planning." (David Nett 1999)

In MMP, technology is a major "focus" in terms of quantifiable goals, formulaic approach and methodological procedures as described in the quotation below:

---

[177] Selected samples are listed below:
- *What's Gone Wrong With the Harvest?: A Communication Strategy for the Church and World Evangelism* by James F. Engel, Wilbert H. Norton (1975)
- *Contemporary Christian communications, its theory and practice* by James F. Engel (1979)

DIASPORA MISSIOLOGY: THEORY, METHODOLOGY, AND PRACTICE

> "Concepts such as 'people-groups', 'unreached peoples', 'homogeneous units', '10-40 window', 'adopt a people' and 'territorial spirits'…express both a strong sense of urgency and an effort to use every available instrument to make the task possible. One way of achieving manageability is precisely to reduce reality to an understandable picture, and then to project missionary action as a response to a 'problem' that has been described in quantitative form." (Escobar 2007:216)

The **"conceptualization"** of MMP is grounded in instrumentalism (Hiebert 1999:36-67)[178] and functionalism (e.g. Malinowski & Radcliff-Brown of British anthropology) with strong emphasis on receptor-oriented and "felt needs" approach in practice (Kraft 1979:81-99, 169-192;). The pragmatic mindset leads to targeting measurable success and quantifiable outcomes. This pragmatic orientation is in line with the research findings of Barna Group in 2010 – one of the "six megathemes" of American Christianity is "growing numbers of people are less interested in spiritual principles and more desirous of learning pragmatic solutions for life" and at the same time "the Christian Church is becoming less theologically literate (i.e. another theme of the six).[179]

In managerial missiology, **strategy** is imperatively important, helping to set measurable goals and priority, aiding in achieving efficiency, etc., according to Peter Wagner (1987:32).[180] Within the strategic framework of managerial paradigm are elements of time, action and planning. Tod M. Johnson, director of the World Evangelization Research Center, writes that the closure idea has been kept "before the Christian public almost continually through the twentieth century in the form of confident slogans, plans and documents" then lists out 20 international gatherings, conferences and consultations during the last century (Hesselgrave 2005:288-289).[181]

In terms of planning, personnel and resources, managerial mission practice places high value in entrepreneurship. Managerial missiology is **functionalistic** (i.e. felt-need and efficiency-oriented approach)[182] (or "instrumentalism" in

---

[178] *The Missiological Implications of Epistemological Shifts: Affirming Truth in a Modern/Postmodern World*, Bloomsbury Publishing USA, 1999

[179] Barna Group, "Six Megathemes Emerge from Barna Group Research in 2010 " @ https://www.barna.org/culture-articles/462-six-megathemes-emerge-from-2010. Accessed Dec. 20, 2013.

[180] C. Peter Wagner, *Strategies for Church Growth: Tools for Effective Mission and Evangelism*, (Ventura: Regal Books, 1987).

[181] David J. Hesselgrave, *Paradigms in Conflict: 10 Key Questions in Christian Missions Today*. Kregel 2005

[182] This is a separate but important aspect of managerial missiology. Enoch Wan's critique of functionalist missiology and receptor-oriented approach in Christian mission practice, please consult two earlier studies:
- Enoch Wan, "Critique of Functional Missionary Anthropology," *His Dominion*, vol. 8, no.3, (April 1982)
  http://www.enochwan.com/english/articles/pdf/Critique%20of%20%20Functional%20Anthropology.pdf   Accessed Dec 20, 2013.

Paul Hiebert's terminology, 1999),[183] receptor-oriented with impactful communication and effective outcomes (Kraft 2005).[184]

Formulating strategy is to be specific, in terms of measurable goals, quantifiable outcomes, well thought through plan, procedures, steps of "how to," etc. in managerial missiology. For example, Edward R. Dayton and David A. Fraser in *Planning Strategies for World Evangelism*, Revised Ed. (Eugene: Wipf and Stock, 1990) propose a 10-step model and have two chapters on "managing the mission."

The mentality of **formulaic** approach leading to desirable outcomes also applies to church planting movement[185] in managerial mission practice for example:

> "One of the "deadly sins" to a Church planting movement: "Inch by, inch step by step…this may be the way to make progress in normal human endeavors, but it is deadly to a church planting movement."
> 2004:243-244)[186]

An example of managerial mission practice is "Short Cycle Planting" which is self-explanatory in the quotation below:

> "the strategic, God-enabled process which seeks to continuously shorten the time needed to develop a mature church…with the aim:
> to develop mature, reproducing churches led by nationals in as short of time as possible. With this approach, the elements of the church-planting process, from language learning to evangelism to leadership development, are undertaken simultaneously and accomplished as efficiently as possible."[187]

In order to reduce time for the sake of **efficiency** in church planting, here is a novelty idea:

> "The shortest distance between two points is not a straight line. It's a wrinkle." Strategy Coordinators engaged in Church Planting Movements have learned to wrinkle time—combining multiple steps into a single model. (Garrison 243-244)

- Enoch Wan, "A critique of Charles Kraft's use/misuse of communication and social sciences in biblical interpretation and missiological formulation," http://ojs.globalmissiology.org/index.php/english/article/viewFile/120/346 Accessed Dec. 20, 2013.

[183] In a milder way of critiquing the receptor-oriented approach, Paul Hiebert used the term "instrumentalism." See Paul Hiebert, *The Missiological Implications of Epistemological Shifts: Affirming Truth in a Modern/Postmodern World*, PA: Trinity Press, 1999.

184 Charles H. Kraft, *Christianity in culture: a study in dynamic biblical theologizing in cross cultural perspective*, Orbis Books, 2005.

[185] Gerald Harris, "Shining the Spotlight on the IMB's Church Planting Movement," *The Christian Index* May 24, 2007 http://www.christianindex.org/3270.article (Accessed Dec. 20, 2013)

[186] David Garrison, *Church Planting Movements: How God is Redeeming a Lost World*, (Arkadelphia: WIGTake Resources, 2004:243-244)

[187] https://avantministries.org/about/short-cycle/ and http://avantministries.org/wp-content/uploads/2013/08/Short-Cycle-Church-Planting-Flyer-2013.pdf Accessed Dec. 20, 2013.

It is important to note that a defender for managerial missiology in the article entitled "What's Wrong with the label 'Managerial Missiology'?" complaints that:

> "It appears to me that the word 'managerial' is being used in a pejorative way. This is most unfortunate since a whole group of Christians who try and develop their God-given managerial gifts for the advancement of God's Kingdom find their vocation placed under such negative light. Management is one of many gifts of the Spirit. Time and again Scripture instructs the believers about the use of their managerial skills....Labeling the kind of reflection that has come out of Pasadena as 'managerial missiology' is reductionist in terms of an intentionally negative categorization of missiological studies. The so-called 'Pasadena group' or 'Pasadena think-tank' represents a wide variety of field experiences. The theories or models that have been proposed by both Fuller Seminary's School of World Mission and the U.S. Center have been tested by that most demanding group of Christian witnesses, namely, the multiethnic group of students and practitioners who have taken these ideas to bear upon their field contexts, and have critiqued and criticized them in papers and dissertations for more than two decades now..." (DeCarvalho 2003:15)[188]

Critique of Popular "Managerial Missiology" & "Managerial Mission Practice"

MMP is an accumulative effect of a long process of wrong contextualization: selling out to the world, sacrificing everything at the altar of measurable outcomes, entrepreneurship and quantifiable success.

A feature of the **"focus"** of MMP is the negligence of the new realiality of the following two major phenomena of the 21st century: the rapid and explosive growth of the phenomena of diaspora and the shifting of center of Christianity from northern hemisphere to southern hemisphere in the post-colonial era. A brief historical review below is informative of "why" a paradigm shift is imperative:

> "Imperial missiology carried on missionary work from a positon of superiority: political, military, financial, technological. While 'the cross and the sword' symbolized it at the height of Iberian mission in the sixteenth century, 'commerce and Christianity' symbolized it at the height of

---

[188] Levi T. DeCarvalho, "What's Wrong with the label 'Managerial Missiology'" *Mission Frontiers*. July-August 2002,
http://www.missionfrontiers.org/issue/article/whats-wrong-with-the-label-managerial-missiology (Accessed Dec. 20, 2013)

Protestant European mission in the nineteenth century. And in our lifetime 'information technology and gospel' has come to symbolize it. In the imperial missiology paragidm, Christianity is thus dependent on the prop and trutelage of another powerful partner…The paradigm shift that this understanding requires is still underway, esepecially among the evangelical missionary establishment." (Escobar 2003:26)

The call for missiological reflection and re-examination by missiologists from the majority world was issued at the historic Iguassu Missiological Consultation[189] which was held in the city of Foz do Iguassu, Brazil, October 10-15, 1999 the leadership of William D. Taylor, Executive Director, WEF Missions Commission. It was attended by 160 participants from 53 countries to examine the way Christian mission is changing at the turn of the millennium.

"The Consultation, however, affirmed newer models of mission, which emphasize the development of mission movements in every country where there is a mature Christian church. The Iguassu Affirmation, a 2275 word declaration, signed Friday by the participants present for the final communion service, reversed the traditional Western to Two Thirds-World flow and advocated the vision of "doing missiology and mission by people of all nations to people of all nations. Participants in the Consultation also endorsed a fuller understanding of the nature of and obedience to the Great Commission; they questioned over-dependence on **managerial methods in mission**…"[190]

It is worth noting that the concept of "five selfs of the church of Christ" was the underlying conviction both for the Iguassu Consultation as well as this compendium volume, i.e. self-supporting, self-governing, self-propagting, self-theologing and self-missiologizing. (Taylor 2011:550)

A key voice at the consultation was Peruvian missiologist Samuel Escobar, according to the report in *Christianity Today*:

"…criticized the 'managerial missiology' practiced by certain North American groups. 'The distinctive note' of this approach to missions 'is to *reduce Christian mission to a manageable enterprise*,' Escobar wrote. Practitioners of this approach focus on the quantifiable, measurable tasks of missions and ask pragmatic questions about how to achieve goals. Escobar called this statistical approach 'anti-theological' and said it "has no theological or pastoral resources to cope with the suffering and persecution involved because it is geared to provide guaranteed success." (David Nett 1999)[191]

---

[189] The papers presented at the Iguassu Missiological Consultation and Iguassu Affirmation were edited by William D. Taylor, *Global Missiology for the 21st Century: The Iguassu Dialogue.* Baker Academic 2011.

[190] "Missiologists Affirm New Models," Press release October 17, 1999 issued by William D. Taylor of WEF.

[191] David Nett in Foz do Iguassu, Brazil reported in *Christianity Today* [posted 12/6/1999 12:00AM] http://www.christianitytoday.com/ct/1999/december6/9te028.html Accessed Dec. 20, 2013.

At the Iguassu Missiological Consultation, W. Taylor of WEF quoted James Engel on "plans to complete the task of evangelism by A.D. 2000" to be "the dark side" in the following manner:

"Quantifiable results soon became a virtual obsession... Organizational public relations machinery geared up to fever-pitch reporting the numbers allegedly reached through crusades, the media, and intensified personal evangelism initiatives...(no) definite evidence that the kingdom of God is being exemplified." (David Nett 1999)

Joseph D'Souza, chair of the All India Christian Council, at the Iguassu Missiological Consultation, also indicted the popular missiological trends of managerial missiology in these words:

"have tended to turn communication [of the gospel] into a technique where we market a product called 'salvation.' The consumer is the sinner and the marketer is the missionary. In the bargain, what is missed is redemptive living in society." (David Nett 1999)

Adopting **marketing** principle and **techniques** in communication and management, managerial mission practice places high premium on "**efficiency**" at the cost of "relationship":

"A formulaic approach to missions that places a high premium on rapidly abandoning tried and tested practices in favor of cutting-edge discoveries in the social sciences or the business world has not benefited missions in the majority world. Instead, the pursuit of efficiency in missions has left behind a trail of broken relationships." (Sills 2010:107)[192]

Practitioners of MMP tend to view Christianity as a commodity to be whole sale to as many "consumer of religion" as possible with efficiency. The element of consumerism in American culture and Christian practice is the major focus of Matthew Chittum's dissertation in the Doctor of Missiology Program at Western Seminary, entitled "Unmasking Consumerism for the Practice of Relational Discipleship within Contemporary American Culture" (April, 2014).

The missionary nature of Christianity will then become secularized, being changed to be **mercenary** and non-relational; instead of missionary and relational. For this reason, Escobar criticizes managerial missiology being **dehumanizing** (Escobar 2003:57) in the following manner:

Its basic tenet is that Christian mission can be reduced to a "manageable enterprise" thanks to the use of information, technology, marketing techniques and managerial leadership. Their effort to visualize the missionary task with "scientific" precision has led to the formulation of concepts such as "unreached peoples," "homogenous units," the "10-40 window" or "adopt-a-people." What I am seeing in the application of these concepts in the mission field is that missionaries "depersonalize"

---

[192] M. David Sills, *Reaching and Teaching: A Call to Great Commission Obedience*, (Chicago: Moody, 2010)

people into "unreached targets," making them objects of hit-and-run efforts to get decisions that may be reported. The difficult tasks of discipleship and building the body of Christ are bypassed in the name of managerial goals that seem designed to give their missionary center in the United States an aura of success. (Escobar 2003:167)

The **"conceptualization"** of MMP is instrumentalism which is non-relational and pragmatic. There is the tendency of empting ministry and Christian mission of relational reality by treating religion/spirituality as program to be delivered and the gospel as commodity to be marketed for consumption based on **"felt need."** Let us heed the warning of James F. Engel who was a main champion for MMP but has made drastic shift to become a critique who observes:

> "One of the final lures of managerial missiology lies in the area of appeal to felt need...it is possible to build a large church quicly and easily by promising that Jesus is the answer to all our hopes and felt need...Crowds thronged around Jeus during his early ministry because of this cvery expectation. However, as he focused on the narrow way, on the true meaning of kingdom living, the crowds dwindles. Christ did take felt need seriously, but this was only the starting point. He quickly moved to the underlying real need and issued a stringent call for commitment and radically altered lifestyle. Numerical growth can slump drastically when we follow his model." (Engel 2014)[193]

Escobar traces the "strong influence of American functional social sciences" in managerial missiology (Escobar 1993:217) which places high value in quantifiable data and strive towards problem-solving:

> "Missionary action is thus reduced to a linear task that is unfolded into logical steps to be followed in a process of management by objectives. Movements that express this trend proliferated as the end of the twentieth century approached, proposing strategies that used the year 2000 as a date to comple evangelization." (Escobar 2007:216)

The obsession for rapid and **quantifiable growth** and spectacular outcomes may mislead practitioners who may end the church planting process disastrously with devastating damage to their sense of calling and career (Escobar 2003:57). Along the same line of thinking, a missionary has made the following observation regarding CPM:

> "Missionaries not experiencing the rapid reproduction of churches get discouraged. This methodology sets up 99 percent of missionaries for

---

[193] James F. Engel, "Will the Great Commission Become the Great Ad Campaign?" *Christianity Today*, 2007:216, http://www.rebuildjournal.org/articles/cmsnorcmpgn.html Retrieved Feb. 20, 2014.

certain failure, because if no CPM occurs, most missionaries feel as though they have failed."[194]

It, according to Cody Lorance in Chapter 18, MMP may also lead to "Babel complex" and "left behind a trail of broken relationships" (Sills 2010:107).

Proponents of MMP embrace a strong Euro-American centric **"perspective"** that has been shaped by the "Christendom" mentality with centuries-long history of western domination internationally. Reinforced by their linear, territorial and spatial cognitive pattern, naturally lead to their insistence on the binary pattern of sending and giving, home and foreign missions, local and global ministry.

The **"orientation"** of MMP is managerially statistical and strategic

There is limitation to the use of statistical method in Christian missions, as Escobar insists:

> In missionary work there are some aspects that cannot be reduced to startistics, but (managerial) missiological approach gave predominance to that which can be reduced to a statistical chart. Some acts of verbal communication of the gospel, such as distribution of the printed page, hours of broadcasting through radio or TV, massive gatherings for evangelism, or groups of new believers organizaed into churches, are all activities that can be counted and registered. It is more differeult to measure the time, energy and sacrifice involved in leadership treaing, personal discipleship or theological creativity, all of the necessary for new churches. (Escobar 207:216)

Statistical data are informative for strategizing but misued managerially will lead to dire consequence as warned by Janel K. Bakker:

> "They are concerned more with statistics, techniques, inventiveness, enterpreneurisalims, leadership strategy, pragmatism, and numerical growth than with theological or anotherpological reflection…the managerial model has fostered numerous mission efforts among evengelicals (who now overwhelmingly dominate international mission endeavors among North Americans) that are 'organized, focused, well-managed, and even scientific' in their approach to ministry."(Bakker 2014:34)[195]

---

[194] Gerald Harris, "Shining the Spotlight on the IMB's Church Planting Movement," *The Christian Index* May 24, 2007 http://www.christianindex.org/3270.article (Accessed Dec. 20, 2013)

[195] Bakker, Janel Dragt. 2014. *Sister Churches: American Congregations and Their Partners Abroad*. Oxford Press.

Summary

In this chapter, we have introduced the popular managerial paradigm in terms of "managerial missiology" and "managerial mission practice" in anticipation of the next chapter when "diaspora missiology paragim" is offered as an alternative.

It is fitting to conlude this chapter with two quotations from two different perspectives for the readers of this volume to consider. The first one represents a positive posture towards MMP:

"Labeling the kind of reflection that has come out of Pasadena as 'managerial missiology' is reductionist in terms of an intentionally negative categorization of missiological studies. The so-called 'Pasadena group' or 'Pasadena think-tank' represents a wide variety of field experiences. The theories or models that have been proposed by both Fuller Seminary's School of World Mission and the U.S. Center have been tested by that most demanding group of Christian witnesses, namely, the multiethnic group of students and practitioners who have taken these ideas to bear upon their field contexts, and have critiqued and criticized them in papers and dissertations for more than two decades now .... All in all, we must be grateful for the criticism leveled against 'managerial missiology.' We have been forced to rethink our assumptions, values, and commitments – in short, our worldviews ..." (DeCarvalho 2002:17)

The second quotation below is critical of MMP:

"Within managerial missiology, statistical anaylysis was used first as a way of measuring the effect of missionary action, in an effort to reduce the lack of clarity that surrounded it and a cerntain fuzziness in the traditional way of defining and evaluating it. The call for measuring was a key component of the necessary process of evaluation required by the missionary enterprise at the middle of the twentieth century. A clafication of goalds and plans was called for in view of bilibal imperatives. The negative aspect of this approach was that such evaluative methodogy was at the service of a concept of mission narrowly defined as the numerical growth of the church. Donal McGavran was the champion of this position, presenting it in contrast to more inclusive definitions of mission that were dominant especially in the conciliar ecumenical movement." (Escobar 2007:216)

Chapter 8

Diaspora Missiology– A Contemporary Paradigm for the 21st Century[196]

Enoch Wan

Etymologically, the term "diaspora" was originally used in the context of the Jewish dispersion, and the Greeks used the term "diaspora" to mean migration and colonization. In the 1960s its usage was extended to refer to the Africans who were taken away from their home continent. Only in the late twentieth century has the term been generalized to include other ethnic groups who have moved away from their homelands. In the 1990s the study of diaspora became a discipline in the academic field.

The original word "diaspora" had a sense of forcible dispersal of a people and their subsequent unhappiness in their countries of exile; more recently the widely used term refers to "the phenomenon of 'dispersion of any ethnic group'."[197] Today, the term often implies a positive and ongoing relationship between migrants' homelands and where they now work and live.

Characteristics of Diaspora Missiology Paradigm

Diaspora missiology emerged as a contemporary paradigm for the 21st century adjusting to the demographic reality of diaspora phenomena found globally; whereas managerial approach in missiology has been slow in strategizing

---

[146] This chapter is adapted from two previous works:
- Enoch Wan, "Diaspora Missiology," EMS *Occasional Bulletin* Spring 2007a.
- EnochWan and Sidira Joy Tira, "Diaspora Missiology and Mission in the Context of the 21st Century," *Torch Trinity Journal* Volume 13, No.1 (May 30, 2010).

[197] Luis Pantoja, Sadiri Joy Tira and Enoch Wan, eds. Scattered: The Filipino Global Presence (Manila, Philippines: LifeChange Publishing Inc, 2004), xxviii.

accordingly. Listed below are the characteristics of diaspora missiology in four dimensions.

Figure 8.1 Four Dimensions of Diaspora Missiology[198]

#	DIMENSION	CHARACTERISTICS
1	Focus	• diaspra phenomena of the 21st century • shifting landscape of "Christendom"
2	Conceptualization	• beyond "melting-pot"(American) & "cultural mosaic"(Canadian)
3	approach & orientation	• "The Gospel from Everywhere to Everyone"[199]
4	Strategy	• viewing & following God's way of providentially moving people spatially & spiritually, strategic Kingdom partnership

The **"focus"** of diaspora missiology is on adaptability and flexibility. The "conceptualization" of diaspora missiology is mutuality and reciprocity because of the change of landscape of Christianity as described by Philip Jenkins:

> "…far from being an export of the capitalist West, a vestige o Euro-American imperialism, Christianity is now rooted in the Third World, and the religion's future lies in the global South." (Jenkins 2007: Preface)

The Euro-centric focus of Western approach in missiology has been slow in shifting their focus to the global south. The new Pope being from Argentina, instead of Western Europe, is one of the signals that a new reality of Christianity in the 21st century requires adjustment of the Euro-centric focus in missiology. Case studies from Asia, Africa, and Latin America and the contributions of 14 world mission scholars from the majority world in *Missions from the Majority World*[200] points to the necessity of shifting focus on mutuality and reciprocity with the global South where diaspora groups in the west originated and the vibrant churches are

---

[198] Modified from Figure 5 in Wan, "Diaspora Missiology," *Occasional Bulletin*, EMS, Spring 2007a; also in *Global Missiology*, (July, 2007a); available at www.GlobalMissiology.org.

[199] C.F. Samuel Escobar, *The New Global Mission: The Gospel from Everywhere to Everyone*, Christian Doctrine in Global Perspective, (Downers Grove: InterVarsity Press, 2003)

[200] Missions from the *Majority World: Progress, Challenges and Case Studies,* edited by Enoch Wan & Michael Pocock (EMS17 - 2009).

awaiting for mutuality and reciprocity in carrying the Great Commission. In the diaspora paradigm, the motto is "The Gospel from Everywhere to Everyone."[201]

Hybridity is another "conceptualization" of diaspora missiology, at variant to managerial approach in missiology which has been dominated by concepts of melting-pot (American) and cultural mosaic (Canadian). The trend in Western countries is moving towards cultural diversity as indicated by the insistence on "ethnic ministry" to categorically cover all sorts of diaspora ministry and diaspora missions. In the 21st century, the concept of ethnicity (e.g. being black or white) is not helpful when encountering cases such as golf-celebrity Eldrick Tont "Tiger" Woods and supermodel Tyra Lynne Banks.[202]

In anthropological literature, "liminality" (from the Latin *limen* – a threshold) to denote "in between" with a sense of "ambiguity," first by Arnold van Gennep[203] then Victor Turner.[204] Though the concept and term began with research on tribal practice of rites of passage, later it has been extended to modern and postmodern contexts in reference to both temporal and spatial dimensions and social identity that are "in-between" (ambiguous and transitional).[205]

In this study, the term "liminality" is used in reference to both the experience and identity of diaspora being complicated by: (a) advance technologies in communication and transportation, and (b) the extensive experiences in migration/immigration. The old paradigms[206], e.g. American melting-pot (assimilationist) or Canadian cultural-mosaic (multiculturalism), are no longer helpful to the 21st century new reality of diaspora who can

---

[201] C.F. Samuel Escobar, *The New Global Mission: The Gospel from Everywhere to Everyone*, Christian Doctrine in Global Perspective, (Downers Grove: InterVarsity Press, 2003)

[202] In is worth noting that the entry 'Tyra Banks ethnicity' is "Googled approximately 500 times per month by curious fans across the globe that turn to their Internet browsers for answers." (http://www.arogundade.com/is-tyra-banks-black-are-her-parents-of-mixed-race-her-ethnicity-nationality-heritage-facts-about-tyra-banks.html, access December 20, 2013)

[203] Arnold van Gennep, The Rites of Passage. Chicago: University of Chicago, 1960 (*Rites de Passage*, 1908) – a study on ritual practice marking the change of individual identity through the cycle of life. See Rosemary Zumwalt, "Arnold van Gennep: The Hermit of Bourg-la-Reine" [originally published in *American Anthropologist*, 84:299-313, 1982] Accessed Dec. 20, 2013.
http://www.aaanet.org/committees/commissions/centennial/history/090vangennep.pdf

[204] The chapter entitled, "Betwixt and Between" In *The Liminal Period in Rites de Passage*" by Victor Turner http://www2.fiu.edu/~ereserve/010010095-1.pdf Accessed Dec. 20, 2013.

[205] Szakolczai, A. (2009) "Liminality and Experience: Structuring transitory situations and transformative events", in *International Political Anthropology* 2 (1): 141-172. www.politicalanthropology.org
Szakolczai, A. (2000) Reflexive Historical Sociology, London: Routledge.
Thomassen, B. (2006) "Liminality", in A. Harrington, B. Marshall and H.-P. Müller (eds) Routledge *Encyclopedia of Social Theory*, London: Routledge, 322-323.
Thomassen, B. (2009) "The Uses and Meanings of Liminality", in *International Political Anthropology* 2 (1): 5-27.www.politicalanthropology.org

[206] Enoch Wan, ""The Dynamics of Ethnicity: A Case Study on the Immigrant Community of N.Y. Chinatown." Unpublished doctoral dissertation. State University of New York, Stony Brook. 1978

simultaneously live in multiple realities and maintain social contacts of people in the homeland, in host country, and place of resident with ease.

In addition, for some professional and sough-after-immigrants by some government, there is less pressures than before for diaspora to: (a) give up one identity in order to acquire a new identity due to restrictive government policy,[207] (b) stay in a new location then lost touch with folks in the homeland socially, (c) give up old way of life culturally, (d) severe old ties with homefolks that bonded psychologically, etc. An individual from diaspora groups can live in multi-reality, maintain multiple identities, extend social networks transnationally…that leads to a state of "luminality"[208] without any hardship psychologically, technically, politically, socially and culturally.

The "approach and orientation" of diaspora missiology is non-spatial and borderless, transnational with extensive networking. Being "non-spatial" is "de-territorialized," i.e., the "loss of social and cultural boundaries" in mission strategy. A practical example of this is the evangelism training in Tokyo among Japanese believers who plan to evangelize Brazilians residing in Tokyo. Brazilians who no longer reside in Sao Paolo have become reachable through Japanese Christians for they are living in Tokyo! Diaspora mission is also "GLOCAL"[209] instead of "sending" and "receiving in managerial approach in missions because diaspora missions is multi-directional.   Unlike the "dichotomisti orientation" of managerial approach, the paradigm of diaspora missiology is not geographically divided to home/foreign, regional/global, urban/rural because diaspora mission is multi-directional, borderless, global in scope and through transnational networking.

The "practice" of diaspora missiology is flexible and adaptive, carried out not only in property on land; but on tour bus in limited access context and on the ocean aboard ships among seafarers.[210]   The "strategy" of diaspora missiology is viewing and following God's way of providentially moving people spatially and spiritually

---

[207] For example, the author of this book is an ethnic Chinese but has four official documents: two passports and two residential identity cards - each from a different government/country.
[208] Ybarrola, Steven. Diasporas & Multiculturalism: Social Ideologies, Liminality, and Cultural Identity." IN The Human Tidal Wave, by Sadiri Joy Tira. Manila: Lifechange Publishing, Inc., 2013.
[209] "GLOCAL" missions is ministry outreach being carried out simultaneously locally and globally, i.e., what we do out there, we do it here simultaneously. See Bob Roberts Jr., Transformation: How Glocal Churches Transform Lives and the World (Zondervan, 2006). Also "Glocal Church Ministry: Bob Roberts has an idea that may change American congregations, if not the world," interview by Mark Galli (posted 8/02/2007); available at   http://www.christianitytoday.com/ct/2007/july/30.42.html
[210] For references to these illustrationsa, see the following publications:
- Otto, Marvin. *Church on the Oceans: A Missionary Vision for the 21st Century*. Carlisle, California: Piquant Editions, 2007.
  - Enoch Wan, "Global People and Diaspora Missiology."In Toyko 2010 Global Mission Handbook. Edited by Yong J. Cho and David Taylor. Published by the Tokyo 2010 Global Mission Consulataion Planning Committee, 2010a. Available at http://www.tokyo2010.org/resources/Handbook.pdf

as explained biblically and theologically in Chapters 4 and 5, practically in Chapters 10-14 and the five case studies.

In managerial missioloogy, scholars tend to emphasize the ccontrast between Jehovah's calling people to Himself as missions in the Old Testament and Jesus Christ's sending of the disciples into the people as missions in the New Testament. Contemporary missiologists distinguish between "evangelism" and "missions" according to the spatial, linguistic, and cultural barriers between the sharer and the recipients of the Gospel, and categorize them linearly into E-1, E-2 and M-1, M-2. In contrast, diaspora missiology is a responsive way to reach diaspora individuals and communities wherever they are found thus more mobile, adapative and flexible including the practice of "glocal" missions.

In addition, the strategies of diaspora missiology includes missions *to, through, by/beyond* and *with* the diaspora – all to be practiced within a relational framework (see details in chapters 11-14 and the five case studies).

Figure 8.2 – "Managerial" & "Diaspora" Paradigms Compared

ASPECTS	MANAGERIAL MISSIOLOGY	DISPORA MISSIOLOGY/MISSION
#1 - FOCUS	<ul><li>negligent of new reality</li><li>marketing approach: commodification of Christianity & consumerism thus "mercenary" instead of "missionary"</li><li>entrepreneurship: efficiency-oriented, outcome based</li><li>technology: formulaic & methodical, dehumanizing</li></ul>	<ul><li>contextual to new reality in the 21st Century: (a) diaspora phenomena, (b) shifting landscape of "Christendom</li><li>holistic Christianity with strong integration of the Great Commandment & the Great Commission, evangelism with Christian charity</li><li>relational: vertical and horizontal relationship, high touch, people-oriented, networking</li></ul>
#2 - CONCEPTUALIZATION	<ul><li>instrumentalism (functionalism): felt needs approach, receptor-oriented</li><li>pragmatism: measurable success & outcome-base</li></ul>	<ul><li>beyond "melting-pot"(American) & "cultural mosaic"(Canadian)</li><li>"deterritorialization,"[211] "glocal,"[212] "mutuality" & "reciprocity," "hybridity," "liminality"[213]</li></ul>
#3 - PERSPECTIVE	<ul><li>territorial: Euro-American centric & spatial</li><li>binary pattern: sending & receiving, home & foreign mission, local & global, etc.</li><li>"Babel Complex"</li></ul>	<ul><li>non-spatial: "borderless," transnational & global</li><li>integrated & interdisciplinary</li><li>"The Gospel from Everywhere to everyone"[214]</li></ul>
#4 - ORIENTATION	<ul><li>emulating the secular business management model.</li><li>humanistic and man-centered mentality</li><li>Managerially statistical and strategic</li></ul>	<ul><li>viewing & following God's way of providentially moving people spatially & spiritually</li><li>"moving mission fields" & mobile/flexible, strategic Kingdom patnersship</li></ul>

---

[211] "deterritorialization" is the "loss of social and cultural boundaries"
[212] See Sadiri Joy B. Tira, "Filipino International Network: A Strategic Model for Filipino Diaspora Glocal® Missions," *Global Missiology*, (October 2004); available at www.GlobalMissiology.org.
[213] See discussion below on "Liminality" – from the Latin *limen* (a threshold, in-between)
[214] C.F. Samuel Escobar, *The New Global Mission: The Gospel from Everywhere to Everyone, Christian Doctrine in Global Perspective*, (Downers Grove: InterVarsity Press, 2003)

Four types of "diaspora missions"

In this chapter, the four types of "diaspora missions" will be introduced as specific strategies in diaspora missiology, i.e. missions *to* the diaspora, missions *through* the diaspora, missions *by* & *beyond* the diaspora, and missions *with* the diaspora.

As a review from Chapter 1, there are two kinds of "diaspora ministry" (see Figure 1.1):

> "ministering *to* the diaspora"- diaspora as recepients from non-diaspora Christians who practice the Great Commendment for pre-evangelistic purpose of serving them in social and spiritual dimensions – focusing on the diaspora by practicing "*to*" and "*through*" strategies.

> "ministering *along* the diaspora" – mobilizing diaspora Christians to partner with others in the fulfillment of the Great Commission beyond their own diaspora group – focusing on recipients outside by practicing "*by & beyond*" and "*with*" strategies.

"Ministering *to* the diaspora" includes the first two types of "diaspora missions" (i.e. "*to*" and "*through*" strategies); whereas "ministering *along* the diaspora " includes the last two types of "diaspora missions" (i.e. practicing "*by & beyond*" and "*with*" strategies*)*.

The strategy of missions "*to*" and "*through*" the diaspora

"Missions to the diaspora" is reaching the diaspora groups in forms of evangelism or pre-evangelistic social services, then disciple them to become worshipping communities and congregations, whereas "missions through the diaspora" is diaspora Christians reaching out to their kinsmen through networks of friendship and kinship in host countries, their homelands, and abroad."

The following summary from a doctoral dissertation[215] is helpful to illustrate these two types of strategy in diaspora missiology. During the 1970s, there were two waves of Vietnamese "boat people" who reached the shores of many lands and were settled in refugee camps in various countries. Individual Christians and congregations in host countries practiced "mission to the diaspora" that led to the formation of many Vietnamese diaspora communities and among them Vietnamese diaspora congregations in the US, Canada, Europe, and Australia. There were sponsoring churches in host countries and

---

[215]Thanh Trung Le, "A Missiological Study of Vietnamese Diaspora," Unpublished doctoral dissertation, Western Seminary, 2013

Christian charitable agencies which served them in multiple ways: housing, schooling, post-trumatic counseling, etc.

Church planting and church growth among diaspora Vietnamese congregations practiced "mission through the diaspora" in evangelism and outreach through their kinship network both abroad and in the homeland. The success of "mission through the diaspora" among diaspora Vietnamese resulted in the formation of Vietnamese Christian parachurch organizations and ethnic departments in many transnational denominations (e.g. C&MA, Baptist, Nazarine, etc.)

Many ministries and missions have been organized by the diaspora Christian Vietnamese to reach out to other diaspora Vietnamese groups. Some of the denominations and mission boards involved in ministries among the Vietnamese diaspora include the Vietnamese National Baptist Fellowship, the United Methodist Church – Vietnamese National Caucus, the Vietnamese District of the Christian and Missionary Alliance, the Vietnamese Mission Board, the Vietnamese Christian Mission Ministry, the Vietnamese Presbyterian Caucus, North America Vietnamese Mennonite Fellowship, Vietnamese Evangelical Churches in Europe, the Association of Vietnamese Alliance Churches in Canada (AVAC), and the Worldwide Association of Vietnamese Alliance Churches (WAVAC). Besides these denominations and mission agencies, several para-church groups or interdenominational ministries are also involved in ministering to the Vietnamese diaspora.

The New Hope Ministry is a case of "mission through the diaspora" for it seeks to minister to the Vietnamese diaspora in Cambodia. Rev. and Mrs. Rick Drummond established this ministry in 1997. New Hope Ministries, an Alliance outreach in the Vietnamese community of Phnom Penh, brings the good news of Jesus to refugees living in desperate poverty. In 1998 Rev. Thu Nguyen and his wife were sent by the C&MA Canada as missionaries to the Vietnamese diaspora in Cambodia. The missionary team also includes two Vietnamese missionaries from Canada and a Vietnamese missionary couple from Australia. The New Hope Ministry now has seven churches with three local pastors and four lay leaders. The various ministries include medical services, Christian school, practical ministry training, computer training, church planting, leadership development, and evangelism training through TEE.

The formation of both the Presbyterian Church of Ghana in New York in the mid-1980s (a global pioneer - the first church outside of Ghana) and the U.S. Presbyterian Church of Ghana were the fruit of practicing "mission to the diaspora" and "mission through the diaspora" among diaspora Ghanaians in the US.216 These two strategies are to be credited for the formation and development of Ghanaians denominations in US, Canada and Europe.217

The strategy of missions "*by & beyond*" the diaspora

"Missions by & beyond the diaspora" is " motivating and mobilizing diaspora Christians for cross-cultural missions to other ethnic groups in their host countries, homelands, and abroad." In this strategy, diaspora individuals or communities are no longer the receipients of (social and other forms) services rendered to them. Instead, they are to be motivated and mobilized to engage in Kingdom ministry to others cross-culturally.

Here is a case study of Dr. Nghia Pham, a Vietnamese medical doctor partnering with CAMA to serve in Mongolia. Only one-half of 1% of the Mongolian population are evangelical Christians. Yet in this spiritually needy climate, people are finding Jesus through the ministry of Alliance workers. The Barong Haraa church is one of several places where Dr. Nghia Pham holds a monthly mobile medical clinic through CAMA. Many new believers who were baptized and made decision to follow Christ because they first heard the Gospel from Dr. Pham. The medical clinic has seen more than 40 people make the choice to follow Jesus, and 15 were baptized in 2007. This outreach has been a powerful tool for the Gospel and for the church in Mongolia.

Dr. Pham also operates a health clinic out of the Darhan CAMA project center. While training three other healthcare workers, he serves hundreds of patients every month in communities where Alliance churches have been planted. The clinic sets high standards for patient care, service, and cleanliness as well as excellence in training new healthcare workers. Dr. Pham also works with short-term medical teams as a means of initial evangelism and church planting. Every patient treated there hears the Gospel and is prayed for. For instance, CAMA Mongolia hosted a medical team from the Sarang church in Orange County, California. Six members assisted Dr. Pham with various aspects of his work in Darhan and Erdenet. More than 600 patients were treated over the course of five days. Dr. Kang and his assistant Tai saw 125 dental patients. The Gospel was shared with all patients, and eight made an initial commitment to follow Jesus. Ongoing community development projects also

---

[216] Yaw Attah Edu-Bekoe, "Ghanaian diaspora: an integrative study of the Presbyterian Church of Ghana congregations in the United States of America." Unpublished doctoral dissertation, Western Seminary, 2011.

[217] *Scattered Africans Keep Coming.* Yaw Attah Edu-Bekoe and Enoch Wan, IDS-USA, 2013.

coincide with the clinic's work.[218] And on February 28, 2010, 10 were baptized at the Tolgoi Good News House Church, Darhan, Mongolia.[219]

---

[218] *The Alliance, News & Stories*. Accessed August 22, 2011.; available at http://www.cmalliance.org/news/?s=Dr.+Nghia+Pham%2C+Mongolia.
[219] Pham Xuan Nghia, Newsletter. Accessed Augsut 22, 2011; available at http://www.northhollywoodchurch.org/Ministries/Mongolia/Truyen_Giao_Mong_Co_Thang_2_

Missions "with" the diaspora[220]

In this revised edition, *"with"* is proposed as an additional strategy in the diaspora paradigm. The key in the *"with"* approach is "bridging and bonding" as shown in Figure 8.3 below. The distinctiveness of this approach is that not all participants are to be exclusively from diaspora group(s) as compared to the other three (i.e. *"to," "through,"* and *"by & beyond"*) in theory and practice. This is an inclusive way of Kingdom ministry regardless of ethnicity, language, culture, class or background or participants.

Figure 8.3 The concept and practice of *"with"* approach

CONCEP-TUAL	PRACTICAL	
	Relational Pattern	Practical Way
Bridging & Bonding	Networking: • Bridging by regional proximity or linguistic/racial affinity • Bonding: kinship/friendship/mutual interest	• Hospitality • Receiprocity • Connectivity & complexity • Solidarity • Unity
	Partnership: • National & transnational individual • Local congregations or institutional entities of multiple variety	

The best way to explain the *"with"* approach is by way of illustrations. It can be an ex-missionary returning home (due to retirement, health or family reason) from Japan but continue to work with diaspora Japanese or Chinese. He/she has the language facility to evangelize (or partner with) Japanese diaspora and the cultural sensitivity to work with Chinese diaspora. A missionary returning to US from South America but continue to work with all kinds of Hispanic Americans. I personally witnessed a Christian ambassador from the Philippines, reaching out to and working with Chinese diaspora in a country in the Gulf Region. I, an American-Chinese, had worked with a Christian engineer from India who drove his own car in a Muslim country to provide transportation for Chinese workers from the "free-zone" area to attend an international church led by a Caucasian pastor from Canada. Another example is Ken Taylor - a Filipino professional musician graduated from

---

[220] The addition of the "with" approach in this revision was publicly introduced by Enoch Wan, "Response to Matthew Krabill & Allison Norton - New Wine in Old Wineskins: A Critical Appraisal of Diaspora Missiology." Regional EMS-Canada, Vancouver, BC, Jan. 24, 2014.

Western Seminary then began missionary service in Japan. He realized the Japanese embrace black gospel music so he formed the "Halleluja Gospel Family"[221] by partnering with Japanese churches and invited Afro-American Christians (including gospel singers and hip-hop dancers) from the US to evangelize through music. Now he has organized gospel choirs in 50 churches across Japan.[222]

Networking and partnership in the "with" approach of diaspora mission may vary in form, size, shape and flavor because our Lord is soeverign over all circumstances, creative and impressively surprising in His miraculous ways of building His Kingdom. We stand in awe when observing how He orchestrated things to His glory and our astonishment.

The key concepts of the "with" approach are "**bridging and bonding**" and the practice may take the relational pattern of networking or partnership. "Bridging" may be based on regional proximity (e.g. same continent such as southasian or South America), linguistic affinity (e.g. Portugese from Portugal, Brazil, Mozambique and Angola), racial affinity (e.g. Hispanic from South America and Spain). Bonding may be based on kinship, friendship or mutual interest. Partnership may occur among national, expatriate and transnational at congregational or institutional entities of multiple variety (e.g. charity or faith-base). Those who practice the Great Commendment among people in needs can bond so strongly that "bridges" are built for long-term relationship. For example, Muslim diaspora from a limited access country (or traditionally called "unreached people-group") in the US will be very ready to introduce a Caucasian American care-giver to be hosted by their Mulim family back home if a visit is arranged to bring greetings, goods and gift.

Practical ways of practicing the *"with"* approach varied according to time, place, occasion, circumstances, available resources and stages of relational formation and cultivation. **Hospitality** of a host family to regugees, orphans, international student may build "bridges" that can be transgenerational and transcontinental for the Kingdom. People from many countries and cultures place high valunue on **"reciprocity"** of gift-giving, favor-exchange, aids of financial and practical nature. The "connectivity" may take the form of friendship, adoption (e.g. godparent in Catholic tradition, sandek of Jewish tradition, *Santería* of Yoruba, 乾爹/乾媽 in Chinese) and other variations. The **"connectivit**y" may grow into **"complexity"** of extending the concentric circle or converging circle to kinsmen and countrymen, neighbors in distant land, mutual friends, business and religious associates, expatriate and compatriot, transcontinental and transgenerational…etc.

---

[221] See link: http://jesuslovesjapan.com/2010/06/black-gospel-music-a-movement-of-god-in-japan/ Retrevied Feb. 20, 2014

[222] Check link: https://www.cbn.com/cbnnews/shows/cwn/2011/August/Gospel-Choirs-Convert-Japanese-Singers-to-Christianity/ Retrevied Feb. 20, 2014

When **"bonding"** is done correctly, it will lead to a sense of **"solidarity"** - the strong bond developed and cultivated on the basis of a variety of factors such as sentiment (e.g. patriotism, nationalism and religiosity) or commitment (e.g. ideological or religious). **"Unity"** is a sense of togetherness and oneness beyond or in spite of all kinds of barriers (e.g. racial, linguistic and cultural nature). Christian unity (John 17; Rom 12; Eph 2, 4;) and Kingdom mentality (Luke 17:20-21; John 13:15; Romans 16:1; Ephesians 5:1; 6:21-22; 1 Peter 2:21; Revelation 21:3-4) are not only key theological themes in the Bible; they frequently are practiced and demonstrated in the **"with"** approach of diaspora ministry and diaspora missions.

While hospitality, reciprocity connectivity and complexity are specific ways to practice the *"with"* approach; solidarity and unity are the practical manesfestation of successful bridging and bonding in diaspora ministry and diaspora missions.

Summary

In this chapter, the popular managerial paradigm has been compared to the diaspora paradigm and found wanting. In the remaining chapters of Part 3, we shall explain diaspora paradigm in more spicific and concrete ways. In this chapter, the four types of "diaspora missions" have been introduced as specific strategies in diaspora missiology, i.e. *"to," "through," "by & beyond" and "with"* approaches. New to this revised edition is the addition of the **"with"** element to the diaspora paradigm.

The increase in human geographic distribution is providing the church in all parts of the world with new opportunities to reach the nations. The people God has put within the church's immediate reach spatially, socially and spiritually to become bridges to the nationsand and partners for Kingdom ministy in the fulfillment of the Great Comission.

Chapter 9

Diaspora Missiology in Progress

Enoch Wan

Introduction: Diaspora Missiology in Action

Efforts in practicing diaspora missions can be illustrated by "Church without Walls"[223] - a Canadian case study on a group of believers who intentionally moved into a neighborhood where 35 apartment buildings housed over 30,000 people. Among them 90% are Asian immigrants who have lived in Canada for less than five years, two thirds of them are South Asians. The believers moved into the neighborhood and ministered to the physical needs of the people. From helping with documents in English and children's homework to shopping in the malls and playing soccer in the park, this group lived out the Gospel daily, holistically and relationally.

The result of this effort was the establishing of a 24/7 church without walls, bringing church into everyday life instead of bringing the neighbors into a church building. Partnership was important in this venture; two groups made the commitment to see a local church established, and another partnered with the Salvation Army to give away winter jackets.[224]

Other examples of diaspora missiology in action can be found in a collection of articles entitled *Missions Practice in the 21st Century*, edited by Enoch Wan and Sadiri Joy Tira[225]. In it Tira describes a case study of diaspora missiology in action by the First Filipino Alliance Church in Edmonton, Canada. He uses the "kangaroo model" to describe this church-birth and development in three stages: 1) pregnancy, 2) preparation, and 3) partnership.

---

[223] de Haan, Charlene. *A Canadian Case Study in Diaspora Missiology*, accessed September 23, 2009; available at http://www.lausanneworldpulse.com/perspectives.php.
[224] "ForestView" is a project of "church without walls" in Toronto, see link: http://www.forestviewchurch.ca/ (accessed Feb. 20, 2014)
[225] Enoch Wan and Sadiri Joy Tira, eds. *Mission Practice in the 21st Century* (Pasadena, CA: William Carrey Inernational University Press, 2009).

Another example is from Lorajoy Dimangondayao, who describes how the Filipino International Network (FIN) is a case of diaspora missiology in action. It embraced the Great Commission as well as acting out the Lukan mandate they call "glocal missions" (Wan and Tira 2009: 236), making disciples in multiple locations and for all people through preaching, teaching, training, church planting, compassionate ministries and other strategies to make disciples of Jesus Christ.

The booklet *Scattered to Gather: Embracing the Global Trend of Diaspora*[226] was passed out at Cape Town 2010 to all delegates. It contained a summary of the growth of diaspora missiology in the last few years. The last section entitled "Next Steps You Can Take" encourages the Church to put diaspora missiology into practice. Enoch Wan introduced the booklet as a ministry guide for outreach to the diaspora in Minnesota and the fruitful outcomes were reported in case study 8, Chapter 20.

Diaspora Missiology: Conference and Development

In the past few years, the relatively new diaspora missiology paradigm was introduced to missiologists and missions leaders through a series of activities (e.g. conferences, meetings and course offerings) as listed below.

The annual meeting of the American Society of Missiology (AMS) in June 2002 chose the theme "Migration Challenge and Avenue for Christian Mission" and the proceedings were subsequently published in the journal *Missiology* XXXI (January 2003), covering matters related to ministry to diaspora. Examples are: Enoch Wan's "Mission among the Chinese diaspora: A case study of migration and mission," Christine Pohl's "Offering hospitality to strangers," Samuel Escobar and Daniel Rodriguez on the Hispanic diaspora nn the United States and Spain. There were case studies, e.g. Jan Jongenee - "The Mission of Migrant Churches in Europe" and Jean Stromberg - "Responding to the Challenge of Migration: Churches within the Fellowship of the World Council of Churches (WCC)."

In Seoul, Korea April 12-15, 2004 at the consultation of Filipino International Network (FIN), missiologists, theologians, and practitioners reported and explored issues related to diaspora missions with a focus on the global phenomenon of the Filipino diaspora. The proceedings were published *Scattered: the Global Filipino Presence*[227] - the first book focusing on the study of diaspora missiology with five parts: historical demography, biblical theology, missiological methodology, global strategy (evangelism and discipleship), and personal stories of Filipino "Kingdom workers ."

---

[226] *Scattered to Gather: Embracing the Global Trend of Diaspora* (Manila: LifeChange Publishing, 2010).
[227] Luis Patoja, Sadiri Joy Tira, and Enoch Wan, *Scattered: Filipino Global Presence* (Manila: LifeChange Puglishing, 2004).

As the chief editor, Enoch Wan develops a missiological methodology to study the phenomenon of diaspora by integrating historic-demographic facts with biblical-theological data. He insists that diaspora missiology is non-spatial, and deterritorialized; not homogenous but multi-cultural; and both multi-ethnic and multi-directional.

In 2004, at the Lausanne Forum held in Pattaya, Thailand, "diaspora" was an issue group for the first time in LCWE (Lausanne Congress of World Evangelization) and produced the first-ever Lausanne Occasional Paper (LOP No. 55) on diaspora entitled "The New People Next Door" (free digital copy is available @ http://www.lausanne.org/docs/2004forum/LOP55_IG26.pdf). This booklet provides a discussion on biblical and theological basis for missions among scattered people and case studies on Chinese, Filipino, South Asian, Persian and international students. The publication of LOP No. 55 is significant in that it helped to place "diaspora missiology" on the global agenda of the Church.

The Filipino Diaspora Missions Consultation took place at the Torch Trinity Graduate School of Theology Seoul, Republic of South Korea, April 12-15, 2004. At the conference, Enoch Wan addressed the matter of ""The Phenomenon of Diaspora: Missiological Implications for Christian Missions" and later was published in the multilingual e-journal *Global Missiology*.[228]

At the Philippine Baptist Theological Seminary, Baguio City, Philippines, the Filipino Theological Educators' Consultation on January 4-6, 2006 was attended by dozens of missiologists and theological educators from USA, Canada, Korea and the Philippines to strategize ways and means to promote both formal and informal education in diaspoa missiology for pastors, missionaries and Filipino Kingdom workers around the world.

Later in the same year, LCWE endorsed the first Global Diaspora Missiology Consultation, sponsored by the FIN (Filipino International Network) that was held at Taylor University College and Seminary (Edmonton, Alberta, Canada) on November 15-18, 2006. At the meeting, case studies were practitioners from major diaspora groups (e.g., Chinese, Jewish, Filipino, South Asian, Kenyan, Korean, Vietnamese, Tibetan, Nepalese, Hispanic, etc). At this consultation, Tuvya Zaretsky of Jews For Jesus convincingly proposed that the Jewish diaspora experience to be a key to the study of diaspora missiology, as demonstrated years later in the case study on Sri Lankans by Ted Rubesh.[229]

---

[228] For the digital version of the paper, please use the link below:
http://ojs.globalmissiology.org/index.php/english/article/view/1036
For information regarding this conference, readers are referred to Joy Tira's paper entirled "Filipino international network: a strategic model for Filipino diaspora glocal® missions" @
http://ojs.globalmissiology.org/index.php/english/article/viewFile/123/356 (Retreived Feb. 20, 2014)
[229] Ted Rubesh, "Wandering Jews and scattered Sri Lankans: viewing Sri Lankans of the G.C.C. through the lens of the Old Testament Jewish diaspora," February 7, 2014

In 2007, Sadiri Joy Tira was appointed as "Senior Associate for Diasporas" by LCWE and the following year completed his dissertation entitled "Filipino Kingdom Workers: An Ethnographic Study" (at Western Seminary, Spring 2008, under the superversion of Enoch Wan) which was later published by William Carey under the same title in the EMS Dissertation Series, 2011.

At the Lausanne Diaspora Educators' Consultation on November 11-14, 2009 at Torch Trinity Graduate School of Theology, Seoul, Korea, "The Seoul Declaration on Diaspora Missiology"[230] was drafted by a task group and approved on November 14, 2009. And a working committee was formed and tasked to produce an official document for the Cape Town 2010 conference. Consequently, the booklet *Scattered to Gather: Embracing the Global Trend of Diaspora* was produced and distributed at Lausanne Cape Town 2010 (a digital version of the book is accessible @ http://www.jdpayne.org/wp-content/uploads/2010/10/Scattered-to-Gather.pdf). Due to a combination of factors, only a few copies of the pre-publication version of the booklet *Korean Diaspora and Christian Mission*[231] were available at Cape Town 2010 and a year later was published by Regnum International Books. Subsequently the Global Diasporas Network was formed under the auspices of the Lausanne Movement in 2010 and Sadiri Joy Tira serves as both the Senior Associate for Diasporas and chairperson for the Global Diaspora Network.

The GDN headquarters/secretariat office in 2011 was established in Manila and officially registered under the Securities & Exchange Commission of the Philippines providing GDN with a legal identity.[232]

And in February 2011, the GDN Advisory Board met for the first time in France to project the "Lausanne Diaspora Missions" for the next 5 years including the Global Diaspora Forum (March 2015) to be held in Manila, Philippines.[233] The Global Diaspora Forum was officially announced during the Lausanne Leadership Biennial Meeting in Boston, MA, June 2011.

> "The 2015 World Diaspora Forum will be held in the Philippines, March 24-28, 2015, and is sponsored by the Lausanne Committee. The GDN plans to invite 500 people from around the world to participate including church leaders, educators, practitioners and donors. If you

---

[230] "The Seoul Declaration on Diaspora Missiology" is accessible at the LCWE site @ http://www.lausanne.org/en/documents/all/consultation-statements/1112-the-seoul-declaration-on-diaspora-missiology.html

[231] S. Hun Kim and Wonsuk Ma (eds.) *Korean Diaspora and Christian Mission*. Regnum Books International, 2011 (excerpts of the book are available @ http://books.google.ca/books?id=boSv9lJz4mIC&pg=PA1&lpg=PA1&dq=filipino+international+network+fin&source=bl&ots=ZGatZT5xxS&sig=KA9SfSAelMxy8WyitNl_2tqtJig&hl=en&sa=X&ei=KuNBU5_1Ku_iyAHY1IHoAw&ved=0CEgQ6AEwBw#v=onepage&q=filipino%20international%20network%20fin&f=false)

[232] http://www.globaldiaspora.org/about_gdn Retreveid Feb. 20, 2014.

[233] http://www.globaldiaspora.org/about_gdn Retreived Feb. 20, 2014.

> have suggestions for people to invite from among the RHP network, contact Paul (Paul@iafr.org) as soon as possible....The GDN will also publish a compendium about the diaspora and the Kingdom of God with sections on theological foundations, current realities, strategic possibilities of the diaspora, the role of the church, and various case studies."[234]

At the third Lausanne Congress in Capetown on October 20, 2012 he was reappointed for a term of five years and the Global Diaspora Network (GDN) was formed - a catalytic organization motivating and mobilizing diaspora Christians to partner for global missions.

GDN hosted "The Far East Asia Educators Forum" in Manila, August 11-14, 2011 in order to gather theological educators to a joint effort in developing courses and curriculum to train workers and researchers to advance the cause of diaspora mission and ministry.[235]

The 8th Korean Diaspora Forum (KDF) met in Johannesburg, South Africa, Feb.14-17, 2012 with the theme "Beyond Barrier, Beyond Generations." KDF has a long history tracing back to its birth in Baltimore, USA in 2004, during which Korean Diaspora churches worldwide participated. Since 2005 KDF met annually: Beijing-2006, Tokyo-2007, Kuala Lumpur-2008, Shanghai-2009, Seol-Ak Mountain- 2010, Los Angeles-2011.[236]

At the Korean Diaspora Forum, May 18-21, 2010, Seoul, Korea, Enoch Wan presented a paper on "Korean Diaspora: from Hermit Kingdom to Kingdom Ministry," challenging Korean participants from a dozen countries engaging in diaspora ministry among Koreans overseas and in cross-cultural contexts. At the International Forum for Migrant Mission (IFMM, May 25, 2010, Seoul, Korea), Enoch Wan gave a presentation on "Diaspora Missiology in Action: A Case Study of Chinese Diaspora Missions & CCCOWE[237] (the first ethnic global network in evangelism since Laussane 1974). He used the case study of CCCOWE to challenge Korean participants to form a global network in diaspora mission.

---

[234] http://www.worldea.org/news/4227/life-on-the-road-updates-from-the-refugee-highway-partnership Retreived March 8, 2014.

[235] http://www.globaldiaspora.org/content/far-east-asia-disapora-educators-met-manila Retreived Feb. 20, 2014.

[236] http://www.globaldiaspora.org/content/gdn-networks-kdf Retreived Feb. 20, 2014.

[237] "In July 1974, some seventy Chinese Church leaders, who came together at the International Congress on World Evangelism in Lausanne, were inspired by the Holy Spirit to commence the movement. In August 1976, the 1st Chinese Congress on World Evangelization was convened in Hong Kong; soon after, the Chinese Coordination Centre of World Evangelism was established to mobilize Chinese churches to spread the gospel to nations all over the world."
http://www.lausanne.org/en/connect/regions/east-asia/cccowe-overview.html Retreived Feb. 20, 2014.

"On May 22nd, 2012 Eurasian Diaspora Study Center has been opened at Ukrainian Evangelical Theological Seminary. Senior bishops of the Evangelical churches, the rectors of theological schools, scholars, and representatives of public organizations of Ukraine attended the opening ceremony."[238]

The theme "Mission On Our Doorsteps" of the 12th Ethnic Ministries Summits was held in Chicago, April 18-20, 2013. Ethnic America Network (EAN) is "a catalytic coalition of Christian ministries and churches from across the USA and Canada" and "Since 2000, we have partnered with local leaders and educators in holding annual Ethnic Ministries Summits, out of which we seek to establish Regional Networks of ethnic ministries."[239] It is interesting to note that it is not hard to draw a parallel between the approach of EAN in ethnic ministry and Donald Anderson McGavran's concept of ethnic diversity of the church in India (1979).[240]

The theme of the Evangelical Missiological Society of 2014 (www.EMSweb.org) is "diaspora missiology" with many papers presented at regional meetings in the Spring of 2014 and from which some will be selected to be included in the national conference and the EMS annual monograph on "diaspora missiology" to be edited by Enoch Wan and Mike Pocock. The theme of the 2014 North American Mission Leaders Conference is "Migration and Mission" with multiple tracks including "Diaspora/Ethnic Ministries" hosted by Missio Nexus, Evangelical Missiological Society (EMS), Ethnic America Network, and Alliance for Excellence in Short-term Mission (AESTM) September 2014 at the Hilton Atlanta, GA.[241]

Recent Researches and Publications on Diaspora Missiology

Recent Publications on Diaspora Missiology

At present there are not many publications on this emerging study of diaspora missiology and listed below are illustrative items to show case some of the recent research and publciation.

The booket "*The New People Next Door*" (LOP No. 55) produced by the Lausanne Forum (2004) is a significant document in that it helped placing the

---

[238] http://www.globaldiaspora.org/content/diaspora-missiology-launched Retreived Feb. 20, 2014.
[239] http://ethnicamerica.com/about/ Retreived Feb. 20, 2014.
[239] Donald Anderson McGavran, *Ethnic Realities and the Church: Lessons from India*. William Carey Library, 1979
[241] http://www.missionexus.org/mission-leaders-conference/ Retreived March 8, 2014.

topic of diaspora missiology on the global agenda of the Church. Later LCWE endorsed the first Global Diaspora Missiology Consultation, sponsored by the FIN (Filipino International Network) that was held at Taylor University College and Seminary (Edmonton, Alberta, Canada) on November 15-18, 2006. At the meeting, Case studies were presented by leaders from major diaspora groups, e.g., Chinese, Jewish, Filipino, South Asian, Kenyan, Korean, Vietnamese, Tibetan, Nepalese, Hispanic, etc. At the Consultation, Tuvya Zaretsky of Jews For Jesus, pointed out that Jewish diaspora experience to be a key to the study of diaspora missiology, as shown in the case study on Sri Lankans by Ted Rubesh.[242]

In the article entitled "Diaspora Missiology" (EMS *Occasional Bulletin*, Spring 2007), Enoch Wan defines diaspora missiology and delineats its contents, distinctiveness, and methodology that laid the theoretical and methodological foundation for his subsequent researches on diaspora missiology.

In July 2007, *Global Missiology* a multi-lingual free online journal, devoted the entire issue to the study of diaspora missiology.[243] In the same year, Atul Aghamkar called for a partnership in witnessing to the Hindu diaspora in North America, as they are one of the most neglected and unreached people in the world; even though they live in relatively close proximity to the church in North America.[244]

Recently, there is a growing number of publications by Christian authors in this area and listed below are some samples:

- Warner, R. Stephen, and Judith G. Wittner. 1998. *Gatherings in diaspora: religious communities and the new immigration*. Philadelphia, PA: Temple University Press;
- Haar Gt. (1998) *Halfway to paradise: African Christians in Europe,* Fairwater, Cardiff: Cardiff Academic Press.;
- Walls AF. (2002) "Mission and migration: the diaspora factor in Christian history," *Journal of African Christian Thought* 5: 3-11.;
- Spencer S. (2008) *Mission and migration,* Calver, Derbys: Cliff College Publishing.;
- Hanciles J. (2008) *Beyond christendom: globalization, African migration, and the transformation of the West*, Maryknoll, N.Y.: Orbis Books.
- Währisch-Oblau C. (2009) *The missionary self-perception of Pentecostal/Charismatic church leaders from the global South in Europe: bringing back the Gospel*, Leiden; Boston:
- Brill.; Kim, S. Hun and Ma, Wonsuk. (2011) *Korean diaspora and Christian*

---

[242] Ted Rubesh, "Wandering Jews and scattered Sri Lankans: viewing Sri Lankans of the G.C.C. through the lens of the Old Testament Jewish diaspora," February 7, 2014
[243] Available at www.GlobalMissiology.com.
[244] Atu l Y. Aghamka, "Partnership in Witnessing to the Hindu Diaspora in Nor th America." *Journal of the Academy for Evangelism in Theological Education*, Vol 22 (2006-2007): 23-48; also available at http://www.aeteonline.org/twentytwo.pdf.

mission, Oxford: Regnum Books.;
- Ludwig F and Asamoah-Gyadu JK. (2011) *African Christian presence in the west: new immigrant congregations and transnational networks in North America and Europe,* Trenton NJ: Africa World Press.;
- Adogame A. (2013) *The African Christian diaspora: New currents and emerging trends in world Christianity,* London: Bloomsbury.

R. Stephen Warner has presented a convincing argument that "migration is not random with respect to religion, Warner R. S. (2000) Religion and New (Post-1965) Immigrants: Some Principles Drawn from Field Research. *American Studies* (00263079) 41.." Along the same line of thought is *Faith on the Move,* a recent study by the Pew Research Center's Forum on Religion & Public Life, focuses on the religious affiliation of international migrants, examining patterns of migration among seven major groups: Christians, Muslims, Hindus, Buddhists, Jews, adherents of other religions and the religiously unaffiliated. Another important document is *The Global Religious Landscape,* 2012 also produced by Pew.[245]

In reference to Korean diaspora, it is worth mentioning several publications. Chan-Sik Park edited the book *21C New Nomad Era and Migrant Mission.* Christianity and Industrial Society Reserch Institute, Seoul, Korea, 2010 and was distributed to all participants of the Korean Diaspora Forum and the International Forum for Migrant Mission in May 2010, Soeul, Korea. Contributors are Korean practitioners and academicians, covering biblical and sociological aspects of diaspora missiology along with case studies in many countries. Another book is *Korean Diaspora and Christian Mission,* edited by S. Hun Kim and Wonsuk Ma. Limited copies of a pre-publication version were distributed during the Lausanne III (Cape Town 2010) congress in South Africa and later published by Regnum Studies in Mission in 2011. Similar to an earlier title, *21C New Nomad Era and Migrant Mission* in structure and nature, *Korean Diaspora and Christian Mission* covers biblical, historical, and strategic matters related to Korean diaspora and diaspora missions, supplemented by several case studies illustrative of "diaspora mission by and beyond" Korean diaspora. Two special issues of *Torch Trinity Journal* were designated to the theme of "Diaspora" with Korean, American and Chinese contributors: Volume 13, No. 1, May 30, 2010 and Volume 12, No. 2, Nov. 30, 2010.[246]

Strangers next door: immigration, migration, and mission by Payne J. D. (2012, Downers Grove, Ill.: IVP Books.) presents helpful demographic data and calls for Christian to actively engage in diaspora mission by reaching out to

---

[245] *The Global Religious Landscape,* 2012 also produced by Pew Research Center, Pew Forum for Religion and Public Life available @
http://www.pewforum.org/global-religious-landscape-christians.aspx.
[246] Key word "diaspora" may be used to search at the link below:
http://www0.ttgst.ac.kr:30000/search/eng/search_result.asp?backdepth=1&history=key_word&query0=diaspora&range=20&page=1&area0=all&material=all&y=18&graph=%B4%DC%BC%F8%B0%CB%BB%F6&x=56&max_srch=135 Retreived Feb. 20, 2014.

incoming migrants and immigrants in our neighborhood. Similar to Payne in passion for evangelism and church planting, Tira and Santos use Greenhills Christian Fellowship of the Philippines to show case the practice of "by and beyond" in diaspora mission extending to Canada –(Tira, Sadiri Joy, and Narry F. Santos. 2011.) "Diaspora church planting in a multicultural city: A case study of Greenhills Christian Fellowship." In *Reflecting God's glory together: diversity in evangelical mission*, edited by A. Scott Moreau and Beth Snodderly. Pasadena: William Carey Library.

Recent Researches at the Institute for Diaspora Studies (IDS-USA) - Western Seminary, Portland, Oregon

In 2007 Western Seminary (Portland, Oregon) launched an Institute for Diaspora Studies (IDS-USA), a joint effort by researchers and practitioners seeking to understand and minister to people of diaspora. A branch of IDS has also been launched at the Alliance Graduate School of Theology in Manila, Philippines at the commencement and Enoch Wan gave an address on Abraham as the prototype of subsequent Jewish diaspora.

Since 2007, courses offered and dissertation research at of Western Seminary are selectedly listed below:

- At Western Seminary, Portland, Oregon: on diaspora missiology, taught by Enoch Wan, Tuvya Zaresky, Sadiri Tira - Summer 2007, 2009 and April 2010; on Hindu diaspora taught by Atul Y. Aghamkar; in February 2010 ; on diaspora missiology, taught by Enoch Wan and Sadiri Tira, April 2010, and team taught by Enoch Wan, Thanh Trung Le, Andy Ponce, Mike Holland, and Randy Mitchel, May 2013.
- At Ambrose University College, Calgary, Canada, a course on diaspora taught by Sadiri Joy Tira, Feb. 2010.

Completed doctoral dissertations under Enoch Wan's supervision at Western Seminary are selectively listed below:

- Tuvya Zaresky, "The Challenges of Jewish-Gentile Couples: A Pre-evangelistic Ethnographic Study," Spring 2004. (Later published by William Carey with the title: *Jewish-Gentile Couples: Trends, Challenges, and Hopes*)
- Sadiri Emmanuel Santiago B. Tira, "Filipino Kingdom Workers: An Ethnographic Study, Spring 2008. (with the same tile, EMS Dissertation Series, William Carey, 2011)
- Yaw Attah Edu-Bekoe, "Ghanaian diaspora: An integrative study of the Presbyterian Church of Ghana congregations in the United States of America," April, 2011. (*Scattered Africans Keep Coming* Yaw Attah Edu-Bekoe and Enoch Wan. April 1, 2013 @ www.amazon.com)
- Mike Holland, "Diaspora mission to Hispanics in the USA," February 11, 2013

- Thanh Trung Le, "A missiological study of Vietnamese diaspora," January, 2013. (Forth coming title: *Mobilizing Vietnamese Diaspora for the Kingdom*. Enoch Wan and Thanh Trung Le, Spring 2014)
- James Mook Sum Lai, "An ethnography of the contextual approach of community projects among the Yunnanese Chinese community in Lashio, Myanmar," (Chinese diaspora), September 15, 2013
- Paul Kyu-Jin Choi, "Towards a paradigm of missional ecclesiology for Korean diaspora," April 2014
- Siu Lun Law, "An ethnographic study of the relief ministries of the Oasis Chapel and missiological implications for relational missiology," (Japanese diaspora), January 2014
- Ted Rubesh, "Wandering Jews and scattered Sri Lankans: viewing Sri Lankans of the G.C.C. through the lens of the Old Testament Jewish diaspora," February 7, 2014 (Forth coming title: Wandering Jews and scattered Sri Lankans: Understanding Sri Lankan diaspora in the GCC region through the lens of OT Jewish diaspora, Spring 2014).
- Ongoing research projects of IDS-USA at Western Seminary under the supervision of Enoch Wan and about a dozen doctoral dissertations are in progress on various diaspora groups such as Hispanic, Korean, etc.

There are ongoing researches conducted by doctoral students in other schools as selectively illustrated below:

- Anthony Francis Casey, "How shall they hear? The interface of urbanization and orality in North American ethnic church planting," The Southern Baptist Theological Seminary, 2013
- Andy Ponce, "Find Home: Envisioning Church Ministry to Left-Behind Families of Oveseas Filipino Workers (OFWs)," Asbury Theological Seminary, 2014.

A branch of the IDS was launched on April 1, 2007 at the Alliance Graduate School of Theology in Manila, Philippines at the commencement as IDS-Asia. Following the launch, Joy Tira taught diaspora-related courses in Manila and elsewhere.

Summary

Diaspora missiology is an emerging strategy in Christian missions and an emerging missiological paradigm in the 21st century. In this chapter, conferences recently held with significance to diaspora missiology have been covered. Recent researches and publications on diaspora missiology are selectively reported to show that there is significant progress in diaspora missiology; though it is a relatively new paradigm.

Chapter 10

Interdisciplinary Research Methodology for Diaspora Missiology

Enoch Wan

Introduction

This chapter begins with a discussion on missiological research methodology in general, then proceeds to introduce the "what" and "how" of an interdisciplinary approach in diaspora missiology. The content of this chapter is an adaptation and synthesis of three previous works:

- Enoch Wan, "Rethinking Missiological Research Methodology: Exploring a New Direction," (Global Missiology, October, 2003b).[247]

- Enoch Wan, "The Paradigm and Pressing Issues of Inter-disciplinary Research Methodology," (Global Missiology, January 2005a).

- Enoch Wan, "Research Methodology for Diaspora Missiology and Diaspora missions," presented at the Regional EMS Conference – North Central, February 26, 2011b, Trinity Evangelical Divinity School, and Deerfield, Illinois.

Three key terms should be defined before going into the details of the interdisciplinary research methodology.

- "Research methodology" - the ways and approaches employed in academic and systematic studies (Wan 2005a: 2).

---

[247] Available at www.GlobalMissiology.org.

- "Missiological research methodology" - the systematic, dynamic, and integrative manner of conducting research in missiological studies" (Wan 2003b:1)
- "Interdisciplinary research" – academic and systematic studies conducted by using elements such as theory and methodology from one or more disciplines in the attempt to achieve a high degree of coherence or unity (Wan 2005a:2).

Interdisciplinary Missiological Research Methodology

The following discussions focus on two research methodologies: the missiological research methodology and the interdisciplinary research methodology. The former is a traditional research method, and the latter is being introduced in this chapter for the study of diaspora missiology.

A diachronic survey of the traditions in missiological research and a synchronic overview of the nature of missiological research have been presented in earlier publications (Wan 2003b: 2005). These research studies fall under two broad categories: qualitative research and quantitative research.

There are three advantages (Wan 2005a:4-5) in conducting studies with interdisciplinary research methodology: disciplinary synergism, mutual enrichment, and research advancement.

1. **Disciplinary Synergism:**
   It integrates into a macro-paradigm what is otherwise a set of independent disciplines of study. Interdisciplinary research methodology enables the researcher to widen the scope of knowledge and see the whole in which the parts interact together. The result is more holistic understanding of reality and better theoretical formulations about that reality. (Wan 2003b)

2. **Mutual Enrichment:**
   In interdisciplinary research, different disciplines are allowed to enter into dynamic interaction for mutual enrichment (Wan 2005a:4-5). The enrichment process also sharpens the focus of the research thus securing results that are more systematic and closer to the subject matter under research.

3. **Research Advancement:**
   The interdisciplinary approach is a helpful tool for understanding the subject matter of inquiry. The reality of the vastness of the created order, the diversity of human culture, and the complexity of human experience are all subjects quite impossible to understand by using merely a single research approach. The combination of multiple disciplines not only enhances coherent

149

understanding but also solves research problems along the way.[248]

The interdisciplinary research methodology is a symphonic approach to interdisciplinary integration: a varied dynamic model. It could be described as:

> "The axiom of all research methodology is that the nature of the data and the problem under research determine that the methodology be either qualitative or quantitative. There is, however, data and problems whose nature does not fit either of these methodologies, but rather requires both approaches. This integration of both methodologies is called triangulation or theoretical triangulation (Leedy 1993:139,143). This integration uses several frames of reference in the analysis of the same data which allows the researcher to test a theory in more than one way so that such a theory may acquire complete scientific validation" (Wan 2003b:8).

Interdisciplinary Research Methodology for Diaspora Missiology

There is much complexity in the cause, process, and consequence of the phenomena of diaspora, and no single disciplinary can enable researchers to explain and apply insights from the challenging undertaking. Thus, by necessity, diaspora missiology is to be interdisciplinary by integrating missiology with related disciplines such as human geography, cultural anthropology, political demography, urban and ethnic studies, communication sciences, etc.

In addition, topics such as globalization, urbanization, ethnic and race relations, conflict resolution of ethnic and religious groups, pluralism, multiculturalism, etc., are all relevant to research in diaspora missiology. These topics are to be explored by the joint efforts of missiologists, social scientists, and humanitarian agents. Factual findings from these studies must be integrated with missiological understanding in ministry planning and missions strategy.

Many sub-fields exist in diaspora missiology when studies are focused on the phenomenon of people moving away from their places of origin. For example, migrant study is one area of diaspora missiology to study people who move internally within a country, such as workers moving from rural areas to metropolitan centers for jobs, residents moving from areas of conflicts to

---

[248] John W. Creswell, *Research Design: Qualitative, Quantitative, and Mixed Methods Approaches,* 2nd ed. (Thousand Oaks: Sage, 2003).

[handwritten at top: The areas are concerning territorial dispersion / deaf culture is mainly sociological dispersed]

shelters for safety. Immigrant study is another area of diaspora missiology. It is the study of people who move across political boundaries and transcontinentally. Another focus of diaspora missiology is the relationships, conflicts, and conflict resolution among ethnic groups that live in close proximity as a result of diaspora. In addition, academic studies related to the "who," "how," "where," and "why" of people moving from their homelands and the missiological implications are within the scope of diaspora missiology.

Castles and Miller, in their work *The Age of Migration*, argue that diaspora studies are intrinsically interdisciplinary, incorporating the dual tracts of the "determinants, processes, and patterns of migration" and "the ways in which migrants become incorporated into receiving societies and resultant change on both sending and host societies this processes causes (Castles and Miller 2009:20-21).[249]   In contrast to theories which see diaspora movements solely in terms of economics or historical structuralism, Castles and Miller exegete the role of networks and families in the migration system.   These systems are formed by "two or more countries which exchange migrants" and are built upon the existence of "prior links between sending and receiving countries based on colonization, political influence, trade, investment, or cultural ties" (Castles and Miller 2009: 27).   Macro-structures (Large scale social and political influences), micro-structures (kinship structures and social networks), and meso-structures (recruiters, sponsors, smugglers, etc.) all work in harmony to fuel, and at times exploit, migrants and the process of migration (Castles and Miller 2009:28-29).

Brettell and Hollified (2007:199) have outlined the usage of different disciplines for conducting research in migration studies.[250] This useful information can also be applied towards the study of diaspora missiology (Figure 8.1).

[handwritten: Where is "home" of a culture?]

---

[249] Stephen Castles and Mark J. Miller, *The Age of Migration: International Population Movements in the Modern World*, 4th Ed. New York: Guilford Press, 2009.   Ian Goldin, Geoffrey Cameron, and Meera Balarajan's *Exceptional People* is just one recent example which focuses on these dual tracts concurrently but not integratively.   (Ian Goldin, Geoffrey Cameron, and Meera Balarajan, *Exceptional People: How Migration Shaped our World and Will Define our Future*.   Princeton: Princeton University Press, 2011)   Judith Brown, in her work *Global South Asians*, provides an example of a theory which is primarily focused on the process of becoming a diaspora through the three step process of establishing new homes and social networks, relating to public life and geography of their new home, and reestablishing their links with their old homeland (Brown: 2007, 173-174).   Bibliography reference: Judith M. Brown, *Global South Asians: Introducing the Modern Diaspora*, (New Delhi: Cambridge University Press, 2007).

[250] Brettell, C. B. and Hollifield, J. F. , eds., *Migration Theory: Talking Across Disciplines*, 2nd Edition (New York and London: Routledge, 2007).

Interdisciplinary Research Methodology and Diaspora Missiology

By nature and necessity, diaspora missiology is to be interdisciplinary in its approach for studying the phenomenon of diaspora. In research conducted on diaspora missiology and diaspora missions, the interdisciplinary approach utilizes more than one discipline and maximizes the advantage of each of the multiple methods employed to study the complex phenomena of diaspora in order to discover emerging challenges and opportunities. Various methodologies and research approaches are used to collect factual data, formulate mission strategy, conduct strategic planning, and draft/implement ministry plans.[251]

There are two ways to employ interdisciplinary research methodology to conduct research in diaspora missiology: (a) integration of multi-disciplinary theory/methodology by a single researcher/ author, and (b) collaboration of researchers, teaming up together to complement one and other with their expertise on a specific aspect of diaspora missiology.[252] We will illustrate each approach with one publication by Christian researchers below.

An example of (a) category above is: *Strangers Next Door: Immigration, Migration and Mission* by J.D. Payne (InterVarsity Press, 2012) who has successfully combined biblical-theological reflection (chapters 4-5), historical review (chapter 6), demographic data (chapters 2-3, 7-8), ethnographic description (chapter 9), and missiological strategizing (chapters 10-13) in a single volume. Payne is to be credited for informing readers "what" opportunities created by global migration, inspiring them by the real-life stories then strategize "how" to take action locally to engage in global mission. It is a good case study of "glocal" mission in diaspora missiology.

An earlier publication in diaspora missiology (an example of category "b" above) is: *Scattered: The Filipino Global Presence* (Pantoja, Tira and Wan 2004) – a compendium volume of the Filipino Diaspora and Missions

---

[251] Research methods (both quantitative and qualitative) and research approaches (e.g. field work, case studies, statistics, surveys, and action research) may be combined to collect factual data (in demographics, ethnography, comparative religions and worldview analysis), and to formulate mission strategy (e.g. evangelism, church planting, discipleship programs), to conduct strategic planning (e.g., church multiplication, leadership development) and to draft/and/implement ministry plans in terms of church multiplication, leadership development and drafting/implementing ministry plans.

[252] *The Human Tidal Wave*, (Manila: Lifechange Publishing, Inc., 2013.) edited by Sidiri Joy Tira is a significant recent publication in the genre of diaspora missiology by evangelical Christians. However, it is not used as an example for this discussion for it is neither "group specific" nor advancing the understanding of a specific aspect of diaspora missiology; a collection of papers from specialists of several disciplines that describe the general phenomenon of diaspora. It "is a continuation of a discussion highlighted at the Third Lausanne Congress for World Evangelization (Lausanne III) held in Cape Town, South Africa from October 17-24, 2010. " (Tira 2013:ix).

Consultation held at the campus of Torch Trinity Graduate School of Theology, April 2004. It is a publication resulted from group-specific research[253] on Filipino diaspora, conducted by practitioners and scholars - ranging from field workers, mission executive, pastor, journalist, government official, evangelist, etc. with specialization in various fields such as anthropology, geography, ESL, theology, missiology, etc.   It was endorsed by Christian leaders, e.g. Ralph Winter, George Verwer, Paige Patterson, Paul Cedar and an one-page "Message" from Her Excellency Gloria Macapagal-Arroyo – President, Republic of the Philippines. It is a pioneer publication advancing the field of diaspora missiology for it was officially presented on stage then freely distributed to all participants of the 2004 Forum for World Evangelization, sponsored by Lausanne in Pattaya, Thailand.

Another group-specific, collaborative study by researchers of various backgrounds is the publication on Korean diaspora, *21C New Nomad Era and Migrant Mission*,[254] which is a collection of research findings of contributors who integrated methodologies from demographic studies, sociology, anthropology, theology, missiology, etc.

---

[254]Park, Chan-Sit and Noah Jung, eds. *21C New Nomad Era and Migrant Mission*. Seoul: Christianity and Industrial Society Research Institute, 2010.

Figure 10.1 Migration Theories across Disciplines
(Brettell and Hollified 2007:199)

DISCIPLINE	RESEARCH QUESTION(S)	LEVELS/ UNITS OF ANALYSIS	DOMINANT THEORIES	SAMPLE HYPOTHESIS
Anthropology	How does migration effect cultural change and affect ethnic identity?	Micro/ individuals, households, groups	Relational or structuralist and transnational	Social networks help maintain cultural difference.
Demography	How does migration affect population change?	Macro/ populations	Rationalist (borrows heavily from economics)	Migration has a major impact on size, but a small impact on age structure.
Economics	What explains the propensity to migrate and its effects?	Micro/ individuals	Rationalist: cost-benefit and utility-maximizing behavior	Incorporation varies with the level of human capital of immigrants.
Geography	What explains the spatial patterns of migration?	Macro, meso, & micro/individuals, households & groups	Relational, structural, and transnational	Incorporation depends on ethnic networks and residential patterns.
History	How do we understand the immigrant experience?	Micro/individuals and groups	Eschews theory and hypothesis testing	Wan and Le (Spring 2014)[255]
Law	How does the law influence migration?	Macro and micro/ the political and legal system	Institutionalist and rationalist (borrows from all the social sciences)	Rights create incentive structures for migration and incorporation.
Political Science	Why do states have difficulty controlling migration?	More macro/political and international systems	Institutionalist and rationalist	States are often capture by pro-immigrant interests.
Sociology	What explains incorporation and exclusion?	Macro/ethnic groups and social class	Structuralist or institutionalist	Incorporation varies with social and human capital.

---

[255] Enoch Wan and Thanh Trung Le. *Mobilizing Vietnamese Diaspora for the Kingdom.* (forth coming, Spring 2014)

Figure 10.2 Interdisciplinary Research Methodology - "Missions *to* the Diaspora"

#	RESEARCH QUESTION	DISCIPLINE	METHODOLOGY	SAMPLE
1	Where are they and how they got there?	- demography - ethno-history	demographic, diachronic, migrant/immigrant studies	Scattered 2004:5-36,[256] Remigio[257]
2	What is their ethnographic profile and social status?	- anthropology - sociology	ethnographic, sociological, case study, field work,	Edu-Bekoe & Wan 2013[258] Adeney[259]
3	How to practice the Great Commandment (pre-evangelism)?	- social work, - holistic missions	community development, holistic mission	De Haan[260]
4	How do we evangelize them?	- missiology	Evangelism	Wan 2003[261] Seim[262]
5	How do we disciple the new converts?	- practical theology	Discipleship	Park & Jung 2010:217-226[263]
6	How do we organize them into worshipping community/ congregation?	- pastoral - theology, - missiology	Leadership development, church planting/ multiplication	Park & Jung 2010:123-148.[264] Edu-Bekoe & Wan 2013

---

[256] Amador A. Remigio, Jr., "A Demographic Survey of the Filipino Diaspora," in *Scattered: The Filipino Global Presence*, eds. Lius Pantoja, Jr., Sadiri Joy Tira, and Enoch Wan (Manila: Life Change Publishing, 2004), 5-36.

[257] Remigio, Amador A. "Global Migration and Diasporas: A Geographical Perspective." IN The Human Tidal Wave, by Sadiri Joy Tira. Manila: Lifechange Publishing, Inc., 2013.

[258] Yaw Attah Edu-Bekoe and Enoch Wan. *Scattered Africans Keep Coming*. 2013 (www.amazon.com)

[259] Adeney, Miriam. "Colorful Initiatives: North American Diasporas in Mission." IN The Human Tidal Wave, by Sadiri Joy Tira. Manila: Lifechange Publishing, Inc., 2013.

[260] Charlene de Haan, *A Canadian Case Study in Diaspora Missiology*, accessed September 23, 2009; available at http://www.lausanneworldpulse.com/perspectives.php.

[261] Enoch Wan, The Chinese Diaspora – A Case Study of Migration & Mission," *Missiology*. 31, no. 1: 35. Pasadena, CA, 2003a. Accessed January 31, 2011; available at http://www.missiology.org/new/wp-content/uploads/2011/01/ChineseDiaspora-Missiology.pdf

[262] Seim, Brian. "Diaspora and the Megacities: A Narrative Mode." IN *The Human Tidal Wave*, by Sadiri Joy Tira. Manila: Lifechange Publishing, Inc., 2013.

[263] Yeong Ae Kim, "Ammi Mission Fellowship" in *21C New Nomad Era and Migrant Mission* ed. Chan-Sik Park and Noah Jung (Seoul, Korea: Christianity and Industrial Society Research Institute, 2010), 217-224

[264] Young-Sang Ro, *The Ecclesiastical Approach for the Integration of Multicultural Society: Intercultural 'Unity in Diversity' in the Multiethnic Ministry,* " in *21C New Nomad Era and Migrant Mission*. Seoul: Christianity and Industrial Society Research Institute, by Park, Chan-Sit and Noah Jung, eds.2010, 123-148.

Figure 10.3 Interdisciplinary Research Methodology for "Missions *through* the Diaspora"

#	RESEARCH QUESTION(S)	DISCIPLINE	METHODOLOGY	SAMPLE
1	How to gage their spirituality & nurture them towards spiritual maturity?	Pastoral	Spiritual formation, Quantitative/ qualitative	Wan & Gross 2008[265] Org, Harvey 2013[266]
2	How to motivate them individually and institutionally to fulfill the Great Commission by evangelizing their kinsmen in their homeland?	Theology of mission	Didactic	Wan & Tira, *Mission Practices*, 2009. pp 231-235.
3	How to mobilize them individually and institutionally to fulfill the Great Commission by evangelizing their kinsmen in their homeland?	missiology	Case study Field research Action research	Park & Jung 2010. pp 282 – 290.
4	How to motivate them individually and institutionally to fulfill the Great Commission by evangelizing their kinsmen elsewhere?	missiology	Case study Field research Action research	Wan 2010. Korean Diaspora Forum.
5	How to mobilize them individually and institutionally to fulfill the Great Commission by evangelizing their kinsmen elsewhere?	missiology	Action research	Thomas, Wan, & Tira. Presentation at LCWE III. Tira 2013

---

[265] Wan, Enoch & Linda Gross. "Christian Missions to Diaspora Groups: A Diachronic General Overview and Synchronic Study of Contemporary U.S." *Global Missiology* vol. 3, no. 2 (2008). Available at www.GlobalMissiology.org

[266] Harvey, Thomas Alan. "Pluralism, Multiculturalism, and the Diaspora Mission: Discovering the Relevance of Apostolic Mission Today." in *The Human Tidal Wave*, by Sadiri Joy Tira. Manila: Lifechange Publishing, Inc., 2013.

Figure 10.4 Interdisciplinary Research Methodology for "Missions *by and beyond* the Diaspora"

#	RESEARCH QUESTION(S)	DISCIPLINE	METHODOLOGY	SAMPLE PUBLICATION
1	How to find out if they have acquired language facility, cultural sensitivity and relational competency in the adopted country?	Linguistics Anthropology Sociology	Ethnography Field research	*Scattered* 2004, pp. 251-271.
2	How to help them improve their language facility, cultural sensitivity and relational competency in the adopted country?	Missiology Anthropology Psychology	Relational approach Cross-cultural orientation	Wan & Tira, *Mission Practices*, 2009. pp 236-241.
3	How to motivate them individually and institutionally to engage in cross-cultural missions in the host society?	Practical theology Missiology	Cross-cultural communication	Wan. *Transformation*, Jan 2011, 28 (1) 3-13.
4	How to mobilize them individually and institutionally to engage in cross-cultural missions in the host society?	Practical theology Missiology	Cross-cultural evangelism	Adelaja, Sunday. *Church Shift*, 2008. Thanh Le, 2014[267]
5	How to motivate/mobilize them individually and institutionally to engage in cross-cultural missions elsewhere?	Practical theology Missiology	Network study Cross-cultural evangelism Partnership	Tira, *The Floating Communities*[268] Tira's dissertation[269]

---

[267] Thanh Trung Le, "A Missiological Study of Vietnamese diaspora," Unpublished dissertation, Western Seminary, 2013, chapter 3.

[268] Sidiri Joy Tira, Tira, "*The Floating Communities,*" http://conversation lausanne.org/en/conversations/detail/10178 (accessed 2.13.11)

[269] Sidiri Joy Tira, Tira, "Diaspora Missiology: An Ethnographic Study of Filipino Kingdom Workers An enthographic study," Unpublished dissertation, Western Seminary, 2008.

Figure 10.5 Interdisciplinary Research Methodology for "Missions *with* the Diaspora"[270]

#	RESEARCH QUESTION(S)	DISCIPLINE	METHODOLOGY	SAMPLE PUBLICATION
1	Who and where are the diaspora groups?	Demographics	Ethnography Surveys	Camarota 2002[271] Remigio[272]
2	How and why did they migrate?	Ethno-history	Ethnography	Boosahda 2003[273]
3	How big is the family? Is it spread across natal lands and in the diaspora as well? To what extent does the family uphold group solidarity and obligation?	Cultural Anthropology, Network Theory	Ethnography Interviews, Archival Research	Patai, Raphael, 2007[274] Cooke & Lawrence 2005[275]
4	What are the bridges and barriers in evangelism?	Missiology, History	Cross-cultural evangelism	Parshall, *Muslim Evangelism*, 2003[276]
5	How does one engage, build relationship and then use these relationships to go overseas?	Missiology, Evangelism, Relational-Paradigm	Network study Cross-cultural evangelism Partnership	Tira's dissertation (chapter 7)[277] Thanh Le, 2014 (chapter 3)[278]

---

[270] Adapted from dissertation in progress: Jacques Hebért, *A New Strategy for Sending Exogenous Missionaries to the Arab Muslim Context: A Diaspora Model*, Western Seminary. For detailed discussion on the "with" strategy in Chapter 8 as presented by Jacques Hebért.

[271] Camarota, Steven A. *Immigrants from the Middle East: A Profile of the Foreign-born Population from Pakistan to Morocco* . Washington D. C.: Center for Immigration Studies, 2002.

[272] Amador A. Remigio, Jr., "A Demographic Survey of the Filipino Diaspora," in *Scattered: The Filipino Global Presence*, eds. Lius Pantoja, Jr., Sadiri Joy Tira, and Enoch Wan (Manila: Life Change Publishing, 2004), 5-36.

[273] Boosahda, Elizabeth. *Arab-American Faces and Voices: The Origins of an Immigrant Community*. Austin: The University of Texas Press, 2003.

[274] Patai, Raphael. *The Arab Mind*. Rev. ed. Tucson: Recovery Resources Press, 2007.

[275] Cooke, Miriam and Bruce B Lawrence, *Muslim Networks: from Hajj to Hip Hop*. Chapel Hill: The University of North Carolina Press, 2005.

[276] Parshall, Phil. *Muslim Evangelism: Contemporary Approaches to Contextualization*. Rev. Ed. Colorado Spring: Biblica, 2003.

[277] Sidiri Joy Tira, Tira, "Diaspora Missiology: An Ethnographic Study of Filipino Kingdom Workers An enthographic study," Unpublished dissertation, Western Seminary, 2008.

[278] Thanh Trung Le, "A Missiological Study of Vietnamese diaspora," Unpublished dissertation, Western Seminary, 2013, chapter 3.

However, this type of research is conducted at the level of trans-disciplinary and multidisciplinary approach or with "mixed methods."[279] It is not conducted at the higher level of integrative study (see Wan, 1998, 2003, 2009[280] and van Kerkhoff, L. 2005[281]).

The five figures provide examples of the application of the interdisciplinary research on diaspora ministry and diaspora missions. Selected sample publications are listed to illustrate how interdisciplinary research methodology have been used by researchers in studying the five approaches of diaspora missiology, i.e. "missions *to* the diaspora," "missions *through* the diaspora," "missions *by/beyond* the diaspora" and "missions *with* the diaspora."

Summary

The complex nature of the diaspora phenomenon necessitates the use of combined methods across disciplines in conducting research in diaspora missiology. Many researchers have found the interdisciplinary methodology essential in the study of diaspora missiology in order to be comprehensive in scope, holistic in perspective and innovative in approach. Sample publications listed in the figures above are illustrative of the use of interdisciplinary methodology in researching and strategizing for "missions *to* the diaspora," "missions *through* the diaspora," "missions *by/beyond* the diaspora," and "missions *with* the diaspora."

---

[279] John W. Creswell, *Research Design: Qualitative, Quantitative, and Mixed Methods Approaches*, 2nd ed. (Thousand Oaks: Sage, 2003).
[280] Enoch Wan, "The Paradigm and Pressing Issues of Interdisciplinary Research Methodology," an unpublished paper presented at the 50th Anniversary of the Evangelical Theological Society, Radisson Twin Towers, Orlando, Florida, November 19-21, 1998, Published as "The Paradigm and Pressing Issues of Inter-disciplinary Research Methodology," *Global Missiology* (January 2005a), available at www.GlobalMissiology. org.; "Rethinking Missiological Research Methodology: Exploring a New Direction," *Global Missiology* October 2003b; available at www.GlobalMissiology.org. Wan 2003; Enoch Wan, "Core Values of Mission Organization in the Cultural Context of the 21st Century," *Global Missiology*, January 2009b, available at www.GlobalMissiology.org
[281] Lorrae van Kerkhoff, "Strategic Integration: The Practical Politics of Integrated Research in Context," *Journal of Research Practice*, 1(2), Article M5. Accessed February 24, 2011; available at http://jrp.icaap.org/index.php/jrp/article/view/14/24.

Part 4
PRACTICE

Diaspora missions is a new strategy for opportunities created by the demographic reality of diaspora in the twenty-first century. Part 4 includes an overview on the history of Christian missions and a proposal for new strategies in response to the phenomenon of diaspora.

Chapter 11

Diachronic Overview of Christian Missions to Diaspora Groups

Enoch Wan

Introduction

In this chapter, a simple theological reflection on diaspora reported in the Bible is followed by a diachronic overview of Christian missions to diaspora groups in eight periods in the history of Christianity.

Diasporas in the Bible

On the surface and from a human perspective, it is tragic for diaspora groups to leave the familiarity and security of their homeland in exchange for a sojourner's hardship abroad. Yet nothing that happens in life (both fortunate and unfortunate) escapes the sovereignty of God, as Joseph reflected on his diaspora experience in Egypt (Gen 45:1-6), and as found in the conviction of the apostle Paul (Acts 17:26-28; Rom 8:28; 11:17-26). The figures below identify some biblical patterns of the scattering and gathering of God's people in the Bible.[282]

---

[282] These figures were presented in lectures delivered in the Philippines in 2005 and later under the title "Korean Diaspora: From Hermit Kingdom to Kingdom Ministry" at the Korean Diaspora Forum, May 18-21, 2010e, Seoul, Korea, Available at
http://www.enochwan.com/english/articles/pdf/Korean%20Diaspora_2010.pdf

Figure 11.1 Scattering (Dispersion) in the Old Testament

#	WHO/WHEN	SIGNIFICANCE			
		WHERE	CAUSE	NOTE	SIGN
1	Adam & Eve, after the Fall (Gen 3:22-24)	From the Garden of Eden	Rebellion & pride	- provision - position of bliss - presence of God	- sweat & toil - child birth - power relationship
2	Cain, after murdering Abel (Gen 4:14-17)	From the presence of Jehovah	Envy & pride	- son Enoch built a city	- spare of his life promised
3	Noah & family, after the flood (Gen 9:1-7)	From the temporary shelter of the ark	Life spared due to obedience	- blessings reassured - post-flood promise	- rainbow
4	Post-plotting & rebellion (Gen 11:1-9)	From the Tower of Babel	Uniformity desired	- confusion of tongues (Gen 10:2-5, 20,31)	- Tower of Babel
5	Chastisement forewarned (Prophetic books of OT)	From the promised land	Idolatry, not obedient	Scattered all over the world	Diaspora

Figure 11.2 Gathering (Calling) in the Old Testament

#	WHO/WHERE	SIGNIFICANCE		
		POSTERITY/ PROSPERITY	LAND	RELATIONSHIP (COVENANT)
1	Bringing Eve to Adam (Gen 2:22)	Blessed with "help-meet" (Gen 2:18-21)	"be fruitful & multipl, rule & sumdue"	Wholenss: "2 shall become 1" (Gen 2:23-24)
2	Calling Noah to the Ark (Gen 8, 9) = temporary shelter	Blessings (Gen 9:1-7)	Fill the land (Gen 9:1, 7)	Rainbow as sign (Gen 9:8-19)
3	Abraham from kindred... (Gen 12:1-3; 15:1-7; 17:1-8)	- nation, name, blessings	Will show you (Gen 12:1, 15:7-8, 17:8)	Circumcision as sign (Gen 17:9-14)
4	- Lot & family from Sodom (Gen 18:1-33) - Isaac (Gen 21:12; 22:16-18; 26:24) - Jacob (Gen 28:13-15) - Calling out from Egypt	- Great & mighty nation, lessons (Gen 18:16-19; 22:17-18) - Isaac (Gen 21:12) - Jacob (Gen 28:4) - free from slavery	The earth, returned to his place (Gen 17:8, 8:25,33; 28:15,33)	Covenant (Gen 17:1-8; 26:24; Exodus 2:24-25)
5	Joshua gathering Isrealites to enter Canaan (Joshua)	Rest (Heb 11, Lev 26:9)	Provided land (Lev 26:6)	City (Heb 11:13-16) Heavenly Jerusalem (Heb 12:18-29)
6	Gathering the remnant	From captivity	Promise land (Deut 28:8-11)	Promising future gathering: Deut 28:7

Figure 11.3 Scattering (Dispersion) in the New Testament

#	WHO/WHERE	SIGNIFICANCE PERSECUTION & HARDSHIP	WHEN
1	Jews from Jerusalem (Acts 8:1-8); Stephen's martyrdom	(Acts 11:19-21)	AD 32
2	Jews from Jerusalem; Persecution from Saul	(Acts 9:1-2)	AD 33
3	Jews from Rome (Acts 18:1-4)	King Herod	AD 46
4	Not of this world (John 18:23-36); Jews from Athens to Corinth (Acts 18:1-4)	Claudius	AD 50
5	Jews in Jerusalem	The fall of Jerusalem	AD 70*

*Mt 14:1-2; 1 Pet (AD 64) and 2 Pet (AD 66)

Figure 11.4 Gathering (Calling, Covenant, Ecclesiology) in the New Testament

#	WHO/WHERE	SIGNIFICANCE
1	John the Baptist (Luke 7:24-35; 16:16)	Announcing the coming of the Kingdom
2	- Calling of the 12 (Mt 11:1-11) - Calling of the 70 (Luke 10:1-20) - Parable of the Kingdom (Mt 13; Mt 15:7-14)	Power demonstrated (Mt 14:15-21; John 6:1-14; Luke 9:1-17;) People being called (1 Cor 2:1-5)
3	- Calling children (Mt 19:1315) banquet (Mt 22:1-14) sinners (Mk 2:13-17; Luke 5:27-32) - Seek Kingdom (Luke 12;29-32) amidst you (Luke 17:21)	Not of this world (John 18:23-36) Disciples fought (Mt 18:1-5; Mk 9:33-37; Luke 9:46-48), James & John (Mt 20:22-24; Mk 10:20-24); at Passover (Luke 22:24-30), Ascension (Acts 1:3-6)
4	The Pentecost (Acts 2)	Reverse of Tower of Babel (Gen 11) The "Church"—called out ones (1 Cor 11:18; 12;28; Acts 15:30h)
5	- Calling of the elect (Mk 13:24-30; John 11:47-53; Ro 9-11) - Kingdom of Christ (the *eschaton*)	-Gathering Jews – 1948; - futher gathering (Ro 9-11); - New heaven & new earth, perfect (Rev 21)

The figures above show the biblical basis of diaspora missiology in both the Old and New Testaments. Theologically, we can see the hand of God scattering many diaspora groups abroad for Kingdom purposes.

"Scattering" in the Old Testament has not always been the consequence of sin. In fact, it was God's design that human kind should scatter. Scattering was actually a blessing from Jehovah before the Fall (Gen 1:26-28). The same blessing was reaffirmed to Noah after the flood (Gen 9:1, 7). Refusing to do so was to be rebellious against God, as seen in the incident of the Tower of Babel and the building of city (Genesis 11:1-9). The consequence was thus judgment from God (Gen 11:1-9)

There were times when scattering of people in the Old Testament was the consequence of sin. This is shown after the fall of man in the Garden of Eden (Gen 3:22-24), the murderous act of Cain against his brother (Genesis 4:13-15) and the Tower of Babel (Genesis 11), and the idolatry practice of the Israelites (Ps 78:54-64; Is 1-5).

The Great Commission is God's design for Christians in the New Testament "to scatter" and to bear the good news to all nations (Matthew 28:18-20; Mark 16:15-17; Luke 24:46-49; John 17:18; Acts 1:8). Failing to do so would incur punishment of being forced to scatter (Acts 9, 11). Thus the "scattering" of Christians could be God's provision for outreach and church planting (Acts 18; 1 Peter and 2 Peter.)

"Calling" in the Old Testament is God's way of gathering his chosen people, e.g. Noah (Genesis 7–8; Hebrews 11:7), Abraham (Genesis 12, 14, 17; Hebrews 11:8-12), Isaac (Genesis 21), Jacob (Genesis 28), the Israelites (Book of Joshua, Hebrews 11), the remnant (Is 40–45), and the church (Ephesians 1–2; 1 Peter 2:1-11). The calling of people unto Himself is an act of grace.

Due to the limitation of this study, detailed explanation and discussion on God's sovereignty and human tragedy of diaspora in Christian missions is not included here. Readers can refer to "Diasporas and God's Mission: A Position Paper," by Lausanne Diasporas Leadership Team.[283]

Selected Precedents of Diaspora in the Bible

Many cases of diaspora are found in the Bible, e.g., Abraham the wanderer from Ur to Egypt and Canaan; Joseph the slave boy from homeland to Egypt, then eventually became the prime minister there; Daniel being taken from his homeland as a captive but turned into a court official in Babylon; Ruth left her homeland and renounced the Moabite god of Chemosh. She was committed to

---

[283] This position paper drafted by Enoch Wan and Elias Medeiros in 2009 was included in the book *"Scattered to Gather: Embracing the Global Trend of Diaspora"* distributed at Lausanne, Cape Town, 2010.

DIACHRONIC OVERVIEW OF CHRISTIAN MISSIONS TO DIASPORA GROUPS

follow her mother-in-law, Naomi, and Naomi's God, the God of Israel.[284] Ruth left her people and eventually also left her people's god.

The story of Priscilla and Aquila is a case study of diaspora missions.[285] They were a Jewish couple on the move: from Pontus to Rome, to Corinth, to Ephesus, and back to Rome. They started out as political refugees from Rome but ended up as church planters in three cities: Corinth, Ephesus, and Rome (Wan 2007a). When they were forced out of Rome under the anti-Sematic law imposed by Claudius (Acts 18:1-2), they took up residence in Corinth. There they hosted the Apostle Paul for 18 months when he was on his second missionary journey (Acts 18:4-11). Afterwards, the couple accompanied Paul to Ephesus where Paul left them for Antioch (Acts 18:18-22). They stayed in Ephesus, where eventually a church emerged, of which they served as founding members. In Ephesus they opened their home to receive another diaspora Jew from Alexandria, Apollos, who was "an eloquent man, and mighty in the scriptures… being fervent in the spirit" (Acts 18:24-25). In their home they provided personal coaching to Apollos because his teaching was limited to "the baptism of John."

In a string of personal greetings in Romans 16, the Apostle Paul made reference to Priscilla and Aquila as "my helpers in Christ Jesus" (Ro 16: 3). Paul used strong language to recount the couple's remarkable ministry to him (Ro 16:3-4). In addition to their labor with apostle Paul in the founding of the churches in Corinth and Ephesus, they later started a house church in their home in Rome (Ro 16:5). This is the consistent pattern of their faithful gospel ministry and church planting effort during their years in diaspora.[286]

The characteristics of Priscilla and Aquila as a diaspora couple are listed as follows:
1. Ready to be mobile for the sake of the gospel while on the move: in Pontus, Rome, Corinth, Ephesus and Rome.
2. Adaptable to circumstances and willing to play multiple roles for the gospel, i.e., tent-making, hosting missionary Paul, coaching Apollos, etc.
3. Faithful and sacrificial service in life-threatening circumstances.

---

[284] Neill, Stephen, *A History of Christian Missions* (New York: Penguin Books, 1986), 13.
[285] Enoch Wan, "Diaspora Couple Priscilla and Aquila: A Model Family in Action for Missions," April 2009, www.GlobalMissiology.org; Originally published in Chinese, *Great Commission Bi-monthly*, vol. 79, April 2009).
[286] For details on this diaspora couple, see Enoch Wan, "A Missio-Relational Reading of Romans," EMS *Occasional Bulletin* Winter 2010e.

Diaspora Groups in the History of Christianity

The face of Christianity has been changing over its twenty-one centuries of existence. It started as a small Jewish sect and has grown to claim over two billion adherents today. And the influence of Christianity has spread from Jerusalem to the rest of the world through various diaspora groups in different periods in history. The following is a brief recount of eight diaspora groups in the history of Christianity: the early church, the apostolic age, the first 500 years, the dark ages, the medieval world, the age of discovery, protestant precursor to missions, and the great century and beyond.

The Early Church

On the day of Pentecost, thousands of Jews traveled to Jerusalem and received Jesus Christ as their Messiah (Acts 2). These Jewish believers of the early Church were the first diaspora people in the Christian world to be dispersed by persecution. After they were scattered, they embraced this opportunity to preach the gospel throughout the Roman Empire.

The Apostolic Age

The period following the ascension of Jesus Christ may be labeled as the Apostolic Age, the initial period of Christian missions. It was characterized by both the apostles and ordinary Jewish believers spreading the good news of salvation in Jesus Christ.[287]

In that period, Christians were dispersed from Jerusalem to Judea, Samaria, and other parts of the earth. They were diaspora people serving the Lord as He guided their journeys from place to place. This was the pattern of evangelism outlined by Jesus in Acts 1:8. In Antioch the first believers were gentiles, not Jewish proselytes. Therefore they were called Christians to be distinguished from a sect of Judaism (Acts 11; Moreau 2011: 439-440).

The Apostle Paul and Barnabas preached the gospel in other parts of the world during their missionary journeys. Paul went to the Jews first, then to the Gentiles. The Pax Romana prepared the political environment and facilitated travel to major commercial and government centers (Moreau 2011:440). The Apostolic Age saw the gospel sent out through diaspora people to various parts of the known world.

Methods in missions that characterized this time period were focused on the apostles' preaching, teaching and the forming of house-churches in homes of Christians.

---

[287] Acts 6:8-8:9ff; 13:6ff; 16:16ff.

DIACHRONIC OVERVIEW OF CHRISTIAN MISSIONS TO DIASPORA GROUPS

The First 500 Years

In this period, the gospel spread quickly from its original location to the Orient (including India), then the West (Europe and the British Isles), and then southward to Egypt and North Africa. Christianity became the dominant religion of the Roman Empire during this period.[288]

Missiologically, during this period, the Christian faith was spread throughout the Roman Empire by diaspora people groups away from their homelands. Their mission efforts were facilitated by local Christians and government leaders, and through commercial contacts and marriages (Terry 1998: 441).

The Dark Ages: 500–1215 A.D.

During this period, the church continued to grow and expanded into new areas including Russia, Moravia, Eastern Europe, Great Britain, continental Europe, and Scandinavia. The Nestorians were the first ones to introduce Christianity to China and Asia. In spite of their heretical doctrines, the Nestorians did gain some temporary favor due to their monastic nature, which was comparable to the Buddhist monastic lifestyle in China.[289]

Challenges of this period included schism in the Eastern church and the irruption of Islam (Terry 1998:187). As a result, many were forced to give up their Christian faith. Other influences leading to Christian apostasy were the social, economic, political, military, and religious pressures from Muslims who dwelled among Christians in North Africa. Under these pressures, many abandoned their superficial commitment to Christ and converted to Islam with devotion to Allah.

In response to the Islamic victories, Crusades were launched to reclaim the Holy Land from Islamic control and to restore the Eastern church into the fellowship. Christianity suffered irreparable damage caused by the brutal conflict between the Crusaders and Islamic forces. The Crusades left a deep and lasting rift between the Islamic world and the Christian church that continues even today. Subsequently, the church fell into a morally low ebb, characterized by cruelty and savagery in its missionary strategy (Terry 1998: 187-188).

In spite of these conflicts, the Christian church continued to grow. Lessons learned from the Dark Ages can shed light on missiological strategies in

---

[288] John Mark Terry, *Missiology: An Introduction*, (B&H Academic, 1998), 183.
[289] Ibid. and Terry, 184-188.

evangelizing the Muslim diaspora in present time. The following are some suggestions:

- Praying and looking to the Lord's leadership in becoming all things to these people.
- Representing Christ the True Savior and God, in hopes that some would be saved (1 Corinthians 10:33).
- Carefully grounding new converts in the Lord.
- Avoid forcing or coercing anyone to follow Jesus Christ as their Lord and Savior.
- Allowing the Spirit of God to do his part when missionaries are to be prepared to do their part.

The Medieval World: 1215–1650 A.D.

By this time, Muslims had gained such strong control over the Middle East that only a remnant of Christians remained. Although Christianity in India and Ethiopia was visible and functional, the work begun by the Nestorians in China was suppressed and had seemingly come to an end, because the time for the gospel in Asia had not yet arrived (Moreau 2010: 442; Neill 80-83). The Crusades' attempts to convert residents in the Holy Land from Islam to Christianity by force resulted in the loss of many lives and brought in enmity between Muslims and Christians that still continues today (Moreau 2010:442).

During this period, some Franciscan missionaries went to China in response to the positive report by Marco Polo. An increased response to the hospel was seen for a brief period, and through the efforts of John of Monte Corvino 100,000 people in China turned to Christ. John of Marignolli took 33 friars from Italy with him to China and carried on the work for a short time, without replacement. Soon after this, in 1362, James of Florence, the Bishop of Zaitun, was martyred. Then in 1369 the last remnant of the Latins were expelled from Peking and China closed its doors to the gospel (Moreau 2010:442; Neill 1986: 107-109). Some of the insurmountable obstacles for Christian outreach in China included the use of Latin in Catholics masses and the imposition of foreign liturgical practices.

Age of Discovery, Reformation and Renaissance: 1215–1650 A.D.

By 1215 A.D. the Western Church, being Roman Catholic in form, had recovered from the Crusades to a great degree. Moreover, the Western church was at its height in both religious and political power. All temporal and spiritual matters were under the charge of the Roman Catholic Church. On the other hand, facing the challenges of Islam and the schism, the Eastern Church merely survived by holding on to a fortress mentality. The Western Church was prepared to reach out to its Eastern counterparts (Terry 1998:188-189).

DIACHRONIC OVERVIEW OF CHRISTIAN MISSIONS TO DIASPORA GROUPS

Martin Luther and other key leaders were credited for their leadership in the Reformation when Luther protested against the Catholic Church, and the Protestant movement was born. The Catholic Church responded by launching a counter-reformation. At the same time, Jesuits emerged as a new Catholic missionary order (Terry 1998:188-189).

On the Protestant side, it is puzzling that reformers such as Luther, Zwingli, Calvin and Knox showed little missionary zeal. Some scholars attribute this lack of interest in missions to the following factors:

1. The reformers believed that the Great Commission had been fulfilled by the Apostles in the Early Church. Such belief caused the Great Omission.
2. Establishing the Reformation involved a life-and-death struggle, and there was no room for missionary endeavor.
3. The Reformers were faulty in their provincial ecclesiology, known as "territorialism," which curtailed the broad view of universal missions.
4. The Reformers held to a faulty eschatology that they were the last generation before the return of Christ. Thus they believed that any missionary efforts at that point would be meaningless and futile (Terry 1998:194-195).

Protestant Precursors to Missions: 1650–1792 A.D.

Spiritual depth was lacking in the Protestant Church immediately after the Reformation. Reformers strived to survive and were distracted from thoughts of mission. However, renewal began with Philip Spencer who initiated pietistic practices in small prayer meetings and Bible study groups. These groups soon grew and spread. Subsequently, the Moravian Mission, the Wesleyan Revival, and the William Carey Baptist Missionary Society came into place. Three Anglican societies also rose in North America for outreach to the Native Americans. In fact, the work of these organizations later became the model for the William Carey Baptist Society. By now the stage was set for the next century when Christian missions blossom into a great expansion.

The Great Century and Beyond: 1792–1910[290]

This period of time was characterized by the expansion of Christianity around the world. Missions societies and organizations were formed in Europe and

---

[290] Terry, 199. *The Great Century* was coined by Kenneth Scott Latourette.

America. The mission work of these societies was missionary-directed, paternalistic, and financially subsidized.

By the late nineteenth century, Christian mission was typified by evangelism, individual conversion, church planting, social transformation, and outreach through education and medicine (Terry 1998:213). Regardless of criticisms directed against the nineteenth and twentieth century missions movements, God used brave heroes of the faith to extend the gospel worldwide (Terry 1998:217-218).

The four diagrams of this chapter (i.e.Figures 9.1, 9.2, 9.3, 9.4), are shown in the two composite frameworks in lineal and cyclical patterns below:

Figure 11.5   History of Humaity in Lineal Progression[291]

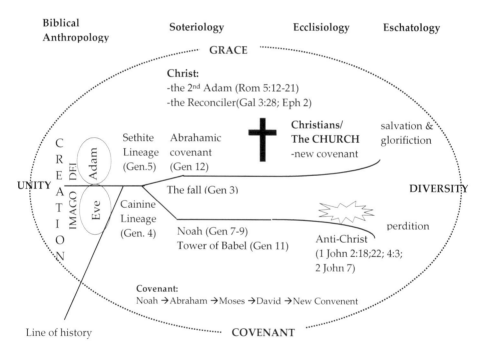

---

[291] Enoch Wan, Sino-theory: A That in the dispensation of the fulness of times he might gather together in one all things in Christ, both which are in heaven, and which are on earth; even in him:Survey Study, *Christian Communication Inc.* Canada 1999:220 (in Chinese)

DIACHRONIC OVERVIEW OF CHRISTIAN MISSIONS
TO DIASPORA GROUPS

Figure 11.6 Gathering and Scattering: Cyclical Development[292]

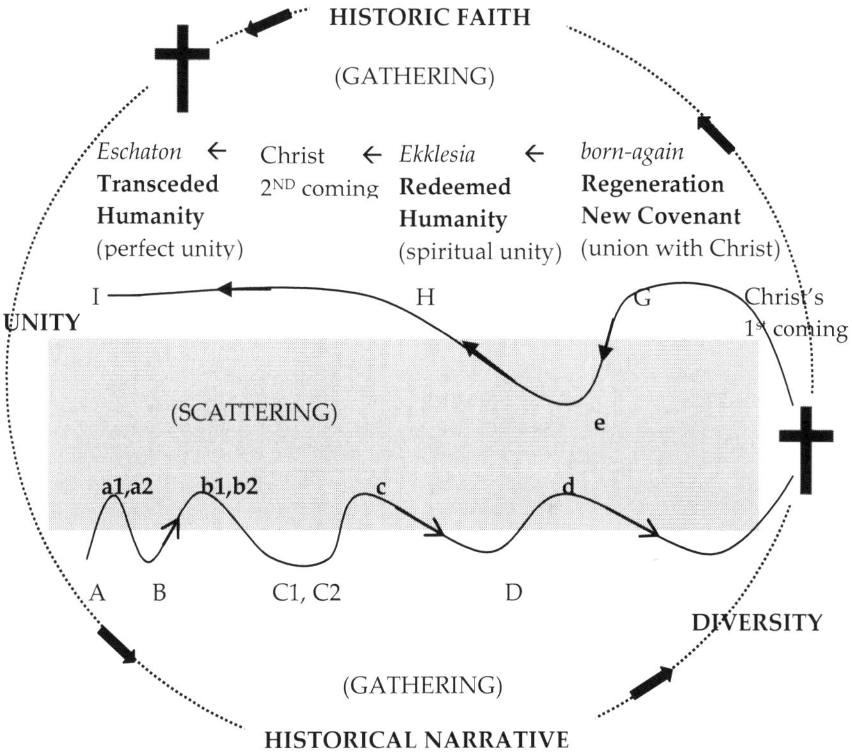

HISTORIC FAITH
(GATHERING)

Eschaton ← Christ ← *Ekklesia* ← *born-again*
Transceded 2ND coming **Redeemed** **Regeneration**
Humanity **Humanity** **New Covenant**
(perfect unity) (spiritual unity) (union with Christ)

I — H G Christ's
UNITY 1st coming

(SCATTERING)
e

a1,a2 b1,b2 c d

A B C1, C2 D

DIVERSITY

(GATHERING)
HISTORICAL NARRATIVE

---

[292] Adapted from Enoch Wan, Sino-theory: A Survey Study, *Christian Communication Inc.* Canada 1999:220 (in Chinese)

Key to Figure 11.6

 -- Scattering

Scattering - OT
- a1 – Adam and Eve scattered from the garden (Gen 3:22-24)
- a2 – Cain scattered from the presence of Jehovah (Gen 4:14-17)
- b1 – Noah and famiy from the temporary shelter after the flood (Gen 9:1-7)
- b2 – Mankind scattered from the city and the Tower of Babel (Gen 11:1-9)
- c- Joseph & Jacob scattered to Egypt (Gen 37-50)
- d- Isrealites scattered from promised land (AD 1948)

Scattering - NT
- e – Jews from Jerusalem (Acts 8:1-8) and from Rome (Acts 18:1-4)

Gathering - OT
- A – Bringing Eve to Adam (Gen 2:22)
- B – Brought Noah and household to the ark for temporary shelter(Gen 8,9)
- C1 –Called Abraham from country, kindred and father's household to Himself (Gen 12:1-3)
- C2 – Called Lot and household from Sodom (Gen 19)
- D – Joshua gathering Isrealites to enter Canaan (Joshus 1-13)

Gathering – NT
- E – John the Baptist calling for repentence to Jordon River (Lk 7)
- F – Jesus calling the 12, the 70, the chidren, sinners to Himself (Mt 11, 13, 19; Lk 10; Jn 7:37)
- G – Jews and god-fearers gathered in Jerusalem, the out-pouring of the HS = reversal of the Tower of Babel (Gen 11; Act 2)
- H – Calling of the elect (Mk 13:24-30; John 11:47-53; Ro 9-11);
  Ekklesia – spiritual unity & new humanity (Eph 1:10, 4:22-24; Col 3:9-11)
- I – Gathering in the New heaven and new earth,
  Eschaton - perect unity & transcended humanity (Rev 21)

Summary

In this chapter we engaged in brief theological reflections on gathering and scattering in the Old Testament and New Testament times, and presented a survey of precedents of gathering ans scattering historically. From the perspective of "unity" and "diversity," human historyhas been outlined in both lineal and cyclical patterns.

Chapter 12

Demographic Reality of Diaspora and the Strategy of Diaspora Missions

Enoch Wan

Introduction

The demographic trend of diaspora in the 21st century is indeed impressive for " More people than ever are living abroad. In 2013, 232 million people, or 3.2 per cent of the world's population, were international migrants, compared with 175 million in 2000 and 154 million in 1990."[293]

This chapter provides a description on the increasing scale, intensity, and frequency of the diaspora phenomenon, and to propose the practice of diaspora mission as a positive response. The content of this chapter is adapted from the following presentations by Enoch Wan:

1. "Global People and Diaspora Missiology," plenary session, "Tokyo 2010" on May 13, 2010, Global Mission Consultation.[294](2010b)
2. "Moving to Reach People on the Move," Multiplex session on October 20, 2010 at "Cape Town 2010"[295] (2010f)
3. "Moving to Reach People on the Move," Lausanne conversation (2010)[296] (2010g)
4. "The Global Status of Diaspora Ministry" in "Global Issues Update" at *Mission Exchange,* Web Seminar, January 2011, (see www.enochwan.com).[297] (2010h)

---

[293] For the UN report, see http://esa.un.org/unmigration/wallchart2013.htm (Accessed Dec. 20, 2013)
[294] The video clip of this presentation is available at http://www.enochwan.com/english/confvideos/index.html.
[295] The video is available at http://conversation.lausanne.org/en/conversations/detail/11438.
[296] Link at http://conversation.lausanne.org/en/conversations/detail/11438.

Globally, the United States remains the most popular destination and the new estimates of a recent UN report include breakdowns by region and country of destination and origin, and by sex and age as follows:

"The North, or developed countries, is home to 136 million international migrants, compared to 96 million in the South, or developing countries. Most international migrants are of working age (20 to 64 years) and account for 74 per cent of the total. Globally, women account for 48 per cent of all international migrants."[298]

More statistical data and demographic information on international migration can be obtained at the following web sites:

- http://www.gcim.org/policy-analysis-and-research-programm/policy-analysis-and-research-programm/
- http://www.ilo.org/
- http://www.imi.ox.ac.uk/
- http://www.imi.ox.ac.uk/projects/research-themes/transnationalism-and-diasporas
- http://www.un.org/esa/population/migration/
- http://isim.georgetown.edu/
- http://www.sourceoecd.org/database/16081269/intmigration
- http://ojs.GlobalMissiology.org/index.php/english/article/view/201/561/

Diaspora Missions – Strategic Response to Demographic Reality of Diasporas

More and more government officials and social scientists are paying attention to the demographic reality of diaspora for the reasons listed below:

"International migration is a global phenomenon that is growing in scope, complexity and impact. Today, virtually all countries in the world are simultaneously countries of destination, origin and transit for international migrants. Traditional migration patterns are complemented by new migratory flows, fuelled by changing economic, demographic, political and social conditions. Changing migration patterns affect the size and composition of migrant populations as well as economies and societies in countries of origin and destination. The rise in global mobility, the growing complexity of migratory patterns and the impact of such

---

[297] Webinar at https://netforum.avectra.com/eweb/shopping/shopping.aspx?site=exchange&shopsearch=diaspora&shopsearchcat=top%20100%20products&prd_key=1781ee1f-0ecd-446c-9898-b5eb7e7e6a12.

[298] See link: See link: http://esa.un.org/unmigration/wallchart2013.htm (Accessed Dec. 20, 2013)

movements on development have all contributed to international migration becoming a priority for the international community."[299] Missiologists are also to be observent to the demographic trend of diaspora though for a more noble reason , i.e. the Kingdom of God. Besides, people in transition are more receptive to the Gospel, thus providing us with opportunities as well as challenges in mission practice (Figure 12.1).

In the demograhpic reality of the 21st century, diaspora groups become "moving mission fields" as Escobar vividly describes.[300] Christian workers are to be mobile and adaptive. The priority of diaspora missions is every person outside the Kingdom everywhere; there is no difference between reaching out to Buddhists in New York or Thailand, Muslims in London or Iran, and communist Chinese in Africa or inside China. The theological assumption of diaspora missions is that it is God who determines where people will live at certain times so that wherever they are located; they can call upon God and find Him (Acts 17:26-28). Escobar (2003) has made this point clear in his book, *The New Global Mission: The Gospel from Everywhere to Everyone.*[301]

In diaspora situations among new comers, the disappearance of geographical barriers makes it possible to carry out missions in our neighborhoods, even to the unreached people groups in the post-Christian industrial west. Many diaspora communities have been reached by Christians who share the Gospel through practicing hospitality and charity in obedience to the Great Commandment. Other creative ways differing from the traditional "soil-based" church planting include bus churches for the diaspora in limited access contexts, and churches in the ocean aboard ships, cruise ships and ocean liners.

Diaspora and "Faith on the Move"

The dimensions of the connection, identity, affiliation, and practice the old religions by diaspora in the new homelands are not to be ignored. Warner and Wittner note:

---

[299] http://www.un.org/esa/population/meetings/twelfthcoord2014/twelfthcoord2014.htm

[300] J. Samuel Escobar "Mission Fields on the Move,"
- *Christianity Today*, April 27, 2010 http://www.christianitytoday.com/ct/2010/may/ Accessed Dec. 20, 2013.
- *Christianity Today*, The Global Conversation. [posted 4/27/2010 2:43PM] http://www.christianitytoday.com/globalconversation/ Accessed Dec. 20, 2013.

[301] Samuel Escobar, The New Global Mission: The Gospel from Everywhere to Everyone. InterVarsity 2003

> As religion becomes less taken for granted under the pluralistic and secular conditions prevailing in the United States, adherents become more conscious of their tradition and often more determined about its transmission. Religious identities nominally assigned at birth become objects of active persuasion.[302]

As the studies of migration and diaspora have been further developed, Pew Research Center has recently released two reports, *Faith on the Move: the Religious Affiliation of International Migrants* and *Rising Tide of Restrictions on Religion*, which focus globally on the impact that religion has in migration. These studies are global in their focus with data to support broad explanations about "why" and "where" people chose to migrate as it pertains to religion. These studies also provide some context to explain the phenomenon that the decline of Christianity in post-Christian western countries is slower than expected because of the high percentage of global diaspora are with Christian background:

- "75 percent of the global population lives in a country that is rated as politically or socially highly restrictive regarding religion" (Pew, *Rising Tide of Restrictions on Religion*, The Pew Forum on Religion and Public Life, September 2012, 9).
- This fact partially explains why 49% of the 214 million global diaspora are from a Christian background and why 69 % of Muslim immigrants, who comprise an additional 27% of the global diaspora, chose to immigrate "laterally" to the Middle East and North Africa (Pew, *Faith on the Move: The Religious Affiliation of International Migrants*, The Pew Forum on Religion and Public Life, March 2012, 11, 26).

The figure below is provided for those who prefer to view the data in diagram format.

---

[302] R. Stephen Warner; Judith G. Wittner. *Gatherings In Diaspora: Religious Communities and the New Immigration* (Kindle Locations 211-214). Kindle Edition 1998.

Figure 12.1 Religious composition of international migrants[303]

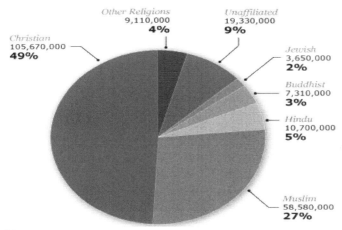

Note:
- Percentage and estimated no. of all migrants who belong to each religious group.
- Population estimates are rounded to ten thousands. Percentages are calculated from unrounded no. and may not add to 100 due to rounding.

Diaspora Missions in Action in the 21st Century

In recent years, diaspora missions initiatives are beginning to take place in churches, mission organizations, and theological institutions. A case in point is the Greenhills Christian Fellowship (GCF) in Toronto, Canada. The church is purposeful in reaching Filipino diaspora groups not only in Toronto but also in other provinces in Canada.[304]

Also in Toronto, Canada, a group of Christians called MoveIn took up residence in neighborhoods where many new immigrants live. With a cup of cold water in one hand and the good news in the other, they are praying that these communities will discover Christ's love. The MoveIn Christians hope that their presence in these neighborhoods will eventually result in churches being planted, missionaries being raised up, and God's Kingdom come upon them.

---

[303] From "*Faith on the Move: The Religious Affiliation of International Migrants,*" The Pew Forum on Religion and Public Life, March 2012, 11, 26 @
http://www.pewforum.org/2012/03/08/religious-migration-exec/ (Accessed Feb. 20, 2014)

[304] Use the link for details, accessed October 1, 2011; available at http://www.gcf.org.ph/pages/about/.

The vision of "diaspora missions" has slowly spread from churches in metropolitan areas to churches in rural areas. The Kelowna Alliance Church in British Columbia, Canada, for example, takes up the opportunity to reach out to the thousands of foreign workers arriving from Mexico to work in the vineyards and orchards in the Okanagan valley.

In 2007, the Filipino International Network (FIN) forged a partnership with Operation Mobilization, Campus Crusade for Christ, the Seamen's Christian Friends Society (ACAS), and the Alliance Graduate School for outreach ministry to Filipinos who work on ships. These Filipinos compose over 25% of the global marine workers. Since then, "churches on the ocean" have been planted on board of various kinds of ships for "people of the ocean." This is an illustration of the multi-directional and trans-national approach to diaspora church planting.

FIN also conducts ongoing evangelism and discipleship training with Campus Crusade for Christ in cities with large Filipino expatriate populations. One of these cities is Tokyo, Japan where close to 200 Filipino and some Brazilians have received training and have gone on to train others. Such is a demonstration of the diaspora missions force resulting in multiplication of disciples, illustrating cases of "missions through the diaspora and "missions by/beyond the diaspora ."

During the last two years, OMF (Overseas Missionary Fellowship) has developed a new department on diaspora missions with dozens of staff workers among diaspora groups; though primarily among Asian diaspora. Also during the period of 1970 to 1989 and in response to the reality of explosive Filipino diaspora as described below, the Philippine Missions Association (PMA) and the Philippine Council of Evangelical Churches (PCEC) were founded.

It had been said that one can find Filipinos in any part of the world as a result of the Filipino immigration. Starting in the mid 70s, Filipinos began immigrating due to employment opportunities in the Middle East. Pushed by the lack of employment at home, coupled with job openings abroad— particularly in Saudi Arabia and other neighboring Arab countries—skilled professional and technical workers started the Overseas Filipino Workers (OFW) phenomenon…As a result of this migration, Filipinos are now is settled in more than 180 countries. The number of Filipino workers is approaching 10 million, the bulk of whom are found in North America, the Middle East, Southeast Asia, Australia and New Zealand. Filipino labor migration began with 36,035 workers in 1975 and swelled to 598,760 in 1990. By 1998, it had grown to 831,643, and by 2003, Filipino labor migration numbered 867,964 workers.[305]

---

[305]"The Philippine Missions Movement c. 2010: From an Evangelical Perspective," presentation by Rey S. Taniajura at Tokyo 2010; available at http://www.tokyo2010.org/resources/Tokyo2010_T1_Rey_Taniajura.pdf

DEMOGRAPHIC REALITY OF DIASPORA
AND THE STRATEGY OF DIASPORA MISSIONS

Figure 12.1   Opportunity: Working with the Diaspora[306]

#	DIMEN-SION	CHARAC-TERITICS	OPPORTUNITY	
			DIASPORA MISSIOLOY	DIASPORA MISSIONS[307]
1	focus	-diaspora phenomena -shifting landscape of "Christendom"	• 21st Century diaspora: large scale, higher % & frequency • decline of the Western church & rise of the global South & East	• motivate & mobilize diaspora without dichotomy of "laity" & "clergy" • not program-oriented, • not performance-oriented • not outcome-based; but relational
2	Concept -ualliza-tion	beyond "melting-pot" (American) & "cultural mosaic" (Canadian)	• principle: - mobility & connectivity, - hyphenated identity & hybridity • flexibility & luminality • preference & practice: -relational-orientation	• principle: - "deterritorialization" - people-oriented - practice: - reciprocity, networking, partnership - Kingdom mentality
3	Approa-ch & orienta-tion	"The Gospel from Everywhere to Everyone"[308]	• principle: - non-spatial, - "glocal" & transnational • preference & practice: - interdisciplinary; not disciplinary compartmentalization; - Kingdom mentality	• principle: - sending and receiving from anywhere; non-lineal, with extensive network & synergy • Practice: - relational accountability & networking for the Kingdom without "unreached people" / "borderless church,"[309] "liquid church"[310] "bus church," "church on the oceans,"[311] "CWW -church without wall,"
4	strategy	view & follow God's way of providentially moving people spatially & spiritually	• "Mission Fields on the Move,"[312] therefore moving along • flexible & adaptive	• strategic with diaspora: - missions to diaspora; "mission on our door step" - missions thro diaspora: networking - missions by/beyond diaspora: "reverse mission" - missions with diaspora & "strategic partnership"

---

[306] Enoch Wan, "Moving to reach the people on the move," Multiplex Session on October 20, 2010 at Cape Town 2010.
[307] "Diaspora missions" is a providential and strategic way to minister to the nations by the diaspora, through and beyond the diaspora."
[308] C.F. Samuel Escobar, *The New Global Mission: The Gospel from Everywhere to Everyone*, Christian Doctrine in Global Perspective, (Downers Grove: InterVarsity Press, 2003)
[309] David Lundy, *Borderless Church: Shaping the Church for the 21st Century* (Authentic Lifestyle 2001).
[310] Ward 2002.
[311] A church was founded by the chief cook brother Bong on board of the container vessel Al Mutannabi in Nov. 2002 (see Martin Otto, Church on the Oceans (UK: Piquant. 2007)
[312] Samuel Escober, *Christianity Today*, April 27, 2010

Local and Global Diaspora Missiology: From FIN to LCWE

Diaspora is a global phenomenon, yet diaspora missiology must begin at the local level and proceed to become global in perspective and in scope. The FIN movement[313] is an example. It began locally in Canada, networking among Christian & Missionary Alliance local congregations, and gradually expanded to become an interdenominational and global organization.

Missiologists, realizing the potential of "ministering to the diaspora and ministering through the diaspora," began to incorporate them as themes for conferences and seminars. Some of these meetings and the resolutions that came out of them are listed below.

At Forum 2004 in Pattaya, Thailand, the Lausanne Committee for World Evangelization (LCWE)[314] recognized "diaspora peoples" as a new track and one of the key issues in global missions. A "Senior Associate for Diasporas'[315] was installed during the Bi-annual LCWE Leadership International meeting in Budapest, Hungary, June 18-24, 2007. In January 2008 the Lausanne Diasporas Leadership Team (LDLT)[316] was assembled to hold its first meeting in Portland, Oregon, hosted by IDS-US (Institute of Diaspora Studies) at Western Seminary.

Subsequently, international migration became one of the global issues discussed at the Lausanne Congress III in Cape Town, South Africa, October 16-25, 2010.

In preparation for the Lausanne Congress III, the LDLT convened for the Lausanne Diasporas Strategy Consultation in Manila in May 2009, hosted by Greenhills Christian Fellowship in Manila, Philippines, and the Lausanne Diaspora Educators' Consultation in November 2009 at Torch Trinity Graduate School of Theology (TTGST) in Seoul, Korea. Furthermore, the editors of the publication *Commission VII: Christian Communities in Contemporary Contexts* recognized diaspora as a reality of Christian mission in the 21st century in the gathering in Edinburgh on June 12-13, 2009.

---

[313] For details of the FIN movement, see the two works below:
- Tira, Sadiri Joy, *Filipino Kingdom Workers: An Ethnographic Study in Diaspora Missiology*. Dissertation, Doctor of Missiology, Western Seminary, Portland, OR, 2008, under the supervision of Enoch Wan.
- Tira, Sadiri Joy and Enoch Wan. "The Filipino Experience in Diaspora missions: A Case Study of Christian Communities in Contemporary Contexts." Commission VII: Christian Communities in Contemporary Contexts, Edinburgh, June 12-13, 2009.

[314] For details of LCWE, see http://www.lausanne.org.

[315] For details of the appointment and role of "Senior Associate for Diasporas," see http://www.lausanne.org/lausanne-connecting-point/2008-september.html.

[316] For details of LDLT, see http://www.gatheredscattered.com/.

Research in Diaspora Missiology

Since the emergence of migration studies in recent years, diaspora missiology has become a research topic in missiological studies. Research has been carried out on the unreached people who are seen as living in a "borderless world" where they move in from everywhere and move to everywhere. "Diaspora missiology" is a new research area not only to study the phenomena of the diaspora people but also to find strategies and practical ways to minister to them. Some of the publications on diaspora missiology are listed below:

- *The World at Your Door: Reaching International Students in Your Home, Church, and School*[317]
- *Missions Have Come Home to America: The Church's Cross-Cultural Ministry to Ethnic*[318]
- *Missions within Reach*[319]
- *Reaching the World Next Door*[320]
- *New People Next Door: A Call to Seize the Opportunities* (free download)[321]
- *A Higher Purpose for Your Overseas Job* (free download)[322]

Diaspora Missions in Practice

The diaspora phenomenon offers many advantages in the practice of missions to the diaspora. Diaspora missions: (1) is economically sustainable; (2) is geographically accessible in reaching the target groups; (3) has fewer political and legal restrictions; (4) involves partnership among people and organizations committed to the Great Commission; (5) is not carried out by just a few "experts" or "international workers;" (6) is a way to encourage self-supported

---

[317] Tom Phillips et al, *The World at Your Door: Reaching International Students in Your Home, Church, and School* (Minnesota: Bethany House, 1997).
[318] Jerry L. Appleby, *Missions Have Come Home to America: The Church's Cross-Cultural Ministry to Ethnics* (Kansas City: MO, Beacon Hill Press, 1986).
319 Enoch Wan, Missions Within Reach: Intercultural Ministries in Canada
(Hong Kong: Alliance Press, 1995).
320 Hopler, Thom and Marcia, Reaching the World Next Door (Downers Grove: IVP, 1995).
[321] "New People Next Door: A Call to Seize the Opportunities, " the *Occasional Paper No. 55*. Produced by the Issue Group on Diaspora and International Students at the 2004 Forum hosted by the Lausanne Committee for World Evangelization in Pattay, Thailand. (Sept. 29 to Oct. 5, 2004).
[322] The free booklet, "*A Higher Purpose for Your Overseas Job*," is most helpful for pre-departure preparation of diasporic Kingdom Workers. It is also available at
http://ojs.GlobalMissiology.org/index.php/english/article/view/215.

diaspora Christians to be "Kingdom workers ," especially those working in limited access contexts; (7) is putting the "priesthood of believer" into mission practice – a heritage from the Reformation.

When diaspora missions are being carried out then many unprecedent opportunities will surprisingly present themselves, as summed up in Figure 10.2 (Wan 2007a).

Figure 12.2 "Missions to the Diaspora"
as "Mission at Our Doorstep" (Wan 2007a:7)

NO	YES
-No visa required	-Yes, door opened
-No closed door	-Yes, people accessible
-No international travel required	-Yes, missions at our doorstep
-No political/legal restrictions	-Yes, ample opportunities
-No dichotomized approach	-Yes, holistic ministries
-No sense of self-sufficiency or unhealthy competition	-Yes, powerful partnership

Indeed missions to the diaspora has encountered unprecedented receptivity to the Gospel of the diaspora. The author's own experience among the Chinese in diaspora serves as a vivid illustration. For three consecutive summers the author was involved in short-term ministry in a creative access country where approximately 20,000 Chinese were engaged in construction, agriculture, and medical services. As a result of diaspora ministries, three churches were established in the duration of merely two years. For several years, the annual conversion rate was around 300. The author had personally witnessed two baptisms taken place, each with over 80 new converts. In one year, 2,200 people attended an outreach meeting to celebrate Chinese New Year, with 1,300 more refused entry into the facility due to fire regulations. Such is the picture of diaspora missions in practice

Missions *to* the Diaspora

One strategy in fulfilling the Great Commission is by means of missions through the diaspora. When practicing diaspora missions, one goes to where God is providentially moving people spatially and spiritually; in contrast to the "sending and receiving" in a mission station. The priority of diaspora missions is "every person outside the Kingdom everywhere;" there is no difference between reaching out to Muslims in New York or Paris, and those in the

Singapore and Hong Kong; especially among contract workers and domestic helpers.

In the fulfillment of the Great Commission, evangelism and discipleship might take place on ocean liners and cruise ships, in refugee camps or ethnic enclaves of metropolitan centers. It is God who determines where people will live, but wherever they are in the universe, they can call upon Him and find him (Acts 17:26-28). It is the Holy Spirit who moves among people who have moved from their homeland to settle in strange places and host countries. Therefore, we must move with the Holy Spirit to bring the Gospel to these people on the move.

Mission *through* the Diaspora

One way to reach the diaspora is through the social networks of diaspora Christian individuals, congregations, and communities. The diaspora Christians, after settling down in the host countries, are the natural bridges to reach out to their kinsmen who are new comers, for they have the advantages of sharing the common language and cultural practices with their non-Christian counter parts.

It is important that diaspora Christians are being motivated, equipped and mobilized to have a passion for the lost and the skills to reach them; especially their kinsmen on the move. They must be mobilized to strategically bring the Gospel to their own groups in diaspora. By equipping diaspora Christians to become Kingdom workers , diaspora missions is accomplished through the diaspora.

Missions *by and beyond* the Diaspora

Diaspora Christian individuals and congregations have the potential to reach not only their kinsmen in diaspora, they also have the potential to expand their mission efforts to participate in cross-cultural missions to reach out to members of the host society. The diaspora experiences have made them adaptive in languages and cultures and thus informally preparing them for cross-culture evangelism.

An example of missions by/beyond the diaspora is found in the Filipino couple Ken and Bola Taylors. Ken was a professional entertainer in Southeast Asia prior to his conversion in the '80s. After he immigrated to the US, he received theological training at Western Seminary (San Jose Campus). Then he went to Japan in 1997 with wife Bola to serve as vocational missionaries of

WorldVenture (formerly known as the Conservative Baptist Foreign Mission Society).

This diaspora couple from the Philippines are gifted in music, Ken a jazz musician and Bola a professional singer. They creatively use African-American Gospel music to reach Japanese non-Christians. Their "Black Gospel Music" is thoroughly contextualized and indigenized for the Japanese in Japan. And they organized the "Hallelujah Gospel Family" (HGF) which is described as:

> "They are self-sustaining, indigenous, and rooted in a local church context. In the ten years between 2000 and 2010, HGF has grown from a single choir led by Ken himself to over forty choirs led by a host of volunteer choir directors" (Fujino 2010:15).

The organization of "Hallelujah Gospel Family" (HGF) [323] is a show case of "relational approach" with a "community based" emphasis (see case studies in Part 4) with "strategic partnership" (see Chapter 14). In partnership with Japanese congregations, the Taylors help churches create indigenous, self-sustaining, multiplying choirs that use gospel music "to develop communities and strengthen relationships in celebration" for the local church.

Ken and Bola Taylor were honored by The Mission Exchange in 2009 for being an example of excellence, innovation, and partnership in missions within the Great Commission community in the US and Canada. Their mministry illustrates the practicing of "diaspora missions" in the forms of "by the diaspora" and "beyond the diaspora" in contemporary Japan – one of the most challenging mission fields of the twenty-first century.

Readers will find more case studies of "missions by and beyond the diaspora" in Part 4.

Missions *with* the Diaspora

Networking and partnership are the relational pattern to carry out the concepts of "bridging and bonding" (see Figure 8.3) in missions "*with*" the diaspora. In the case studies of Part 4, there are ample examples of practical ways of practicing "missions *with* the diaspora"in terms of: hospitality, reciprocity, connectivity and complexity, solidarity and unity.

---

[323] For those who are interested to learn more about HGF, see links listed below:
- -http://jesuslovesjapan.com/black-gospel-music-a-movement-of-god-in-japan
- -http://jesuslovesjapan.com/black-gospel-music-a-movement-of-god-in-japan
- -http://web.mac.com/taylorjapan/Site/Home.html
- -http://www.youtube.com/watch?v=eL3a2ml_2K4&noredirect=1
- -http://www.youtube.com/watch?v=gZRCSiFO554
- -http://www.design-gate.com/en/showcase/48-blog/135-hgf-concert-2009

DEMOGRAPHIC REALITY OF DIASPORA
AND THE STRATEGY OF DIASPORA MISSIONS

Summary

This chapter proposes "diaspora missions" as a strategy in response to the reality of the demographic trend of diaspora in the 21st century. Diaspora missions includes "missions to the diaspora," "missions through the diaspora" and "missions by and beyond the diaspora." Examples cited in the chapter illustrate how these three types of diaspora missions are carried out among various ethnic groups in different countries.

It had been said that one can find Filipinos in any part of the world as a result of the Filipino immigration. Starting in the mid 70s, Filipinos began immigrating due to employment opportunities in the Middle East. Pushed by the lack of employment at home, coupled with job openings abroad — particularly in Saudi Arabia and other neighboring Arab countries — skilled professional and technical workers started the Overseas Filipino Workers (OFW) phenomenon...As a result of this migration, Filipinos are now is settled in more than 180 countries. The number of Filipino workers is approaching 10 million, the bulk of whom are found in North America, the Middle East, Southeast Asia, Australia and New Zealand. Filipino labor migration began with 36,035 workers in 1975 and swelled to 598,760 in 1990. By 1998, it had grown to 831,643, and by 2003, Filipino labor migration numbered 867,964 workers.[324]

---

[324] "The Philippine Missions Movement c. 2010: From an Evangelical Perspective," presentation by Rey S. Taniajura at Tokyo 2010; available at
http://www.tokyo2010.org/resources/Tokyo2010_T1_Rey_Taniajura.pdf

Chapter 13

Relational Paradigm for Practicing Diaspora Missions in the 21st Century

Enoch Wan

Introduction

The "relational paradigm" is proposed in this chapter as the appropriate choice for practicing diaspora missions in the 21st century. Eight reasons are presented below, along with discussions on each, except for the last two which are covered separately in Chapter 12. Key terms in previous chapters that are defined within the theoretical framework of relational paradigm are explained in the next section.

This chapter is a synthesis of publications on the topic by Enoch Wan, as listed below:

- Enoch Wan and Mark Hedinger, "Understanding 'Relationality' from a Trinitarian Perspective," *Global Missiology*, (January 2006). www.GlobalMissiology.com.
- Enoch Wan, "The Paradigm of 'Relational Realism'," *Occasional Bulletin*, EMS, vol. 19, no. 2 (Spring 2006):1-4.
- Enoch Wan, "Relational Theology and Relational Missiology," *Occasional Bulletin*, EMS, vol. 21, no 1 (Winter 2007): 1-7.(2007c)
- Enoch Wan, "A Missio-relational Reading of Romans," *Occasional Bulletin*, EMS, Vol. 23, no. 21 Winter 2010:1-8.(2010e)
- Enoch Wan & Nary Santos, "A Missio-relational Reading of Mark," *Occasional Bulletin*, EMS vol. 24, no. 2 (Spring 2011):1-26.

Relational Paradigm: An Appropriate Choice for Practicing Diaspora Missions

In Western society today a lack of "relational reality" can be socio-culturally observed: (a) high mobility in general and high density of population in urban centers; (b) the prevalence of failed marriages and broken/dysfunctional families; (c) the prevalence of virtual relationship over actual personal interaction, e.g., the popularity of social networks such as Facebook and Twitter; (d) the Christian church's obsession with programmatic and managerial aspects of ministry for quantitative growth instead of "body life" of genuine Christianity and "personal touch;" (e) the increasing popularity of the "gospel of health and wealth" without relational intensity.

Firstly, the rediscovery of "relationalship" in Christian faith and practice is desperately needed. It is necessary to integrate the relational paradigm into Christian faith and practice in order to put into action the Great Commandment and to fulfill the Great Commission in the context of practicing diaspora missions. The relational paradigm is deemed the most appropriate choice in the practice of diaspora missions in the 21st century for the following reasons:

Secondly, it is an excellent Christian response to the cry for relationship from people of the twenty-first century.

Thirdly, it is a practical way to rediscover "relationship" which is the essence of Christian faith and practice.

Fourthly, it has been proven to be effective in ministering to diaspora communities and individuals in need of Christian charity. (See case studies in Part 4)

Fifthly, it is a paradigm that enables the synthesizing of diaspora missiology and diaspora missions.

Sixthly, it is transculturally relevant to societies in the majority world which are highly relational.

Seventhly, it nurtures a Kingdom orientation and strategically fulfills the Great Commission (a vertical relationship with the Sovereign Lord), and a working relationship with fellow "Kingdom workers" (horizontally with one and other).

Eighthly, it enables the practice of "strategic stewardship" and "relational accountability" (Chapter 14).

Ninely, In light of the various approaches in diaspora missions (e.g. *to, through, by/beyond* and *with*) which are all "relational" in nature as shown by the use of

Lastly, in light of the shift of Christendom's center from the West to the majority world, strategic partnership and synergy require the practice of relational paradigm; instead of the popular managerial tendency and entrepreneurship of the West (Chapter 13).

Theoretical Aspects of the Relational Paradigm

The philosophical element of the relational paradigm is based on "relational realism" (Wan 2006) and the methodological element is based on "relational theologizing" (Wan 2007c).

Theologically, the relational paradigm is grounded on the fact that man was created in the image of God and his existence (ontologically) is solely dependent on God at all times (Gen 1:26-27; Ro 11:36; Heb 1:3). His ability to know (epistemologically) and his undertaking in missions (missio Dei) are all dependent on God, who is the great "I AM" (Ex 3), as stated in the following three statements (Wan 2007c:3):

- "'I AM' therefore i am" ontologically[325]

- "'I AM" therefore 'i know'" epistemologically

- "'I AM' (*missio Dei*) therefore 'i am'" missiologically[326]

These three statements are in contrast to the rationalist's maxim of Descartes — "I think therefore I am" (Wan 2006:2).

The motto, "I think therefore I am" provided an impetus for the rationalist orientation ("I think") and existential element ("I am") with its individualistic and humanistic tendency based on the capital "I" in the entire undertaking.

The relational paradigm is based on "relational realism" which is different from the "critical realism" of Paul Hiebert (1999:37-38) because both assert realism yet in different ways (Figure 13.1).

As shown in the table below, critical realism is too closely align with science epistemologically and empically. The "umpire's response" in critical realism is too man-centered, too dependent on human perception and human objectivity (i.e. "I call it the way I see it). In contrast to critical realism, "relationa realism" is God-centered both ontologically, epistemologically and extentially.

---

[325] The "I AM" is God's self identification and "i am" (lower key) is an intentional designation for man in contra-distinction to "I AM"

[326] Our Triune God is characterized by love, communion, commission (sending) and glory. Also see Kevin Daugherty 2007, John A McIntosh 2000.

Figure 13.1 – Hiebert's "Critical Realism" vis-a-vis Wan's "Relational Realism" (Wan 2006:2)

2 KINDS OF REALISM	NATURE OF KNOWLEDGE	RELATIONSHIP BETWEEN SYSTEMS OF KNOWLEDGE	THE UMPIRE'S RESPONSE
Critical realism	"The external world is real. Our knowledge of it is partial but can be true. Science is a map or model. It is made up of successive paradigms that bring us to closer approximations of reality and absolute truth."	"Each field in science presents a different blue-print of reality. These are complementary to one another. Integration is achieved, not by reducing them all to one model, but by seeing their interrelationship. Each gives us partial insights into reality."	"I call it the way I see it, but there is a real pitch and an objective standard against which I must judge it. I can be shown to be right or wrong."
Relational realism	The external world is real but that reality is based primarily based on the vertical relationship on God & His created order (Acts 14:14-17, 17:24-31), secondarily based on horizontal relationship within the created order (i.e. spirit world, human world and natural order). God is the absolute Truth. Science is a road map and may provide human-based paradigm that cannot exclusively claim to be the only way to closer approximations of reality and absolute truth. Scientist, with a modernist orientation, has neither monopoly to truth nor can dogmatically/ conclusively/ exhaustively make pronouncement on reality.	God is the Truth: His Word (incarnate with personhood, inscripturate & revealed in written form) is truth, His work (creation, redemption, transformation, etc.) is truthful. Therefore, truth and reality are: multi-dimensional, multi-level and multi-contextual. All human efforts & disciplines (science, theology, philosophy, etc.) without vertical relationship to God (the Absolute Reality) at best are defective ways to approximate truth and reality (for being unidimensional = horizontal; single-level= human plain field; uni-contextual = shutting out the spirit world of God & angels (Satan & fallen angels included). Truth & reality are best to be comprehended and experienced in relational networks of God & the created 3 orders, i.e. angels, humanity and nature.	Man, without God and His revelation (Incarnationate and inscripturate Word) and illumination (H.S.), can be blinded to truth & reality. Therefore, he is not the umpire to make the final call of being: real or illusion, truth or untruth, right or wrong, good or bad. No human judgment is final, nor can it be dogmatic /conclusive; without the vertical relationship to God—the absolute Truth & the most Real.

Christian Response to the Cry for Relationship in the 21st Century

The relational paradigm is a timely Christian response to the general cry for relationship in the twenty-first century. Factors contributing to the relational deprivation in the 21st century include: failed marriages, broken families, and agrowing sense of alienation resulted from urbanization and globalization. Communication technology and social media have enabled people to be connected in real time virtually; but not face-to-face human interaction. The growing acceptance of virtual relationships is an indication of relational deprivation in our time. A common phenomenon is siblings texting with one another from separate rooms under the same roof; insteqad of interacting with one another face-to-face. It is within this socio-cultural context that the relational paradigm is offered as a timely approach to rediscover relationship of the Christian faith and practice when reaching out to individuals and communities in diaspora.

Rediscovering "Relationship"—the Essence of Christian Faith and Practice

The relational paradigm provides a way to rediscover relationship in Christianity—the essence of Christian faith and practice. If Christianity is likened to "chicken soup" and "relationship" is the genuine chicken (with flesh and bone), then the contemporary Christian church and individual believers have often settled for chicken soup that only has a resemblance to the chicken in canned chicken soup. The use of "chicken soup" analogy was included in video presentations by Enoch Wan at presentations at Tokyo 2010 and Cape Town 2010.[327]

A personal touch and relational intimacy are part of the uniqueness of Christianity. Individually, every human being is known before birth by God and every Christian is intimately called by God before the foundation of the world. He/she is God's beloved, chosen in Christ by the Father (Eph 1:4), destined to be a joint heir with Christ the Son (Rom 8:17), known to the Good Shepherd by name (John 10:3), transformed by the Holy Spirit (Eph 4:3, Rom 12:1-4) and indwelled by the Spirit as His temple both individually and collectively (1 Cor 3:16-17; 6:19).

Collectively, the Church is the bride and body of Christ (Eph 5:22-33), purchased by His precious blood (Acts 20:28), interceded by the High Priest before crucifixion (John 17) and now interceding at the right hand of the Father (Rom 8:34). However, over the course of time, as the churches focused on quantitative growth, relied on programs and management skills, and steeped in the secularization process, the relational distinctiveness of Christianity was gradually lost.

---

[327] Chicken soup is valued in most majority world cultural traditions, see my presentations at Tokyo 2010 (Wan 2010b) and Cape Town 2010f.

An Alternative to "Managerial Missiology" of the West

The relational paradigm is an alternative to managerial missiology of the West which undermines the relational nature of Christian faith and practice

The relational paradigm is proposed as an alteranative to the problems listed above. Furthermore it will serve as a corrective within the cotext of the relationally deprived post-Christian west and helpful in reaching diaspora from the majority world characterized by relationship culturally.

An Effective Means in Ministering to the Diaspora

The relational paradigm has been proven to be helpful in ministering to diaspora communities and individuals by practicing the Great Commandment and fulfilling the Great Commission. For details, see the case studies in Part 4.

An Effective Synthesis of Diaspora Missiology and Diaspora Missions

In this book, the relational paradigm is employed as the theoretical framework to synthesize diaspora missiology and diaspora missions at the levels of theory and practice. The figure below presents a synthesis of relational paradigm (left side) and diaspora missiology and diaspora missions (right side). If the relational paradigm is likened to the skeleton (as in biology) or syntax (as in linguistics), then diaspora missiology and diaspora missions is the flesh/face (as in biology) or word/sound (as in linguistics).[328]

---

[328] For an explanation this figure, refer to Enoch Wan, "Global People and Diaspora Missiology," In *Handbook of Global Mission: Consultation, Celebration*, May 11-14, 2010b: 92-106. Video clip available at http://www.ustream.tv/recorded/6897559.

Figure 13.2 Relational Paradigm:
Synthesizing Diaspora Missiology & Diaspora Missions

RELATIONAL PARADIGM		DIASPORA MISSIOLOGY & DIASPORA MISSIONS
5 ELEMENTS	**5 RELATIONAL ASPECTS**	
PARTICIPANTS Triune God & Christians carry out the Great Commission resistant: Satan, fallen angels	**RELATIONAL NETWORK** Triune God is the originator of relationship; the center and foundation of all networks two camps: God, obedient angels & Christians ← → Satan	not programmatic, not entrepreneur, not outcome-based strong emphasis on relational dimensions between person Being (the triune God) and beings (of humanity and angelic reality) recognizing the dimension of spiritual warfare
PATTERN (→sending) Father → the Son & together → H.S. Father → the Son → Christians (Jn 17: 18), Christians obeying H.S. sending: Acts 10:19; 13:2 Christians empowered	**RELATIONAL DIMENSIONS /CONTEXT** vertical dimension to God horizontal dimensions within the Church & beyond multi-context: divine, angelic, human; changing human contexts due to globalization, diaspora movement, etc.	vertical dimensions, e.g. "relational accountability" "glocal" missions in the globalized context non-spatial, "borderless," no boundary to worry, transnational different approach: integrated ministry & interdisciplinary study of Missiology learning of new demographic reality of the 21st Century & strategize accordingly with good stewardship
PRACTICE Christians participating in God's mission, carrying out the "Great Commission"	**RELATIONAL REALITY** God: reconciling the world to Himself in Christ through Christians Satan & fallen angels at enmity with God and His followers.	new reality in the 21st Century viewing & following God's way of providentially moving people spatially & spiritually. moving targets & move with the targets (diaspora)
POWER God's love transforms Christians and compels them carrying out His mission	**RELATIONAL DYNAMICS** doing missions out of love for God and compassion for the lost empowered by the H.S.	micro: love, compassion, Christian hospitality macro: partnership & networking holistic Christianity with strong integration of evangelism with Christian compassion & charity
PROCESS God: plan of salvation provided & the Church carrying out God's mission	**RELATIONAL INTERACTION** God's calling, Christ's commissioning, H.S. empowering Christians obedient to God, Satan resisting God's mission	"Great commission" + "great commandment" diaspora mission: ministering **to** and **through and by/beyond** & **with** the diaspora relational accountability strategic stewardship and partnership

Cross-culturally Relevant and Practical

The relational paradigm is cross-culturally relevant because most societies in the majority world are highly relational in operation, i.e., intricate networks interwoven at multiple levels. This aspect of relational paradigm is portrayed in the case studies in Part 4.

Nurturing the Kingdom Orientation

A person with Kingdom-orientation is someone who embraces the perspective, sentiment, and motivation of the Kingdom at heart and in action. Kingdom-orientation enables practitioners of diaspora missions to overcome denominationalism, parochialism and territorialism. It will remove relational barriers in communication and reduce the tendency of being managerial and paternalistic thus being impersonal. The relational paradigm will aid the cultivation of relationship among all parties. It will nurture partnership between the dwindling church in the West and the thriving church in the global south.

With kingdom-orientation, diaspora Christians and congregations can be motivated and mobilized to become Kingdom workers and Kingdom partners.[329] With the exception of refugees, most diaspora people are gainfully employed. As Kingdom workers, their Kingdom-orientation will help multiplying mission forces without draining the scare resources of mission agencies, and at the same time fulfilling the Great Commission. For example, approximately 7% of Filipino working overseas are evangelical Christians, and they are potentially a significant mission force if they are being nurtured to become Kingdom workers (Tira 2008). This aspect of relational-base ministry to the diaspora individuals and communities are clearly delineated in the case studies of Part 4 and the IDS-Series on Ghannian, Vietnamese and Sri Lankan.

Summary

The relational paradigm is essential in implementing diaspora ministry and diaspora missions. It also provides theoretical coherence for the various parts of this book and be a balm to heal all who suffer "relationship deprivation" in the 21st century. Its practical outworking is illustrated in case studies in Part 4.

---

[329] See two publications for elaboration: Enoch Wan, "Korean Diaspora: From Hermit Kingdom to Kingdom Ministry," Korean Diaspora Forum, May 18-21, 2010, Seoul, Korea;
Sadiri Emmanuel Santiago B. Tira, "Filipino Kingdom Workers: An Ethnographic Study in Diaspora Missiology." Unpublished dissertation, Western Seminary, 2008.

Chapter 14

Diaspora Missions, Strategic Stewardship and Strategic Partnership

Enoch Wan

Introduction

In light of the shift of Christendom's center from the West to the majority world, traditional approaches to missions, which have had the tendency to be paternalistic, hierarchical, and unilateral, must be replaced by the context-relevant mission approaches of the twenty-first century. Reasons for the change are: first, mission resources of personnel and finance from the post-Christian West are declining rapidly; and second, citizens of the majority world are more receptive to the gospel and churches are growing at a faster rate than the post-Christian West. Therefore traditional approaches must be modified for conducting mission work in the post-colonial era.

In this chapter the mission strategies of "strategic stewardship" and "strategic partnership" are proposed to modify traditional mission strategies.

Partnership Should Mimic the Trinity

"The relational reality of the Trinute God figures prominently in both the Old and New Testaments scriptures."[330] Seven principles can be derived from the model of the Trinity for the practice of ministerial partnership as shown in the figure below:

---

[330] Enoch Wan, "Partnerships Should Mimic the Trinity, " *Faith Today, July/August* 2010:27

Figure 14.1 Partnership in light of the Trinity[331]

PRINCIPLES	PRACTICE OF MINISTERIAL PARTNERSHIP
1. relationship	know, confer, plan with one another
2. unity	spiritual unity leading to unity of goal
3. diversity	difference in gifting and distinct roles
4. interdependence	not self-sufficient
5. love	self-sacrificial love within the Trinity and beyond
6. peace	harmony; freedom from anxiety and inner turmoil
7. joy	Christians are to be joyfully serving God and others

The Father, Son and the Holy Spirit relate to one and other in perfect unity; though distinct from one and other with diverse roles and operating interdependently. This theological understanding of the Trinity has practical implications for the practice of strategic partnership in diaspora missions.

Strategic Stewardship

According to Jenkins (2002), places where Christianity is thriving and mutating are also places where population is shifting. He projects that this demographic trend will continue throughout the next century. Given this global demographic trend, the Church must strategically minister to receptive people in developing nations where population and church are growing at a higher rate than the post-Christian West. This strategy also applies to ministries to diaspora groups who are usually more receptive to the gospel while on the move from the security of their homeland.

Christian stewardship has two dimensions: entrustment by God **vertically** and entrustment by others **horizontally**. Strategic stewardship (Luke 12:32-48) and relational accountability (Luke 15;1- 16:13) also have vertical and horizontal aspects. Resources, spiritual gifts, and ministry opportunities are all originated from God thus those who are custodians of various measures of grace from the Father (Jam 1:16-18), the Son (Eph 4:7-11) and the Holy Spirit (1Cor 12:1-11) are to be good stewards. Therefore, Christian individuals and institutions are accountable to the Triune God for their stewardship of endowments and entrustments vertically and strategically.

Likewise, resources and ministry opportunities oftentimes come from other Christian individuals and institutions by means of contribution, donation, and entrustment. There is to be strategic stewardship on the part of recipients who are accountable horizontally to the contributors and donors.

---

[331] Enoch Wan, "Partnerships Should Mimic the Trinity, " *Faith Today, July/August* 2010:27

DIASPORA MISSIONS, STRATEGIC STEWARDSHIP
AND STRATEGIC PARTNERSHIP

Biblical Basis of Relational Accountability[332]

Relational accountability is the understanding and practice of accountability within the relational paradigm. It consists of two dimensions: vertical and horizontal dimensions. The relational paradigm is contextually more relevant within the context of "Missions in the Majority World"[333] than modernist, post-modernist or rationalist paradigms. The reason is that in the socio-cultural context of the majority world, social structure is primarily the interwoven of myriads of networks at multiple levels.

The Old Testament contains many illustrations of "relational accountability." For example, Joseph was faithful to God in the household of Potiphar in Egypt (Gen 32) and later in the entire country of Egypt (Gen 42-45). He was vertically accountable to God (Gen 45:1-15) and horizontally accountable both to Pharaoh (Gen 41:37-57) and the well-being of his family (Gen 50:15-25). Likewise, Moses was found faithful in the household of God (Heb 3:2) and was held accountable to God for his ministry vertically (2 Cor 3:1-18). However, he failed horizontally as the leader of the Israelites when he disobediently struck the rock for water (Deut 20:10-13; 34:1-8) and failed in parenting.

In the New Testament, Jesus Christ systematically taught his disciples and the multitudes the vertical and horizontal dimensions of responsibility and accountability (Mt 5–7; Mark 9:33-55; Luke 6, 11; John 13–15). The apostle Paul served exemplarily in Ephesus for other elders to follow (Act 20:17-35), he was accountable to God vertically and to shepherding the flock horizontally. The Corinthian Christians were to be followers of the apostle Paul horizontally, as he was a follower of Christ vertically (2 Cor 11:1).

The Pauline epistles teach that Christian leaders are accountable to God vertically in their calling, and are to be faithful and exemplary horizontally among fellow Christians, their households, and non-Christians (1 Tim 3–4; Tit 2). The apostle Peter also addressed the issue of leadership and accountability both vertically and horizontally, i.e., shepherding and modeling horizontally while accountable to the Chief Shepherd vertically (1 Pet 5:1-6). Christians are vertically accountable to God in integrity, and horizontally accountable to God's people by refusing to be a stumbling block to them (Rom 14; 1 Cor 10:23-33).

In the "code of household," both the apostles Paul (Eph 5:21-6:9; Col 3:18-4:6; 1 Tim 6:1-2; Tit 2) and Peter (1 Pet 3:1-7) address the vertical dimension to God and the horizontal dimension in the dyadic relationships between

---

[332] The content of this section is adapted from "Global People and Diaspora Missiology" Tokyo 2010 Global Mission Consultation, Plenary Session, Tokyo, Japan, (May 11th-14th 2010): 92-106.
[333] See Enoch Wan and Michael Pocock (eds.) *Missions in the Majority World*. William Carey Library, 2009.

husband and wife, parents and children, masters and servants. There is the accountability horizontally in the network of human relationships.

There is both a vertical accountability and a horizontal accountability in the "code of household" of Eph 5:21-6:9.[334] All members of the household are to submit to one another horizontally "in the fear of God" (Eph 5:21) vertically. Horizontally, there is mutuality to one another horizontally within marriage (5:22-33), between parents and children (6:1-4), and between masters and servants (6:5-9)—all because of their "fear of God" vertically.

The most obvious pattern of interwoven relationships both vertically and horizontally is found in Eph 6:8-9 where the apostle Paul admonishes the masters that both they and the servants are to subordinate to the lordship of Christ vertically, although the servants are horizontally accountable to their masters.

Traditionally, mission agencies in the West were accountable to donors and not vice-versa. When Western mission organizations are hard pressed by dwindling resources in finance and personnel, accountability is no longer based solely on finance from the West. A new pattern of relational accountability between partnering entities in the West and the majority world is to replace the pattern of Western paternalism and dominance. When the relational paradigm is being practiced in diaspora missions, mutual "relational accountability" is to replace the traditionally "unilateral accountability" by entities of the majority world to those of the West.

For example, historically, Western-based mission agencies had always funded mission operations in the majority world. They, as the dominant force, often ignored issues and concerns raised by the local people. The only relational accountability for these missionaries from the West was to their own sending agencies in the West. The relational paradigm and relational accountability proposed in this book is to counter such "one-way" relationship.

Strategic Partnership and "Reverse Missions"[335]

"Partnership" is a "unique opportunity" to work with the Triune God and the Body of Christ to accomplish the *missio Dei* under the power and direction of the Holy Spirit."[336] "Strategic partnership" is "partnership" characterized by wise use of

---

[334] This discussion is based on an earlier publication in Chinese: Enoch Wan, *Questions and Answers to Christian Marriage: Practical Guide to Christian Family*. CA: Publisher of Overseas Magazine, 2000.
[335] Enoch Wan, "Diaspora Missiology and Missions in the Context of the 21st Century ," *Torch Trinity Journal*, Volume 13, No.1, May 30, 2010i): 46-60. Also in *GlobalMissiology*, October, 2010; available at www.GlobalMissiology.com.
[336] For detailed discussion on "partnership" see the 3 articles below:
Enoch Wan & Kevin P. Penman,"The 'why,' 'how' and 'who' of partnership in Christian missions," *GlobalMissiology*, April 1, 2010; available at www.GlobalMissiology.com;

DIASPORA MISSIONS, STRATEGIC STEWARDSHIP AND STRATEGIC PARTNERSHIP

God-endowed resources and God-given opportunity to His glory and for Kingdom extension.

Strategic partnership is a fitting replacement for Western paternalism and Euro-centric style missions. Members of thriving diaspora churches in host countries must be challenged to practice "reverse missions." It is the carrying out of mission work in the post-Christian West by diaspora Christians or Christians of the global south. It is also the sending of members of diaspora groups to their homelands and to other countries for mission work. Success of these mission endeavors depend on the collaboration and partnership among parties concerned, i.e. mission entities from the West, maturing congregations in the global south, and diaspora churches. The synergy from such partnership will enhance Christian stewardship and advance Kingdom ministry.

A good case of "reverse missions" is the trend of church planting by Africans in Europe that began in the latter part of the last century with momentum:

> "The 1990s witnessed the rise of New Pentecostal Churches (NPC) with African origins. For example, one of the largest Churches in Western Europe is Kingsway International Christian Centre (KICC) founded in 1992 by Pastor Matthew Ashimolowo (Nigerian); also one of the largest Churches in Eastern Europe was founded in 1994 by an African, Sunday Adelaja pastor of Embassy of God in Kiev, Ukraine. African Churches in Europe are making many contributions and are bringing renewal to a continent that is fast loosing its Christian roots and values. The contributions of African Churches can be seen in the following areas; Church growth, social cohesion among ethnic minorities, community development, women's ministries and discourses, immigration services, *diaspora* studies, revival, missions and a host of others."[337]

It is, therefore, critically important for churches in Europe and North America to practice strategic partnership with the vibrant diaspora churches in the context of post-Christian west and for the fulfilment of the Great Commission globally.

Summary

Approaches to missions in the 21st century, especially approaches to diaspora missions, must be context-relevant by practicing strategic stewardship, relational accountability, and strategic partnership, even reverse missions partnership.

Enoch Wan & Johnny Yee-chong Wan, "Partnership—a relational study of the Trinity and the Epistle to the Philippines," *GlobalMissiology*, April 1, 2010a; available at www.GlobalMissiology.org;
Enoch Wan and Geoff Baggett, "A theology of partnership: implications for Christian mission & case study of a local congregation," *GlobalMissiology*, April, 2010, available at www.GlobalMissiology.org.
[337] "Reverse Missions: African Churches in Europe" (Accessed Dec. 20, 2013)
http://israelolofinjana.wordpress.com/2012/01/25/reverse-missions-african-churches-in-europe/

Chapter 15

Case Study 1: Diaspora Jews

Tuvya Zaretski

Introduction

No *diaspora* study is complete without an examination of the Jewish people. In this chapter we consider the unique relationship of the Jewish people with the experience of *diaspora*. A short study like this can perhaps shed light on the purposes of God in scattering peoples at various times. We must describe the demographic trends in the Jewish diaspora of the 21st century. Where are the Jewish people and in what directions are they moving? We will find that the concept of "homeland" is taking on a new symbolic definition for world Jewry.

We then want to provide ethnographic descriptions of trends in Jewish diaspora missiology. What are the fresh and exciting approaches for ministry to segments of Jewish people that are open for diaspora ministry? We will look at ways that ministry is being done now to diaspora Jews, with some additional suggestions for stimulating Christians to engage in diaspora ministry as well. We will also present a few case studies of ministry taking place through the Jewish diaspora today. Our hope is that others will see potential for partnering in Jewish Evangelism. This chapter concludes with a description and invitation for partnering in an existing Jewish evangelism network—perhaps the most significant to arise in the modern mission movement—The LausanneConsultation on Jewish Evangelism.

Definitions

I find it helpful, when discussing matters that relate to the Jewish people and Israel, to begin with a set of definitions. It helps to have a clear and common understanding of the terms, since meanings are culturally defined and may vary between what Jews and non-Jews have ordinarily thought. We use the following terms as defined here.

Jews – the ethnic people descended from Abraham, Isaac, and Jacob.

Jewry – the collective term for Jewish people or distinctive elements among them (i.e., world Jewry, Israeli Jewry, or Sephardi Jewry).

Jewish – the descriptive term for that which is distinctive of the specific group of ethnic people known as Jews (i.e., Jewish people, Jewish customs, or Jewish symbols).

Judaism – the traditional monotheistic religion of Jewish people dating from roughly the fourth century A.D. Contemporary Jewish leaders define it much more broadly than the way we are using it here. In their perspective, Judaism has been integrated into Jewish identity, incorporating "culture, customs, ethics, sense of self," along with faith and rituals.[338] However, just as the term *Jewish* is descriptive of segments within the ethnic community, we view *Judaism* as one cultural component held in various forms among members of that ethnic community.

Israel – the name for the sovereign political state in the Middle East established in 1948 (i.e., the *State* of Israel). This term "Israel" may also be used for "the Jews" in speaking of the biblical descendants of the patriarch, Israel (i.e., the *people* of Israel). Care must be used in distinguishing between an intended meaning for Israel the ancestral *people*, Israel the modern *state*, the *citizens* of that sovereign state ("Israelis"), the *patriarch* (formerly Jacob) and the *northern kingdom* of Israel that went into Assyrian captivity in 722 B.C.[339]

Historical Review of Jewish Diaspora

Diaspora in the Jewish Experience

The term *diaspora* is uniquely identified with one ethnic group—the Jewish people. In almost any American English dictionary, the historic Jewish dispersion, or "scattering," is spelled with a capital letter—*Diaspora*—and defined as "the dispersion of the Jews." The same term is used with a lower-case 'd' in reference to "any scattering of people with a common origin, background, beliefs, etc…"[340] Diaspora has been a characteristic of the Jewish people from the very beginning of their history.

---

[338] Stephen Wylens, *Settings of Silver: An Introduction to Judaism* (New York: Paulist Press, 1989), 3.
[339] For further examination of the term see, Tuvya Zaretsky, "Israel the People," in *Israel the Land and the People* (Grand Rapids: Kregel Publications, 1998), 36-39.
[340] *New World Dictionary of the American Language*, Second College Edition, ed. David B. Guralnik (World Publishing, 1978).

CASE STUDY 1: DIASPORA JEWS

Abram, later called Abraham, was the original Hebrew diaspora patriarch. God called him to leave his homeland and his family in Ur. God asked him to trust and follow the Lord to a new land. Abram's tribe was scattered from the land of Padan-Aram to subsequently live amidst Canaanite and Egyptian peoples.

Moses too was a wandering child of scattered Israel. At God's command, around 1450 B.C., he led his people out of their four-hundred year sojourn in the land of Egypt. By then, the tribe had become a nation, yet still without a new homeland. The Lord subsequently fulfilled His promise to Abraham, bringing one of his descendant tribes into their new homeland after forty years roving the Sinai wilderness. Through their rootless years, Yahweh proved faithful to Abraham and his descendants. So He commanded the Jewish people to remember their patriarch and recall their history with the words, "My father was a wandering Aramean…"[341]

The term *diaspora* is particularly fixed within the history of the Jewish people dating from the first Israelite exile in 722 B.C. That marks the fall of Samaria, the Northern Kingdom of Israel. The Assyrian empire, by policy, dispersed large populations that they conquered. In exchange, they displaced and relocated other defeated nations. So, the ten northern tribes were scattered across regions of Asia. Foreign peoples, who became known as the mixed-race Samaritans, came to occupy their homes in the land of Israel.

In 586 B.C., the military of Babylonia invaded and conquered the two remaining southern Israelite tribes that made up the Kingdom of Judah. They too were carried away from their land, east into Mesopotamia, as captives. Jewish historian H.H. Ben-Sasson asserts that these two cataclysmic dispersions in Jewish history set a new pattern of Jewish life that would hold true for more than 2,500 years.[342]

The Roman Empire, after crushing the Jewish revolts in 70 and 135 A.D., carried out policies and persecuted Jews in the Levant, intending to wipe out the bond with their homeland.[343] The identity of Jewish people as a scattered nation was fixed in that period and continues through history until the twentieth century.

Israel as Jewish "Homeland"

Since the destruction of Jerusalem in 70 A.D., diaspora has been the prominent condition of Jewish existence. The Jewish people were scattered outside of their

---

[341] Deuteronomy 26:5
[342] H.H. Ben-Sasson, ed., *A History of the Jewish People*, (Cambridge, MA: Harvard University Press, 1976), 182.
[343] Ibid. 333-335.

promised eternal homeland, living among other nations until the establishment of the State of Israel in 1948. That event changed the perspective of world Jewry.

Journalist David Zax notes the nuanced distinction between two terms that are commonly used for the Jewish dispersion. He points out that Israeli scholars often speak of the "captivity" or "exile" of the Jewish people using the Hebrew words *golah* or *galut* (גולה or גלות). Zax, an American Jew, describes this as an "inept translation" since "exile" has a more negative connotation than merely a people who are "dispersed" or "scattered abroad" as in *diaspora* (διασπορα).[344] Historically, "captivity" is the descriptive term for those who have been relocated as outsiders, from the vantage of those who remain within the Jewish homeland.[345] In a theological sense, the Bible speaks of those Jews who were relocated or moved out of their homeland as people who had been "scattered" according to the Lord's purposes.[346]

In recent years, the State of Israel has once again become the largest Jewish population center of any country in the world. Israeli citizens consider the other sixty-two percent of world Jewry as choosing to remain in exile. Demographic studies have shown that non-Orthodox diaspora Jewry is trending toward intermarriage, declining birth rates and disaffiliation from Judaism. Such a shift in Jewish identity prompted an Israeli leader to inform American Jews that, "The only hope for the Jewish people in the diaspora is Israel."[347]

Theological Observations on Jewish Diaspora

Most of the theological dimensions associated with exile and diaspora are beyond the scope of this chapter. However, it is helpful to make a few relevant observations. First, Adam and Eve were exiled from the Garden of Eden as part of God's purpose and an expression of His grace. Their removal from the garden was to prevent them from eating of the Tree of Life and thereby making permanent their fallen state.[348]

Also, according to God's purpose Abram's descendants were promised that they would be temporary sojourners in a foreign land.[349] The first purpose was to allow the iniquity of the Amorites to become complete. Thus, God would be just in removing them from their land and giving it to the Israelites. Second, God nurtured the number of Israelites during their sojourning in Egypt. Though only seventy Jews originally went down into Egypt, after 430 years they had become a nation numbered more than 600,000 men plus their wives, children

---

[344] David Zax, "Whose Diaspora is it Anyway?" *Moment Magazine* (October/November 2007).
[345] See Ezra 1:1, 2:1 and 2 Kings 17:23
[346] See Deut. 28:64 and James 1:1
[347] Binyamin Netanyahu, "No Future for the Jews in the Diaspora," *Arutz 7 – IsraelNationalNews.com* (6 October 2006).
[348] Genesis 3:22-24
[349] Genesis 15:13-16

CASE STUDY 1: DIASPORA JEWS

and extended families.[350] So scattering the nation into Egypt served to incubate its growth.

Some would complain that God was pointless or cruel in His dispersion of the Jewish people—even periodically—from the land of promise. Nevertheless, both the Assyrian and Babylonian dispersions of 722 and 586 B.C. were within the plan of God. Isaiah was Yahweh's messenger to warn and comfort Israel before both dispersions. In spite of temporary removals from the Land, the Lord preserved a faithful remnant. This prefigured those of Israel who would ultimately return, trusting in Yahweh's Messianic Redeemer, saying "a Redeemer will come to Zion, and to those who turn from transgression in Jacob".[351]

That Redeemer is the promised Seed of the woman seen in Genesis 3:15. God's plan was to send that Anointed One through the Jewish people in the person of the Messiah Jesus. He was to be the blessing to the nations through Abraham's seed.[352] A faithful remnant of Israel did trust in Him as recorded in Acts 2. During the Jewish feast of *Shavuot* (Pentecost), diaspora Jews came to Jerusalem to observe the festival. When they heard the good news that the Redeemer had come to Zion, many believed in Him on that day.[353]

Subsequently, those new Messianic believers went back out to their diaspora communities carrying the gospel message with them. So, through the scattered Israelite nation, the Lord first spread news of Messiah Y'shua (Jesus) among other Jews and some gentile proselytes in their synagogues and remote diaspora communities.

The Lord used diaspora Jewish believers to further spread the gospel after the persecution of Stephen. Jewish followers of Jesus were under pressure, hunted and threatened by traditional Jewish leaders because of their faith in the new Messianic Redeemer. A cohort of Messianic Jews moved from Jerusalem to Cypress and then to Phoenicia, finally making their way to the diaspora community in Antioch. Through their testimony "a large number who believed turned to the Lord" in that city.[354] So, even persecution of that first Jewish remnant served as an evangelistic ministry to spread the good news into the diaspora where Jews and Gentiles continue to receive it today.[355]

---

[350] Exodus 12:37, 38:26
[351] Isaiah 59:20
[352] Genesis 12:3
[353] Acts 2:36-41
[354] Acts 11:19-21
[355] See Oskar Skarsaune, "We have found the Messiah! Jewish Believers in Jesus in Antiquity," MISHKAN (Jerusalem) no. 45 (2005): 17-20.

Figure 15.1 Demographics of the Jewish Diaspora

Country	1970	2005	2010[356]
World	12,633,000	13,033,000	13,428,000
Israel	2,582,000	5,235,000	5,703,700
North America	5,686,000	5,652,000	5,650,000
United States	5,400,000	5,280,000	5,275,000
Canada	286,000	372,000	375,000
Latin America	514,000	398,000	335,100
Argentina	282,000	185,000	182,300
Brazil	90,000	97,000	95,600
Mexico	35,000	40,000	39,400
Other countries	107,000	76,000	17,800
Europe non-FSU	1,331,000	1,161,000	1,118,000
France	530,000	494,000	483,500
United Kingdom	390,000	298,000	292,000
Germany	30,000	115,000	119,000
Hungary	70,000	50,000	48,600
Other EU	171,000	150,000	174,900
FSU	2,151,000	380,000	315,700
Russia	808,000	235,000	205,000
Ukraine	777,000	84,000	71,500
Rest FSU Europe	312,000	40,000	20,600
FSU Asia	254,000	21,000	18,600
Asia (rest)	104,000	19,000	19,200
Africa	195,000	79,000	76,200
South Africa	118,000	73,000	70,800
Oceania	70,000	109,000	115,100
Australia	65,000	102,000	107,500

---

[356] Source: Sergio DellaPergola. World Jewish Population, 2010 (Connecticut: Berman Institute – North American Jewish Data Bank No. 2 (2010): 60-62.

CASE STUDY 1: DIASPORA JEWS

Diaspora Jewish Ministry

Diaspora Jewish ministry began in the first century, and was comprised of two complimentary purposes. First, the original scattering of Jewish believers in Jesus was used of God to spread the gospel *to* the Jewish diaspora. The Great Commission started from within the Jewish homeland, under the power of the Holy Spirit, and spread outward. As noted above, many diaspora Jews and proselytes who were visiting Jerusalem during *Shavuot* came to faith in Jesus.[357] Then, from Jerusalem they carried the good news back to diaspora Jewish centers in Mesopotamia, Asia Minor, Northern Africa, the Mediterranean regions, Southern Europe and the Arabian Peninsula. This is an example of historic ministry *to* diaspora Jewry.

Second, the Lord used Jewish believers who were residents of Israel to spread the gospel into the diaspora *through* both Jews and gentiles after the persecution of Stephen. Disciples traveled out into Cyprus, Phoenicia and Antioch, and Luke reported that many gentiles in Antioch turned to the Lord.[358] This is an example of ministry *through* means of the Jewish diaspora.

Diaspora ministry has historically penetrated *into* and *through* Jewish communities. As such, it is worth noting some demographic data regarding the centers of Jewish people today.

Ethnographic Profiles of Diaspora Jewry

According to demographic data, approximately 13.4 million Jewish people are in the world today. The two largest Jewish communities, Israel and the United States, comprise 82% of Jewish world population. Selected regional ethnographic descriptions follow with an emphasis on population growth or decline, movement, and gospel receptivity.

Jewish Diaspora in the U.S.

The U.S. Jewish population has declined by 300,000 in the last decade, even though 300,000 Jews, mostly from the former Soviet Union (FSU), immigrated to the U.S. in the 1990s.[359] The U.S. Jewish birth rate of 1.8 children per couple is not keeping pace with the death rate, resulting in a Jewish population net loss of about 50,000 people per year.

---

[357] Acts 2:5, 8-11, 37-42
[358] Acts 11:19-21
[359] Yair Sheleg "World Jewish Population Drops by 300,000" at Judaismonline www.simpletoremember.com/vitals/jewpopdrops.htm. Emigration figures are from www.ujc.org/content_display.html?articleid=83403.

The American Jewish community is undergoing sociological and spiritual transitions. Physical movement is modest, as retirees move out of the Northeast and to the Southeast and Southwest of the U.S. The 2000/2001 National Jewish Population Survey (NJPS) showed a highly educated, more affluent, and older community than the average American.

It is also a population in decline, disconnecting from Judaism and frequently intermarrying.[360] Two-thirds of American Jews are unaffiliated with any Jewish institutions. Barely twenty percent of American Jews give philanthropically to Jewish causes. Most significant of all, over half of all American Jews who married in the past 20 years have married gentiles. More than a third of all married American Jews are intermarried. American Jewish leaders recognize that the "Jewish people are at a critical juncture" as the community is shrinking.[361] Public policy debates in the U.S. Jewish community explore what can be done to save American Jewry from these trends.

Since the 1970s, the American Jewish community has been in spiritual transition toward secularism. A climate of diversity in America encourages spiritual exploration and acceptance of nontraditional options. The post-war baby generation led the way in eroding traditional cultural taboos. The 2001 American Jewish Identity Survey concluded "secularism is a serious source of conviction for some Jews... (and)... a serious existential condition for a great many more."[362] Some have suggested that in America the Jewish Diaspora is ending. "Jews are creating new homes and futures in intimate, symbolic, and national ways" that are no longer defined by a homeland in Zion.[363] New ideas of Jewish identity are being shaped by transitional experiences within host cultures and contemporary business climate. As American Jews are moving away from Judaism and traditional forms for defining Jewish identity, the transitional times are opening doors for diaspora ministry.

Russian-Speaking Jewish Diaspora

Jewish people from the former Soviet Union (FSU) took the opportunity to leave once the doors for immigration were opened in the 1990s. The largest population migration, about 1.2 million, went to Israel. Another 402,000 exchanged one diaspora for another in the U.S. The remaining FSU Jews have been moving back into Germany and Poland, where Jewish diaspora flourished before the Holocaust.

---

[360] 2000/2001 NJPS is posted at <www.ujc.org/content_display.html?ArticleID=60346>
[361] Michael Steinhardt, "On the Question of Crisis" in Contact: The Journal of Jewish Life Network. Vol. 5, No. 3 (Spring 2003): 8-9.
[362] Felix Posen, "Concluding Reflections," in the 2001 American Jewish Identity Survey Report: Mayer, Kosmin and Kesar, editors, 50.
[363] Caryn Aviv and David Shneer. *New Jews: The End of the Jewish Diaspora*. (New York: New York University Press, 2005), 173.

CASE STUDY 1: DIASPORA JEWS

The Russian-speaking Jewish population in the FSU is not only in decline, but large-scale movement is contributing to social and religious shifts. After seventy years under communist religious and ethnic suppression, it is apparent that FSU Jewry for the most part had little or no connection with the former religious traditions of Judaism. Many are more familiar with the spirituality of Eastern Orthodox Christianity than with the rites of Judaism.

FSU Jewish people are largely secularized, and they have generally resisted attempts in Israel and the Diaspora to reconnect them with mainstream Judaism. Some of that resistance may be due to an unusually high intermarriage rate of 80% among Jews from the FSU. Thus, they are likely to continue to assimilate in the U.S. and Europe.[364]

The culture of "openness" was proclaimed throughout the FSU in 1990. That opened a door for spiritual ministry among Russian-speaking Jews wherever they are found today.

Israeli Diaspora

The state of Israel is a young nation. While it is the traditional Jewish homeland, it is also the refuge for many of the dispersed Jewish populations. Diaspora communities have entered Israel in waves, as a flood of Holocaust survivors from Europe, a tidal flow of refugees from the Middle East and North Africa during the time of statehood, and, in the last thirty years, as smaller waves from Iran, Ethiopia, and the former Soviet Union.

The Jewish population of Israel more than doubled just in the last thirty years. Whole segments of Jewish population have been uprooted from the dispersion, only to become the next generation in transition within a new Jewish homeland. While Israel is now home to the largest concentration of world Jewry, it has yet to settle on a unified vision for Jewish life at home and at peace. It is a state composed of the formerly scattered people who are sociologically in transition, surrounded by hostile neighbors and seeking a secure future.

Social research has shown an Israeli population that is spiritually divided between 62% secularists and 38% that profess a strict adherence to Judaism.[365] Israeli society is sociologically and politically at odds between those who want more religious influence in daily life and those who want a purely secular country. As a country that is ideologically in transition, and is still absorbing significant numbers of new immigrants, Israel provides a surprisingly fruitful field for diaspora gospel ministry.

---

[364] Source: Division of Jewish Demography and Statistics, The A. Harman Institute of Contemporary Jewry, The Hebrew University of Jerusalem, cited in DellaPergola, Dror and Wald, 12.
[365] Charles S. Liebman and Elihu Katz, *The Jewishness of Israelis: Responses to the Guttman Report*, (Albany: SUNY Press, 1997).

It is worth noting an Israeli diaspora. Field studies have shown that large, gregarious communities of native-born Israeli communities exist in New York, Los Angeles, London, Paris, Sydney, and Berlin. Israelis, for the sake of educational development or business opportunity have moved out of Israel and exist as "transnationals," as Stephen Gold refers to them in *The Israeli Diaspora*.[366] They have preserved a cultural identity as Israelis within foreign host cultures, thus representing a unique category of diaspora Jewry.

Israeli youth and young adults are quite open to study different and nontraditional spiritual options. Their families originally came to Israel from diverse cultural backgrounds in the diaspora. Israelis in general appear to be more open than American Jews to discuss and consider the diverse cultural and spiritual experiences of Jews who came from other lands.

Also, Israel is a small country, no larger than the American State of New Jersey. Therefore, Israelis look beyond their borders for the refreshment of foreign travel. Young and old seek new perspectives outside the limits of Israeli geography and Jewish social life.

Israeli youth spend the last of their teenage years in the defining experience of compulsory military service within the Israel Defense Forces. Immediately after leaving such a regimented life, these young people typically travel abroad for extended periods. They tour with family or in small peer-flocks to exotic destinations like Bali, the beaches of Goa India, Thailand, the U.S., Latin America, and Brazil around the time of Carnival. In these settings, post-Army Israeli trekkers are quite receptive to non-traditional spiritual perspectives and discussion when it is offered. Such open encounters can have serious missiological implications.

The New Age Movement (NAM) is evident in Israel. Historically it was introduced as early as the 12th century in the mystical form of Judaism known as Kabbalah. It incorporates Jewish Gnosticism, which is fascinating to modern Israelis and resonates in their thinking with other Gnostic teaching in the Far East, especially Buddhism.[367] Walking the streets of Tel Aviv today, one can find shops offering alternative medicine therapies, astrologers, diviners, palm and tarot card readers and varieties of NAM bookshops. Wicca and small satanic cult groups also function in Israel.

Jewish-Gentile couples are another potentially open Israeli subpopulation. Rabbi Yisrael Rozen has claimed that the intermarriage rate in Israel is 7%.[368] The general assumption is that a large number are Jews from the FSU, but no precise data is available. Much more will be said about ministry to this sector of Jewish life later in this chapter.

So, Jewish diaspora today is far more than the Jewish population outside of the Land of Israel. It is immigrant families that move from one diaspora location to

---

[366] Stephen Gold, *The Israeli Diaspora* (Seattle: University of Washington Press, 2002), viii.
[367] Finn Barr, "The New Age and Similar Movements in Israel," *MISHKAN* 38 (Jerusalem 2003): 16-23.
[368] Jonah Mandel, "Think of non-Jewish Immigrants as close kin," Jerusalem Post online, 4/27/2011 at http://www.jpost.com/JewishWorld/JewishNews/Article.aspx?id=218017

another. It involves a younger generation of Israelis who are in transition as post-army trekkers, New Agers, curious secularists, and sojourners in other lands. Jewish diaspora is much larger and more complex than would be appreciated without the diaspora focus on people who are scattered or are otherwise in transition. Attention to the cultural complexities and potential entry points for Great Commission ministry makes world Jewry a worthwhile missiological study.

Next we will consider some mission models and case studies being employed in present-day Jewish evangelism practice. The gospel of the Messiah Jesus is being effectively communicated in a variety of creative and appropriate ways to diaspora Jewry and among Jews who are experiencing transition.

Ministering to Jewish Diaspora

The following is a brief introductory presentation of missiological approaches to diaspora Jewry. Following the model presented by Enoch Wan, we consider them according to diaspora ministry practices that *minister to* Jewish people in diaspora and *ministry through* the natural diaspora networks or kinship groups that exist at home and abroad. In this section we look at strategies that are pre-evangelistic and evangelistic in nature. They offer services to Jewry in need and in transition to create the possibility for relational ministry that leads to making disciples of Messiah Jesus. Among the common practices, we consider humanitarian aid, liturgical and artistic outreach events, apologetic forms, outreach to seekers and trekkers, and Jewish-Gentile couples ministry. A few short case studies are included for illustration.

Humanitarian Aid

A variety of ministries have been created to give humanitarian aid to the Jewish people, especially in Israel. For example, The Joshua Fund extends reconciliation ministry to Jews and Muslims in the Middle East in the name of Messiah Jesus. The Joshua Fund web site explains that their mission is to give humanitarian relief, educational resources and prayer support to people who are in physical and spiritual need.

> Since our founding in 2006, The Joshua Fund has invested millions in blessing poor and needy Jews, Muslims and Christians in the epicenter; in training and encouraging pastors and ministry leaders in the epicenter; and in educating and mobilizing Christians around the world to bless Israel and her neighbors in the name of our Lord Jesus Christ.[369]

---

[369] http://www.joshuafund.net

Liturgical and Artistic Events

Liturgical outreach events are a common form of Jewish mission practice. Appropriate public liturgical services are offered for the fall season High Holy Days, weekly Sabbath services and Passover banquets in the springtime. They are offered through mission stations or in conjunction with messianic congregations of Jewish believers in Jesus.

High Holy Day Services

Liturgical services conducted in keeping the High Holy Days of Rosh Hashanah and Yom Kippur have become a staple of Messianic congregations and Jewish mission agencies. The ten-day period leading up to the Day of Atonement is one of the most spiritually solemn and reflective times of the Jewish year. Diaspora Jewry in Europe, Latin America, Austral/Asia, the former Soviet Union, South Africa, and North America can experience these events in special mission-sponsored events and through the services of established Messianic congregations.

In one case, two Los Angeles based Jewish missions and one Messianic congregation collaborate annually to promote and host High Holy Day services.[370] They promote the events through street banners, their organizational newsletters and personal invitations. Jewish seekers attend these events. Some have returned the following year to give testimony of their journey of coming to faith in Christ.

Passover Banquets

Passover banquets are another appropriate cultural, religious and social occasion to invite Jewish seekers for exposure to the gospel. Most Messianic congregations and Jewish mission agencies, along with some churches, present Passover banquets where Christian friends or mission workers invite Jewish neighbors and contacts for a *seder*—a traditional Passover service, meal and remembrance. Passover liturgy tells the story of the redemption of Israel from Egypt. Woven into the Passover story is an explanation of the Passover Lamb and the importance of blood for redemption. It is very easy to introduce the gospel in such a setting. This is an example of diaspora Jewish ministry that is *to* Jewish people and, in the congregational setting, it is also ministry *through* the networks and kinship arrangements that already exist.

---

[370] Congregation Adat Y'shua HaAdon, Chosen People Ministries, and Jews for Jesus

CASE STUDY 1: DIASPORA JEWS

Artistic Outreach Events

In addition to holiday and Sabbath services, some congregations and missions have hosted public outreach events utilizing the arts. They have featured *klezmer* or Israeli folk music concerts in the U.S., Poland and FSU. Hear O' Israel Ministry produced a series of music festivals throughout Eastern Europe, India, Africa and South America. According to their website "over a dozen new Messianic Jewish congregations have been birthed in the former Soviet Union through these outreaches."[371]

Jews for Jesus offered exhibits with discussion of spiritual nuances evidenced in the works of the artist Marc Chagall.[372] These events create an opportunity for curious Jewish seekers to experience alternative perspectives of Jewish spiritual life that are outside of their traditional rituals or artistic understanding. They are able to receive spiritual benefit in familiar formats while learning of sound reasons for putting faith in Jesus.

Apologetic Forms

Debates, evangelistic ads and specialized literature are also used to present the gospel among diaspora Jewish people and those in life transitions. We consider a few examples of these apologetic forms below.

Debates

One sad chapter in church history reports the deleterious effects of the thirteenth century Jewish-Christian disputations.[373] However, in recent years, successful and respectful debates have been conducted on subjects like "Jesus and the Jewish people." In October 2004, Rabbi Shmuley Boteach and Dr. Michael L. Brown, a Messianic Jew, were featured debaters at the Harvard Club in Boston, Massachusetts. The title of their program was "Can Jews Believe in Jesus: a Debate."[374] A follow-up debate at Scottsdale, Arizona, in April 2005, brought the two together again to debate the question, "Can Jews Accept Jesus as the Messiah?"[375] A Messianic Jewish scholar, Brown has engaged in three separate debates with rabbis on these topics. They are worth reviewing for his

---

[371] Source: Jewish Voice Ministries International website www.jewishvoice.org/about_jb.php
[372] See http://jewsforjesus.org/publications/issues/4_5/jesusinart
[373] H.H. Ben-Sasson, *A History of the Jewish People*, (Cambridge: Harvard University Press, 1976), 385-8.
[374] Source: www.shmuley.com/viewproduct.php?id=65
[375] Benjamin Leatherman, "Rabbi, Evangelist Debate Jewish View of Messiah," *Jewish News of Greater Phoenix* Vol. 57, No. 33 (April 15, 2005).

gracious manner, sharp intellectual skills, and deft handling of the biblical content.[376]

Rabbi Boteach, a strident and sharp-witted orthodox Jew, has a television and radio following among religious Jews in America. However, he and Brown have enjoyed the role of respectful adversaries, while developing a mutual friendship off-stage. Their public interactions have been a healthy airing of the issues, without coercion or defamation.

Evangelistic Advertising

Evangelistic advertising has been used effectively to reach Jewish people with the gospel. In the early 1970s, the American Board of Missions to the Jews, now Chosen People Ministries, utilized a full-page newspaper advertisement to raise Jewish awareness about Jesus. The question "Why are all these Jews smiling?" was a device pointing to the Messiah. That same mission has conducted campaigns to draw attention to Isaiah 53, the amazing chapter of the prophet with poignant Christological images. Other Jewish missions have used evangelistic advertising to lift high the name of *Y'shua*—"Jesus" in Hebrew.

Congregations and missions around the world have used newspaper ads and forms of outdoor advertising to publicize services and outreach events. Congregation Adat Y'shua HaAdon in Southern California has used light pole banners to publicize their High Holy Day services. It is a common format for notifying the public of religious services in their area. As a result, Jewish seekers come to the services, attracted by the offer of admittance without cost.

Some advertising is not event-driven. Jews for Jesus has used handheld street banners to proclaim "Jesus for Jews." The same slogan was used on thirty subway station kiosks between Grand Central Station and Times Square in New York in July 2006. Media begets media. The ads created a large enough "buzz" to prompt television coverage that amplified the message to an even broader audience. It made the debate, "Can a Jew believe in Jesus?" a matter of public discourse. News media outlets carried it as a public service.

Billboards, another form of outdoor advertising, have also been used effectively. Jews for Jesus specialized in billboard ads throughout a five-year evangelism campaign to reach every city in the world, outside of Israel, with a Jewish population of 25,000 or more. Messages were thought provoking, like "Be More Jewish—Believe in Jesus!" Another offered a free video with the testimony of Holocaust survivors who believe in Jesus.

Missions have used newspaper and magazine advertisements to offer books containing testimonies of Jews who have come to faith in Jesus. Yanetz Publishing, in Jerusalem, has had a very effective ministry in this manner, offering free books in Hebrew. HaGefen Publishers in Israel produces books to

---

[376] See http://www.realmessiah.com/Debate

CASE STUDY 1: DIASPORA JEWS

help children understand the story of Jesus in a culturally appropriate framework.

Advertising leaflets are mailed and hand delivered to offer free copies of the *Jesus* film by Campus Crusade for Christ. In Israel, they have been produced in Hebrew, Russian, and Amharic. Or b'Aretz (Light of the Land) was a team, formed in Israel, to distribute flyers offering the "Yeshua" video for free.[377] The *Jesus* film was also dubbed in Yiddish for distribution to the Ultra-Orthodox Jewish community in New York City in 2006. 80,000 flyers were mailed to religious homes. In this way, adherents of the strictest religious sects of Judaism were able to view the gospel story in the solitude of their homes.

Literature in Hebrew, English and Russian

At least four Messianic Christian publishing houses serve the Jewish missions. Two are in Israel and two in the U.S. Lederer/Messianic Jewish Communications is based in Maryland and on the web.[378] Purple Pomegranate Productions are in San Francisco.[379] The Israeli publishing outlets mentioned above produce materials for Jewish people in Hebrew, English, and in Russian.

Yanetz Press was the first modern Christian publishing house in Jerusalem. They produce devotionals, biographical materials, evangelistic literature, Bibles, and apologetic texts, many of which are reprinted from valuable historical works. Under the directorship of Victor Smadja, books are distributed through individuals, mission workers, congregations, youth camps and their own newspaper advertisements.[380]

The Christian Witness to Israel ministry established HaGefen Publishing. They major in evangelistic, expository, theological, and devotional material, also providing a variety of useful services and resources to the evangelistic cause in Israel.[381]

In addition to these publishing houses, the Caspari Center for Jewish Studies in Israel offers study services and important publications to Christians to aid the cause of Jewish evangelism in Israel and the Diaspora.[382] The Pasche Institute now publishes the semi-annual journal, *MISHKAN: A Forum on the Gospel and the Jewish People*. MISHKAN focuses on issues for Christians focused on missiology, history, theology, and trends in Jewish evangelism.[383] Several of

---

[377] Jan Mortensen, "Large-Scale Jesus Video Project in Jerusalem" *LCJE Bulletin* Issue 69 (August 2002): 6-10.
[378] See: www.messianicjewish.net
[379] See: store.jewsforjesus.org
[380] Baruch Maoz, "Trends and Circumstances within the Hebrew speaking churches in Israel," MISHKAN 28 (Jerusalem: Caspari Center 1998): 82-83.
[381] www.cwi.org.uk/HaGefen/hagefen_publishing.htm
[382] http://www.caspari.com
[383] http://mishkanstore.org/store/product_info.php?products_id=30&osCsid=fpcjdwte

the international Jewish missions publish outreach literature and web pages for Jewish seekers. For one example, see Jews for Jesus' bi-monthly newsletter specifically for Jewish seekers called *ISSUES: A Messianic Jewish Perspective*.[384] It offers excellent archives of articles. Also valuable are the excellent apologetic videos and articles produced through the ministry of the above-mentioned Messianic scholar Michael L. Brown, available at RealMessiah.com.[385]

Ministry Through the Jewish Diaspora

Congregational Outreach

Elements of the traditional Sabbath synagogue liturgy are a comfortable and familiar Jewish religious observance. They are now a key feature of Messianic congregations, or assemblies for Jewish believers in Jesus. Messianic congregations are now found in every major diaspora Jewish community in the world and in Israel. A 1999 survey found more than 130 Messianic congregations functioning in the State of Israel.[386] In the United States, the numbers are in the hundreds and growing. Most are small and independent. However, three denominations of Messianic congregations have been established—the International Alliance of Messianic Congregations and Synagogues, the Union of Messianic Jewish Congregations, and the Association of Messianic Congregations.[387]

Congregational ministry, as an outreach of local Messianic communities, has an important role in reaching Jewish people with the gospel today. Congregations provide opportunities for gospel engagement through ongoing programs, events and services. They can also encourage those of their members who are gifted evangelists to reach other Jewish people.[388]

A challenge of the Messianic congregational model, in some cases, is presented when cultural elements of Jewish ritual or Torah-observant Judaism are allowed to overshadow the gospel of grace in the Messiah Jesus. In an effort to stem confusion, a helpful publication was released in 2005 entitled *The Messianic Movement: A Field Guide for Evangelical Christians*.[389]

---

[384] http://jewsforjesus.org/publications/issues

[385] http://www.therealmessiah.com/

[386] Kai Kjær-Hansen and Bodil F. Skjott, "Facts and Myths about the Messianic Congregations in Israel," *MISHKAN* 30-31 (Jerusalem: 1999).

[387] Source: www.iamcs.org; www.umjc.net; www.messianicassociation.org

[388] See Mitch Glaser, "Community Based evangelism – A Model for 21st Century Jewish evangelism," *LCJE Bulletin* 84 (June, 2006): 13-16.

[389] Rich Robinson, Ed. *The Messianic Movement: A Field Guide for Evangelical Christians*, (San Francisco: Purple Pomegranate Publications, 2005).

CASE STUDY 1: DIASPORA JEWS

Field Outreach to Israelis on the Move

Jewish youth, in the diaspora and within Israel, are often in cultural transition. Young Israelis travel the world on post-Army adventures during which they are open to new spiritual experiences. In this section we will introduce the Cochebamba House, New Age outreach in Asia, and New Age festivals in Israel.

Post-Military-Service Israel Trekkers

After their Army service, Israeli adventurers head off to different parts of the world in small groups. They have actually published informal journals, and they also pass along word-of-mouth information about new and interesting experiences. One of the more popular treks is to South America for mountain climbing, river tours and a hedonistic party week during Carnival in Brazil. On the way, some find the "Israeli House" in Cochebamba, Bolivia.

In 1983, Bob and Joyce Wilhelmson of New Tribes Missions saw a door of opportunity open to them. They were serving as missionaries to one of the tribes near Cochebamba, and they noticed a large number of young Israeli travelers coming through their station.

They began to offer the Israeli youths a warm welcome, the hospitality of an overnight accommodation, and an Israeli dinner followed by a two-hour Bible lesson. During this lesson, the missionaries begin by describing their mission work to learn the language and customs of the Bolivian tribe. They then ask the Israelis if they would like to know what the tribal people are taught about the Bible and the Jewish people. The offer usually gets a positive response, followed by a talk that begins in the book of Genesis. They describe the eternal love of God and His plan of salvation for everyone in Jesus the Messiah.

Conversations continue with the visitors until they head off to sleep. Everyone is offered a New Testament to take along the journey. Each group is photographed together and the pictures are kept in an album. Subsequent groups enjoy looking through to seek any of their friends who might have passed by earlier. In this way, the mission workers at Israeli House have been able to document approximately 11,000 Israelis who have passed through the mission station since 1983.[390]

In 2008, Jews for Jesus launched the Massah Israel Outreach as a discipleship course for Messianic Jewish young adults and as an outreach to young Israeli trekkers in India. The summer-long discipleship project allows for cross-cultural exposure between Israeli adventurers and American Messianic

---

[390] Joshua Pex, "The "Israeli" House in Cochebamba," *MISHKAN* 38 (Jerusalem 2003): 64-66

Jews.[391] The Messianic youth build relationships with Israelis at Indian youth hostels, along the mountainous hiking trails and at food stops or "chai houses." They then have used social network media like Facebook to stay in touch with these acquaintances after the summer ends.

Outreach to New Agers in the East

Gentile Christians have also effectively been able to meet Israeli youth taking the eastern routes to beach cities in Thailand and in Goa, India. In 2001 and 2002 the Danish Israeli Mission composed a Danish youth team that volunteered to go to Thailand and India. The project was called "Jews in the East."

Each team had one month of training in Jerusalem at the Caspari Center. They were introduced to Israeli customs, rites and values. They flew the same routes as the Israeli young people, to the beaches in the Far East coastal resorts. It was very easy for the young Danes to engage young Israelis in English conversations. They offered free literature and New Testaments in Hebrew.[392]

New Age Festival Outreach

The New Age movement (NAM) has touched the Jewish people in Israel. The syncretistic amalgam of pantheism, the esoteric, the occult, magic, pop psychology and Gnosticism has influenced modern Jewish spirituality. Two expressions of the NAM are Kabbalah Judaism and a Jewish fascination with Tibetan Buddhism. A taxonomy of new terms includes Hinjews (Jewish Hindus), JUBUS (Jewish Buddhist) and New Age Judaism (Kabbalah Judaism).[393]

New Age festivals have become a place to extend ministry to NAM Israelis. In 1997, the first New Age festival was held in Israel and was attended by 4,000 people. The Beresheet ("in the beginning") Festival takes place during the fall season, corresponding with the High Holy days around Rosh Hashanah, the Jewish New Year. More than 25,000 people annually attend this festival on the Galilee seashore.

Another New Age festival called Boombamela is held during Passover week on the beach near Ashdod. It draws as many as 30,000 Israelis and is modeled after a Hindu religious feast.

Israeli Messianic congregations and mission workers have responded with immersion outreach into these festivals. Local Jewish believers in Jesus purchase booth space and open chai shops to welcome Israelis for tea and conversation about the Messiah Y'shua. They offer a warm welcome and a

---

[391] See http://massahoutreach.org/about
[392] Renz Hartmut, "Annual Report for LCJE Europe 2002," *LCJE Bulletin* No. 71 (February 2003): 16.
[393] Heinrich Pedersen, "Hinjews, Jubus and New Age Judaism," *MISHKAN* 38 (Jerusalem: 2003): 39-46.

non-judgmental opportunity to discuss, in Hebrew, the Good News that Jesus has come as Lord God, Savior and Messiah.

A distorted Israeli news story about the latest festival reported, "The largest and only air-conditioned tent at the festival is run by Jews for Jesus and offers free non-kosher food and baptisms."[394] The NAM Festivals present a mission opportunity that is so large that Israeli outreach teams report that the field is white unto harvest and the workers are all too few.[395]

Ministry to Jewish-Gentile Couples

Ministry to Jewish-Gentile couples is one of the most exciting missiological opportunities now present throughout the diaspora. In the United States, the declining birth rate no longer repopulates a Jewish community that is graying and dying. An exodus from Judaism has left less than one-third of American Jews attached to any Jewish institutions. Most dramatic of all, demographic reports indicate that over the past 25 years, more than half of American Jewish people who married have taken non-Jewish spouses.

Demographic data on intermarriage rates in Europe (40-60%), the former Soviet Union (80%) and Latin America (45%) are similar.[396] Responses from traditional Jewish sources have been vigorous, but far from effective. A large number of gentiles have entered Jewish communal life through marriage, yet without absorbing the culture or religion of Judaism. As a result, diaspora Jewry is changing.

Christian mission workers have been slowly stepping up to this challenging opportunity. In 2004, an ethnographic missiological study sought to understand the challenges that Jewish-Gentile couples face. We found confusion over identity differences, tension over religious differences, disagreements over life-cycle celebrations, challenges to family harmony, and discord over the training of children. Most importantly, we found that couples were desperate to discover some way of experiencing spiritual harmony that was mutually satisfying.[397]

Jewish partners did not want to convert to something that appears to be a foreign religion, as they saw Christianity. Gentile, or Christian, partners did not want to embrace Judaism if it meant giving up Jesus.[398]

Some Messianic congregations, like Son of David in Rockville, Maryland, and mission efforts like Jews for Jesus in Los Angeles, have hosted small-group

---

[394] Meir Schwartz, "Israeli Festival Becomes Jewish Encounter," Arutz 7-IsraelNationalNews.com, 10/16/06.
[395] Lisa Loden, "The New Age in Israel at the Beginning of the 21st Century," *MISHKAN* 38 (2003): 24-38.
[396] DellaPergola, 12.
[397] Wan and Zaretsky, 2004.
[398] Tuvya Zaretsky, "Relations and Tension: Research on Jewish-Gentile Couples," *LCJE Bulletin* No. 77 (September 2004): 9-14.

discussions for Jewish-Gentile couples that focus on biblical truths about marriage and family life. A discussion begins in the biblical text. In this way, solutions to spiritual disharmony are focused in the God of Abraham, Isaac, and Jacob and His biblical resources.

Through Existing Social and Kinship Networks

Some congregations are hosting *Havurot* (pl.). A *Havurah* is a small fellowship group that traditionally stands alongside synagogues or Jewish community centers. It is typically a place where social, family and spiritual issues can be discussed in practical terms. This is a fitting mission form for Jewish-Gentile couples to explore culturally appropriate spiritual options in a comfortable learning setting.

Children's ministry is an area where Jewish-Gentile couples report significant cross-cultural tension. Conflict often focuses around how to enculturation children when there are two faith traditions and cultures in the household. Several good models for Jewish-Gentile children's ministry have emerged.

For more than thirty years, one of the Messianic congregations in Israel has sponsored summer youth camps in Jerusalem. In the diaspora, the Jews for Jesus ministry has sponsored Camp Glial, a program for children ages eight through eighteen. Ariel Ministries conducts Camp Shoshanna, focusing on Bible exposition for youth and families in New York State.

Weekly daytime Bible clubs are also used to reach Jewish children in Israel and in the diaspora. Parents are informed that children are receiving instruction in the Bible, including the New Testament and the teachings of Jesus. A Messianic ministry in Chicago originated *Club Maccabee*, which follows a similar model with its own curriculum and outreach to Jewish children.[399] These methods have opened additional avenues for ministry to intermarried parents.

Strategic Mobilization for Jewish Evangelism

Enoch Wan has called attention to a new missiological paradigm to meet the opportunities and challenges that are encountered in diaspora missiology. It is worth considering this multi-directional, multi-dimensional and "diaspora management" missiological paradigm of networking and partnership in the context of Jewish evangelism.[400]

---

[399] Kirk Gliebe, "Children's Outreach: Past, Present and Future," LCJE Bulletin 65 (September 2001): 17-25

[400] Enoch Wan, "The Phenomenon of Diaspora: Missiological Implications for Christian Missions," in *Scattered: The Filipino Global Presence*, (Manila: LifeChange Publishing, 2004), 110-115.

CASE STUDY 1: DIASPORA JEWS

The Multi-Directional Approach

We have shown that Jewish communities in the diaspora and even in Israel are shifting populations. Jewish communities are flowing, growing, moving and experimenting with new forms of spirituality. Our mission approach to Jewish people must include an apostolic lifestyle of availability, vulnerability and mobility. It also must include strategies for reaching out to the Jewish people wherever they are. Specifically, approaches should come through appropriate structures that provide ways for communicating into currently existing Jewish networks.

We are seeing a new era in cross-cultural mission opportunities through the Jewish diaspora relationships currently in place. It is time to mobilize the resource of Jewish Believers in Jesus (JBJ) in the diaspora who can move with the Jewish population flow. Iranian JBJs in Los Angeles can effectively minister to other Iranian Jews in the U.S., in Iran, and among new Israeli émigrés or visitors. Another case in point is the influx of Ethiopian JBJs to Israel. Approximately 90,000 *Flash*, or "exiled" Ethiopian Jews moved to Israel in the 1990s. Among their community are *Flash Mura*, Ethiopian JBJs. They have established Christian congregations in Israel and are evangelizing Ethiopian Jews and other Israelis.

Inside the state of Israel, we find Russian, Farsi, Spanish, Amharic, German, and Hebrew-speaking Jews who are coming to faith in Jesus Christ. They are well qualified to go out into the diaspora to carry the gospel just as it was borne by the earliest disciples. They can reach out to the diaspora from the Jewish homeland.

Europe is also presenting opportunities for multi-directional, cross-cultural diaspora outreach. Jewish believers in Jesus from the FSU are more easily able to move to Poland and Germany where the new immigrant streams of Jewish diaspora communities are moving. In the early 1990s, Jewish missions were sending American gentiles and Jews to the eastern bloc countries to learn Russian language for ministry there. Now, native Russian-speaking Jewish believers are capable of moving across European lines carrying the gospel with them.

During the summer of 2006, Jews for Jesus (JFJ) conducted an outreach campaign in metropolitan New York. Specialized teams of Hebrew-speaking Israelis and Russian/Ukrainian-speaking workers from the FSU came to minister the gospel among the Israelis and Russian-speaking Jews in Manhattan and the surrounding areas. One team of mission staff from the FSU remained behind in Brooklyn to continue discipleship and outreach ministry, completing the work that began in the summer. In fact, JFJ is also deploying staff from their FSU branches to help evangelize the growing Russian-speaking diaspora Jewish community that is now moving into Hungary and into Berlin and Essen, Germany. Availability, vulnerability, and mobility are important values for a multi-directional approach to mission.

Multi-Dimensional Approach

Ministry among Jewish-Gentile couples and their families requires outreach that is multi-dimensional in approach. The extension of ministry must be appropriate to the challenges of intermarried parents and for the different needs of their children. In this way, we can encourage mission through existing networks and kinship relationships of the Jewish diaspora.

Traditional Jewish community approaches presume a one-size-fits-all methodology. They seek to bring Jewish-Gentile couples into closer conformity with rabbinic Judaism or at least to make Jewish life choices. Whether they call for outreach or conversion, the goal ignores the cross-cultural distinctions that are present in the Jewish-Gentile couple matrix.

A holistic mission approach is needed which extends Christian love of the couple (the greatest commandment) and offers the gospel as the resource for the spiritual isolation from God and one another (the Great Commission).[401]

We have already seen, in the case of the New Age trekkers in the diaspora and the spiritual seekers at Israeli New Age festivals, the need to find emotional acceptance in the course of their spiritual search. The polemical approach is inferior to relational interactions with diaspora Jews and those in spiritual transition or on the road to assimilation.

Networking and Partnership

Networking and partnership are among the reasons that the LausanneConsultation on Jewish Evangelism (LCJE) came into existence. In fact, in 2005 they added the qualifying words, "Networking Jewish Evangelism" to the organizational title. The LCJE is a network of people and agencies that are enthusiastic about reaching Jewish people with the gospel.

LCJE originated from a task force on reaching Jewish people that met during a LCWE conference in Patty, Thailand, in 1980. Today, the membership is composed of Jewish mission agencies, missionaries, congregations and denominational representatives that are engaged in Jewish evangelism. They are scholars, authors and individual mission workers in the field. Members pay dues as either agencies or individuals.

The purpose of the LausanneConsultation on Jewish Evangelism is foremost to encourage networking. It is the only global organization in existence today that brings together people who are involved in the field of Jewish evangelism. The membership has five clearly stated functions:

- Share information and resources
- Study current trends

---

[401] ibid. 112

CASE STUDY 1: DIASPORA JEWS

- Stimulate one another's thinking on theological and missiological issues
- Strategize on a global level so that more Jewish people will hear and consider the Good News of Jesus.
- Arrange consultations that are useful for accomplishing the purposes of the LCJE.

LCJE Conferences

An international coordinating committee (ICC), composed of four elected members, does the business of LCJE. The ICC plans and coordinates international conferences every four years. The Ninth International LCJE Conference was held at the historic High Leigh Conference Center in Huddleston, England, in August 2011. The theme was "Jewish Evangelism: Always and Everywhere." Papers from this and past conferences and the 2011 *Conference Statement* are available online at the LCJE website.[402]

Regional networks have been established in Europe, North America, Austral/Asia, Japan, Latin America, South Africa, and Israel. Volunteer coordinators submit reports on behalf of network members laboring in the cause of the gospel in their regions.

Regional LausanneConsultations on Jewish Evangelism meetings are generally held annually. At the request of member mission leaders, the ICC has planned and convened three LCJE CEO conferences between international meetings during 2001 in Oslo, 2005 and 2009 in France. A network for LCJE younger leaders also meets periodically.[403] The LCJE also sent representation to the LausanneForum 2004 in Patty, Thailand, and the LCWE Cape Town Conference in 2010.

LCJE Publications

LCJE produces useful publications for their membership and others engaged in Jewish evangelism. It maintains and periodically publishes a *Directory* of the membership. The *LCJE Bulletin* is published and distributed four times a year. LCJE also maintains an internet home page for conference registration and an archive of past *Bulletins* and conference papers.[404] LCJE has also produced the two LausanneOccasional Papers.[405]

---

[402] See www.lcje.net
[403] See LCJE Bulletin 71 (February 2003): 4-5.
[404] www.lcje.net
[405] David Harley, editor, LOP 7 Thailand Report – Christian Witness to the Jewish People, 1980 and Tuvya Zaretsky, editor, LOP 60 Jewish Evangelism: A Call to the Church, (Lausanne Committee for World Evangelization, 2005).

The *LCJE Bulletin* is published four times a year: in February, May, August, and November. An annual subscription is $15, although it is provided free to all individual members. Regional reports of LCJE network activities are published in the *Bulletin*. Book reviews help membership stay current on literature that addresses Jewish evangelism. Articles on relevant issues, media updates and theological subjects arising from regional network meetings aid information sharing. The *Bulletin* also commends other valuable resources in the field, such as the publication *MISHKAN: A Forum on the Gospel and the Jewish People*, the *Caspar Center Media Review*, and the Jewish Mission History On-Line Library[406] (an online digital library that hosts primary source materials from the history of Jewish evangelism[407]).

Enoch Wan urged attention to diaspora mission management in order to enhance cooperation and partnership. The late Jewish mission leader, Moshe Rosen, used to say, "If there were no such entity as the LausanneConsultation on Jewish Evangelism, then we would need to create one." It is an organization that does not evangelize. However, it effectively brings people together to strategize, share information, study trends, form partnerships and plan together to fulfill the Great Commission among Jewish people in the diaspora and undergoing transitions.

Summary

This study has described historical background and provided data regarding Jewish diaspora. Ethnographic descriptions highlighted missiological trends to show where mission opportunities are emerging among world Jewry. A sample of current Jewish mission practices illustrated some of what is being done to meet those opportunities. We hope that these suggestions will stimulate and encourage further creative thinking and practice in Jewish evangelism.

---

[406] <www.caspari.com> and < www.lcje.net/cgi-bin/gsdl/library?>
[407] Rich Robinson, *LCJE Bulletin* No. 71 (February 2003), 9-14.

Chapter 16

Case Study 2: Missiological Implications of Chinese Christians in Diaspora

Kim-Kong Chan

Introduction

Christianity (Protestantism) in China began with the contemporary mission movement in the mid-nineteenth century. The Christian population in mainland China was not significant until the reported huge Christian growth of the recent three decades. During the past quarter century, all religious groups in China have been growing, with the Christian (Protestant) community[408] growing the fastest, from a tiny group in 1980 (estimated at 3 million) to recent count of at least 23 million, according to a survey by the Chinese Academy of Social Science.[409] Some Christian scholars claim that there are more than 80 million Christians in China. A communist scholar even suggests that the number of Christians will increase to 200 to 300 million in the coming 20 years and will become one of the largest clusters of Christians in the world.[410] Concurrently, the centrality of global Christianity is shifting from traditional Western countries such as those in Europe and North America to non-Anglo-Saxon countries such as Korea, Nigeria, and Brazil where the fastest

---

[408] This paper deals only with the Protestant (hereafter refer to as Christian) community in China and the discussion on Catholic community is not included for the Catholics in China are involved with the complicated issue of Sino-Vatican diplomatic tension.

[409] Chen Jia, "Over 23 Millions Christians in Country" in *China Daily*, 12 August 2010; available at http://www.chinadaily.com.cn/usa/2010-08/12/content_11144948.htm

[410] Lu Daji, foremost expert on religion in Chinese Academy of Social Science (CASS), made such suggestion on an internal report to the United Front Work Department, as quoted by Ma Hucheng, "An Analysis of the Reasons for Rapid Growth of the Protestant Church in Today's China," *Studies in Religious and Minority Questions in Modern China* (Beijing: CASS, 2010).

growing[411] and largest churches are found.[412] With this increasing prominence, some missiologists predict that the Chinese Christian community may well become one of the major centers of Christendom in this century, as it is one of the main contributors to this global trend.[413]

During the same period of time, China has emerged from economic obscurity with virtually no significant economic impact to being the world's second largest economic entity, just after the U.S. It is one of the world's fastest growing major economies over the past 30 years. China is also the largest exporter and second largest importer of goods in the world. China became the world's top manufacturer in 2011, surpassing the United States. From 1980 to 2006, its GDP increased from U.S.D 147 billion to U.S.D 2.225 trillion, a fifteen-fold increase,[414] and in 2010 its GDP reached 5.87 trillion, more than double in less than five years or forty-fold in 30 years! Currently China is the largest single holder of U.S. debt, more than 1 trillion U.S.D![415] Many countries have already felt China's unprecedented economic growth, with Chinese goods flooding the world market and China's economic tentacles in the form of investments and purchasing reaching virtually every part of the globe.

If one considers China's economic-political expansion together with her Christian development, one can hardly ignore the missiological ramifications of Chinese Christians for future global mission. Some, like David Aikman, venture to suggest that perhaps the Christian community in China—one of the fastest growing churches situated within one of the most powerful economic entities with global vision—may one day also become the largest exporter of missionaries to have the last frontier for Christianization. This last mission frontier, popularly known as the 10/40 window,[416] is an area that embraces the predominantly Islamic region stretching from Central Asia to the Middle East and North Africa.[417] Will the current export of commodity goods and services such as clothing, shoes, refrigerators, TVs, cars, electronic goods, infrastructure construction, investments, engineers, entrepreneurs, and construction laborers from China to this region one day be augmented to or followed by the religious

---

[411] Cf. Philip Jenkins, *The Next Christendom: The Coming of Global Christianity* (Oxford: Oxford University Press, 2002).

[412] The largest Congregation is the Yoido Full Gospel Church in Seoul with membership of more than 850,000 as of August 2011, personal visit, August 2011.

[413] For example, see "Let the 21st Century be the Mission Era of the Chinese Church," available at http://www.Gospelherald.com.hk/news/mis_350.htm., February 21, 2007.

[414] See President Hu Jintiao's speech at Yale University on April 22, 2006; available at http://www.peacehall.com/news/gb/intl/2006/04/200604220826.shtmi

[415] David Barboza, "China tells U.S. 'It must cure its addiction to debt,'" *New York Times*, August 6, 2011; available at http://www.nytimes.com/2011/08/07/business/global/china-a-big-creditor-says-us-has-only-itself-to-blame.html

[416] The 10/40 Window is an area of the world that contains the largest population of non-Christians. The area extends from 10 degrees to 40 degrees north of the equator, and stretches from North Africa across to China, see http://1040window.org/main/whatis.htm.

[417] See David Aikman's *Jesus in Beijing: How Christianity is Transforming China and Changing the Global Balance of Power* (Washington, D.C.: Regency Publishing Inc, 2003).

counterpart of these commercial activities, namely, Chinese missionaries and the gospel message? Will this merger of Christian revivalism, economic growth, global commercial ambition, and increasing numbers of Chinese for expanding Chinese diaspora communities in virtually every country result in a missiological movement of significance that would shape the global Christendom?

Several possible mission thrusts exist for Christians in China: direct sending of missionaries to oversee the mission field, mission through diaspora communities, or "business as mission"(BAM). Currently some missionaries are already being directly sent, such as the "Back To Jerusalem Movement" (BTJ or BJM) which is predominantly operated by autonomous Christian communities of China that are mostly non-registered with the Government. These Chinese Christian communities are not included in this chapter.[418]

This chapter will study missiological implications of the development of diaspora Chinese Christian communities, especially during the past 25 years, as large numbers of Chinese from mainland China choose to live overseas in various countries, thus greatly expanding the diaspora Chinese community. It will examine the BAM model of Chinese Christian business people overseas as typified by Chinese Christian merchants from the Wenzhou areas of Zhejiang Province.

Chinese Global Commercial Activities and Missions: The Case of Wenzhou Christians

Wenzhou is a municipality within the Zhejiang Province with population of about 7.5 million in 2005.[419] It has increased to 9.1 million, according to the census of 2011.[420] Wenzhou residents speak a unique dialect that few outsiders

---

[418] For those who are interested in this topic, see Chan Kim-kwong, "The Back-To-Jerusalem Movement in Mainland China," in *Emerging Mission Movements: Voices of Asia*, ed Bambang Budijanto (Colorado: Compassion International/Asian Evangelical Alliance, 2010), 101-122.
[419] Mr. Yang Shangming, Deputy Director of the Liaison Office of the Wenzhou Municipal Government, supplies all figures about population profile of Wenzhou. Mr Yang is the expert on this topic as he keeps track of the Wenzhou natives not only in China, but also their whereabouts all over the world. There is no reliable published data on this subject due to the dynamic nature of the Wenzhou people in their movements. Unless indicate otherwise, all data on Wenzhou in this paper is supplied by Mr Yang. Personal interviews, November 24-26, 2005.
[420] The figures on population of Wenzhou need to be qualified. The Chinese government has a registration system which regards one's origin as the place where their grandfather was born (three-generation, paternal side). Such system has been in practice for centuries and has only begun to face challenges in recent times, as there has been a high degree of people migration due to rapid social changes. If we count those who are of Wenzhou origin, there are about 7.5 million, as the older census in 2005 only counts such number. However, with the increase of internal migrants, current practice of

of this region comprehend. They are entrepreneurs by tradition, and led China's economic reform policy by establishing the first batch of private enterprises in China in the late 1970s. They have the highest per capita income in China, and the highest percentage of merchants in their population. Virtually there is someone in every family who is engaged in business or private enterprise.[421] More than 93 percent of Wenzhou's GDP is from the private sector, surpassing the national average of around 60 percent. Wenzhou people are perhaps the richest people-group in China, with at least RMB 800 billion (8 RMB = 1 U.S.D) liquidity floating around and waiting for investment opportunities.

Furthermore, Wenzhou people carry their age-old tradition as itinerant merchants wherever business opportunities exist. Wenzhou merchants not only set up business in every major city in China, they also set up business in at least 140 countries. Of these 7.5 million Wenzhou residents, 1.5 million are scattered throughout all parts of China doing business, from the rich Chinese coastal provinces such as Jiangsu to the harsh plateaus of Tibet. Another 500,000 are doing business in more than 140 countries all over the world, from Morocco[422] to Montenegro.[423] No wonder they are called the "Jews of China!"[424] At the same time, at least 3.5 million migrant laborers from other provinces work in factories in Wenzhou. Therefore, at least 9 million people physically live within the Wenzhou municipality as permanent residents in an area of about eleven thousand square kilometers.

The Wenzhou Christians

Wenzhou has the highest percentage of Christians among all municipalities in China, with an official figure of 1 million,[425] or about 11 percent of the

---

Chinese Government counts those who live in a place of more than half of the days in a year as permanent residents. In this way, we have the figure of 9.1 million included those internal migrants who are from outside of Wenzhou areas, such as factory workers. See
http://www.wenzhouguide.com/wenzhou-the-largest-city-by-population-zhejiang/

[421] Field observations in November 2005, and March 2006, and interviews of more than 100 families, substantiate the high entrepreneurial spirit of Wenzhou people as virtually every family, which this author visits, runs some kinds of business, usually small ones!

[422] "Attention, les Chinois débarquent!" in *Aujourd'hui Le Maroc*, September 15, 2004.

[423] This writer traveled to Kotor, a medieval town in Montenegro in August, 2004, and saw a Wenzhou business man who operated a shop in the local market.

[424] There are about 2 million Wenzhou natives living outside of Wenzhou. However, the official figure is 1.35 million as it excludes those Wenzhou people who obtained citizenships or resident status elsewhere or in other countries/region. See http://news.hexun.com/2011-05-10/129462195.html.

[425] Rev. Matthew Deng, President of Zhejiang Christian Council, gave the figure of 770.000 on March 24, 2006. This figure does not include the unregistered ones, as well as those Wenzhou Christians who are not living in Wenzhou—about 27% of the Wenzhou people! This author interviewed several Wenzhou church leaders in April 2011 in Zhejiang Theological Seminary while giving lectures to these church leaders, and they all suggested that there are well over 1 million Christians within the registered churches and at least another .5 million within the non-registered sector. Since all these leaders are from the registered churches, they may have a rather conservative figure on the non-registered sector. The actual figure would be higher.

CASE STUDY 2: MISSIOLOGICAL IMPLICATIONS OF
CHINESE CHRISTIANS IN DIASPORA

population. Reliable sources suggest that there are currently at least 1.5 million Wenzhou Christians, from both registered and non-registered churches which amount to about 20 percent of the population in Wenzhou. Visitors to the region can find church buildings literally in every village. If at any given time the 1.5 million Wenzhou Christians were to spread out and live as internal migrants in China, there would be about 300,000 Wenzhou Christians living in every major city and remote town all over China. Wenzhou Christians often establish gathering points (house churches) among themselves in new places where there is no Christian presence. For example, Wenzhou Christians formed perhaps the first Government-sanctioned Christian meeting point at Lhasa, Tibet where at least a thousand now gather every Sunday. Some share the Christian faith with local inhabitants who had never been contacted by missionaries before. Many Wenzhou Christians combine their business practice with missiological aims: to share the Gospel in places where they have business ventures, especially newly developed markets in remote places.[426] Some deliberately establish business in areas with no Christian presence so as to spread the Gospel and establish Christian churches.[427]

Wenzhou Christians in Diaspora

With the increase of Wenzhou migrants in more than 140 countries now numbering at least half a million, about 20 percent of them are Christians. It is estimated that 100,000 Wenzhou Christian "merchant-cum-missionaries" are currently carrying the good news of inexpensive Chinese products as well as the Good News of free salvation to all corners of the world. They are also the founders of many new Chinese congregations in Europe, including one in Bucharest, Romania in the late 1990s and one in Cairo, Egypt in 2008. Will they, through their global commercial activities and their strong evangelical zeal, be a natural army of missionaries to bear Christian witness in places hard to access by conventional mission channels? Will countries that forbid conventional mission activities and entry of missionaries, and countries that are inaccessible to the West be opened to Wenzhou Christians merchants? Will the Chinese BAM become the counter part of the Moravian Brethren in Europe ?

---

[426] See Kim-kwong Chan and Tetsunio Yamamori, *Holistic Entrepreneurship in China* (Pasadena, California: William Carey International University Press, 2002), 65-72.

[427] In 2005 and 2011, the author met merchants residing in sensitive areas (boarder areas, military zones). They successfully established viable Christian communities among the locals, some of whom came from minority groups which have no Christian churches. Thus, for security reason, names, locations, and interview dates have been omitted.

BAM – A Bumpy Road for Diaspora Wenzhou Christians

In the history of contemporary mission movements, when Christian mission work was associated with Western political and economic forces (especially during the nineteenth century), mission activities benefited from and were protected by colonial powers. Missionaries preached along the trade routes established by their political and commercial counterparts in the mission frontier. After the Second World War, people in the developing world gained national independence from Western colonial powers. Western-backed Christian activities were often rejected by xenophobic and nationalistic new regimes. Christian communities in China in the 1950s is a good example of the negative consequences from close alliance between Christian mission and secular political/economic powers. The Chinese Church was accused of being the agent of imperialists in undermining Chinese sovereignty. Will the new China be playing the reverse role and be perceived as economic aggressors, which lead to the emergence of sinophobic sentiments affecting all Chinese—including missionaries—in host countries? The following examples seem to indicate such a possibility.

The current large volume of inexpensive Chinese goods in international markets has become a threat to many countries, as these goods undercut local industry which often lacks a competitive edge against Chinese imports. A global sinophobic sentiment is in the making in recent years, and China-bashing has become a common political gesture to distract public attention from internal economic problems. In many countries around the world, anti-Chinese sentiment has been the result of global commercial activities of China.

In 2004, Moscow police "confiscated" more than U.S.D 30 million worth of goods from Chinese merchants in Ismira Market on the outskirt of Moscow.[428] Furthermore, the presence of about half a million Chinese in Siberia has stirred up strong sinophobia in Russian society resulting in numerous abuses against Chinese in that region, such as blocking roads to Chinese markets.[429] Chinese merchants in Russia have found it increasingly difficult to engage in business activities.[430] Such harassment of Chinese continued in 2010 when Moscow's government suddenly decided to close off the largest outdoor market in the country, Cherkizovsky, of which 90 percent was operated by Chinese. Fifty thousand Chinese were affected, and they were given no compensation for their confiscated goods. As extreme nationalism emerges in Russia, beating of

---

[428] See the Chinese report "Reflection on the Elche Incident," available at http://news.sina.com.cn/c/2004-10-07/11433847992s.shtml

[429] For example, see Vilya Gelbras's interview in *Vladivostok News*, October 25 2001, available at http://vn.vladnews.ru/arch/2001/iss280/News/upd25.HTM; or "Chinese Consul Investigates Protest," in *Vladivostok News*, April 23 2002; available at http://vn.vladnews.ru/arch/2002/iss306/News/upd23_3.HTM.

[430] Yu Chen, "Reports on the Situation of Chinese Merchants in Far East Siberia," 11 November 2004; available at http://peacehall.com/news/gb/chinese/2004/11/200411111357.shtml.

CASE STUDY 2: MISSIOLOGICAL IMPLICATIONS OF CHINESE CHRISTIANS IN DIASPORA

Chinese and other non-white individuals has become common practice these days.[431]

In May 2004, district police in Bucharest cordoned off a section of the huge Europa market (currently the largest commodity market in Europe, with 95 percent of shops owned by Chinese), and literally robbed every Chinese merchant within the cordoned areas.[432] Local authorities used all sorts of excuses to fine Chinese merchants, and Romanian employers withheld Chinese employees' salaries, citing obscure regulations backed by authorities.[433]

In September 2004, Moroccans urged their government to take active measures to curb importation of Chinese goods in order to protect their own industry.[434] At the end of September 2004, several hundred Spaniards in Elche took to the street to protest against Chinese merchants. They attacked Chinese-run stores and burned Chinese-made shoes worth a total of U.S.D 1 million, while the local police took no action.[435] Many shouted insulting and xenophobic racist remarks such as *"chinos fuera"* or *"chinos de mierda."*[436] Anti-China sentiment spread to Madrid and Barcelona in May 2006 as both municipal governments closed off hundreds of Chinese shops to protect local commercial interests.[437]

In 2003, anti-Chinese activities[438] took place in Rome during which shoes were taken from Chinese stores and burned. Police in Milan arrested and injured many Chinese based on some minor disputes,[439] and in 2010, some Italian stores even hung signs banning Chinese from entering their stores.[440] Such scenes are increasingly common not only in Europe but also in Latin

---

[431] See Video: The Life of Chinese Merchants in Moscow, available at http://blog.wsj.com/chinarealtime/2010/02/09/video-the-life-of-chinese-merchants-in-moscow.

[432] This writer personally interviewed many victims of this incident in August, 2004. The Chinese embassy stepped in to stop the abuse of the local police against the Chinese merchants. See the statement issued by the Chinese Embassy in Romania in *Ziarul "Chinezi Europeni"* (Chinese In Europe), July 20, 2004, p. 1.

[433] See http://8ok.com/bbs/200901/studyeu/535.shtml. In December 2008, the Chinese communities in Romanian came to rescue those Chinese workers strained in such situation.

[434] The recent arrival of more than 1,000 Chinese merchants triggered a whole series of anti-China articles appearing in local newspapers. For example, see Adam Wade, "Les chinois coulent la plasturgie marocaine," in *Aujourd'hui Le Maroc*, September 17, 2004; or Bensalem Fennassi, "Menace sur l'industrie locale," in *Aujourd'hui Le Maroc*, September 17, 2004.

[435] Katya Adler,"Spanish fury over Chinese shoes," in BBC News, September 24, 2004; available at http://news.bbc.co.uk/2/low/europ/3687602.stmle/

[436] *"Protesta xenofoba en Elche,"* available at www.carteleralibertaria.org/articulo.php?=1005&more=1&c=1

[437] The tension between Chinese-run shops and local shops in both cities has been escalating for many months leading to the Spanish Government to take drastic actions. The Chinese Embassy has sent strong words of protest, and the disputes are still unsettled as of May 2006. See *Mingpao* May 5, 2006.

[438] Jose Gonzalez Mendez, "*La pesadilla China*," in *La Jornada*, October 11, 2004.

[439] See http://8ok/bbs/200812/eulife/1301.shtml.

[440] See http://hk.yahoo.com/article/100122/4/g9a4.html.

America, Africa, and Pacific countries where Chinese commercial activities are gaining momentum. Also, in recent years, a new avalanche of literature on China-threats has become best sellers in the EU and U.S.

These increasing anti-Chinese sentiments have had several damaging effects on Chinese merchants, especially the Wenzhou merchants who operate small scale family business. First, the flow of Chinese merchants has been slowed down. Second, harassment from host countries has caused bankruptcies among many Chinese enterprises and factories engaging in export-oriented manufacturing.[441] Bankruptcies became more acute after the 2008 financial tsunami, as the U.S. and EU greatly reduced their consumer spending. It seems that the volatility of the global market no longer provides long-term sustainability for these Chinese 'merchants-cum-missionaries' in the mission field,[442] especially when political tensions in host countries escalate along with Chinese merchandise flooding the post-WTO global market. Currently, more and more Chinese commercial engagements in global economic activities are huge enterprises, such as Sinopec (China Petroleum) and CICB (China Industrial and Commercial Bank), with strong government backing. Small-scale commercial operations such as those run by Wenzhou merchants are no longer mainstream. Only large-scale enterprises with fewer on-site operators and those with an optimal scale of economy have a good chance of survival in such a volatile business environment. These large-scale enterprises exclude most small size operators and almost all Wenzhou merchants, thus gradually reducing the number of Chinese merchants in foreign lands.

Diaspora Missions – Wenzhou Style

Recent field studies on Chinese Christian congregations developed by Wenzhou merchants in emerging market countries reveal the following features: 1) these congregations are more ethno-centric than ecumenical in spirit, as Wenzhou Christians would gather together while Chinese Christians of other dialects worship in separate groups; 2) these congregations provide social functions along with spiritual care for Chinese communities and often serve as the only means of social support to merchants who are far from home; 3) these congregations experience diasporic growth rather than cross-cultural growth, as almost all new converts are of similar ethnic origin, if not dialect; 4) most of these Christian merchants are struggling to survive socially, spiritually, and financially ; 5) because of difficulties in establishing long-term business and residency, these congregations

---

[441] Wang Jin and Xian Yuanhong, "Bitter Winters for Three Major Shoe Manufacture Capitals," January 16, 2005, available at http://finance.sina.com.cn/chanjing/b/20050116/11501297523.shtml.
[442] One recent case is the leadership crisis of several Chinese churches in Eastern Europe caused by change of local commercial policy resulting in departure of many Chinese merchants of which some are church leaders. Personal field research/interview, August 2004, Romania.

are unstable communities with a high rate of membership turnover; and 6) these congregations are ambivalent to the local host community.

Missions to the Diaspora

In light of the above characteristics, diaspora Wenzhou Christian communities are in desperate need of pastoral care to consolidate their presence. There is a need for "mission to the diaspora" rather than "missions through the diaspora" or "missions beyond the diaspora."[443] Therefore, the main contribution of Wenzhou Christian communities is to serve as a self-propelled society for transient Chinese merchants away from home and not as a cross-cultural mission impetus for world Christendom. Furthermore, the stability and the sustainability of these communities are more directly related to the volatility of the global market than to any strategic mission agenda. For example, the first Chinese Church in Egypt was established in 2007 by a Wenzhou merchant who came to Cairo from Prague to start a new business. He left the business he had operated for more than ten years in the Czech Republic when the business environment became unfavorable.[444]

Missions through the Diaspora – To the Motherland

The direct beneficiaries of the overseas Wenzhou Christian merchants are Christian communities back in China. As the Wenzhou merchants build churches in host countries, they draw other diaspora Wenzhou people and ethnic Chinese into the Christian faith, resulted in large number of baptism. These new Christians, when return to their hometowns, bring their newfound faith with them. This in turn enhances the existing local Christian communities in China (registered or otherwise). Also, it is not uncommon for some of these new Christians to receive their theological education in Europe or elsewhere and return to China to start new unregistered congregations, simply because these trained pastors find it difficult to operate within the rather rigid government sanctioned institutions such as the Three-Self Christian Council. Furthermore, these overseas churches often look to churches back in Wenzhou for help in pastoral care. The home churches would then respond by sending to them pastors through legal and creative means. One can hardly define such exchanges between the home and overseas Christian communities as foreign

---

[443] Dorottya Nagy, a Romanian-Hungarian, has done her doctoral dissertation at the University of Utrecht on Chinese Christian communities in Eastern Europe, and completed in 2008. The above findings are result of her fieldwork which Dr Nagy had shared with this writer.
[444] Personal Interview, July 2007, in Cairo, at the first Sunday Worship of this Church.

religious infiltration, for it is the ethnic Chinese who are conducting these exchanges. However, such exchanges surely enhance the diversity of Christian communities in China, and challenge the exclusive claim and sanctioning power of the Chinese government. Perhaps it can be regarded as an unintended consequence of reverse mission through diaspora.

Missions through the Diaspora – To Diasporas around the World

Currently, at least 40 million overseas Chinese live in diaspora outside of Greater China (mainland China, Taiwan, Hong Kong, and Macao).[445] Among these, at least 20 million mainland Chinese migrants[446] have settled all over the world since 1985. The estimated distribution of these populations is as follows: Europe 1.5 million, U.K. 0.5 million, Latin America 1 million, Africa 0.5 million, North America 7 million, Australia and Oceania 0.1 million, Asia 30 million.[447] During the past 15 years, there has been a sharp increase in mainland Chinese who emigrate by various means, legal or otherwise, to countries not on the above list. Chinese Christian communities have traditionally existed in areas with large populations of Chinese, including the U.S., Australia, Canada, Japan, Thailand, Indonesia, Singapore, and Malaysia. As more mainland Chinese settle overseas, the Christian communities of Chinese in diaspora outside the Greater China Circle are also on the increase, paralleling the growth of their counterparts in mainland China.[448] The conversion rate among overseas mainland Chinese is very high—up to 30 percent in the U.S. The high rate of conversion to Christianity among mainland Chinese immigrants makes

---

[445] The Overseas Compatriot Affairs Commission of Republic of China (Taiwan) has 39.46 million as of December 31, 2009. Available at www.ocac.gov.tw.

[446] There were 28 million overseas Chinese migrants in 1985, and 35 million in 2000. The majority of these new migrants came from Mainland China. If one uses the conservative increasing rate of these 15 years, there would be at least 15 million Mainland Chinese migrants in 2005 and 20 million in 2010.

[447] This author tabulates this rough estimate from various sources. It is just a rough estimate for there is no agency that dedicates to keep track of such figures.

[448] Enoch Wan has done perhaps the best published estimates of Chinese in diaspora and the Chinese Christian community in Diaspora, in "Mission among the Chinese diaspora—Case Studies of Migrant & Mission," (pre-publication version), *Missiology*, January 2003. Some of his estimates seem to be on the low side as this writer checked Wan's figures against field research and other sources. For example, Wan listed 5,000 Chinese in Portugal and there were, in 2005, at least 15,000, and only 5,000 in the Netherlands, yet the figures in 2006 suggest a high number of more than 100,000, and now at least 120,000 (interview with local church leaders in September 2010). Wan has no figure of Chinese in Russia, and there were at least 200,000 Chinese in Russia in 2005, and up to 400,000 in 2010. Wan has listed one Chinese church in Romania, and this writer founded at least three Chinese Christian groups in Bucharest in 2004. Surely such new information was not available in 2002 as Wan did this paper. Furthermore, this writer interviewed a Chinese Catholic priest in Rome (December 3, 2007) who had been in Italy for 5 years, and his estimate of Chinese in Italy was more than 500,000 with a daily increase of 200 to 300 new arrivals just in Rome alone. However, reliable statistics are hard to come by in this highly fluctuating field of mission work as many new Chinese churches are establishing in diaspora communities especially in recent years as discussed in this paper.

CASE STUDY 2: MISSIOLOGICAL IMPLICATIONS OF CHINESE CHRISTIANS IN DIASPORA

Christianity the largest bloc of religious practices identified by Chinese Americans. More than 30 percent of Chinese Americans claim to embrace the Christian faith, and as many as 3,000 Chinese churches exist in the U.S.[449]

In recent years there have been records of sustainable Chinese Christian communities in many countries with no previous records of Chinese churches, including Mongolia, nations of the former Soviet Republic, and even in the Crimea where traditionally few Chinese students and no Chinese Christian communities were present.[450] New Chinese Christian churches are now reported to emerge in most major cities in European countries,[451] totaling 250 churches and about 1.5 million Chinese Christians.[452] Other new Chinese churches have been established in Polynesian nations, Middle East countries, half of all South American countries, and a dozen African countries. In countries such as Italy, Chinese Christian churches are several dozen in number and they have formed their own national association of Chinese churches. A preliminary comparison of figures from 2002, 2006, and 2010 for the same countries strongly suggests a trend of rapid increase of Chinese people in diaspora, as well as Chinese churches.[453]

The number of Chinese language seminaries and Bible schools are also on the rise. Reports show that during the last 15 years, Bible schools and training programs have been established in the U.K., U.S., Australia, Canada, Korea, Burma, Thailand, Indonesia, Singapore, Malaysia, Panama, the Philippines, Brazil, Surinam, South Africa, Russia, Hungary, Rome, France, Italy, Germany, and Spain to serve the growing needs of Chinese churches in the diaspora.

---

[449] See Yang Fenggang's excellent study on this topic, *Chinese Christian in America* (University Park: Penn State U Press, 1999). Figures quoted here are from Professor's Presentation at the IAHR 2005 Tokyo Conference, March 2005.

[450] There has been a Chinese Christian Church at Kiev in Ukraine established already for a decade and there is a substantial number of Chinese living there. However, this writer recently came across a VCD on the Third Anniversary celebration of the founding of the Simferopol Mandarin (Chinese) Church in the Crimea Republic of Ukraine; and Simferopol, with a small population of 330,000, has already have sufficient Chinese living there to sustain a Chinese Christian Church!

[451] For example, see Mary Wang, "Recent Situation of Chinese Mission Work in Europe," in *Great Commission Bi-Monthly* no. 61 (April 2006): 3-13, containing perhaps the best estimated figures on Chinese and Chinese churches in Europe. However, it only includes the 10 countries where Chinese Overseas Christian Mission (founded by Mary Wong) established their work. There is no figure on the other 20-plus European nations. However, the figures in almost all of these 10 countries are much higher then what Enoch Wan had quoted in 2002, perhaps a reflection of the rapid increase.

[452] This is an estimate given by a missionary who works in Europe and shares these figures in 2007 at a mission conference. See http://www.Gospelherald.com.hk/news/mis_359.htm. It seems that this figure is higher than what Wang (see previous footnote) gave in 2006, perhaps a sign of rapid increase of Chinese migrants in Europe since 2005.

[453] Figures of 2002 are from Wan (2002) and figure of 2006 is from Wang (2006). CCCOWE did an update in 2010, see *Chinese Church Today* (February 2011): 8-10.

Ministering to Four Diaspora Chinese Groups

The increasing number of mainland immigrants in diaspora has caught the attention of the more mature Chinese Churches in U.K., U.S., Canada, and Hong Kong. They regard these new immigrants as mission targets—an opportunity for "missions to the diaspora." Four main different groups exist among the new migrants: intellectuals (students, scholars, and professionals), merchants, temporary project workers, and manual laborers (legal or otherwise).

Immigrants in the first group are often the target of mission organizations, both on campuses and in the Chinese communities, and the result is a high conversion rate. A common feature of this group of Chinese Christians is that they are highly educated, as many of them hold advanced degrees earned in their host countries. Most of them learned about Christianity when they were not in China, precluding any root, understanding, or connection to any Christian communities in Mainland China. Most of them belong to independent churches, a popular ecclesiastical model for overseas Chinese churches, also a model similar to those of the non-registered churches in China. While many Christians from this group settle in their host countries, almost all maintain intimate ties with families, colleagues, or business back in China. Since 2008, many have returned to China where economic prospects continue to improve, and many participate in local church activities.

Diaspora Wenzhou merchants dominate the second group. More churches among this group are established by the Wenzhou merchants who have roots in China than by mission agencies overseas. They share their faith with fellow merchants of similar linguistic and cultural backgrounds. Their church mode is, in many ways, a replica of the one in Wenzhou. Hymnology and Bibles are brought from China. For example, even though they may live in Rome, the ancient center of Christianity, their church life and activities seem to be thousands of miles and hundreds of years apart from fellow Christians in their host countries. These Chinese churches seem to be more of a global extension of Wenzhou churches in China than an expression of Christian faith from migrant Chinese.

The third group—temporary project workers—includes Chinese construction workers, seamstresses, exported manual laborers, and staff members of large construction projects or mining projects such as railways, highways, hospitals, clothing factories, copper mines, and oil drilling platforms. These projects take place all over the world, particularly in the Middle East, Africa, and Latin America. They are supervised by either Chinese construction companies or contracted under foreign companies. These workers usually live in secluded compounds and have little interaction with local populations. For example, 40,000 such workers lived in Libya's oil fields in the beginning of 2011 before they were evacuated at the outbreak of the civil war there. These people are an extension of Chinese state-owned enterprises in the host country and they all return to China once the project is finished. There is little opportunity to reach them because they live in isolated compounds. Christians among these project workers sometimes manage to hold worship services and conduct small group Bible studies. Some, with the help of Chinese missionaries, even manage to organize themselves to attend local Chinese church services. For example, Chinese construction workers in Dubai are regularly bussed to local Chinese church services, and they hold evening meetings in the middle of the desert where their compounds are situated.[454] However, in most host countries, there are few reports of Christian activities among these Chinese migrants other than occasional attempts to evangelize some of them, with unknown results.[455]

Few studies have been conducted on the last group of Chinese migrants, as almost all of them are either illegal migrants and hence difficult to study, or they live at the fringe of society and are often difficult to track down. Due to their illegal status, they are not included in official statistics. They are often in hiding and are afraid of being caught. Many end up staying in the underground world and are abused by others. Some Chinese women end up as prostitutes,[456] and many men as slaves in sweatshops or restaurants. These individuals are too ashamed to tell the truth to people back home. Few pay attention to this hidden group living on the fringe, which numbers in the tens of thousands, and so far no mission has targeted this deprived group. Chinese authorities have also chosen to ignore them, as they are illegal people not under the jurisdiction of the consular service of the Chinese Embassy.

Missions through the Diaspora – Impacts on Mainland Chinese Churches

The increasing number of Chinese Christians and their newly established churches have significant impacts on overseas Chinese communities. These Christian communities often become the most powerful bloc of Chinese overseas groups, such as in the U.S., and the sole organized Chinese institution among the migrant population, especially in remote areas with small Chinese migrant populations, to provide social services for newcomers. It is not uncommon for Chinese churches to operate Chinese language schools as part of the Sunday school program to provide Chinese language and cultural studies to

---

[454] This writer visited such Christian groups in 2007 and 2008.
[455] Some Zambian pastors who requested gospel literature in Chinese to give to the many Chinese construction workers in his hometown approached this writer in 2009.
[456] This writer witness literally hundreds of Chinese prostitutes standing near the harbor areas in Dubai, in 2008. A staff of the Chinese Embassy in a Gulf State told this writer that in 2008, a Chinese reporter of the Xinhua News Agency saw this situation and wrote a report but was censored by the Chinese ambassador for disgracing the work of the Embassy. This reporter was later demoted and recalled back to China.

children of new immigrants who often want their children to retain the Chinese cultural identity. In addition, the free Chinese meal after Sunday service in many Chinese churches in the Middle East and Europe is a rare treat that offers a taste of home. The apolitical, cultural, and charitable nature of these Christian churches are often more popular than other Chinese associations in diaspora which usually have political affiliation with either Taiwan or mainland China. These churches are also the key players in the Chinese diaspora communities, especially in Western countries where churches are respected by civil authorities. So these Chinese diaspora churches serve not only in the spiritual aspect, but also in the social aspect among diaspora Chinese communities. In this way, mission to the diaspora is carried out in the host countries. Other than the establishment of a few Chinese churches, the impact of diaspora Christians is virtually not felt beyond the Chinese communities, for contacts between Chinese Christians and their counter parts in the host countries are often minimal. Therefore, growth of these new Chinese Christian communities on the host country Christian landscape produces little effect other than their token or symbolic presence. It is not uncommon for these new Chinese Christian groups to be under-reported, as ethnic Christians groups often are, by the host country Christian communities for the simple reason that there is a lack of contact between each other. Even though the number and the extent of coverage of these Chinese Christian communities are on the increase, their influence so far is limited among and within the Chinese community, and seldom goes beyond the ethnic boundary.

However, the impact of these new groups can be felt in China as more of these newly converted overseas Chinese return to China to start businesses either short-term or long-term. These Christians, while in China, usually do not participate in government-sanctioned registered churches simply because they are not accustomed to their style of religious activities, with the exception of perhaps the Wenzhou Christians. These Christian returnees establish their own groups, usually among their colleagues or friends belonging to professional or intellectual classes and possessing a certain degree of affluence. These clusters of highly educated Christians would form cell groups with theological stance identified more with overseas churches than with Chinese churches in mainland China. Their presence is already being felt in certain circles in China, including business, higher education, and professional circles. They belong neither to the government-registered Three-Self/Christian Council nor to the traditional non-registered networks. They often set up their own churches with more links to overseas Christians than to local Chinese Christians.

With increased participation in globalization activities by Chinese citizens, these diaspora groups will also be on the rise. Their presence will contribute to the increasingly diverse Christian community in mainland China. These groups bear a strong international favor and intellectual atmosphere—both of which are characteristics currently lacking among Christian communities in China. Perhaps in the long run, such characteristics will help to shape the Christian communities in

CASE STUDY 2: MISSIOLOGICAL IMPLICATIONS OF CHINESE CHRISTIANS IN DIASPORA

China into groups with strong global perspective and in time will instill a sense of global mission among Chinese Christians in China. Furthermore, these bi-culturally trained Chinese Christian returnees are ideal potential recruits for cross-cultural mission work.

As for the missiological potential among diaspora Chinese Christian communities, it seems that the Christian population among the diaspora community is still on the low side in most places; for example, there are only 800 Christians among 200,000 Chinese in South Africa, a mere 0.3 percent.[457]

Missions by/beyond the Diaspora

The current growth in Chinese diaspora communities seems to be more of a target for mission to the diaspora and mission through the diaspora but has not reached the potential of "mission by and beyond the diaspora." Mission movements from diaspora Chinese churches have been in existence for some time, especially among the more established Chinese churches in U.K., U.S., and Canada. These churches mainly focus their mission efforts in new diaspora Chinese communities made up of mainland Chinese immigrants in Europe, Africa, Latin America, and North America. In fact, most of the new Chinese diaspora churches owe their existence to these older diaspora Chinese Churches. For example, the Chinese church in Bucharest was established by COCM, a mission agency founded by Chinese Christians in U.K. with the goal to carry out evangelistic work among diaspora Chinese in the U.K. and Europe.

However, a lack of coordination among various Chinese mission agencies resulted in their targeting the same diaspora Chinese communities. A lack of understanding on the demographic patterns and characteristics of the diverse diaspora Chinese population also hampers the efficiency of the mission efforts. Furthermore, a lack of ecclesiological vision often leads to difficulties in establishing sustainable church polity and administrative structure, thus resulting in fragmentation and division among some of the diaspora Chinese churches.

These diaspora Chinese congregations not only provide spiritual and social support to Chinese communities in diaspora, they also provide high moral standard and inner strength to church members to enable them to sustain hardship in their diaspora journey. To the host countries, these congregations act as a bridge to link the often self-contained Chinese communities with local communities through their common basis in religious aspiration. They also serve as a channel of goodwill from the Chinese communities to the host society

---

[457] A mission agency has made this figure available on 30-01-2007 at a mission recruitment meeting; available at http://Gospelherald.com.hk/news/mis_345.htm

so to ease the negative feelings held by local populations. For example, the Chinese Church in Bucharest supports the local orphanage as a sign of goodwill on behalf of the Chinese community. Such benevolent deeds have earned the Chinese a positive image, counteracting the typical greedy image popularly held by Romanians.

Chinese in diaspora is part of the great population migration trend since the late twentieth century and will certainly continue in this century. This population movement will not only rewrite the ethnic and population profiles of many countries, but will also reshape the contour of the Christian world. The increasing diaspora Chinese population cannot be ignored, as it enjoys one of the highest conversion rates in Christian churches. To meet the needs and challenges presented by these diaspora groups, several actions must be taken. More emphases must be placed on missiological teaching among the diaspora churches to instill a global worldview so to balance the current ethnocentric attitude commonly found among the Chinese diaspora churches. More studies should be conducted on this migration trend in order to form effective mission strategies. There should be more cooperation among mission agencies to maximize resources for outreach and church planting. With the establishment of more sustainable Chinese Christian communities in diaspora and bi-culturally trained Christians, perhaps this new contingent of Christians living in virtually every country in the world will become a new wave of missionaries not only reaching its own kinsmen, but also reaching other ethnic groups.

Summary

In conclusion, this chapter analyzes the impacts of these missiological phenomena, from mission to the diaspora, then to mission through the diaspora, and finally the possible mission beyond the diaspora in the context of the future shaping of world Christendom.

China is undoubtedly emerging as a major economic and political power in the international community. Christians in China together with other non-Western Christians may write the next chapter of world Christendom. However, the Christian community in China is but a minority group among the diverse Chinese population of 1.3 billion, and is still far from being an influential social group even within the Chinese social milieu.

In recent years, some Chinese Christians are establishing footholds overseas and taking advantage of China's global economic expansion, such as the Wenzhou Christian entrepreneurs and the Chinese new migrants. These Christians face the difficult task of survival in the host countries before they can have religious influence among the diaspora Chinese population. Only after they are firmly established, perhaps even into the second or third generation, can they have sufficient resources to reach the local population or

CASE STUDY 2: MISSIOLOGICAL IMPLICATIONS OF CHINESE CHRISTIANS IN DIASPORA

beyond. Many of these newly established Christian communities still rely on support from their home churches in China or funding from mission agencies. Furthermore, the emergence of sinophobic sentiments among nations with increasing Chinese global political-economic presence has negative impacts on the survival of diaspora Chinese communities, hence Chinese Christian communities in such context are often rather unstable. Even in extremely stable international business and political environments favoring Chinese merchants and migrants, it will take a long ecclesial development process before diaspora Chinese Christian communities are able to exert significant influence in world Christendom via cross-cultural evangelizing to host country populations and beyond. At the present moment these congregations are often just an extension of existing Christian communities from mainland China, Greater China, or other diaspora communities. They are composed mainly of newly arrived Chinese migrants. Their current tasks are surviving, expanding and consolidating.

Chapter 17

Case Study 3: Missions among the Urban Muslim Diaspora in the West[458]

Moussa Bongoyok

Introduction

We live in a very interesting time in the history of missions. The golden age of Western missionary[459] enterprise seems to be over. The center of Christianity has shifted to the global south. Western Christianity is declining and many people are very pessimistic about the future of the church and missions in the West.

However, the condition of Christian mission in the West is not hopeless. God is acting in an amazing way and creating unique opportunities for mission in the West to regain vitality and to have a greater impact on global Christianity, particularly when it comes to reaching the unreached people groups. Millions of Hindus, Buddhists, Muslims, and followers of other religions have moved and are continuing to move to the West. In this chapter, I will focus on the Muslim people groups. Islam is the second largest religion in the world after Christianity and the West hosts a large number of Muslim diaspora. While the presence of Western missionaries in Muslim nations and highly Islamized regions is becoming more and more dangerous, especially after 9/11, Muslims are settling in and building mosques in European and North American cities where none existed before.

Many church leaders are worried. A large number of Christians are panicking. Many view the phenomenon as a real threat and are doing their best to stop the "Islamic invasion" of their neighborhoods. Church leaders and members have

---

[458] This chapter is adapted from an unpublished paper presented at the South West Regional EMS Meeting at Biola University on March 18, 2011.
[459] In this chapter, I focus on Europe and North America, namely, Canada and the United States of America.

personally approached me many times and asked me what to do, how to react when Muslims start to build mosques near their church buildings or when a large group of Muslims move into their cities. In a suburb near Houston, five hundred Iranians moved to a Christian neighborhood and people did not know how to handle their presence. Although there are many friendly Christians who provide support to Muslims and welcome them in their communities, a majority seems to be afraid, suspicious, or openly hostile to them. Islamophobia is a tenacious reality.

One of the main questions the Church in the West must seriously ask relates to the perception of the growing number of urban Muslim diaspora in the cities of Europe and North America. Is it a threat or an opportunity? The main thesis of this chapter is that the increasing number of Muslim diaspora in Western cities is a unique opportunity. To demonstrate it, I will describe some of the key characteristics of Muslim diaspora in Europe and North America and expand on why it is important to reach out to them. Finally, I will make some recommendations as to how to conduct missions among urban Muslim diaspora in Europe and North America.

Urban Diaspora Muslims in Europe and North America[460]

The Muslim population is growing rapidly across Europe and North America, and immigration plays a great role in this growth.[461] According to statistics provided by Mandryk (2010:74, 194, 862),[462] there are 5,177,550 Muslims in the U.S., and they constitute 1.63% of the total population (in contrast, there are 246,553,012 Christians and they constitute 77.62% of the total population). There are 982,803 Muslims in Canada and they constitute 2.90 % of the Canadian population (Christians are 24,424,341, totaling 72.07% of the population). In Europe, there are 44,381,426 Muslims and they are up to 6.07% of the total population. (Christians are 522,017,165 and they constitute 71.34% of the total population).[463]

Although the encounter between Islam and the West goes back to 711 A.D. (when Islam conquered Spain), one must take into consideration the fact that most of the Muslims are first and second-generation immigrants. Schmidt

---

[460] David Claydon, "The Uniqueness of Christ in a Postmodern World and the Challenge of World Religions" Lausanne Occasional Paper No. 31(2005).
David Claydon, *Moving Europeans: Migration in Western Europe since 1650*, 2nd ed. (Indianapolis, IN: Indiana University Press, 2003).
Jane Smith, *Islam in America*, 2nd ed. (New York, NY: Columbia University Press, 2010).
[461] Lesslie Page Moch (2003:189) observes that "The absolute number of foreign residents increased by 13 percent in West Germany (between 1974–1982), by 33 percent in France (1969–1981), and by 13 percent in Britain (1971–1981)."
[462] Jason Mandryk, ed. *Operation World* (Pasadena, CA: William Carey Library, 2010).
[463] Garbi Schmidt, *Islam in Urban America* (Philadelphia, PA: Temple University Press, 2004).

CASE STUDY 3: MISSIONS AMONG THE URBAN MU.S.LIM DIASPORA IN THE WEST

(2004:5), commenting on Islam in the United States, writes: "The establishment of an Islamic community in the United States is highly influenced by thoughts and ideas from elsewhere in the world." In Europe, urbanites are 73% of the population, in North America 82% (Mandryk, 2010:43, 74). Therefore, mission among Muslims in the West largely concerns urban immigrants, although some Muslims are converts from native groups or families well established in the West for ten generations or more, and many Muslim diaspora in Europe live in rural areas where they work on farms. It is a fact that the overwhelming majority of Muslim diaspora in the West live in large cities.

Muslim diaspora[464] in the West come from a variety of countries. In Europe, most of them come from North Africa, the Balkans, West Africa, the Middle East, Turkey, and South Asia. In North America, most of them come from South Asia and the Middle East.

> Immigrant Muslims are ethnically extremely varied, coming from virtually every country where Muslims live, or well over 100 countries in all. The largest numbers of immigrants derive from three main sources: South Asia, Iran, and the Arabic-speaking countries. The single largest group of Muslim diaspora is from South Asia (meaning Bangladesh, India, and Pakistan). They are followed by perhaps 300,000 Iranians and 600,000 from the Arab countries. Shi'is, who make up about 10 percent of the worldwide Muslim population, probably make up about the same percentage of the U.S. Muslim population. (Pipes and Khalid, 2002:1)[465]

Although the population of African Muslim diaspora in North America is relatively small in size, in comparison to other ethnic groups in accordance to U.S. Census Bureau it is on the rise since the 1990s (Cf. Stoller, 2001:231)[466]. Muslim diaspora have the tendency to settle in large cities. The higher concentration in the U.S. is found in the following states: New York, California, Texas, Maryland, Virginia, New Jersey, and Massachusetts. In Canada, they are mostly found in several provinces: Ontario, Quebec, British Columbia, and Alberta.

Muslim diaspora come to Europe and North America for a variety of reasons. Many of them come as refugees. They are pushed by unrest, civil wars, and ethnic and religious persecutions. They are looking for a safe haven, a place where they can live a peaceful life. Others are looking for economic

---

[464] Rima Berns McGown, *Muslims in the Diaspora: The Somali Communities of London and Toronto* (Toronto: Toronto University Press,1999).
[465] Daniel Pipes and Khalid Durán, "Muslim Immigrants in the United States" in *Immigration Studies* (Washington D.C.: Center for Immigration Studies, 2002).
[466] Paul Stoller, "West Africans: Trading Places in New York," in *New Immigrants in New York,* ed. Nancy Foner (New York, NY: Columbia University Press, 2001).

opportunities (a better life), education, or a host of personal reasons. Some Muslims, especially Islamists, are actively involved in the spread of Islam (Islamic da'awah). Sookhdeo (2008:59)[467] identifies the Muslim Brotherhood and its affiliates among the "large Islamist movements that actively seek to gain adherents in all Muslim communities worldwide and appear in almost all Western countries." Some Islamic sectarian groups are also very active in the West (Haddad and Smith, 1993:1-22).[468]

Most Muslim diaspora are non-Arabs. Generally Muslim diaspora in North America are highly educated and have decent job opportunities. Many among them are business peoples, professors, lawyers, medical doctors, and high-ranking officials. In Europe, there are a large number of less-educated immigrants, and most of them are doing subaltern jobs (farming, housekeeping, security guard, etc.). Some Muslim diaspora come from cities. Others come from rural areas. Some Muslim diaspora are highly educated and fluent in many languages while others are illiterate. Among them, many are nominal believers in Islam while others are more zealous. The Muslim community is really diverse and, to add to the complexity, "Muslim immigrants continue to bring with them their own form of Islam, contextualized in their country of origin" (Schmidt, 2004:191-192). All these aspects must be considered in the development of effective mission strategies for urban Muslim diaspora.

After 9/11, Muslims began to face strong hostility, or Islamophobia, although the level of unfriendliness is not the same in every city or neighborhood. Islamophobia "polls of American attitudes toward Muslims conducted after 9/11 attest to the widespread mistrust of the religious beliefs and values that many non-Muslim Americans believed motivated Muslim's behavior." (Ghanea Bassiri, 2010: 365).[469] The same reality is true in Europe (see various articles in Haddad, 2002:19-186).[470]

Immigrants face a number of challenges in their host countries. Most of them struggle to learn the languages spoken in the West, to adjust to a new culture, to make friends in a context of suspicion or hostility, and to meet their material, medical, and financial needs.[471] In the conclusion of an article on Muslim dilemmas in North America, Roland Miller points out that Muslims are concerned about issues such as "the creation of good relations with the majority religion" or "the struggle against discrimination" amongst others. (1996:142)[472]. They appreciate

---

[467] Patrick Sookhdeo, *Faith, Power and Territory*. (McLean, VA: Isaac Publishing, 2008).
[468] Yazbeck Haddad, and Jane Idleman Smith, *Mission to America: Five Islamic Sectarian Communities in North America* (Gainesville, FL: University Press of Florida, 1993).
[469] Kambiz Ghanea Bassiri, *A History of Islam in America: From a New World to the New World Order* (New York, NY: Cambridge University Press 2010), 365.
[470] Yvonne Yazbeck Haddad, *Muslims in the West: From Sojourners to Citizens* (New York: Oxford University Press, 2002), 19-186.
[471] Read Stoller 2011: 237-247 for interesting details.
[472] Miller, Roland. "Understanding Muslim Dilemmas in North America," *World and World*. Volume XVI. No 2, (1996).

CASE STUDY 3: MISSIONS AMONG THE URBAN MU.S.LIM DIASPORA IN THE WEST

friendly Christians who come alongside them, show genuine love to them, teach them the language and the culture, and assist them without imposing Christianity on them. Some argue that Christians should not evangelize them at all. But, do we have the call to share the Good News with them?

Why Should We Practice Missions to Urban Diaspora Muslims?

The impact of postmodern views is visible in the West. Many non-evangelical theologians are allergic to the idea of preaching the gospel to non-Christians. Philosophically, they think that it does not make sense because there is no absolute truth. They teach that all religions are equally valid. They also view the act of proclaiming the gospel as an arrogant judgment of followers of other religions.

God clearly communicates a different message. First of all, He shows that He is love. He loves all humans, without discrimination (John 3:16; 1 John 4:9-11). He does not force people to believe in Him or to obey Him. He cares about them to the point of sending His only Son to this world. He became flesh, and lived among us, died and rose again on our behalf in order to save those who believe in Him, Muslims included. Muslims deserve to know about the special love that God has for mankind.

Secondly, the Bible teaches that our Lord Jesus Christ is the only Savior. Jesus himself said it (John 14:6) and the apostles, under the inspiration of the Holy Spirit, proclaimed it (Acts 4:12; 1 Tim 2:5-6). When Jesus and the apostles spoke, there were a plurality of religions existing at that time. In fact, Christianity only had a minority of adherents during the first four centuries. But that did not prevent the Lord and the apostles from proclaiming that there is no other way to come to God besides Jesus. Furthermore, Christians are not preaching salvation through a religion, not even Christianity, but through the historical person of the Lord Jesus Christ. This statement clearly contradicts the discourse of inclusivists and pluralists who think that each religion is equally valid and that Jesus may be a cosmic Christ present in every religion. As far as the uniqueness of Christ is concerned, a clear choice needs to be made. I think that it is safer to listen to God who created us. He is omniscient and will ultimately judge the living and the dead.

Thirdly, the Lord did not only declare that He is the way, the truth and the life, thus stressing His uniqueness,[473] He also commanded His disciples to go

---

[473] I agree with the view of uniqueness of Christ developed in The Lausanne Occasional Paper No. 31 entitled "The Uniqueness of Christ in a Postmodern World and the Challenge of World Religions," ed. David Claydon.

and preach the Good News to all the ethnic groups (including Muslim people groups) and to the whole world (Matthew 28:19-20; Mark 16:15; Acts 1:8). Those who claim to be His disciples cannot help but obey His command (cf. John 10). Urban Muslim diaspora need to hear the gospel, and for the message to get to them, Christians need to go and preach to them (Romans 10:14-16). Christians are called to witness through their words and deeds.

Besides biblical commands, there are many other reasons for taking the Good News to urban Muslim diaspora . One reason is that the Muslim field is ripe for harvest. Since the 1990s, more Muslims have become followers of Jesus than in the previous fourteen centuries. This is the result of a combination of factors. Christians around the world are mobilized in prayer on behalf of the Muslims. The Christian movement of Thirty Days of Prayer for the Islamic community during the month of Ramadan is bearing fruit:[474] more and more Muslims come to Christ through dreams, visions, and miracles. And entire villages are following Christ. Converts from Islam are openly witnessing and their testimonies are convincing.

With the phenomenon of globalization, there is more freedom. It is harder to prevent any community from communicating with other communities around the world. It must also be said that when peaceful Muslims see violence that radical Muslims perpetrate in the name of Islam, they are more inclined to explore alternatives. Muslim people groups have never been so close to the kingdom of God than they are now.

Urban Muslim diaspora in the West are even more receptive because they do not face the same type of cultural and family pressure that they endured in their countries of origin. Many Muslims are thirsty for God. But the problem is that there are not enough friendly and educated Christians to facilitate their conversion by being good examples and leading them to the Lord.

Freedom of religion is one of the advantages that people have in the West. Technically, even in Islam there is a freedom of belief. One of the classical verses quoted by Muslim and Christian scholars to defend this idea is Qur'ān 2:256, which states: "There is no compulsion in religion…" There are also several Hadiths that say the same thing (see Shirazi, 2001: 107-109).[475] But in many Islamic countries and regions, it is strictly forbidden to leave Islam. Those who do it usually face expulsion from the community, severe persecution, imprisonment, or death. Such threats do not exist in the West thus it is easier for Muslims to become followers of Jesus. The follow-up of Muslim converts is also easier. This should be an encouragement to Christians who are witnessing to Muslims.

Ministry among urban Muslim diaspora is highly strategic. Most of the Muslim graduates of Western universities become leaders in their nations and

---

[474] See http://www.30-days.net for more details on the prayer network.
[475] Muhammad Shirazi, *War, Peace & Non-Violence: An Islamic Perspective*. (London: Fountain Books, 2001).

CASE STUDY 3: MISSIONS AMONG THE URBAN MU.S.LIM DIASPORA IN THE WEST

have a greater impact on their fellow citizens. In the same line of thought, John Algera writes: "Those moving to New York today are more open to the Gospel and spiritual things than the longer established European immigrants of a generation ago. These new immigrants will also become the power brokers of New York in the next twenty years." (Algera, 2009:191)[476]. The same observation is true for London, Madrid, Paris, Chicago, Los Angeles, Ottawa, Toronto, and all major cities in the West. Reaching out to immigrants is a very strategic move with huge impact on the future of the nation. It is worth investing time and resources in such a ministry.

God is opening doors of opportunities for missions among the Muslims through the growing number of urban Muslim diaspora . As Rogers pointed out in his reflection on immigration in the United States, "People from nearly every culture on the planet are pouring into the United States at rates that are unprecedented in history. And while some people see the present level of immigration creating serious social and economic challenges, should not God's people see this as an opportunity?" (Rogers, 2006:6)[477]

This is clearly an opportunity and it should not be wasted. However, it does not suffice to know that God wants Christians to carry out mission among the Muslims. It is equally important to know how to proceed. This is the focus in the third and last section of this chapter.

How Should We Practice Missions to Urban Diaspora Muslims?

Mission among urban Muslim diaspora in the West requires a basic understanding of each people group, city, neighborhood, and even individual. There is no one uniform approach for all occasions and locations. Each individual is unique and each circumstance different. Each context requires special dispositions, godly wisdom, and divine guidance.

A careful examination of the encounters of the Lord Jesus Christ with people in the Gospels shows that He had different approaches for different people. Jesus did not share the gospel with Nicodemus the same way he did with the Samaritan woman at the well or with Zacchaeus. His approach varied pending on individual cases and specific circumstances. A sound knowledge of Muslim neighbors, their beliefs, their culture, and their personal struggles and aspirations is important. Christians must know what to do and what to avoid in

---

[476] John A. Algera, "The Ends of the Earth Have Come to New York: A Church Multiplication Movement in the NY Metro Area" in *Globalization and Its Effects on Urban Ministry in the 21st Century* (Pasadena, CA: William Carey Library, 2009).
[477] Rogers Glenn, 2006 *Evangelizing Immigrants*. Estherville, IA: Mission and Ministry Resources.

relating to their Muslim neighbors. For example, a Christian must avoid offering pork to his or her Muslim friend. It can be interpreted as an insult.

Daily contact with Muslims is very important because, as Larry A. Poston (2000:222)[478] writes,

> "Some of the most significant reasons why Muslims do not convert to Christianity are sociological rather than theological, and personal contact with Christians on a day-to-day basis is what Muslims need."

However, even though personal and regular contact with Muslims is important, every conversion is a miracle because only the Holy Spirit can ultimately convince a Muslim that he or she needs to repent and follow the Lord Jesus Christ. For this reason, even before making contacts with Muslims, Christians must rely on divine enablement to love the Muslims and to serve our Lord. Nobody can offer what he or she does not have. Before reaching out to Muslims, each Christian must ask: "Did I personally give my life to the Lord Jesus Christ or am I a Christian in name only?" That is why I think Christians in the West must "reach in" first, i.e., to re-evangelize nominal Christians, then "reach out" to the diaspora Muslims. If every Christian takes this task seriously, churches in the West will be spiritually renewed and will have a great impact on evangelizing diaspora Muslims around them.

Likewise, before developing strategies or making contacts with Muslims, prayer is fundamental. Christians need to pray for God to open the spiritual eyes of Muslims, destroy all the theological and cultural barriers that constitute obstacles to their conversion, draw them to the Lord Jesus Christ and be granted the necessary wisdom to reach the Muslims effectively.

One area in which the church can help and develop relationships with urban Muslim diaspora in the process is language acquisition. Even immigrants of the second and third generation are struggling with the languages of the host countries, especially those who live in the ethnic enclave. Christine Schirrmacher (2008:106)[479] observes: "Many young people of the second and third generation speak too little German (or French, Spanish, or Dutch) to be successful in vocation."

Ministry among students, refugees,[480] prisoners, diplomats, business people, and hospital patients can provide unique opportunities to lead urban Muslim diaspora to the Lord Jesus Christ. Many Muslim converts who are elites of their nations came to Christ while they were studying in the West. One of

---

[478] Larry F. Poston, with Carl F. Ellis, Jr., *The Changing Face of Islam in America* (Camp Hill, PA: Horizon Books, 2000
[479] Christine Schirrmacher, "Muslim Immigration to Europe –The Challenge for European Societies – Human Rights – Security Issues – Current Developments," MBS Text 106, Martin Bucer Seminar, 2008.
[480] For those who are considering the possibility of ministry among Muslim refugees, a good book to read in order to familiarize with the unique realities that they face is *Muslims in the Diaspora: The Somali Communities of London and Toronto* by Rima Berns McGown.

CASE STUDY 3: MISSIONS AMONG THE URBAN MU.S.LIM DIASPORA IN THE WEST

them, Mamadou Karambiri, a Muslim convert from Burkina Faso, came to Christ when he was a student in Toulouse (France). Today he has one of the most dynamic ministries in French-speaking nations. Through his ministry, many churches were planted, a large number of people came to Christ, and mission among unreached people groups is growing. There are many Muslim background believers who were students, diplomats, and business people, and they came to Christ while studying or working in the West. Today many of them are pastors, church leaders, or committed believers, all making a difference in countries and regions where the majority of the population is Muslim. Some of the converts chose to remain in the West and continue to witness to the members of their ethnic groups who are still Muslims. These are examples of fruits that the involvement of the Western churches among the urban Muslim diaspora can produce.

In the West, Christian immigrants who come from Muslim cultures can help to reach out to the urban Muslim diaspora. Glen Rogers (2006:103) is right when he states:

> One of the effective ways to reach diaspora communities is to mobilize Christians in diaspora groups to reach out to their kinsmen and form ethnic congregations. Those who have contacts with diaspora people in their jobs should be equipped for effective ministry among them. [481]

This is true not only in the U.S. but also in Canada and Europe as well. While not all ministers are knowledgeable in evangelism, some Muslim background believers (MBB) are very effective in reaching out to the urban Muslim diaspora. In order to better prepare Christians for this task, there is a need to make changes in theological institutions and to organize seminars for church leaders and church members so that they are equipped for outreach. As Greenway (1989:87)[482] points out,

> "Theological education that trains leaders to minister beyond the traditional 'white' middle-class church and is adaptable to the needs of ethnic congregations must be developed and expanded."

In fact, each local church and each group inside the local church must move toward that direction. Church leaders and Christian educators should provide

---

[481] Glen Rogers, *Evangelizing Immigrants: Outreach and Ministry Among Immigrants and Their Children*, Estherville, (IA: Mission and Ministry Resources, 2006).

[482] Greenway, "Goals of Urban Ethnic Evangelism" in Roger S. Greenway and Timothy M. Monsma, *Cities: Mission New Frontiers* (Grand Rapids, MI: Baker Book House, 1989).

training to Christians on how to witness to Muslims and how to disciple them after they become Christians.

While carrying out mission among Muslims in urban settings, it is important to keep in mind that all Muslims do not necessarily think and act like urbanites.

> "Today Muslims, many from rural traditional areas, comprise the bulk of non-European immigrants to Europe. Even those who have settled in cities retain a village mentality and are seen as backward by the business and cultural elites in their countries."(Ben-David, 2009:15)[483]

Besides urban missiology, there is a need to develop "rurban missiology," a combination of rural and urban missiology, in order to better reach those who live in cities with a village mentality. In Christian strategizing, it is important to keep in mind that urban mission needs to be incarnational, holistic, cooperative and globally as Colin Marchant (1998: 31-33)[484] outlined in his article "Talk a walk." In it he followed the steps of Van Engen (1994:254-255)[485] who wrote:

> "So the first step in our method involved a commitment to view the city systemically, holistically, and critically, while we searched for biblical values and insights to inform our life and ministry in our cities."

For this reason, partnership is of utmost importance. A single denomination, a local church, or an individual must not pretend that it, he, or she can reach a city alone. It takes an organized groups of people, churches, and Christian organizations to share the same vision, acknowledge their strengths and weaknesses, and to work together in humility, love, and unshakable commitment for the kingdom of God and the glory of His mighty name. Together this joint force must pray strategically for the city, to reach out to the Muslim ethnic groups present there, to strategize and to carry out all the practical aspects that entail proclaiming the Good News, planting churches, and discipling new believers.

New believers from unreached people groups should be encouraged to maintain contacts with communities in their countries of origin. Those who feel God's calling will eventually return for a short or long term mission trips in order to bring the gospel to their own communities. Those who cannot go can help develop contextual materials that can be made available on the internet or

---

[483] Esther Ben-David, "Europe's Shifting Immigration Dynamic," *Middle East Quarterly* Vol XVI. Number 2 (2009).

[484] Marchant, Colin, "Take a Walk: Urban mission in the United Kingdom," in *Serving the Urban Poor* , ed. Tetsunao Yamamori, Bryant L. Myers, and Kenneth L. Luscombe (Monrovia, CA: MARC, 1998).

[485] Charles Van Engen, "Constructing a theology of mission for the city," in *God So Loves the City,* ed. Charles Van Engen and Jude Tiersma, (Monrovia, CA: MARC, 1994).

CASE STUDY 3: MISSIONS AMONG THE URBAN MU.S.LIM DIASPORA IN THE WEST

through a variety of means accessible to their ethnic group. In doing so, they will grow even more in the Christian life and impact their people in unique ways. Others Christians should support both spiritually and materially those who decide to return to their homelands. The best support is to help them start and develop self-supporting projects so that the initial support will not become a long-term burden.

Lastly, I would like to share an experience I had in ministering among urban Muslims in Africa. Now that I live in the West, I realize that the same principles are applicable in this context as well. In 1994, I gave a series of seminars on the importance of sharing the Good News with our Muslim neighbors in a city in the northern part of Cameroon where 80% are Muslims. People from three denominations took part in the seminars. At the end of the series, those who attended felt that we needed to start an organized movement. I initiated the movement "Les amis de Issa" (The Friends of Jesus). The movement started with a group of volunteers and was built around five key principles: commitment to pray daily for the Muslims in the city, commitment to partner with like-minded followers of Christ and local churches, commitment to develop friendship with Muslims, commitment to do outreach in teams of two at least once a week, and commitment to follow up the converts. We set up a committee in which all three denominations were represented. We agreed to have a monthly meeting for further training, prayer, feedback, and mutual encouragements. We scheduled special prayer meetings for the Muslims during the month of Ramadan. We also agreed to adopt all the mosques in the city and to pray five times a day for the conversion of those who attend these mosques. During the five years I spent in that city, we saw many conversions among Muslims. I recommend that each city in the West start such a movement. It is simple and yet effective. Other models exist, such as COMMA in southern California and Urban Impact in New York City. If the task of reaching urban Muslim diaspora is taken seriously, and if a group is started in each city, the results will be amazing.

Actually, the Church must not worry about the results. Christians are expected to do their best and leave the result to God. The Christian responsibility is to share the Good News. It is the Holy Spirit who does the miracle of conversion. Each Christian must be a faithful witness wherever God puts him or her in society. We should witness with wisdom, faithfulness, humility, gentleness, and patience. Above all, we are to minister to Muslims through prayer and love.

Summary

An African proverb says: "When the rhythm of the drum changes you must change the way you dance." The rhythm of the missionary drum in the West must follow the intensity of immigration. It is time to adjust the dance steps. Non-Christian immigrants in general and urban Muslim diaspora in particular present Western Christianity with an opportunity to develop its spiritual muscles, to be revived and to bring the Good News to people whom God loves so much and for whom our Lord Jesus Christ died on the cross. Instead of Westerners going far, God is sending unreached people groups to the West. God has provided the entire spiritual, human and material resources needed to meet this challenge. The Lord is not only sending, He is also going with those who follow Him according to his wonderful promise in Matthew 28:20. Why are many Christians in Europe and North America still hesitant to go and carry out missions among the urban Muslim diaspora? Why do they feel threatened?

The presence of Muslim diaspora in European and North American cities is not a threat. Rather, it is a golden opportunity for the Western Church to be revitalized and to reach out to people who are difficult to reach in their homelands. If Western churches take this opportunity seriously and do their best to reach out not only to the urban Muslim diaspora but also to all non-Christians who live in their immediate neighborhood, the churches will regain vitality to survive in the post-Christian era and even to reverse the current religious trend. If the strategy takes into consideration the importance of re-evangelizing nominal Christians, making disciples, and training believers, the result will be a renewed spirit which will encourage brothers and sisters in the non-Western World, further the kingdom of God and glorify the Lord. God is speaking loudly through the growing number of Muslim diaspora in the West. Yet the question is: Are we willing to listen to His voice and seize this unique opportunity?

Chapter 18

Case Study 4: Reflections of a Church Planter among Diaspora Groups in Metro-Chicago: Pursuing Cruciformity in Diaspora Missions

Cody C. Lorance

Introduction

Scenes from the Diasporic Ministry of Trinity International Baptist Mission

> *He made from one man every nation of mankind to live on all the face of the earth, having determined allotted periods and the boundaries of their dwelling place, that they should seek God, in the hope that they might feel their way toward him and find him. Yet he is actually not far from each one of us, for "In him we live and move and have our being"; as even some of your own poets have said, "For we are indeed his offspring" (Acts 17:26-28 ESV).*

Scene 1: From Militant to Missionary by Way of Mae La

Soe Rah was born in Kawthoolei, "the land without evil," better known as Burma or Myanmar by non-Karen speakers. From a Buddhist monastic background, he found Christ at a young age and slowly grew to be a natural leader in his village, attaining such rare accomplishments such as a high school education and a civil service job. This success, however, was halted after Soe Rah participated in the pro-democracy protests of 1988. The strongly violent reaction by the Burmese government meant he had to flee his village, family, and everything he had ever known. After years of hiding in the jungles, struggling to survive, carrying a gun as his constant companion, Soe Rah eventually made his way to the safety of a refugee camp in Thailand.

He wasn't content, however, to simply idle his life away in a makeshift hut, living on rations and imbibing hopelessness. Soe Rah's heart went out to his fellow Karen. He knew of many still hiding in the jungles of Burma, lacking food and medicine and unable to safely cross over into Thailand. Soe Rah began to make risky excursions across the border to deliver these needed items. By this time, he had become something of a warrior survivalist—a rugged militant who knew how to navigate the sweltering jungles, how to avoid the notice of military patrols, and how to use his gun. But soon it seemed that the medicine and food weren't enough to truly satisfy his scattered kinsmen in hiding. They were asking him to pray, to read Scripture to them, to lead hymns and even to preach. Having prayed for years for the end of violence in his country, Soe Rah began to realize that it was peace with God that people most desperately needed. So he put away his gun and took up the cross, convinced that God had called him to serve the Kingdom of Christ.

It was more than a quarter of a century ago that Kawthoolei Karen Baptist Bible School and College was founded in Burma's Karen state, but due to increasing violence and oppression in that land it has become "a theological institution displaced" (Kawthoolei Karen Baptist Bible School and College, 2010). It has been relocated and re-established in Mae La, one of nine refugee camps in Thailand just across the border from Burma. The school's new beginning and survival in the camp is a result of the generosity of Christians from around the world who have sent money, resources, administrators, and teachers over the years. For Soe Rah, who eventually enrolled in the Bible college, it was the missionary theologians from South Korea who made the most lasting impact as he was discipled, equipped, and empowered for ministry.

Soe Rah's ministry blossomed in the camps. He became an evangelist, a chaplain, a pastor, and a Bible school teacher. Strangely, he felt himself settling into a rhythm of life and ministry that was joyful, fruitful, peaceful—even, in a sense, comfortable. However, in 2007, the resettlement of refugees from the Mae La camp to the United States began. Initially unwilling to leave the camp and his ministry, Soe Rah became convinced of God's calling when a group of South Korean missionaries from the Bible college laid their hands on him, prayed, and commissioned him to go to the United States to preach the Gospel and plant churches among the Karen there.

CASE STUDY 7: REFLECTIONS OF A CHURCH PLANTER AMONG DIASPORA GROUPS IN METRO-CHICAGO: PURSUING CRUCIFORMITY IN DIASPORA MISSIONS

The Trinity International Baptist Mission (TIBM)[486] team met Soe Rah and his family on the day they arrived at their new home—an overpriced and under-maintained apartment in the Chicago suburbs. TIBM, a small group of diaspora-focused missionaries and lay people based in Chicagoland, had been focusing primarily on working among South Asian Hindus and Muslims.

However, through a variety of providential circumstances, on that busy day the team found themselves carrying household goods and secondhand furniture into the otherwise empty apartment. Amid improvised lessons on the use of refrigerators, stoves, light switches, and toilets, they began to exchange stories with Soe Rah and his family. Soon came the realization that both groups were in Chicagoland for the same conscious purpose—to serve Christ by proclaiming His gospel to diaspora peoples. It was long after the home Bible study group became a church and the church became two churches that Soe Rah told the leader of the TIBM team what that first meeting had meant to his faith: mere hours after touching down in a strange and frightening new land came confirmation from the Holy Spirit that God had indeed brought Soe Rah to the United States for a purpose. That day, Soe Rah determined in his heart to live in Chicagoland with missional intention among his new neighbors of many nations.

Scene 2: A Suburban Lhotshampa and a Sanskritized Savior

Southern Bhutan has been the traditional homeland for thousands of ethnically Nepali "Lhotshampas" for generations. It was there in the plains surrounding the tiny city of Galephug that Krishna Magar grew up. He managed to finish high school and marry before the anti-Nepalis government used violence and oppression to force his family to leave their prosperous five-acre farm and flee Bhutan. Krishna, along with his parents, six older brothers, and thousands of other Bhutanese-Nepalis eventually made their way through India across the Nepalese border, where they settled in refugee camps established by the United Nations High Commission for Refugees (Photo Voice; Bhutanese Refugee Support Group 2010).

Once in the camps, Krishna's education enabled him to work as a teacher in one of the schools established for refugee children. For a decade he taught science and mathematics before finally being promoted to be the headmaster, a position he held until he left the camps for good. This happened late in 2008, when the United States granted asylum to Krishna, his wife, and their three adult children. Packing up whatever they could fit into a few duffle bags,

---

[486] For more information about Trinity International Baptist Mission, visit their website at http://tibm.org.

they bid their family, friends, and neighbors a teary farewell and set out on their long and uncertain journey to America.

Krishna and his family had been living in the Chicago suburbs for about a month when the TIBM team met them. Upon moving into their new apartment, Krishna's three children were quickly befriended by their next-door neighbors, a Karen family active in the church Soe Rah was leading. Hungry for friendship in the strange and lonely land, they were eager, in spite of their Hindu faith, to accept the invitation of their new friends to attend a Bible study.

That night's study was like no other. Cody Lorance, the senior pastor and church planting leader of TIBM, had been co-pastoring the new Karen Baptist Church with Soe Rah during its first year of existence, and it was Lorance's turn to teach the midweek Bible study. Ordinarily, he would teach in English with Soe Rah providing translation into S'gaw Karen. However, the presence of their Bhutanese-Nepali guests required a change in strategy. It seemed that only one of them—Krishna's son—could speak any English at all, but he was altogether unfamiliar with English religious terminology. Lorance was forced to draw upon his limited vocabulary of Sanskrit religious terms, something he had picked up from working among Indian immigrants. Lorance explained the Bible lesson to Krishna's son while Soe Rah was translating for the Karen speakers. Krishna's son, who, like most Nepali Hindus, was somewhat familiar with Sanskrit religious terminology, then translated it all into Nepali for his sisters. The result, actually somewhat less chaotic than it sounds, served to open the door of the gospel for the new diaspora group.

That night, Lorance drove his new Bhutanese-Nepali friends back to their home and met their father. Krishna would tell Lorance much later that in those early days of their resettlement in Chicagoland, he and his wife were willing to allow their children to explore and even follow Christ because they hoped that Jesus would be able to heal their daughter of the frequent seizures that had plagued her for a long time. When she was baptized two months after that first meeting, the seizures left and Krishna was encouraged to explore Christ for himself. The contextualized worship gatherings developed by the TIBM team and other diaspora-focused missionaries made it easy for him, and people from the local Bhutanese-Nepali community to join in. Eventually, Krishna and his wife gave their lives to Christ and were baptized. Some months later, on Christmas Day 2009, just over a year since their arrival in the United States, Krishna was—to the delight of the entire Bhutanese refugee community—ordained to serve as one of the first deacons[487] of the new Nepali-speaking church, a position he continues to serve with great faithfulness.

---

[487] Note: The Nepali-speaking church that was started, TriEak Parmeshwar Mandali, does not actually use the term "deacon" to describe Krishna's role. He was ordained as an *aguaa-sevak* (अगुआ-सेवक) or "servant-leader." This designation has proved to be a contextually fitting way to emphasize the

CASE STUDY 7: REFLECTIONS OF A CHURCH PLANTER AMONG DIASPORA GROUPS IN METRO-CHICAGO: PURSUING CRUCIFORMITY IN DIASPORA MISSIONS

Scene 3: Of First Fruits and Future Harvest

Ganesh Powdyel sat on the sofa in a crowded living room and nodded his head; his eyes were locked on Timothy[488], a veteran Christian leader and pastor/church planter from Ethiopia who was teaching on the subject of spiritual warfare in ministry and missions. Soe Rah sat next to Ganesh, and interjected to share an experience with the group that seemed to resonate with everyone. Moved by what was being shared, Ganesh finally spoke up, insisting that the issue at hand was so critical that it had to be diligently taught in all of their churches. Ganesh had been part of TIBM's peer mentoring network for several months; this monthly gathering of about a dozen pastors, church planters, and other leaders who are all deeply engaged in diaspora missions in the Chicago area and beyond was clearly becoming a critical means by which God was equipping them for ministry in the context of diaspora.

Ganesh, a native of Bhutan, lived in the same refugee camp with Krishma Magar in Nepal and worked as a teacher in the same school. When he and his family first came to the United States in the spring of 2009, Ganesh discovered that his former headmaster had begun to follow Christ. Krishna shared the message of Jesus with Ganesh and encouraged him to attend the weekly Nepali worship services. The use of Sanskrit mantras, bells, incense, narrative preaching, and *bhajans*[489] were familiar and welcoming to Ganesh, a high-caste[490] Hindu, and allowing him to draw near to both the message and the messenger of Christ with his heart and mind. It wasn't long before Ganesh began to follow Christ and was baptized along with his wife and parents. Months later, he was ordained as a deacon along with his old friend, Krishna. Now a newly licensed pastor, Ganesh has begun teaching the Bible and providing strong missional leadership for the young Bhutanese-Nepali church in Chicagoland. In addition to the dozens of Bhutanese-Nepali Hindus who have begun to follow Christ within their own small diaspora community, promising spinoff efforts have now begun among Bhutanese-Nepali immigrants in other North American cities, and opportunities to plant new contextualized churches among the Bhutanese-Nepali diaspora abound.

---

biblical role of deacons as those who serve the local church by mobilizing the body to identify and meet needs of various kinds.

[488] A pseudonym.

[489] A *bhajan* is a particular style of devotional singing especially common in South Asian Hindu communities. For more on this topic, read "Aradhna: From Comfort to Discomfort, from Church to Temple" by Chris Hale, 2007; available at http://www.ijfm.org/PDFs_IJFM/24_3_PDFs/147-150Hale.pdf.

[490] In Nepal, the "Powdyel" surname belongs to the *kshatriya* (क्षत्रिय) or "warrior" caste.

A Brief Introduction to the Concept and Theology of Diaspora Missions

The above case studies provide a compelling look at the dynamics of diasporic movement and mission. Soe Rah, Krishna, Ganesh, Timothy, and their families represent the "people on the move"—the estimated 214 million individuals now residing outside their countries of origin (George 2011). Together their stories illustrate the providential opportunity of diaspora missions and highlight key missiological considerations such as mission "to," "through," and "beyond" diasporas (LCWE 2010)[491] and the "push and pull" factors[492] of diasporic movement (Wan 2007a). These and other concepts form the emerging and multidisciplinary field known as "diaspora missiology." In the 2009 *Seoul Declaration on Diaspora Missiology*, the Lausanne Diasporas Educators Consultation defined diaspora missiology as "a missiological framework for understanding and participating in God's redemptive mission among people living outside their place of origin" (2009). Thus, diaspora missiology is focused exclusively on understanding what God is doing among scattered people and how Christians can faithfully join Him in this Kingdom work.

Diaspora missiologists have worked hard to ground the church's understanding of diaspora missions firmly in Scripture. It is, at heart, a "biblical" field of study, and our engagement in diaspora missions must be "informed by, integrated with, and conformed to biblical and theological foundations" (LCWE 2010).

In this chapter, I want to present the fruit of my theological reflection within the context of diaspora missions in metro-Chicago by proposing "the pursuing cruciformity" in terms of eight major biblicalmotifs as shown in Figure 19.1. The term "cruciformity" of Figure 19.3 is a reference to the imitation of Christ's incarnation and crucifixion—a model of cruciform movement for faithful engagement in diaspora missions. It is the needed antidote to "the Babel Complex" (Figure 19.2) of centripetality and ethnocentrism.

A survey of current diaspora theology reveals at least eight major biblical motifs emphasized by diasporalogists, as shown in Figure 19.1.

---

[491] The concept of missions "to," "through," and "beyond" has become a key framework for understanding diaspora mission strategy. Mission "to" the diaspora refers primarily to efforts of Christians in host countries to reach out to diaspora communities with the gospel. Mission "through" the diaspora refers to diaspora Christians who reach out to their own people in their new host country, in their homeland, or in another country. Mission "beyond" the diaspora refers to diaspora Christians who participate in cross-cultural mission either to people native to the host country or to other diaspora communities (LCWE, 2010).

[492] Wan explains that people move both voluntarily, such as for education or economic betterment, and involuntarily, such as in cases of refugees and human (Wan 2007a). It is important to understand human movement as precipitated by a complicated combination of factors that "push" a people out of their place of origin and "pull" them into a particular host country.

CASE STUDY 7: REFLECTIONS OF A CHURCH PLANTER AMONG DIASPORA GROUPS IN METRO-CHICAGO: PURSUING CRUCIFORMITY IN DIASPORA MISSIONS

For the remainder of this chapter, we will be expanding on the "Babel Complex" motif, using the narrative of the Tower of Babel (Genesis 11:1-9) as an antitype for faithful engagement in diaspora missions. We will further introduce a ninth biblical motif, that of "cruciformity," as a sorely needed antidote to the Babel Complex. Four movements will be presented in which diaspora missionaries—whether ministering "to," "through," or "beyond" the diaspora—can abandon the Babel Complex and proceed toward cruciformity. Finally, an evaluative tool will be suggested that could potentially provide a means for Christians, either individually or corporately, to assess their cruciformity as it relates to diaspora missions in order to identify strengths and areas in need of development. In the end, we will find that cruciformity critically informs how Christians must participate in diaspora missions if they want to be Christ's disciples and follow His footsteps.

Pursuing Cruciformity in Diaspora Missions

"Then they said, 'Come, let us build ourselves a city and a tower with its top in the heavens, and let us make a name for ourselves, lest we be dispersed over the face of the whole earth'" (Genesis 11:4 ESV).

Understanding the Babel Complex in Diaspora Missions

When God created the first man and woman, He gave them a clear commission to multiply and "fill the earth" (Genesis 1:28). His vision was that the entire planet would teem with the crown of His creation—His image-bearers. Even after the Fall and the Flood, when sin had seemed to have irreversibly wrecked this vision, God re-commissioned Noah and his family to go and "fill the earth" (Genesis 9:1). The divine plan had not been thwarted.

From the beginning, God's purpose has been missional. With the manifested movement of humanity into all the earth, there should be no place in which His image is not. Under the New Covenant, this movement is particularly important as it facilitates the scattering and intermingling of God's ambassadors—Christians, to spread among lost people the fragrance of the knowledge of Christ (2 Corinthians 2:14). Far from haphazard, this scattering is superintended by a sovereign God who determines the precise times and places in which people will live in order to accomplish His missional purposes (Acts 17:26-27). "Since the creation of the world, therefore, till today, diasporas have been an indispensable means by which God has accomplished his redemptive purposes through Jesus Christ" (LCWE 2010).

Figure 18.1 Major biblicalMotifs of Diaspora Missions Theology

Biblical Motif	Description
The Doctrine of the Trinity	Key diasporalogical concepts such as migration and integration are to be understood as fundamental to the nature of God as Father, Son, and Holy Spirit. God is revealed to us through Scripture as the "migrant God" in the incarnate Son and in the sending of the Holy Spirit. He is the God who moves. (LCWE, 2010) Beyond this, we may consider the perichoretic nature of God—the interpenetrating movement of God with God through the three persons of the Godhead—as a vision of integration in the context of diaspora in which "essential differences are neither obscured nor allowed to become the cause of division or exclusion" (Jackson, 2011).
The Sovereignty of God in scattering people (Acts 17: 26-28)	God sovereignly decrees and orchestrates the movements of all people throughout all times for His own missional purposes. The geographical and chronological particulars of all people are in His hands. Thus, the phenomenon of diaspora is to be understood ultimately as having its origin in the counsels of God and as being intentionally directed by Him towards the fulfillment of the "Great Commission." (LCWE, 2010) (Thomas, 2010) (Wan, Diaspora missiology, 2007)
The "Fill the earth" mandate (Genesis 1:28, 9:7)	God has, from the beginning of creation, desired to fill the earth with His image-bearers. His command to Adam and Eve to "fill the earth" is repeated post-Flood to Noah. Diaspora, thus, is part of God's original plan for humanity and obedience to Him normally requires geographic movement.[493] (LCWE, 2010) (Pocock, Van Rheenen, & McConnell, 2005) (George, 2011)
"The Babel Complex"[494] (Genesis 11:1-9)	The centripetal tendency to resist diasporic movement is in accordance with the prevailing attitude of those would-be builders of the "Tower of Babel" who considered their own agenda of "name-making" as primary over and against God's purpose of filling the earth with His image-bearers. God's response to the disobedience of Babel was to forcibly scatter the people—an act of judgment but also of mercy as it prevented further depravity and set humanity back on the track of obeying God's "fill the earth" command. (LCWE, 2010) (Pocock, Van Rheenen, & McConnell, 2005) (Casino, 2011) (Jung, 2010) (George, 2011) (Howell, 2011) (Wan, Korean diaspora: From hermit kingdom to Kingdom ministry, 2010)

---

[493] Adam and Eve's expulsion from the Garden of Eden (Genesis 3:24) combined with the description of the garden as being situated near four rivers (Genesis 2:10) leads to the assumption of the garden being a definite geographical location. While this may be true to a point, the pre-Fall command to fill the earth (Genesis 1:28) suggests that we understand the garden as at least not geographically-bounded. Eden may have indeed had a geographic center (Genesis 2:8-14), but the "territory" of the garden is to be understood as having more to do with Adam and Eve's spiritual condition than with latitude and longitude (Waltke, 2001). Thus, pre-Fall, we may conceive of Adam and Eve fulfilling the "fill the earth" mandate without having to "leave" Eden in the sense of crossing the border into a land that is geographically "not-Eden." Before the Fall, the whole earth is Eden, the domain in which "human beings enjoy bliss and harmony between themselves and God, one another, animals, and the land" (Waltke, 2001).

[494] The term "Babel Complex" is taken from the book *Scattered to Gather: Embracing the Global Trend of Diaspora* where it is simply defined as "the desire to be centripetal; never centrifugal" (LCWE, 2010).

Figure 18.1 (Continued)

Models & Heroes of Diaspora (includes sojourner, alien, and stranger concept)	The biblical narrative is replete with examples of people in diaspora which may be considered as case studies and sometimes as diasporic heroes. Examples include: Adam and Eve, Cain, Abraham, Jacob, Joseph, Moses, Ruth and Naomi, Daniel, Esther, Jesus, Paul, Priscilla and Aquila, and others. Such examples serve to illustrate the fact that God's people have a rich migratory tradition and that the Church has been diasporic from its inception. The people of God are by nature aliens, strangers, and sojourners upon the earth with their citizenship in heaven (Philippians 3:20, Hebrews 11:13, 1 Peter 2:11). (Jeong, 2010) (Jackson, 2011) (Jung, 2010) (Casino, 2011) (Adeney, 2011) (Pocock, Van Rheenen, & McConnell, 2005) (Thomas, 2010) (LCWE, 2010) (George, 2011) (Wan, Korean diaspora: From hermit kingdom to Kingdom ministry, 2010) (Song, 2010)
The Jewish Dispersion	The Exile of the Israelites from the promised land is often considered to be a kind of prototypical case of diaspora. It is sometimes likened to stories such as Adam and Eve's expulsion from Eden, Cain's being condemned to a life of restless wandering, or the scattering of people from Babel as cases of judgment-induced diaspora. Nevertheless, while judgment is clearly a key component to understanding the dispersion of the Jews, so is God's commitment to fulfill his original missional purpose through diasporic movement. Thus, even the Exile has hopeful outcomes as seen especially in the stories of Daniel's witness in diaspora context and in the role of Jewish diasporic communities in the spread of the gospel during Paul's missionary journeys. (George, 2011) (Choi, 2011) (Casino, 2011)
New Testament Mission (Great Commandment & Great Commission themes)	Christian mission from its beginning is to be understood as inherently diasporic in nature. It is rooted in the migratory experience of the incarnate Christ, inaugurated in the multicultural context of Pentecost, spurred on by the centrifugal commands to make disciples of all nations and to go into all the earth (Matthew 28:18-20, Acts 1:8), and modeled by the evangelistic journeys of Philip, Peter, Paul, and others. This mission of the early Church is also informed by the "great commandment" to love one's neighbor as oneself (Matthew 22:39)—a command with strong implications for the Christian's interaction with sojourners and exiles towards whom we are called specifically to show compassion, hospitality, and advocacy (e.g. Zechariah 7:10, Malachi 3:5). (George, 2011) (Connor, 2006) (Casino, 2011) (Thomas, 2010) (Wan, Korean diaspora: From hermit kingdom to Kingdom ministry, 2010) (LCWE, 2010) (Wan, Ministering to Scattered Peoples - Moving to Reach the People on the Move, 2010) (Wan, Korean diaspora: From hermit kingdom to Kingdom ministry, 2010) (Wan, Diaspora mission strategy in the context of the United Kingdom in the 21st century, 2011) (Howell, 2011) (Adeney, 2011)
Scriptures written in or to diaspora contexts	Scripture itself was often inspired and written in the context of diaspora. In some cases, the authors were living in diaspora. Examples include Moses's writing of the Pentateuch, Ezekiel's prophecies, and Paul's prison epistles. Other books of the Bible, such as the epistles of James and Peter, were written specifically to people living in diaspora. As Scripture is to be understood as originating from the Holy Spirit, these examples serve to underscore the centrality of diaspora in God's salvation-historic purposes. (George, 2011) (LCWE, 2010)

It is against this backdrop of diaspora as "a missional means decreed and blessed by God" (LCWE, 2010) that we must attempt to understand the sin of Babel. We have been told that the narrative of Genesis 11:1-9 is an example of God's disdain for human hubris, the quest to make a name for oneself rather than to glorify God. While this is certainly part of the story, it is only a part. On the whole, we see exhibited in the builders of Babel a conglomeration of sinful attitudes which oppose God's diasporic missional purposes and lead humanity to rebel against His "fill the earth" command.

This "Babel Complex" is marked by at least four interrelated attitudes. First, the builders of Babel display a marked centripetality—they do not want to move, to "fill the earth." It must not be missed that the underlying motivation for the construction of the tower is not to "make a name" for themselves but rather to prevent their global dispersion (v.4). They fear their scattering for the loss of safety and security, loneliness, and vulnerability it would certainly bring (Waltke, 2001).

Second, the individuals in our narrative have exchanged the surpassing value of God's diasporic missional vision for their own small-minded agenda. God wants to fill the earth with His image-bearers "as the waters cover the sea" (Isaiah 11:9), but they seek security, prosperity, comfort, and a name that will be remembered for all generations. Having tasted the hardship of migration (v.2), the builders cannot conceive of anything good that could come from diaspora. They have seemingly lost touch with the grand metanarrative of God as creator, redeemer, and sovereign, and are looking to write their own story with baked bricks and bitumen.

A third attitude exhibited by the builders is the nearly universal tendency toward convenience. It is a hallmark of sin to seek one's own pleasure above pleasing God (Genesis 3:6), to take the path of least resistance instead of the hard road of obedience. The builders' brief experience of migration was enough to tell them that it would be much easier, safer, and more beneficial to settle together in the fertile plain of Shinar rather than to scatter over all the earth. Once settled, they utilized their collective ingenuity in an attempt to secure a comfortable and prosperous existence through the technological advancements of brick-baking, city-constructing, and tower-building. Any thought of obedience to God's diasporic call was far from their minds.

A final attitude in the Babel Complex that must be considered is the urge to cling to one's own culture as superior to all others, to demand absolute assimilation and conformity and reject any semblance of diversity. The seed of this attitude is apparent in the Babel narrative among the builders who are described as "one people" with "one language" (v.6). This uniformity was so highly prized among the people that when it was removed, they found it impossible to either live or work together. The seed planted at Babel has of course developed into the full-grown ethnocentrism of today which inspires all manner of fear, racism, discrimination, hatred, and genocide. This attitude dangerously obscures our view of the multicolored wisdom of God, which is

CASE STUDY 7: REFLECTIONS OF A CHURCH PLANTER AMONG DIASPORA GROUPS IN METRO-CHICAGO: PURSUING CRUCIFORMITY IN DIASPORA MISSIONS

manifested in people from every culture who find unity *in* diversity around the person and work of Jesus Christ, and causes us to view diasporic phenomena as a threat to the cultural homogeneity that is regarded today as so precious.

The Babel Complex continues to plague humanity today. In the Church, it is the most significant obstacle to our faithful engagement in diaspora missions. The centripetal Christian resists God's outward call to cross national borders and cultural barriers, preferring instead the safety and familiarity of home. Other believers move out diasporically, but only for education, economic reasons, or even as refugees, all the while oblivious to God's greater redemptive purposes for their movement. Still others view diaspora as merely a convenient way to engage in mission without having to sacrifice much in the way of the comforts they've grown accustomed to. They do not participate in diaspora missions because they feel called to do so, but because it is cheaper, closer, and less time-consuming and does not require the pain of learning another language or culture. Finally, some Christians in their practice of diaspora missions still manifest the kind of cultural superiority that should be anathema in the body of Christ. They demand assimilation to the host society, prefer the role of benefactor to partner, and have no patience for contextualization. The figure below illustrates the four prevailing attitudes that characterize the Babel Complex.

As illustrated above, the Babel Complex is inherently self-centered. Its diabolical design is to create distance between gospel-bearing Christians (whether diasporic or not) and diaspora peoples (whether Christian or not) through cultivation of sinful attitudes which, by their nature, foster alienation. If we are to faithfully join in God's redemptive mission among diasporas, we must find a way to descend this tower and draw near to the people on the move. This can only be accomplished as we learn to follow the "migrant God" (Jackson 2011) who left heaven for Calvary and, in so doing, modeled for His disciples the very attitudes that we must prayerfully cultivate in our lives as diaspora missionaries.

Understanding Cruciformity in Diaspora Missions

The antidote to the Babel Complex is the cross. Engagement in diaspora missions that is faithful to the mission of Jesus requires cruciformity—the imitation of Christ's incarnation and crucifixion. He is our diasporic forerunner who experienced "exile, social marginalization, and a sense of rootlessness in and through [His] incarnate life" (Jackson 2011). The Commission on World Mission and Evangelism has noted well that:

> The migration of Jesus to our world was not simply a journey but a way through which God reconciles humanity with himself . . . This

event shapes the entire missionary activity of the Church and is indeed the foundation and charter for its very existence (2010).

Moreover, Christ is the one who moved away from the security of Jerusalem and "suffered outside the gate" (Hebrews 13:12). Christians are called to acknowledge that like Him "here we have no lasting city" and to "go to him outside the camp and bear the reproach he endured" (Hebrews 13:13-14). The *Carmen Christi* may be well-applied as a model for diaspora missions:

> Have this mind among yourselves, which is yours in Christ Jesus, who, though he was in the form of God, did not count equality with God a thing to be grasped, but made himself nothing, taking the form of a servant, being born in the likeness of men. And being found in human form, he humbled himself by becoming obedient to the point of death, even death on a cross. Therefore God has highly exalted him and bestowed on him the name that is above every name, so that at the name of Jesus every knee should bow, in heaven and on earth and under the earth, and every tongue confess that Jesus Christ is Lord, to the glory of God the Father (Philippians 2:5-11 ESV).

Here is Christ submitting to the centrifugal movement of God the Father by leaving heaven. He enters the world with the Father's plan of redemption and of self-glorification His only aim. Forsaking self-gratification and ease, Jesus takes the form of a servant and is obedient to the Father's call, even to the point of death on a cross. And far from clinging to His glorified pre-incarnate state, He empties Himself and becomes a man—fully contextualized to those He is called to serve.

As the Babel Complex consists of four interrelated attitudes of self-interest, so cruciformity in diaspora missions requires a departure from each of these. We are to be, as it were, dispersed from Babel but with crosses borne, pursuing the migrant Savior who goes before us to the scattered people of the world. This cruciform dispersion consists of four movements: towards centrifugality, consciousness of divine purpose, a sense of calling, and contextualization. We have illustrated these four movements in the figure below.

In contrast to the Babel Complex's marked self-interest, God is the focus of cruciform movement in which the self is thereby mortified. The cultivation of these new, Christ-like attitudes naturally impels the Christian out to the diasporas by eliminating such isolating attitudes as centripetality and ethnocentrism. The point is clear: whatever you do second in diaspora missions, first you have to die.

Yet what does cruciform movement actually look like? We must turn our attention now to an elaboration upon these four movements. In so doing, we will begin to see how Christians may leave Babel for Calvary in our mission among diasporas.

CASE STUDY 7: REFLECTIONS OF A CHURCH PLANTER AMONG DIASPORA GROUPS IN METRO-CHICAGO: PURSUING CRUCIFORMITY IN DIASPORA MISSIONS

Four Movements towards Cruciformity in Diaspora Missions

"My Place or His Place" – Moving from Centripetal Tendencies to Embraced Centrifugality

When Soe Rah was first offered the opportunity to move his family to the United States, his natural instinct was to stay put in the Mae La refugee camp. There in his adopted home of Thailand he had forged for himself a life that was reasonably comfortable and predictable, as well as a ministry that was bearing fruit. It took the fervent prayers and the wise counsel of diasporic Korean missionaries whom he respected to overcome his centripetal tendencies and convince Soe Rah to embrace the centrifugal leading of the Holy Spirit.

We have already seen that God is behind the global movement of humanity, that He is orchestrating it for the sake of mission. We are "called to embrace and even to engage" this centrifugal, diasporic movement (Pocock, Van Rheenen, and McConnell 2005) and to "move along with God" (Wan 2010j).

The natural inclination of human beings, as we have seen in the Babel narrative, is centripetal. We see this in some cases on an international scale, as in Soe Rah's former mindset, and in some cases of Christians at home in their own country who in one way or another resist God's call to engage the diaspora peoples around them. The attitude of centripetality is characterized by such attributes as:

- *Immovability* –especially when a Christian or group of Christians (such as a church) resists large or small scale geographic movement in favor of the comfort, security, predictability, and/or familiarity of home.

- *Inflexibility* – when Christians are unwilling to change plans, routines, strategies, structures, traditions, customs, policies, and more for the sake of engagement in diaspora missions, they are exhibiting a kind of centripetality that greatly hinders their missional effectiveness.

- Unhealthy *"long-termism"* – the nature of mission among people on the move often requires a mission methodology that is also "on the move." That means that permanency is not always possible or even preferable. A church or ministry planted among seasonal migrant workers or international students may only last several months or a few years before the congregation moves elsewhere, but it must be planted nevertheless. Churches that minister to diasporas may find themselves needing to adjust policies and re-design ministries frequently to keep up with the constantly evolving needs of diaspora peoples. These churches must not be discouraged from always seeking to engage in the hard work of developing detailed and circumstantial short-term ways of engaging in diaspora missions (Jackson 2011).

Diaspora is central to God's redemptive mission and the fulfillment of the Great Commission (LCWE 2010), but embracing diaspora missions demands that Christians embrace centrifugality—a kind of death. In this, we are to take up our cross and follow Christ, who left the splendor of heaven for the dusty roads of Palestine.

"My Plan versus His Plan" – Moving from Competing Agendas and Contingencies to a Prevailing Consciousness of God's Diasporic Purposes

When Krishna Magar first moved to the United States from Nepal, he had in mind the "American Dream." He envisioned a future of economic prosperity for himself and educational opportunities for his children. He dreamed of life in a democratic and developed country where he and his family would be free from oppression, discrimination, and poverty.

Once Krishna became a follower of Christ, his perspective on his diasporic situation began to change. Eventually, he became a champion for the resettlement of his relatives in the Chicago area. Krishna had become convinced that "if they move here, they will become Christians." Indeed many of his relatives have begun to follow Christ, and gradually Krishna has come to see diaspora phenomena as primarily about God fulfilling his redemptive plan among all peoples.

Enoch Wan has explained that people move either voluntarily or involuntarily in response to various factors that may either "push" them out of their place of origin or "pull" them into a new land (2007). Some of the numerous factors that may be involved include economic and educational opportunities, war, human trafficking, family reunification, natural disasters, and more. Sam George has summarized these as either the "pursuit of opportunity" and the "allure of a better, freer life" or the "running away from misery" (George, 2011). But all of these factors denote an essentially *unconscious* participation in diasporic movement that is orchestrated by God.

At this point, it will be helpful to contrast two migratory episodes from the life of Abraham. In the first (Genesis 12:1-9), Abraham is thoroughly aware that as he moves diasporically, he does so in response to God's call and in connection with God's purpose to bless "all the families of the earth" through him (v.3). Thus, in every place, Abraham is said to have built an altar to worship the Lord, a powerful testimony to all those around him. In the second episode (Genesis 12:10-20), Abraham migrates to Egypt because of a famine in Canaan. There is no mention here of him building an altar to the Lord. Instead,

CASE STUDY 7: REFLECTIONS OF A CHURCH PLANTER AMONG DIASPORA GROUPS IN METRO-CHICAGO: PURSUING CRUCIFORMITY IN DIASPORA MISSIONS

Abraham's time in Egypt is marked by a deceptive lifestyle that is ultimately harmful to the inhabitants of the host country (v.17). Abraham may have left the nation materially enriched, but this he did at the expense of the people to whom he was called to be a blessing.

From the examples of Krishna and Abraham we can see that faithful engagement in diaspora missions requires more than mere centrifugal movement. Both diaspora Christians and their fellow believers who are natives of a given host country must be awakened to God's missional purposes for diaspora. They must become convinced that no facet of human migration is more significant than that of the Holy Spirit who has decreed all such migrations for the sake of mission. When this consciousness develops, all competing agendas and contingency plans fade from view. Even biblical examples such as Daniel and Joseph, whose diasporic situations resulted from the horrors of human trafficking, were able to see the hand of God in their movement and to be positive witnesses for truth (Genesis 50:20). Writes Tereso Casino:

> Ministry-sensitive Christians will find migration as a strategic channel for doing their own share of the missionary task. Geographical mobility, whether forced or unforced, voluntary or involuntary, may be interpreted as a God-given opportunity to spread the good news (2011).

As the quote above suggests, diaspora Christians in particular must be "motivated and mobilized," as they constitute one of the "most strategic missionary forces in the history of missions" (LCWE 2010). In the first place, Miriam Adeney has argued that the inherent liminality of diaspora creates certain cross-cultural strengths in a person that can "blossom into mission" (Adeney 2011). These "liminal, hyphenated, polycentric, multilingual Christians" are the "natural bridge-builders" who can effectively lead in cross-cultural mission endeavors to other diaspora communities (2011). Hun Kim has added that diaspora Christians tend to be "more attuned to religious plurality than their Western counterparts," a trait that "enhances their missionary capacity to maintain effective Christian witness in the face of religious pluralism" (2011). Beyond all this, Thomas Harvey has pointed out that through their non-religious vocations, diaspora Christians can gain access to nations that block access to traditional missionaries (2011).

Many missiologists have also suggested that the influx of diaspora Christians into Western host nations may be a providential means for the revitalization or re-evangelizing of host post-Christian societies (Choi 2011; Pocock, Van Rheenen, and McConnell 2005; George 2011; Casino 2011; Kim 2011; Tan 2011; Jackson 2011). If this is true, it calls for Christians in host countries to awaken to God's purposes in bringing diaspora Christians to their nations, and to seek to establish new missional partnerships built upon humility and reciprocity.

In spite of the compelling potential for mission that diaspora presents, Christians often struggle to give God's plan for diaspora the attention it deserves. Competing agendas and contingencies need to be held in check. In particular, Christians need to guard against:

- *Unawareness* – Perhaps a very simple problem to solve indeed, it is nevertheless the case that most Christians (diasporic or not) are unaware of God's redemptive purposes for human migration. Christian leaders must provide thorough biblicaleducation along these lines at every level. Without proper discipleship regarding diaspora, Christians are disconnected from the grand biblicalmetanarrative of God as creator, redeemer, and sovereign who orchestrates all the movements of humanity for his own missional purposes.

- *A Negative-only Perspective* – The tendency to see human migration only in a negative light must be replaced with a view of diaspora that is always hopeful that regardless of how bad the circumstances may be, God's mission will not be thwarted and He will prove able to use even the worst of situations to His glory.

- *Self-interest* – Most diaspora people have only selfish or earthly interests in mind when they consider their own diasporic movement. If they are followers of Christ, they must not only be informed of God's purposes for diaspora, but they must also be exhorted to embrace God's purposes as infinitely superior to their own.

Min-young Jung has written of diaspora Christians that "diaspora is where they are not by chance, not by human plan in pursuit of worldly dreams, not by unfortunate random twist of history. They are there for a reason, for a great purpose, for the ultimate cause" (2010). But diaspora Christians and their host country counterparts need to be converted from "self-serving" to "missional" in their perspective toward diaspora phenomena. This is also a kind of death, a move toward cruciformity in pursuit of the one who could say, "Father, not my will, but yours be done" (Luke 22:42).

"My Pleasure versus His Pleasure – Moving from Mission as Convenience to Mission as Calling

The ministry highlighted in the opening cases studies, Trinity International Baptist Mission, began in 2004 when Cody and Katherine Lorance, who were at the time preparing for "overseas" missions, responded to what they felt was a clear call from God to "bring the hope and wholeness of Christ to people of all

CASE STUDY 7: REFLECTIONS OF A CHURCH PLANTER AMONG DIASPORA GROUPS IN METRO-CHICAGO: PURSUING CRUCIFORMITY IN DIASPORA MISSIONS

nations—beginning in Chicagoland" (Trinity International Baptist Mission, 2010). They were later joined by team members who had previously set their eyes on mission fields in Tibet, Indonesia, Ethiopia, and elsewhere. For each missionary who joined TIBM, engaging in diaspora missions was a matter of obedience to God's call, and not for geographic, economic, or cross-cultural convenience.

Unfortunately, the "language of convenience" has too often been associated with diaspora missions. It has been suggested that diaspora missions can be practiced "easily" as "mission at your doorstep" which doesn't require linguistic or cultural border-crossing (Wan 2011a). In particular, Christians in Western host countries have been told that they "no longer have to look beyond their own local context"; they don't have to go to the world because "the world has come to us" (Howell 2011). Elsewhere it has been emphasized that diaspora missions means that the nations are "easily within reach" and "with relatively small input toward their immediate needs, tangible results can be produced" (Baeq, Lee, Hong, and Ro 2011). Moreover, it is described as safer since there is "no political danger" in engaging in diaspora missions in Western nations like the United States (Baeq, Lee, Hong, and Ro 2011).

Yet this kind of language obscures the fact that while certain strategic advantages may be presented by the context of diaspora missions, we do not engage in it *because* it is cheaper, easier, closer, safer, or less time-consuming. In many cases, we find that diaspora missions can be significantly less convenient. For example, it is usually more expensive to live in global cities such as Chicago, Paris and Singapore (where large diaspora populations reside) than in relatively homogenous rural villages. Migrant churches have also found it to be a huge investment of time and financial resources to bring in indigenous pastors from their home countries to lead migrant congregations. When one factors in the unique diasporic realities of forced displacement, human trafficking, intergenerational conflict, ethnic tension and conflict, and psychological distress, a picture of diaspora missions begins to emerge that is anything but "easy."

No, the reason Christians must embrace diaspora missions is because they are called to do so. Phillip Conner has made it clear that the Church's response to diaspora movement should be to make disciples of all nations—that we are called to show hospitality, compassion, and justice and to proclaim the gospel because the "eternal destiny of millions is at stake" (2006). Adds T.V. Thomas, "Whatever the size, wherever they go, we have a responsibility to reach out to them with the gospel . . . the Great Commission demands that we reach out to people on the move" (2010).

Diaspora missions should not be understood as a convenient opportunity to "dabble" in cross-cultural mission in lieu of "the real thing." It should not be used by Western Christians to assuage their guilt by, for example, giving some old clothes to a refugee so that they can feel "missional" without sacrificing much in the way of comfort, time, or wealth. Diaspora missions is something Christians are called to. It is a matter of obedience first. Issues related to economics, strategy, and the like come much later. To guard against the attitude of "missional convenience," diaspora missionaries should be on the lookout for:

- *The pursuit of comfort and ease.* Very often Christians involved in outreach to their immigrant neighbors do so on their own terms, when their schedule permits, and so long as it doesn't impede their pursuit of health, wealth, and happiness. Many avoid diaspora missions involvement that would seem too difficult. Thus, fewer American Christians may be found reaching out to refugees who live in crime-infested inner cities than in relatively safer suburban areas. Homes of immigrants that are overrun by cockroaches or bedbugs are avoided by many host nation Christians. But the selfless Christian is willing to pick up their cross and serve in true, painful sacrifice their neighbors of many nations.

- *A preference to get "what I want."* At least unconsciously, many Christians engage in diaspora missions in order to satisfy their own wants and agendas. A youth group may need a good mission trip idea, or a Bible study fellowship needs to do a service project. Adopting a refugee or immigrant family for a short period of time, ignorant of God's larger plans for that family and their community, can often do more harm than good. Volunteer Christians may then walk away feeling a sense of gratification as a result of their cross-cultural encounter, but God's purposes in mission are often left unaccomplished. Christ-followers must make God's will their primary pursuit.

- *Language of convenience.* We must be wary of verbiage that seems to suggest that the reason to engage in diaspora missions is that doing so is cheaper, safer, less time-consuming or otherwise more convenient, and instead seek a greater conviction of God's call on our lives to diaspora missions.

One particular story from the history of TIBM has emerged as rather paradigmatic for their team's understanding of the move from convenience to calling in diaspora missions. Some years ago one of their missionaries, a North American, was spending time in the apartment of a Muslim family who were refugees from Burma. The missionary had spent considerable time cultivating a reciprocal relationship of mutual trust, respect, and love. One day in particular, he had already spent hours with the family—grunting and struggling through broken English, downing endless cans of orange *Fanta*, and consuming plenty

CASE STUDY 7: REFLECTIONS OF A CHURCH PLANTER AMONG DIASPORA GROUPS IN METRO-CHICAGO: PURSUING CRUCIFORMITY IN DIASPORA MISSIONS

of spicy food. After some time, there was a knock at the door. The head of the household, Muhammad,[495] opened the door to find an unknown 'white' American man. The visitor began to tell Muhammad that he was a Christian and that his church was donating free food to needy families. Muhammad was invited to come out to the parking lot and take what food he wanted. Muhammad stared blankly at the man for an uncomfortably long time before the American repeated the invitation, more slowly this time, emphasizing the words "free" and "food." Finally, Muhammad replied with a rough "Okay," and slammed the door. The TIBM missionary heard Muhammad mutter something under his breath in Burmese before returning to his place on the sofa and to his can of *Fanta*.

Would-be diaspora missionaries must ask themselves on which side of the door they wish to do ministry. If on the inside, H.L. Richard has noted that there is a "cost to [such] ministry . . . the cross hurts" (2010). One must learn not only to extend hospitality but to receive it, to welcome diaspora peoples and to go to them. To meet with them not only for 15-30 minutes but to stay there with them until your efforts to speak their language and their efforts to speak yours have been completely exhausted. To stay until tea has become lunch and lunch has become dinner. To stay until their bedbugs have become your bedbugs and then to stay longer. Only a deep sense of divine calling will prove powerful enough to carry us far away from our comfort zones. But here again, Christ is our predecessor who gave up the pleasures of heaven and submitted to the call of crucifixion.

"My People versus His People – Moving from Cultural Clinging to Contextualization / Incarnation

When Ganesh Powdyel first encountered the contextualized, Christocentric Nepali *satsang*, the weekly worship service of TriEak Parmeshwar Mandali,[496] he was greatly surprised. Most Nepali Hindus of his caste had long ago written off Christianity as a foreign religion that was opposed to Nepali culture. But here was an American Christian chanting Bible verses in Sanskrit, singing *bhajans* about Jesus Christ, and using fascinating stories to teach spiritual truths. Incense and candles burned on an altar, giving Ganesh the sense that even in his displacement as a refugee, this was a sacred time and here was a sacred place. Beyond this liturgical contextualization, Ganesh found the missionaries of TIBM pursuing a kind of relational or personal contextualization as well. They worked hard to learn how to develop relationships that the Bhutanese-Nepalis

---

[495] A pseudonym.
[496] TIBM started TriEak Parmeshwar Mandali, a Nepali-speaking church plant, in 2009.

understood to be close. They entered into life with the refugees. They not only worked to assist the newcomers in their efforts to integrate into American society but also engaged in *inverted assimilation*—striving to learn the language and adapt to the culture of Bhutanese-Nepalis. Gradually, all those long-standing cultural barriers between Ganesh and the knowledge of Christ fell away. He and his household came to know Christ and were baptized.

It has been suggested that crossing linguistic and cultural barriers isn't necessary in diaspora missions (LCWE 2010). Brian Howell has argued somewhat against the pursuit of contextualization in diaspora missions, writing, "I would argue that a better approach to mission work and ministry generally is through biblicalvirtues practiced by the established [host country church] rather than starting with principles of contextualization to be employed by mission specialists" (Howell 2011). Howell's case against contextualization is built upon four primary contentions:

1. Strategies of contextualization will become "rapidly obsolete as populations respond to the wider context" (Howell 2011).

2. Contextualization limits participation in diaspora missions to a relatively small number of "mission specialists" (Howell 2011).

3. Contextualization is powerless to "illuminate complex situations of globalization, cultural change, and hybridity" and will tend to exclude concerns for power, economics, gender, race, and inequality (Howell 2011).

4. It is better to emphasize biblicalvirtues such as compassion, hospitality, and justice (Howell 2011).

But all of these contentions must be rejected. In the first place, we have already spoken about the importance of embracing short-term ways of engaging in diaspora missions that are nevertheless detailed and circumstantial (Jackson, 2011). Whether second generation immigrants will speak Nepali or not is irrelevant to the fact that newly arriving immigrants speak it now and will more readily understand the message of Christ in their heart language. Besides this, Howell may be suggesting too strongly the inevitability of cultural assimilation that renders contextualization "obsolete." Sam George has argued instead that very often the experience of migration, uprooting, and alienation contributes to a heightened need for identity and community (2011). Tereso Casino has added that diaspora peoples tend toward "strong ethnic group consciousness sustained over a long time" (Casino, 2011). Other missiologists have cited specific examples of the Jewish, Korean, and Chinese diasporas which have tended to maintain and even intensify their distinct cultural identities (Oh 2011; Choi 2011; Baeq, Lee, Hong, and Ro 2011; Tan 2011). Darrell Jackson has explained that while some migrants choose assimilation, others consciously seek to integrate with the host society in a way that allows for the preservation of their unique cultural distinctiveness, and still others prefer

CASE STUDY 7: REFLECTIONS OF A CHURCH PLANTER AMONG DIASPORA GROUPS IN METRO-CHICAGO: PURSUING CRUCIFORMITY IN DIASPORA MISSIONS

instead to intentionally organize themselves around specific cultural or religious allegiances (2011).

Secondly, the suggestion that the pursuit of contextualization limits diaspora missions engagement to "missionary specialists" begs the question why. Howell says that "the goal of missiology should always be to empower the local church to engage in mission," but that the use of contextualized strategies in diaspora missions "excludes the North American church from having much of a role" (2011). Howell does not explain why he believes this is the case, but we can't help but conclude that he believes that the pursuit of contextualization is simply too difficult for most North American Christians. It is too difficult to develop cross-cultural competencies and learn a new language, to engage in respectful interreligious dialogue, and to seek to deeply understand one's neighbor from another nation in order to better communicate the love of Christ in a way he or she can understand. That may be so, but we remember that the call to diaspora missions includes the demand to abandon any notion of "convenient mission." It is a shame that most North American Christians can speak only English, while their churches' ESL classes are often filled with new migrants who are learning English as their third, fourth, or fifth language.[497] Howell may be correct in suggesting that empowering host country Christians to pursue contextualization in their practice of diaspora missions is somewhat impractical, but, as he has said elsewhere, "pragmatics do not make good theology, nor I would argue, do they make good missiology" (Howell 2011).

Howell's third contention is that contextualization is powerless to "illuminate complex situations of globalization, cultural change, and hybridity" and will tend to exclude concerns for power, economics, gender, race, and inequality (Howell, 2011). This may be true if contextualization is pursued only liturgically and not in a holistic and relational sense. However, when contextualization is pursued as incarnation and, particularly among diasporas, as *inverted-assimilation*, it lands the cross-cultural worker right in the middle of the lived experience of migrant people. It is not just to be a friend as the Christian from the host country might understand friendship, but to be a friend *contextually*, "to know and to care about what truly matters to the other person" (Jeong 2010). When contextualization is pursued as incarnation, issues of power, inequality and hybridity are indeed illuminated because the missionary shares these experiences alongside her migrant friends. Her advocacy and works of compassion and hospitality are consequently of greater resonance to the diaspora in which she ministers because they are done by her as an insider with intimate understanding of the needs and heartbeat of the community, rather than simply as a well-meaning foreigner.

---

[497] One wonders why we even use the term "English as a Second Language" when it is only rarely a student's second language.

Finally, Howell suggests that it would be better for Christians to emphasize "biblical virtues" such as compassion, hospitality, and justice rather than to pursue contextualization in diaspora missions. But this contention has two problems. First, Howell himself admits that virtues such as hospitality and compassion must be practiced "with an eye toward how particular actions and attitudes take on meanings in a given context" (Howell 2011). This insight must not be glossed over, as "well-meaning" Christians are *not* always understood to be so. Contextualization is essential if we desire to effectively communicate compassion, hospitality, and love to our migrant neighbors. But beyond this, Howell neglects the fact that the pursuit of contextualization itself is undergirded by clear biblical values. For example, contextualization values cultural diversity and the unique gifts of each people (Ephesians 4:7, Revelation 21:26). Contextualization promotes an integration that preserves cultural distinctiveness, not an assimilation that obscures them. In so doing, it allows for host Christians to be greatly enriched by their correspondence with Christ-followers from other nations who are encouraged to bring with them their own culturally-contextualized expressions of discipleship and their own "local theologies" (Jackson 2011). Thus contextualization sees the migrant as a "hallowed person" (Sydnor 2011) who is not the mere recipient of charitable acts, but someone with a story, value, and gifts and experiences to share. However, above all, contextualization uplifts the biblical virtue of clear and understandable Gospel proclamation. At its heart, contextualization is about illumination of biblicaltruth and becoming all things to all people so as to reach as many as possible (John 1:9, 1 Corinthians 9:22).

In fact, many missiologists have called for contextualization in diaspora missions (LCWE 2010; Lorance 2010; Richard 2010; Connor 2006; Casino 2011; Song 2010; Jackson 2011; Tan 2011). To be sure, pursuing this holistically will be difficult and costly. The following reflections were written specifically about ministry to diaspora Hindus, but many of the insights are broadly applicable to diasporas of all kinds.

Sacrificial relationship-building is indispensable for maintaining the kind of dialogue that is necessary for true disciple-making. That is to say that the pursuit of contextualization must greatly influence the way we engage in relationships.

Contextualization is essential for the initiating, deepening, and maintaining of these relationships. To some extent, in order for Jesus to become "owned" by the Hindus, the messenger of Jesus also must become "owned." A cognitive distinction must be gradually made in the minds of our Hindu friends between the cross-cultural worker and "most Americans" or even "most Christians." The missionary must, for his/her part, painfully accept the increasing dissonance between him/herself and other non-Hindus as the necessary cost for becoming more embedded and therefore more faithful as an incarnation of Christ among Hindus.

CASE STUDY 7: REFLECTIONS OF A CHURCH PLANTER AMONG DIASPORA GROUPS IN METRO-CHICAGO: PURSUING CRUCIFORMITY IN DIASPORA MISSIONS

A final word that deserves more treatment refers to the importance of cultivating reciprocity and, consequently, indigenous ownership of the Christian faith in our ministry to Hindus. In word, deed, and relationship, we cannot do without reciprocity. Missionaries to Hindus must not only speak but listen, not only give but receive, not only love but be loved . . . I am fully convinced that there can be no sustainable progress of our missionary endeavors to Hindus without all three. If Hindus really feel that they are heard by me, if they feel they can give to me, and if they truly and deeply love me, then I am theirs—an insider to their community. This, in turn, means that I follow Jesus as one of them rather than as a foreigner. So, Jesus too belongs to them. Such sparks of reciprocity must be fanned into flame if disciple-making is to be sustained (Lorance 2010).

Of course, our natural human urge is not to contextualize but rather to cling to our own cultural preferences, biases, and traditions. If we are to pursue cruciformity in our engagement in diaspora missions, we must guard against the following:

- **Demanding assimilation** – This is the desire for everyone else to conform to our own cultural preferences. Instead, we are to be those who advocate for integration that promotes unity and preserves diversity.

- **Ethnocentrism** – Instead of assuming that our own cultural preferences and traditions are the only legitimate way to do things or that our presumptions are the only proper lens through which to view things, we must move toward the radical practice of inverted assimilation in which Christians seek to enter into the cultural context of their diaspora neighbors through language and cultural acquisition and holistic, incarnational contextualization.

- **Benefactor mentality** – This is the false assumption that migrants are to be viewed only as objects of charity. Instead we must move toward the cultivation of reciprocal relationships.

Once again, the costly nature of cruciform diaspora missions is modeled by Christ, who did not consider equality with God "a thing to be grasped," but entered into human flesh, taking the form of a servant (Philippians 2:7). If we are to follow Him, we too must be willing to let go of our cultural preferences and walk the difficult road of incarnation.

Toward an Evaluation of Our Cruciformity

It may seem somewhat counterintuitive to attempt to assess the level of one's cruciformity in diaspora missions. Nevertheless, it is undeniable that being able to identify specific areas in need of growth would be helpful. The following table represents a first step toward the development of such an evaluative tool.

In it, the four prevailing attitudes characterizing the Babel Complex are set against their cruciform counterparts. To each of these major sections are then added specific attributes that may be considered hallmarks of each attitude. The goal is to create a tool that will allow for the assessment not only of individual Christians (both of diaspora and host-country backgrounds) but also of groups of Christians, churches, and organizations. (See figure 18.2).

Figure 18.2 Self-Assessment Questions
My primary reason for migration is self-interest

Strongly disagree	Disagree	Neutral	Agree	Strongly agree
1	2	3	4	5

Or:

I feel especially called by God to diaspora missions

Strongly disagree	Disagree	Neutral	Agree	Strongly agree
1	2	3	4	5

A possible next step in the development of this evaluative tool could be to develop a list of self-assessment questions based on each of the attitudes (see figure 18.3). Questions could be formatted as *Likert items*, for example:

CASE STUDY 7: REFLECTIONS OF A CHURCH PLANTER AMONG DIASPORA GROUPS IN METRO-CHICAGO: PURSUING CRUCIFORMITY IN DIASPORA MISSIONS

Figure 18.3 Evaluating Cruciformity

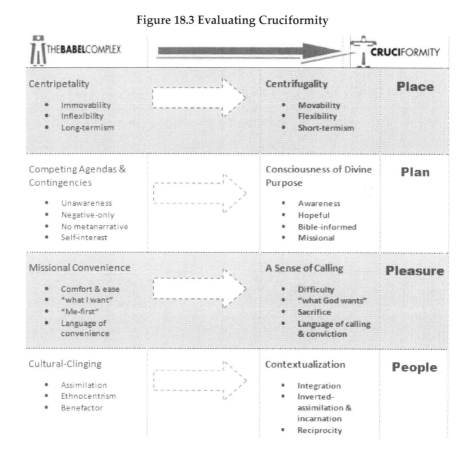

Summary

We have perhaps drifted quite far from the days of impassioned missionaries who packed their belongings in their own coffins as they boarded ships bound to some unknown port in a mysterious land. We feel ourselves so far removed from the times of Judson and Carey, who buried wives and endured harsh persecution; of Moon and Aylward, who forsook marriage and scorned difficulty, poverty, and mental and physical hardship; and of Ricci and de Nobili, who so thoroughly embraced Christ's incarnational model that their own native cultures became something of a distant memory. By the end of his life and decades-long missionary career among the Hindus of southern India, Roberto de Nobili had become fluent in Sanskrit, Tamil, and Telugu. But in writing home to his own family, he found it necessary to make use of a translator, as he had all but forgotten his native Italian (Cronin 1959). Writes de Nobili:

> Let others crave for and seek the temporal goods which I have given up, let others enjoy them. As for me, I have decided to spend my days unknown in some obscure corner and to sacrifice my wretched life for the salvation of souls (Rajamanickam 1968).

These models must not become mere relics of mission history. We must recapture the cruciformity inherent in all true Christian mission—foreign, domestic, and diasporic. Christ's call to ambassadorship is a call to imitation, incarnation, and crucifixion for the sake of the Gospel. The Lausanne Covenant has stated well that "the church which preaches the cross must itself be marked by the cross" (The Lausanne Movement 1974). This call to cross-marked mission is of particular importance in the realm of diaspora, where temptations toward convenience and self-interest, dabbling and volunteerism are so strong, subtly suggesting that in our modern, technologically-advanced, and globalized society, "taking up the cross" in our missional activity may no longer be all that necessary. We who are of Christ must reject the very notion of such things. Paul's diasporic mission was one of laying down his life every day (1 Corinthians 15:31). So should ours be.

Amy Carmichael, herself well-acquainted with the cost of Christian mission, left us with a few poignant lines that are worthy of our reflection as we consider our mission among "the people on the move":

> *No wound? No scar?*
> *Yet, as the Master shall the servant be,*
> *And piercèd are the feet that follow Me;*
> *But thine are whole: can he have followed far*
> *Who has no wound nor scar?*
> (Carmichael, 1936)

Chapter 19

Case Study 5: Diaspora Missions in Minnesota: Local Actions with Global Implications

Randy G. Mitchell

Introduction

It has long been my belief that *diaspora missiology is most certainly global in its implication but it is local in its application*. For this reason, it is imperative that everyone, from local church leaders to local church members, must recognize how *what God is doing on a global level involves them at a local level*. It is at this level that diaspora missiology finds its practical application as we love our new global neighbor.

The reality is that if people in diaspora are going to be reached, it will require a synergistic relationship between local church and mission structures. We will need to bring to bear the extensive experience and vast resources of these structures together with the local context and human contact of the local church. It is time to see mission organizations and individuals working together with local churches to gather the needed information to "formulate mission strategy, conduct strategic planning and draft and implement ministry plans."[498]

Our objective therefore must be to simplify our understanding of diaspora missiology and to clearly communicate it in such a way that the average layperson

---

[498] Enoch Wan, "Diaspora missiology," EMS *Occasional Bulletin* (Spring 2007a). Also in *Global Missiology* (July 2007); available at www.GlobalMissiology.org.

in our local churches can begin to practically take steps for living as a witness to the people in diaspora they already come into contact with. Mission organizations alone cannot effectively reach these displaced persons. Even though they may typically have access to much needed resources and may possess great understanding of how to reach these people in their native lands, agencies lack the local context to reach people in diaspora.

Diaspora Missions and Local Churches

Therefore, I submit that the Church is the crucial link to reaching peoples in diaspora and what is needed today is a strong working relationship between local churches and traditional mission structures.

It is important to make it clear that the local church I am referring to is not a particular denomination, organization, or institution. It is not a location or an event; it is a believing community gathered for the purpose of worship. So, when I say the local church is the crucial link to reaching people in diaspora, I am speaking to the importance of educating, mobilizing, and equipping local believers to be Christ's ambassadors in a cross-cultural context.

This understanding is extremely important because our motivation cannot be to add individuals to our membership or to further the mission function of our denomination. I would further suggest that we need to be careful that our objective is to present Christ and God's Kingdom and not merely the religion of Christianity. We do not set out to produce a religious proselyte, one who has externally adapted themselves to the tenets of a particular belief system. We are not promoting a particular religion, a set of rules, the dogma of an institution, practices particular to our own culture, or a religious identity acquired through affiliation. Rather our message is Christ and the cross. It is the love of the Father expressed in Christ's life and death on the cross as a sacrifice for the sins for the world. Those who believe that message are not required to worship as I worship or pray in the manner I pray or even self-identify as anything other than believers in God and followers of the biblical Christ.

Here in the U.S., One World Missions works to catalyze diaspora missions initiatives by educating churches concerning the opportunities for reaching ethnic minorities as a result of changing demographic trends. Over the years, we have tried to raise awareness concerning the opportunities that local churches have to carry out Christ's redemptive mission among various people groups, some of them typically classified as unreached and least reached. The response we have had from most of our churches has historically been one of ambivalence. Most of their leadership did not fully recognize the opportunity and quite frankly did not believe that it merited much attention. Some acknowledged the ethno-shift that was occurring within their communities but assumed that the church was already equipped to reach the growing number of ethnic minorities within their communities. They assumed that their current methods of engaging people with the living Christ would suffice, when in reality many times their methods were producing only a little fruit among a very limited spectrum of their community. This could be proven by the homogeneous complexion of their congregation. They have failed to see that society (unlike many churches) is very heterogeneous. It is increasingly made up of more and more diverse ethnic people groups and each of these individual groups poses unique challenges for the church desiring to engage them.

Certainly, it should be the objective of a local community church to minister to whole of its community. Not every local church may completely reflect the ethnic diversity of our community, but we should never allow prevailing attitudes, fears and prejudices to keep us from being salt and light to the whole of our community. I heard a pastor once comment that the most segregated time and place in America is our local churches Sunday morning. This should not be.

Paradigm Shift in Local Churches and Church Leaders

In recent years, we have begun to witness a paradigm shift in the thinking of local churches and church leaders. I believe this shift directly corresponds to the increasing emphasis on diaspora missiology. Pastors are realizing that their communities are much more ethnically diverse than they ever knew. For some, this realization has been difficult to navigate as leaders find themselves ill-equipped to minister in their newly formed multi-cultural communities.

For some these shifts are further complicated as they are forced to confront existing prejudices and growing hostilities within themselves and among their parishioners. One pastor remarked, "We simply cannot allow these issues to pass, prejudicial statements to be made, jokes to be told without our saying a word. If we say nothing we quietly voice our approval." Church leaders are being forced to take a stand for righteousness. Communities are being made to realize that as the complexion of a community changes, the community itself experiences enormous pressure as its identity is transformed. A community cannot help being a reflection of its citizenry.

A portion of the community may become entrenched and resistant to this change, but the community will change; again it is no more than a reflection of the present reality. To deny this is to simply be out of touch with reality. There is a shift occurring in the very fabric of the society and the community can never again be what it once was. It is important to note that *communities never react as quickly as they change.* With this type of immigration occurring we witness huge swings in the percentages of ethnic minorities that make up a community. However, it can take years for the community to catch up with these shifts, as people discover and define their changing roles and as new business and community services develop. One community leader described it this way, "In southwest Minnesota there has been some tug and pull."

There are many significant benefits to having immigrants in our workforce and contributing culturally but we do see some tension in the community because things are not turning around quickly. We have made plans that draw a lot of immigrant workers. Resources are needed to connect these immigrants to the community."[499] In the meanwhile, there are bound to be people who find it difficult to adapt and others who will flat out resist the change that is occurring; this often can result in increased tensions within the community.

One local representative described it this way, "Racism and fear are big obstacles here. There is always a group that we seem to be afraid of and there seems to be a mindset among certain people that say or do things that will not help."[500] For some this change is painful, and when faced with this type of ethno-shift people will sometimes respond in a very un-Christian manner. During these times, people's prejudices are often revealed as they resist what they perceive to be a threat to the status quo. It is at this point that our spiritual leaders, like the pastor mentioned earlier, need to challenge people to face their fears of the unfamiliar, set aside their political views and ask God to purify their hearts of prejudice so that they can simply respond with the love of God.

Reaching these diaspora communities will require deep heart changes and practical shifts in the way we think about evangelism, the church and our witness in our communities. It will require the church to become sensitive to people's history, cultural identity, localized social structure, historic religious identity, and so forth. This requires churches and church leaders to first know their communities before they ever think about trying to reach them. As one pastor remarked to me, "We are going to have to get out of our churches and into our communities."

History of Immigration in Minnesota

Minnesota has often been characterized as primarily an Anglo state with little diversity, historically populated by persons of European ancestry. "Data from the 2000 census confirm that the vast majority of Minnesotans are 'white' non-Hispanics (89%) and that 86% of Minnesota residents claim European ancestry."[501] However, over the last 20 years this has begun to change dramatically. Minnesota now has a larger percentage of immigrants who are refugees than any other place in the country. "Since 1989, the percentage of immigrants who are refugees has ranged from 14% to 44% in Minnesota

---

[499] Greg Owen, Jessica Meyerson, and Christa Otteson. A *New Age of Immigrants—Making Immigration Work for Minnesota* (Saint Paul, Minnesota: Wilder Research, 2010).
[500] Ibid.
[501] Katherine Fennelly and Helga Leitner, "How the Food Processing Industry is Diversifying Rural Minnesot," JSRI Working Paper, Vol. WP-59 (East Lansing: Michigan State University, 2002).

compared to the 6% to 16% in the U.S. as a whole."[502] "This form of immigration presents its own unique set of challenges as refugees often bring a high demand for services because of high rates of disease, trauma, torture or persecution."[503]

Consequently, Minnesota has been the primary or secondary site of relocation for large numbers of refugees from Asia, the successor states of the former Soviet Union and the countries of Africa. Asians were among the first refugees to arrive in Minnesota in significant numbers. "In the mid-1970's, after the U.S. withdrawal from Indochina, large numbers of Hmong, Vietnamese and Laotians came to the United States, and several thousand were resettled in Minnesota."[504] Minnesota is now home to the largest urban population of Hmong in the world. "Thousands of Cambodians were also displaced by the Indochinese war and by political turmoil and famine under the Khmer Rouge regime."[505]

In recent years, Minnesota has sheltered successive waves of asylum seekers from Bosnia, Liberia, the Sudan and (most recently) Somalia and Burma (Myanmar).[506] Today as many as 70,000 Somalis call Minnesota home, making Minnesota the de facto "capital" of the Somali community in North America. "It is estimated three out of every four Somalis in Minnesota relocated here after having been placed in one of 23 other U.S. states from the camps in Kenya and Ethiopia."[507] It has been observed that this present wave of diaspora peoples may not be assimilating into the proverbial "melting pot" as previous ethnic groups have. Some have pointed out that historically the majority of ethnic populations settling in Minnesota were largely of European descent with a Western worldview.

Nowadays, Minnesotans frequently come from non-Western cultural and religious backgrounds, resulting in cultural conflicts not often encountered in previous waves of immigration. Increasingly we recognize that the traditions and practices of some groups are sometimes in conflict with the traditional practices of the predominantly Western European groups represented by many native Minnesotans. This of course draws attention to how important it is that we work to build bridges into these new communities. Some have suggested that rather than a "melting pot," what is needed is a different paradigm concerning assimilation, one that represents a "salad bowl" where peoples are not assimilated but rather mixed into the whole, all the while maintaining their individual characteristics, customs, cultures, practices, etc. Although it is beyond the scope of this article, I do believe these concepts could dramatically impact our understanding of the diaspora dynamics at work in American culture as we look to the future, and further study needs to be done on this issue.

---

[502] Helga Leitner and Katherine Fennelly, 2002.
[503] Greg Owen, Jessica Meyerson and Christa Otteson, 2010.
[504] Fennelly, Katherine and Helga Leitner, 2002.
[505] Ibid.
[506] http://www.somaliawatch.org/archivedec00/001221101.htm
[507] http://www.somaliawatch.org/archivedec00/001221101.htm

Small Rural Communities in Minnesota

This massive influx of diaspora peoples is not limited to large cities as some might expect. There are now very few mid-size rural communities (those with populations of less than 50,000) who have not seen a rapid increase in ethnic populations. "The diversity of many of Minnesota's small towns challenges the perception of rural communities as homogenous and unchanging; indeed, most of Greater Minnesota has weathered a dizzying array of transformations in recent decades."[508] Especially during the past 15 years, increasing numbers of immigrants and refugees have moved to small towns and communities.

A case can be made that this introduction of various diaspora populations into rural Minnesota has been closely associated with the changing geography of food processing. The relocation and expansion of food processing plants into rural areas in Minnesota and the Upper Midwest creates a demand for low wage labor that cannot be met locally.[509] Food processing businesses attract minorities seeking jobs. The work does not necessarily require proficiency in English, special job skills, or previous experiences and the wages are attractive when compared to other available jobs. Poultry processing plants in rural areas not only meet these criticism but also offer longer-term employment than the jobs typically available in urban areas.[510]

However, it is important to note that factors that drive relocation are varied and complex, and cannot be reduced to simple economic calculations based on jobs and wages. One Somali woman described it this way, "What I like about living here is that it's a calm place, and it's walking distance to everything—for example schools and work. It is good for my children because there is no violence."[511] In truth, the qualities that draw many of us to small, rural communities are the same factors that attract diaspora peoples.

Willmar, a small rural farming community of approximately 20,000, is a regional hub located about two hours west of Minneapolis. Over the past 20 years, the face of Willmar has changed significantly as they have seen an increase in ethnic population. Looking at the population growth from 1990 to 2000, the minority population more than doubled.[512] One citizen described it this way, "As most everybody has noticed, the make-up of Willmar has changed, some view the changes as positive, some not so positive. However, we cannot ignore the fact that it has changed." While Willmar has made significant progress toward instituting a positive approach to diversity and integration,

---

[508] Greg Owen, Jessica Meyerson and Christa Otteson, 2010.
[509] Fennelly and Leither, 2002.
[510] Louise Lamphere, Alex Stepick and Guillermo Grenier, eds., *Newcomers in the Workplace: Immigrants and the Restructuring of the U.S. Economy* (Philadelphia: Temple University Press, 1994).
[511] Dianna J. Shandy and Katherine Fennelly, "A Comparison of the Integration Experiences of Two African Immigrant Populations in a Rural Community," *Social Thought* 45(1), (2006).
[512] Abdirahman Aynte, "Missing Youth Still Haunt Minnesota Somalis," May 13; Available at www.mshale.com.

strong currents of misunderstanding, resentment and tension remain throughout the community.

The persistence of these kinds of conflicts points to the complicated and multi-layered nature of cross-cultural relationships in communities such as Willmar, and the need for ongoing dialogue to foster greater understanding.[513] Fennelly and Federico point out, "There is evidence that native-born residents in rural communities are more likely to hold negative views of immigrants, including perceptions of the foreign-born as less-hardworking and a 'burden' on the country's labor market and infrastructure."[514] Current research conducted in a number of similar communities shows that rapid immigration of poor and culturally distinct workers and their families creates tensions.[515] Many established residents resent the influx of new immigrants. There is no doubt that rural communities like Willmar have struggled to redefine community in the wake of so much demographic change. However, the impact of immigration is typically not just a short-term phase that communities experience and then recover from.[516] Instead, increasing diversity related to immigration is a trend that will likely continue in the coming years, and is a very real issue to be addressed.

The Latino Community

Like many towns in America experiencing increased diversity, the first newcomers to Willmar in 2010 were Spanish-speaking Latinos coming directly from Mexico, many of whom were "settling out" of the migrant labor stream. As the Latino community grew, drawn in part by the recruitment efforts of local turkey processing plant Jennie-O and in part by families seeking to reunite, tensions within the community surfaced. "Schools were sorely unprepared to serve Spanish-speaking families, the limited supply of affordable housing swelled to overflowing, trailer parks became racially-marked 'eyesores' and ultimately, socially marginalized 'danger zones' that local police were reportedly hesitant to patrol."[517]

To date, the Latino population in Willmar has grown to over 4,000 persons, representing almost 21 percent of the total population. The number of Hispanics has increased 42.9 percent from 2000 to 2010.[518] This has occurred at the same time that population growth has increased at a very modest 2 percent among the Anglo

---

[513] Greg Owen, Jessica Meyerson and Christa Otteson, 2010.
[514] Katherine Fennelly and Christopher M. Federico, " Rural Residence as a Determinant of Attitudes Toward U.S. Immigration Policy," *International Migration,* (February 5, 2008): 46: 1.
[515] Leitner, Helga and Katherine Fennelly, 2002.
[516] Greg Owen, Jessica Meyerson and Christa Otteson, 2010.
[517] Greg Owen, Jessica Meyerson and Christa Otteson, 2010.
[518] Kandiyohi Co. Demographic & Economic Profile Page 1 of 14 DEED Analysis & Evaluation Office.

community. The area's Hispanic population is expected to more than double (128 percent) between 2000 and 2030.[519]

One very exciting development in Willmar is unification of area churches, including the Latino congregations. Beginning in 2011, a network of churches from the Latino and Anglo communities began meeting and planning a citywide event focused on bringing the two communities together and serving as an outreach for the entire area. This event has been exciting to witness, as we see churches from differing cultural and spiritual backgrounds come together in a true spirit of unity that I have never seen.

The churches in the area are really beginning to work together, and surely this is another key to reaching the entire community. If we are to reach the whole of our community, it must begin with us realizing that there are differing churches and each express the differences in our communities. We recognize that the body of Christ is to be diverse even as our community is diverse, and we need to be able to respect these differences, be they cultural or theological. Rod and Annette Rice, local pastors in Willmar, stated, "Since introducing this event to our local ministerial association, there has been a total change of perspective in our community. Our churches are working together in a manner never seen before." They went on to say, "We know that the relationships that are being formed will last well beyond a single event. We believe that this event is unifying the believing community of Willmar."

When asked what impact this event was having on their church, the pastors commented, "First of all it has totally changed us, we have been stretched, we have grown and we know that this is just the beginning. As for our church, there is such a different spirit. We always had Latino families in our congregation, but they have been re-energized as they feel affirmed as an important part of our local church. Our church is excited about reaching out to our whole community and each of these minority peoples are part of our community." One area Latino leader commented, "We have felt that we existed on the margins of our community, it is so wonderful to be able to play such an important role in what God is doing throughout our community."

Certainly, we are seeing opportunity among the diaspora Latino community for diaspora ministry to them through this event, but we are now exploring the possibilities for diaspora ministry through them, by them and beyond them.

The Burmese Community

Willmar has recently made plans to receive 1,500 Burmese refugees. This plan involves relocating families from Minneapolis, but is currently being held up because adequate housing is not available. The Willmar paper, the *West-Central*

---

[519] Greg Owen, Jessica Meyerson and Christa Otteson, 2010.

Tribune, reported, "Most of the refugees in Willmar are Karen (kah-RIN), an oppressed minority in Burma, and they are predominantly Baptist. The Karen and other groups have left Burma, also called Myanmar, during more than 50 years of war in the country."[520] This diaspora represents an entirely different scenario. Local churches in communities where diaspora people come from evangelized backgrounds must rethink their roles. Although many of these diaspora people may be believers, the local church and church leaders still need to demonstrate to them a Christ-like response.

Local churches need to think about how to welcome such individuals and assist them as they join our community. Even among believers, we must understand that certain barriers to integration exist. They may need assistance navigating governmental agencies, enrolling children in school, finding and furnishing affordable housing, securing employment, caring for non-school age children, obtaining a driver's license, etc. As these people settle into their new environment, the believers among them will undoubtedly begin to think about gathering for worship. Willmar First Baptist pastors welcomed recent refugees to the church, offered help, and invited the refugees to come to church services.

However, almost all of these individuals lack the language skills necessary to integrate into the local church, and some may find that the Western model of church does not adequately reflect their cultural expression of worship. For this reason, the ethnic community may very well desire to formulate an independent church that best suits the needs of their community. This church needs to be welcomed into the believing community and their differences in religious perspectives and practices respected. Many of these new fellowships, especially among the immigrant communities, may initially lack the resources to establish new churches.

It should be our desire to assist diaspora believers without consideration of denomination or affiliation. We should strive to assist them in maintaining their independence so that their uniqueness can be preserved within the community. We should also be careful not to allow the sharing of resource to become a means of creating dependency. Some local churches have opened their facilities for these Burmese believers to congregate during hours in which the facility would not normally be in use.

Our understanding of diaspora missions does not limit us solely to direct evangelistic efforts. By serving these believing communities, we can further participate in diaspora missions as these diaspora Christians minister directly to those in diaspora both within their local community and as they reach back to their country of origin. We also recognize the potential effectiveness of equipping diaspora believers to reach out to people in other diaspora communities.

---

[520] Linda Vanderwerf, "Refugees from Burma settling in for work at Jennie-O store," *West Central Tribune* November 13, 2010.

The Somali Community

The modern nation of Somalia gained its independence in 1960.[521] "For much of the next three decades, Somalia was entangled in Cold War politics. Civil war erupted while the Soviet Union was collapsing; atrocities and natural disasters—famine, flood, drought—forced more than a million Somalis to seek refuge in neighboring countries such as Kenya and Ethiopia. Somalia has not had a recognized government since 1991."[522] Most Somalis who now live in Minnesota came to the United States as refugees. As refugees, Somalians are unable to return to their countries of origin due to ongoing famine and war. "Those that have relocated to Willmar, find greater limitations as they attempt to access U.S.-based social networks because rural towns generally lack both established communities of co-ethnics and the panoply of services available in cities. The arrival of African refugees in rural areas, therefore, introduces new challenges for social workers practicing in these settings."[523]

The U.S. census reports the population of Somali in Willmar at over 1,100 individuals;[524] however, in a conversation with Mayor Frank Yanish, he placed the population at 3,500. As with statewide estimates, it is often difficult to arrive at an exact count due to the fact that in any census Somalis are grossly undercounted. This occurs for several reasons. First, Somali families tend to live together under one roof. For they fear eviction when census workers or social workers inquire about their numbers, they tend to underreport. Secondly, due to "in-migration" or "secondary migration," the Somali community has proven quite fluid, moving from the original state of their placement to other cities and towns.

The Somali diaspora move from community to community within Minnesota seeking job or educational opportunities. One Somali man voiced this attitude: *"In the name of God, if we could find jobs other than in the processing plants ... we could stay here. Wherever you go in the United States, it's the same, it doesn't matter to us—although there is a difference between a big city and a small town—a small town is better than a big city."*[525] This transient lifestyle that many have been forced into is terribly destructive to the social fabric of the Somali community. I have observed many young men working in Willmar who have little or no local family ties. This is important because unlike other diaspora populations, many African refugees do not have extended family in the United States. *"Those who do have family ties still have kin networks that are truncated*

---

[521] See map of Somalia in appendix courtesy of http://www.nationsonline.org/oneworld/map/somalia-political-map.htm
[522] "Immigration in Minnesota-Discovering Common Ground," The Minneapolis Foundation; Available at www.MinneapolisFoundation.org.
[523] Dianna J. Shandy and Katherine Fennelly, " A Comparison of the Integration Experiences of Two African Immigrant Populations in a Rural Community," *Social Thought* 45 (1) (2006).
[524] Kandiyohi Co. Demographic & Economic Profile Page 1 of 14 DEED Analysis & Evaluation Office
[525] Shandy and Fennelly, 2006.

compared to what they experienced in Africa. In these situations the mosques serve as important institutions helping immigrants to meet basic needs."[526] For those participating in diaspora missions this represents a great opportunity for families to extend friendship and relationship to individuals who are in much need of family networks. Often we have seen that family lends us context and assists in bridging cultures. Churches and Christian organizations have also recognized the opportunity that this presents to demonstrate the love of Christ by meeting immediate, felt needs of individuals entering a new community.

Challenges to Integration

It is important to note the factors that contribute to diaspora peoples successfully integrating into a new community. Understanding these factors helps us better formulate strategies for reaching these peoples. One expert stated, "When immigrants move to rural communities they not only need housing and social services, but also ... links of incorporation ... secure employment, family formation, the establishment of credit, capital accumulation, competency in English and legal status. If these links remain out of the reach of workers in low-wage jobs, the result will be a marginalized population and increasing frictions between new and long-term residents."[527]

As important as integration strategy is, we cannot ignore the significance of the attitude of the local communities as they assume an active role in receiving people in diaspora. In their research, Downs, Schwei and Fennelly highlighted the need for, "More intentional and focused attention to the education of 'white,' U.S.-born residents. In most communities, cross-cultural work is focused on services for immigrants, without recognition of the ways in which the attitudes of U.S.-born residents facilitate or impede these efforts."[528] This proves that no amount of resources or services or government effort will prove successful in integrating diaspora peoples if the heart and attitude of the populace do not exemplify charity and compassion.

Language and Education

Educational opportunities play a significant role in the integration of people in diaspora into a new community. For school age children this is addressed through free public education. The school systems have proven remarkably

---

[526] Ibid.
[527] Leo R.Chavez, "*Shadowed Lives: Undocumented Immigrants in American Society,*" JSRI working Paper Vol. WP-59 (Orlando, FL: Holt, Rinehart and Winston, Inc., 1992).
[528] Tamara Downs Schwei and Katherine Fennelly, "Diversity Coalitions in Rural Minnesota Communities," *CURA Reporter* (Center for Urban and Regional Affairs: University of Minnesota, Winter, 2007).

effective in educating and integrating school age children into the community, but often schools can be overwhelmed and—like the community —slow to respond. Willmar is now one of the most diverse school districts in Minnesota, with 35 percent of the students being minorities in 2007.[529]

"In 2008, Willmar Public Schools reported minority enrollment increased from 455 in 1990 to 1,478 in 2006—an increase of more than 300 percent."[530] It is believed that studying demographics in K-6th grade can serve as an indicator of immigration trends. Enrollment for the 2011–2012 calendar year shows that 53 percent of incoming kindergarteners are non-Anglo and almost 20 percent are unable to speak English. This greatly stresses the educational system and local resources that fund education. "Studies show that the federal government benefits most from taxes paid by immigrants, but it has devolved many of the costs of basic services to states, counties and municipalities, thus placing a disproportionate burden on localities experiencing rapid immigration."[531] All of this challenges local community in the integrating of a rising immigrant population, and perpetuates the stereotype of immigrants being a burden on society.

Among adults, the problem grows much more complex. Opportunities are fewer, the learning curve is much steeper and there are many more obstacles to older individuals becoming proficient in English or accessing educational opportunities, be it remedial education for the illiterate or higher education. Yet language proves to be one of the most important factors in community integration, and the language barrier needs to be responded to. As it has been mentioned, smaller communities such as Willmar do not have the same access to resources as larger cities such as Minneapolis. This can be readily seen in the discrepancy in English proficiency between small towns and large cities.

A recent study conducted in a rural community of similar size and ethnic makeup as Willmar reported that only 14 percent of Somalis rated their English as "good" or "excellent." In contrast, the English language abilities of Somali residents in the Minneapolis-St. Paul area were much higher. There, 70 percent of Somali respondents stated that they could speak English well or very well.[532] It has already been mentioned that the types of jobs that initially attract Somalis to Willmar do not require high levels of English proficiency. However, this does not lessen the fact that a lack of English language skills constitutes a formidable barrier to other forms of incorporation, such as finding housing, getting a driver's license, interacting with non-Somali on businesses, reading newspapers, and making friends.

One Somali woman said *"We don't speak the same language; we do not chat. We have nothing to do with one another ... What is there to speak about if we cannot*

---

[529] Kandiyohi Co. Demographic & Economic Profile Page 1 of 14 DEED Analysis & Evaluation Office.
[530] Greg Owen, Jessica Meyerson and Christa Otteson, 2010.
[531] Fennelly, Katherine and Helga Leitner, 2002.
[532] Shandy and Fennelly, 2006

understand each other?"533 Providing additional educational resources such as tutoring for school age children and English language courses for adults has proven a successful method to assist diaspora groups such as the Somalians to integrate into local communities. This also provides us with a great opportunity to build relationships with individuals and opens the door for personal witness.

Culture and Religion

For the diaspora people, the barriers stretch far beyond language. There is a tremendous difference in culture, views on family, and of course religion. These barriers can be quite formidable because the fear of loss of one's culture can be overwhelming. In order to understand this, it is necessary to understand the mindset of refugees. One Samolian remarked, *"So many people in diaspora are just lost; we are striving to survive. We have lost our homes, our families, our heritage. We have very little left."* They feel like their culture, their very identity is under assault and they are just trying to hold on to all they have left. This survivor mode serves as a barrier, and fear is a mighty motivator. Isolation serves as a natural obstacle against loss of identity. These cultural norms we see reflected in Islamic dietary laws (only eating halal, religiously sanctioned meat), men's and women's clothing (hejab for women and the koofiyad for men). These practices, together with the fact that Somalis observe a daily prayer schedule and share a common language, serve to strengthen the cohesion of their diaspora community, but these ethnic practices also limit opportunities for Somalis to interact with non-Somalis and result in greater segregation from other U.S. and foreign-born residents of the community.

To quote one Somali,

> *"What keeps us apart is the fact that we belong to a different culture. For example, we do not go to parties, churches, bars or restaurants. Thus, [...] we don't become friends because they want to lead that kind of life, but we do not. They want to go to those places, but we don't believe in that kind of thing."*534 Another added: *"We cover [our bodies] while their women don't. They socialize by drinking alcohol at parties, while we go to the mosque and worship Allah (God). They celebrate Christmas, Memorial Day, and other holidays, which we don't."*535

Another Somali woman stated,

---

[533] Dianna J. Shandy and Katherine Fennelly, "A Comparison of the Integration Experiences of Two African Immigrant Populations in a Rural Community," *Social Thought* 45.1 (2006).
[534] Shandy and Fennelly, 2006.
[535] Ibid.

> *"People who believe in Islam and these [other] people are not the same at all ... Even if they have ten different beliefs, it all comes down to Christianity. They all belong to one another whether they agree or disagree, but we are different from them. We are Muslim people, followers of Muhammed."*

Unfortunately, for some Somalis it goes beyond language or cultural or even religious barriers. Some Somali leaders pride themselves on Somali separateness, and in some cases demonstrate distaste at the notion of interacting with non-Muslim neighbors. For example, in Minneapolis some religious leaders have been instructing Somalis not to respond to a non-Muslim's greeting of *salam alechem* (roughly translated as "Peace be unto you"). They state, "We should give no peace to the infidel." At the same time, social distance between Somalis and European residents is strongly reinforced by some "Christian" rural residents who view Muslims as "terrorists" or "beyond the reach of God," and the "unchurched" (in the words of one rural pastor). I have found that this divide exists in both the diaspora and the local communities.

On a recent visit to Willmar, I stopped in the local Somali grocery store where we have been making efforts to build bridges, and as I was visiting with some of the Somali men I noticed that some were staring out the window. I walked over to see what had captured their interest and realized that a parade was going by. The parade was a scheduled event celebrating the community. I asked the men what was happening and they responded, "We have no idea, we think it is some type of cultural event." Such cultural divide that exists is the perfect environment for breeding mistrust, fear and prejudice. Tension has been on the rise and the divide appears to be growing wider. One Somali community leader summed it up in this manner, "*It is total culture shock running both ways.*" The Somalis live in almost complete isolation. They have little or no social contact outside of their own community and the local people are baffled at best by their presence. "*Each group is completely foreign to the other.*"[536]

Affordable Housing and Business Development

Changing demographics often bring major changes and shifts in urban planning community development. Providing sufficient decent and affordable housing to the new immigrants constitutes a major challenge for host towns. Historically Minnesota has had one of the lowest rental vacancy rates in the United States.[537] After finding a place to live, African tenants may have difficulty retaining their apartments due to conflicts with their U.S.-born landlords over cultural concepts of space and family. Some Somali residents

---

[536] http://www.adcminnesota.org/page/success-stories/willmar
[537] Fennelly and Leitner, 2002.

had problems with their landlords over friends or relatives who came to stay with them. As one man commented, "Landlords do not know our culture. Sometimes we welcome other people [to stay with us] but here it is often against the rules. Having many people stay at your apartment is not part of American culture." Other housing issues reflect cross-cultural differences in gender and family norms. "Somalis come from patrilineal, patrilocal extended family residency systems. In the United States, they are expected to conform to neo-local conjugal family norms."[538] In Willmar, a highly contentious new low-rent housing community called West Wind was recently completed. Residents in the vicinity fought the new complex, fearing a rise in crime and a drop in property values. Units do have strict occupancy limits and the qualification process is extensive; however, this did little to quell the fears of local residents. Since its completion, West Wind has been 100 percent occupied, with many more on a waiting list. One city official stated that since its opening there have been very few occurrences of police involvement, but single-family dwellings in the surrounding area have been harder to sell.

Tension has also arisen over the formation of new businesses in the historic downtown section of Willmar. New Somali businesses have begun to cluster in the formerly empty downtown business district. One resident describes it this way, "Downtown has undergone encouraging revitalization with Latino- and Somali-owned businesses (restaurants, groceries, bakeries and clothing stores) moving in next door to Scandinavian gift shops and old-time coffee counters."[539] But what should be hailed as a rejuvenation of downtown is being met with anger and mistrust, as many people view "*their*" downtown as being "*taken over.*" Some in the community complain of the Somali "*loitering*" in front of stores.

However, what some may refer to as loitering the Somali call community. This reminds me of a true story I recently heard from a resident of Willmar. He was sitting in a local barbershop when a Latino man walked in and sat down for his regular haircut. He remarked to the barber, "What are we going to do with all of these Somalis? It is getting to the point where I am afraid to go out at night. I am not sure what they might do. I don't feel safe anymore and I fear for the safety of my wife and children." The barber responded, "You know it wasn't too many years ago we were saying the same thing about you."

This true story illustrates that yesterday's immigrants can become today's citizens. It also illustrates that many times the arriving ethnic peoples and existing immigrant populations experience various unique tensions. Typically, you would never see an Anglo person eating in the Somali restaurants or frequenting their shops. Interestingly enough, the Latino community do frequent the Somali businesses. This is not entirely surprising, as the two communities overlap in the

---

[538] Shandy and Fennelly, 2006.
[539] Greg Owen, Jessica Meyerson and Christa Otteson, 2010.

workplace and the Somali grocery stores carry Latino commodities. Although the history of relations between the Latino and Somali communities has been mixed, this raises interesting questions about the possibility of building bridges from the Latino community to the Somalis, and outreach strategies partnering with Latino leaders.

Complex Circumstances

One factor that has complicated efforts to reach out to the Somali community is that Somalians are peoples of Muslim backgrounds. Since 9/11/01 negative perceptions of followers of Islam have grown very strong,[540] and with ongoing conflicts in the Middle-East the environment remains continually strained because all Muslims are essentially judged the same. This causes many within the Muslim community to distrust our efforts and question our motives. Among the Somali community, this has been further exacerbated by a series of events in 2008 in which about 20 Somali youth raised in Minnesota were recruited by the terrorist organization, Al-Shabah to travel back to Somalia to fight. "Al-Shabab (The Youth) is an al-Qaeda ally that deliberately emulates its mentor organization—down to its reliance on training camps, a safe haven, the use of the internet for propaganda purposes and suicide attacks."[541]

Two of the youths who left later went on to kill others in suicide attacks and rumors were spread across Minnesota that these students were being radicalized and would be sent back to the U.S. to carry out terrorist acts. Since then, the Somali community has come under intense scrutiny by the FBI. These incidents inflamed public suspicions that Somali immigrants might somehow be linked to terrorism. This also happened just as many Somalians were moving into smaller communities when had a strong sense of patriotism. One Somali leader sitting in a coffee shop stated, "In Minnesota, Somalis are increasingly associated with terrorists … Businesses are raided. Friends and family members are being interrogated by law enforcement agencies. Mosques are under surveillance."

More recently, FBI agents raided money transfer businesses in Minnesota that serve as a key lifeline for millions of Somalis in the home country who depend on monthly remittances from loved ones in the diaspora. This episode was another blow to a community shaken by fear, confusion and uncertainty.[542] It has resulted in the Somali community being very suspicious of outsiders. Many times this anxiety is apparent when talking with Somali men. They will strive to appear overly patriotic and peace-loving, asserting and reasserting

---

[540] Shandy and Fennelly, 2006.
[541] Paul Schmelzer, "Al-Shabab, Minneapolis Somali youth highlighted in new terrorism," September 10, 2010; available at www.Minnesotaindependent.com.
[542] Abdirahman Aynte , 2009.

their desire to live peacefully in the U.S. One Somali friend commented, "I love America, it is my country, we would never do anything against America. We just want to live in peace and raise our families."

Finally, clan structure has produced some challenges to reaching into the Somali community. While Minnesotans may view Somali immigrants as a monolithic group, Somali society is actually composed of multiple groups, affiliated by language, culture, geography and other commonalities.[543] "Somalis belong to clans and sub-clans. These hierarchical descent groups, each said to originate with a single male ancestor, are a central fact of Somali life."[544] Understanding how Somali people relate to one another requires some knowledge of the clan system.

Unfortunately, little is known about the clan structure among Somali diaspora. The Somali community tends to minimize the importance of clan, opting to present a more unified front. In Somali society, clans serve as a source of great solidarity as well as conflict. The Somali clan organization is an unstable system characterized by changing alliances and temporary coalitions. Although historic clan divisions exist, there appears to be little outward conflict among the Somali that could be directly attributed to clan. This solidarity could possibly be understood by grasping the ever-shifting world of clan politics. A popular saying among nomads captures this: "My full brother and I against my father, my father's household against my uncle's household, our two households (my uncle's and mine) against the rest of the immediate kin, the immediate kin against non-immediate members of my clan, my clan against other clans and my nation and I against the world."[545] Far removed from traditional lands, extended family and the strong ties of clan, Somalis have unified against the world. However, this unity is ever shifting and characteristically unstable. The society of the Somalis is also fundamentally democratic. Traditionally, decisions are made by councils of men. These councils are egalitarian, sometimes to the point of anarchy, although age, lineage seniority and wealth can have influence. Anthropologist I.M. Lewis points out that in these councils, "All men are councilors and all men politicians." Somali egalitarianism permeates all aspects of society.[546] This information could explain the difficulty in identifying community leaders. There is much conflict even within the Somali community over who has the right to represent their interests. Civic leaders have commented, "We would love to have a better dialog between civic government and the Somali community if we could only identify who to talk to." As we have endeavored to interface with the Somali community, we often find it very difficult to discern

---

[543] Immigration in Minnesota: Discovering Common Ground. Available at www.MinneapolisFoundation.org.
[544] "The Somali social Structure," available at http://somaliaholland.free.fr/somali_social_structure.htm
[545] Ibid.
[546] Ibid.

who the community leaders actually are. I suspect that much of this can be traced to clan distinctions as well as the egalitarianism of the society. Where traditionally you would find the head of a clan or a ruling council of elders capable of granting access to the community, the structure of the Somali society in diaspora has become much more fragmented, with various leaders representing small contingencies of Somali as they are able to exercise influence.

Missions to the Diaspora

As I have stated, I believe that the local church serves as the crucial link between our diaspora communities and the message of God's love. We must understand that we have a tremendously important message. Our message is "Good News," but it is only "Good News" to those who hear it. Currently our message is drowned out by so much noise and interference that there is little hope of it ever reaching the heart. We need believers who are praying and working together to develop a strategy to make the crucial connection between our heavenly Father and people living in diaspora.

Local Churches as Bridges

Imagine a truck heavily loaded with desperately needed supplies. Our desire is to deliver our cargo to its destination, but between us and them exists an impossibly wide gulf. We will need a bridge, but not just any bridge. Every bridge has a load capacity. The bridge we build needs to withstand the weight of our load. Here the old adage is true, you cannot drive a 20-ton truck over a 10-ton bridge. The bridge must be strong enough to support the load of our cargo. That bridge we are building is the genuine caring relationship one develops with an individual. It should be a relationship built upon mutual respect and complete honesty, and it should also be a relationship built upon love and honorable motives. There can be no ulterior motives, no hidden agenda. We love people because Christ loves them. We love people because they are lovely in His sight. We love people genuinely from the heart and demonstrate that love in our kindness and with acts of goodness. As the relationship develops, our honesty will give us opportunity to share our lives and to communicate our faith in a very natural manner. As we build relationships, we are building bridges.

Local Consultations

A few years ago, One World Missions was approached by a local pastor in Willmar concerning the mounting tensions between the Somali and Anglo communities. We recognized that it was an opportunity to engage a community of believers with the understanding of diaspora missiology. Our desire was to help the church understand the manner in which God has been historically and contemporarily working among peoples both *"spiritually and spatially"* to draw them nearer to Himself.[547] We laid the basic framework for understanding the theology of diaspora missiology and we addressed the opportunity that diaspora missions affords the local believing community.

Our first consultation was attended by a small contingency from three churches. The purpose of our forum was to address strategic ways that the church could engage all the diaspora populations of Willmar, but our focus was mainly on understanding the least understood ethnic group in the city, the Somaliians. We addressed the existing prejudice and fear and contrasted it with the love that Scripture commands be demonstrated with not only our words but our actions as well. We addressed many of the historic misconceptions that exist about Muslim peoples as well as many of the misconceptions that might exist in the mind of the Somali community concerning followers of Christ. We challenged the attendees to be part of the solution and not to contribute to the problem by participating in the rhetoric. We began with challenging the faith community because we believe that the change must begin with us. As I pointed out in the section "Challenges to Integration," no amount of resources or government intervention will help diasporic peoples integrate successfully into a society as long as the existing population remains antagonistic toward their entry.

The believing community must begin to stand for tolerance, patience, acceptance and love. Our faith leaders must stand against bigotry, fear and prejudice. One attending pastor commented, "It is up to us as the spiritual leaders in this community to take a stand against the hatred and the bigotry and the fear that has gripped this community." He said, "People are afraid of the Somali community. Fear dominates their conversation and interaction. But we should not be afraid, they are people just like us and Christ died for each and every one because God loves them and that is a message they need to hear." We challenged believers to work toward building bridges into the community and concentrating on developing relationships. We felt that we could not sit back and wait for others to initiate movement.

The meeting was the first step towards purposefully engaging peoples in diaspora as Christ went out of His way to engage the Samaritans of his day in John 4. It was a recognition that we are surrounded by our own figurative Samaritans. Hopefully, the church will have eyes to see and a heart that perceives that our own Samaritan fields are ripe for harvest. Much prayer and much discussion are needed concerning strategy for engaging diaspora peoples. There needs to be interaction among mission structures as well as local churches

---

[547] Enoch Wan, "Diaspora missiology," EMS *Occasional Bulletin* (Spring 2007). Also in *Global Missiology* (July 2007); available at www.GlobalMissiology.org.

as we seek to become better equipped to engage diaspora communities. One fact is for sure, we cannot do this in our own strength or through our own limited resources. It will take a concerted effort of many people working together.

Continued, Fervent, Heartfelt Prayers

One indispensable key to reaching diaspora people is continued, fervent, heartfelt prayer.[548] Seek out like-minded believers and form coalitions to pray for the community. Because relations between ethnic peoples tend to be layered and complex, we should pray for purity of heart and motive. We should also pray for city government and spiritual leaders in the community to come together in a unified effort to represent Christianity in a manner that reflects Christ. We should pray for God's wisdom and doors of opportunity to open for us to demonstrate the love of God in tangible ways. We should pray for individuals willing to build bridges both from the Christian community and from the diaspora community.

Lastly, we should pray that God will raise up individuals from the diaspora community willing to reciprocate in the spirit of the "man of peace."[549] The "man of peace" is that individual who is willing to receive you and your message in a welcoming manner and demonstrates it by reciprocating the relationship. These are individuals in which the Spirit of God is already at work in their hearts. For this reason, it is important to never forget that as we are looking and praying for the man of peace, they in turn are inwardly and unbeknownst to them looking for us. Pray that there will be opportunities for God to reveal Himself and His nature to individuals through either answered prayer or dreams and visions. Do not miss opportunities to pray for and on behalf of others.

All around the world, we hear stories of how people come to faith in Christ after having experienced dreams and visions. However, it is very important to note that these experiences are not a replacement for the preaching of the gospel. These occurrences only open the heart to the truth concerning Christ. Someone must be positioned in their lives to bring understanding of the truth that saves. So we should pray that God is preparing the heart through all measures to bring the diaspora to Himself. Pray that what blinds them to the truth may be removed so that their eyes may be opened to the truth. In the words of one Willmar area pastor, "God, please show us how to break down the walls and show us how to build bridges into their lives."

---

[548] James 5:16 in the Amplified version says, that the continued, fervent, heartfelt prayer of the righteous makes great power available.
[549] Jesus instructed his disciples to seek out the Man of Peace in Luke 10:5-8.

Crossing Cultures without Crossing Oceans

In order to reach people in diaspora, we have to successfully cross the expanse of culture that separates us. The cultural divide is a formidable barrier because it renders us and our message as foreign. Culture is the way that each of us interacts with the world. Culture exists as a shared set of beliefs, feelings and values of a community of people. My culture dictates the way I see and interact with the world. As I pointed out in my introduction, for diaspora people who have left everything behind, culture is the one element that gives them their identity—it may be all that they have left.

Typically, people will respond to differences in cultures by assuming that their own culture is superior or more advanced or enlightened; this is called ethnocentrism. "Ethnocentrism is the tendency to respond to differences by using our own affective assumptions and reinforce our responses with deep feelings of approval or disapproval."[550] We need to acknowledge our tendency to assume that we are always right, that our ways are the best ways. Now we need to learn to appreciate the differences in the cultures we encounter. Begin with the assumption that there is no perfect culture. We should look for elements within every culture from which we can learn. As we set out to truly understand another culture, we can set aside our cultural biases and appreciate the good we find in these cultures.

This journey across the cultural divide begins with the person being honest about his own culture and his own ethnocentricity. It is necessary to be able to acknowledge that one's own culture is imperfect. There are certainly aspects of every culture that do not measure up to the biblicalstandard to which Christ calls us. Realizing this helps us to be open to how others may be perceiving our culture, and rather than trying to defend our culture, we need to recognize the opportunity it presents to shine a light on God's glorious standard. We need to understand what others' perceptions of our culture are, either right or wrong. This will give us an opportunity to dispel misconceptions and remove prejudice in both parties. As we are trying to draw near to the diaspora people, we also have to work to remove the stereotypes that keep them from moving toward us. Then we can prepare to step across the cultural divide with a genuine love for them and their culture.

Moreover, in order to reach people in diaspora, we need to possess at least a rudimentary knowledge of the diaspora community's history, culture, language, religion, customs, and norms within society. Knowing something about their history, their country, and their culture will demonstrate that we care for them and will remove much of the threat they feel. Other actions include making a decision to reach out, learning basic greetings in their native

---

[550] Paul G. Hiebert, *Cultural Differences and the Communication of the Gospel-Perspectives of a World Christian Movement*, 3rd ed. (L.A: William Carey Library).

language, frequenting their places of business, and eating at their restaurants. With the Somali we offer the common greeting *salam alechem* and to shake their hand. We encourage people that, if the pronunciation is too difficult, just smile and say "hello." Even by just being willing to adapt ourselves to another culture, eating unfamiliar foods, learning common Somali phrases and not being afraid to smile and greet them, we can begin to establish rapport. It is a simple task to learn people's names, ask about their families, cultural norms, and practices.

Many great resources from various mission organizations can help to navigate the nuances of culture. The best guide for understanding their culture is to contact them. Ask lots of questions and you will be amazed at how much you learn when you begin to listen. Return to them regularly and interact with them and bring in family and friends who will be sensitive to your new relationship with these people. The fact that you have a family gives you context and helps them to better relate to you as a father or mother.

Over time, as the relationship develops, there will be opportunities to witness. We should be honest about who we are, our faith, and our life. Let them observe our lives, our piety, and our devotion to God. Look for opportunities to further the relationship. One man told me he was speaking with a group of Somali men when one stated that he did not really know any non-Somali individuals and he did not understand their culture." The man commented in return, "Well, I should have you over for a barbecue." It is this type of interaction, extending hospitality and showing kindness that will begin to open doors—but you must follow through.

Quite often this type of bold invitation will be met with smiles and polite acceptance with no intention of ever following through. We have to be persistent and should not make one attempt and give up. At times, crossing cultures will prove quite difficult especially when mistakes are made. Then we apologize. As long as there is no violation on major cultural norms, relationship should be able to weather it. The most important thing is to have a genuine, caring, and loving relationship.

Ministering Cross-Culturally

Some have made the mistake of believing that they could simply apply an evangelistic method—some soul-winning strategy—and easily "convert" diaspora peoples. The reality is much more complex. Our objective should be not to produce a religious proselyte, one who has externally adapted themselves to the tenets of a particular belief system. Our objective is that they come into the right relationship with their loving heavenly Father by coming to know Christ as personal Lord and Savior.

Once that cultural divide has been crossed to begin a relationship, it is time to ask questions about their faith, their beliefs, and their practices. Most

Christians have no idea what Muslims really believe. Many believe that all Muslims must be terrorists or at least sympathizers. In turn, Muslims look at the behavior typical of our Western society and assume that it represents the beliefs of true Christians. Their assumption is that all non-Muslims are Christians and all Christians are the same. We want them to begin to see that not everyone who calls himself Christian is a 'true' follower of God. This is important because in time this allows them to acknowledge that not everyone who calls himself a Muslim is a true follower of Allah. It is at this point the question can be asked, *"Who are the true followers of God and how do we get into His kingdom?"*

When we build relationships with Muslims, they have the opportunity to see our devotion and the difference that Christ makes in our lives. We also have the opportunity to ask questions that help us understand Islam. Then we can gently open our lives as a testimony. In time, this will provide enable us to share about our own faith. We should focus on any similarities they may share about their faith. It is far more effective to begin with our similarities than with the differences. Although we differ on many important issues, but if we are to build bridges we will have to start out on common ground. Next we need to learn to contextualize our message. This calls for bypassing the interference to communicate the truth in a culturally relevant way. It means to seek out methods for framing the message in a manner that is not wholly inconsistent with their worldview. Doing so allows the Muslim hearer to absorb the message rather than rejecting it. Once the message is received and understood, it can be internalized, and will go to work transforming the way they think and live. Our objective is not that we change them and their culture but that they receive in their hearts the resurrected Christ.

It is important to remember that no one can do it alone. One of the ways to avoid the myriad of pitfalls is to draw up resources from people experienced in cross-cultural ministry to diaspora people, for example, develop relationship both locally and internationally with organizations that have a history of ministering successfully among the target people group. It is beneficial to learn from their practical experience and to borrow their tools such as witness aids, literature, videos, and Bibles in their native language. There is no shortcut in the outreach process. Only the Holy Spirit can draw the diaspora people to the Father. Our job is to be patient and let the light of the Gospel shine on the darkness of their heart. The task requires Christians willing to work together, churches willing to lay aside their differences, and mission organizations willing to interface with local churches.

Summary

Diaspora missiology is most certainly global in its implication. However, this case study demonstrates that diaspora missiology is also local in its application. In recent years, some have suggested that diaspora missions are a phenomenon limited to large urban centers. The small town Willmar in Minnesota proves that the diaspora trend covers towns and cities large and small. It is hoped that by studying what God is doing in one small rural community in Minnesota we can gain deeper understanding on the role the local church plays in reaching out to diaspora communities.

God is at work among people groups around the world, and through mission to the diaspora we made to understand that what God is doing on a global level involves us at a local level. In Willmar we see the unprecedented opportunity to fulfill God's redemptive mission. We must be willing to set aside our fears and prejudice to take part in ministering to the diaspora.

What good does it do if God brings the diaspora people thousands of miles across the globe to us, only to find us unwilling and unequipped of building a bridge to reach out to them?

Part 5
CONCLUSION

Chapter 20

Conclusion

Enoch Wan

This book begins with a description in Part 1 and Part 2 on the two demographic phenomena in the 21st century: the increasing significance of the global trend of diaspora, and the shifting of the Christian church's center of gravity from the West to the majority world. In this section, an alternate theoretical framework to traidtional missiology is proposed, along with research methodology for the emerging paradigm of diaspora missiology and diaspora missions. The necessity and viability for the undertaking described above are illustrated by eight case studies in Part 4.

Theoretical Framework and Methodological Considerations

In response to the demographic reality presented in Chapters 2 and 3, diaspora missiology is proposed in Chapter 7 as an alternative missiological paradigm to supplement the traditional missiological framework. This theoretical framework is founded on the biblical studies and theological reflections in Chapters 4, 5, and 6.

Diaspora missiology is a different way of conceptualizing Christian mission of the global demographic trend of "diaspora" as part of God's sovereign design to accomplish His mission. It is

> "…taking advantage of the current situation of the mass relocation of peoples throughout the world due to war, famine and economic issues. This new missiological approach is a strategic way of ministering to

peoples who are providentially relocated to new places and taking advantage of increased receptivity to the gospel."[551]

Diaspora missiology is a different way of conceptualizing and strategizing Christian missions that is corrective to managerial missiology. It seeks to answer questions on the "who?" "what?" "when?" "where?" and "how?" concerning the phenomenon of diaspora. In the research process it requires a combination of approaches such as biblical study, theological reflection, historical overview, socio-anthropological inquiry, economic assessment, ethical discernment, etc. Therefore, interdisciplinary approach in research is recommended for the study of diaspora missiology and for formulating strategies to reach and mobilize the diaspora.

Case Studies

This volume includes eight case studies that vary from being country-specific to group-specific to location-specific. They are reports of actual events with practical details, insightful understanding, and pragmatic guidelines for both researchers and practitioners. Unfortunately, limitation of space does not permit more worthwhile and valuable case studies to be included; but will be made available in the IDS series on diaspora missiology.

Call for Action

To meet the challenge of the two demographic phenomena of the 21st century, the Church is called to take action in: (1) implementing the proposed diaspora missiology paradigm,[552] the relational paradigm, strategic stewardship, and strategic partnership; (2) practicing diaspora missions of ministering to the diaspora and through the diaspora.

Promote Studies of Diaspora Missiology

Since the size and significance of diaspora have increased in the twenty-first century (see Chapters 1 and 2), missiologists must grapple with related issues by pursuing further studies on diaspora missiology as an emerging paradigm to correct managerial missiology. This new orientation and approach require

---

[551] Enoch Wan, Interview by J.D.Payne, April 19th, 2010; available at http://www.jdpayne.org/2010/04/19/diaspora-missiology-part-1/
[552] The free booklet, *"A Higher Purpose for Your Overseas Job,"* is most helpful for pre-departure preparation of diasporic Kingdom Workers. It is also available at http://ojs.GlobalMissiology.org/index.php/english/article/view/215.

intentional pursuit and collaborative effort. Hopefully, by integrating diaspora missiology into regular missiological curriculum, a new generation of missiologists and missions leaders will rise up to meet the challenge and present us with timely research findings.

Seize New Opportunities Created by the New Demographic Trend

Many new opportunities have been created by the new demographic trend of diaspora, and diaspora people are becoming more receptive to Christian witness (see Chapters 1 and 2). When they are in transition with dire needs, the practice of the Great Commandment combined with the practice of the Great Commission often brings spiritual conversions and church planting outcomes among them.

As the global trend of migrant population moving from south to north, and from east to west, people from the 10/40 window are no long the "unreached." They have come to the doorsteps of Christians in industrial west and developing countries thus created tremendous opportunities for practicing diaspora missions. Consequently, opportunities to minister to the diaspora bring forth three closely related aspects: missions to the diaspora, missions through the diaspora, and missions by and beyond the diaspora (see Chapters 7 and 10).

First, the church must motivate God's people to have compassion on the diaspora and minister to their needs, both spiritual and physical (see Case Study #8 on local churches in Minnesota). Then, the church must mobilize diaspora congregations to realize their potential in carrying out the Great Commission to their diaspora kinsmen in host countries and their motherlands. Finally, the church must equip and empower mature diaspora Christians to take the Gospel across cultures to other ethnic groups in the host society and elsewhere.

Practice Strategic Stewardship and Strategic Partnership

As the Christian world's center of gravity shifts from the northern hemisphere to the south and from the west to the rest, the church must search for available resources and implement effective strategies. In doing so, the church may consider the practice of strategic stewardship and strategic partnership. Mobilizing local churches to minister to the receptive people among the diaspora is one way of practicing strategic stewardship. Equipping diaspora Christians to become gospel bearers to fellow kinsmen in diaspora and native land is utilizing untapped resources both economically and spiritually.

All diaspora missions should be carried out with a Kingdom-orientation towards global missions. Mission entities in the West must collaborate with churches in the global south and cooperate in strategic partnership. In some cases even encourage the practice of reverse mission (see Chapter 12).

Suggestions for Future Research and Further Studies

This book is an introduction on the theory, methodology, and practice of diaspora missiology. Only two global demographic trends are described and theorized: the phenomenon of diaspora and the shifting of Christianity's center of gravity. From the two trends, a paradigm of diaspora missiology is formulated, along with missiological implications and diaspora missions strategies.

There is much to be studied on the multifaceted phenomena of migration, immigration, and transcontinental movement of people. The challenges and opportunities arise from these phenomena call for thorough explorations by mission practitioners and Christian leaders. With the frequent occurrence of disasters, outbreak of wars, and the forces of globalization, the phenomenon of diaspora will continue to increase in scale, significance, and scope of influence. Researchers and practitioners alike must collaborate in their research effort and cooperate in their delivery. More case studies must be collected, studied, and compared to provide a holistic picture on diaspora. More theological reflection, theoretical formulation and practical colaboration should be encouraged for Kingdom purpose.

It is hoped that this book, a humble beginning on the studies of diaspora missiology, will draw the attention of many, and together we will further God's Kingdom by ministering to the diaspora and engaging in: missions to the diaspora, missions through the diaspora, and missions by and beyond the diaspora.

Epilogue

I come from a diaspora Chinese family. I was born in China, grew up in Hong Kong, and was educated in Hong Kong and the U.S. My family history is a story of global diaspora. On my father's side, because of poverty, my two uncles immigrated to Cuba and Myanmar respectively, my cousin immigrated to PEI, Canada, and my niece to New York City. My father also left his village in south China to look for a better life. Subsequently, he brought the family with him to Hong Kong.

My stepmother was sold by her father at a young age to distant relatives in Southeast Asia. She worked as a servant girl there for many years until her elder sister redeemed her and sent her back to their village in China, and then another sister took her to Hong Kong.

My journey in the study of diaspora began with my doctoral dissertation in cultural anthropology on New York's Chinatown. As a student I was intrigued by the complexity of the diaspora phenomena there. Between 1978 and 1981 I traveled for short-term ministries among diaspora Chinese in Southeast Asia. And during the 1980s I launched the Centre for Intercultural Studies in Canada. The Centre focused on five ethnic groups: First Nations of Canada, Chinese, Vietnamese, South Asian, and Filipino. In 1993 I also coordinated in Toronto the National Conference for Intercultural Ministries in Canada and edited the compendium volume *Missions Within Reach: Intercultural Ministries in Canada* (1995). These experiences were further enriched further when I spent my sabbatical year in the Philippines and Australia in 1988–1989. Since then, for more than two decades, I have made frequent trips to evangelize, train, and teach various diaspora groups including Chinese, Filipino, Vietnamese, Korean, and Nepalese in Asia, South America, the Middle East, and Europe.

In June 2002, I was invited to participate in the annual gathering of the American Society of Missiology to address the theme of "Migration Challenge and Avenue for Christian Mission," and I did a presentation on "Mission among the Chinese Diaspora" which was published in 2003 in *Missiology* (Wan 20003a).

However, I did not begin serious and systematic studies on diaspora missiology until 2006 when I took my sabbatical at OMSC as "scholar in residence" and spent much of my time in the Yale Divinity School Library. At OMSC I gave my first public lecture on diaspora missiology. During the same period I also gave another lecture on the same topic at Andover Newton

Theological Seminary. The result of this early research effort was published in the article "Diaspora Missiology," in the *Occasional Bulletin* of EMS, Spring 2007, vol. 20, no. 2:3-7. Since then I have been actively involved in researching, presenting, and organizing conferences on diaspora missiology.

In the past two years (2010-2011) I have had many opportunities to give public addresses and presentations on the topic of diaspora missiology on various occasions, including lectureship at the Oxford Centre of Mission Studies – April 2010; presentation at Korean Diaspora Forum in Seoul, Korea – May 2010; plenary session in Tokyo 2010 – May 2010; dialogue sessions and multiplex in Cape Town 2010 – October 2010; commencement at William Carey International University – January 2011; annual retreat of Japan Evangelical Missionary Association (JEMA) – February 2011; lectureship at Tokyo Christian University – March 2011; and presentation at The North American Mission Leaders Conference – September 2011.

My research on issues related to diaspora, such as "relational paradigm," "strategic stewardship," and "strategic partnership" emerged from personal experience and participation in international organizations such as the AD 2000 Movement, FIN, and LCWE, and academic and professional involvements at the Evangelical Missiological Society and the American Society of Missiology.

It is most encouraging to witness the emergence of diaspora missiology as a missiological paradigm for the 21st century after the publication of the article "Diaspora Missiology" (Wan 2007a). In the same year, it gave me great pleasure to launch the IDS (Institute for Diaspora Studies) at Western Seminary and to speak at the commencement of the Alliance Graduate School in Manila where IDS-Asia was launched. And the July 2007 issue of the multi-lingual online journal *Global Missiology* (www.GlobalMissiology.org) was devoted to the studies of diaspora missiology.

Diaspora missiology has proven to be a missiological paradigm that is contextually relevant for the demographic reality of the 21st century. The future of diaspora missiology is bright, for it has been given a place among practitioners and academicians, in international conferences, major magazines, and mission organizations.

This book is a progress report on my research in diaspora missiology and practice in diaspora missions in the past few decades. It is presented with the hope and anticipation that many more practitioners and missiologists will come together to collaborate in the research on diaspora missiology and to cooperate in diaspora missions.

Bibliography

Abella, Manolo. "Labor Mobility, Trade and Structural Change: The Philippine experience." *Asian and Pacific Migration Journal* vol 2 no 3 (1993): 249-268.

Adelman, Howard. *The Indochinese Refugee Movement: The Canadian Experience.* Toronto: Operation Lifeline, 1980.

Adeney, M. "Colorful initiatives: North American diasporas in mission." *Missiology: An International Review*, (2011): 5-23.

Adler, Katya. "Spanish fury over Chinese shoes." BBC News, September 24, 2004; available at http://news.bbc.co.uk/2/low/europ/3687602.stmle/

Adler, Leonore Loeb and Uwe P. Gielen, eds. *Migration: Immigration and Emigration inInternational Perspective.* Praeger, 2003.

Aghamka, Atul Y. "Partnership in Witnessing to the Hindu Diaspora in NorthAmerica." *Journal of the Academy for Evangelism in Theological Education*, Vol 22 (2006-2007): 23-48; also available at http://www.aeteonline.org/twentytwo.pdf

Agoncillo, Teodoro A. *History of the Filipino People.* Quezon City: GAROTECH Publishing, 1990.

Aikman, David. *Jesus in Beijing: How Christianity is Transforming China and Changing the Global Balance of Power.* Washington, D.C.: Regency Publishing Inc., 2003.

Albright, William. "King Jehoiachin in Exile." In *The Biblical Archaeologist Reader*, vol.1. Edited by David Noel Freedman and G. Ernest Wright. Garden City, New York: Doubleday, 1961.

Alburo, Florian. "Remittances, Trade and the Philippine Economy." *Asian and Pacific Migration Journal*, vol 2 no 3 (1993): 269-284.

Alden, Chris. *China in Africa: Partner, Competitor or Hegemon?* London, UK: Zed Books, 2007.

Algera, John A. "The Ends of the Earth Have Come to New York: A Church Multiplication Movement in the NY Metro Area." In *Globalization and Its Effects on Urban Ministry in the 21st Century.* Pasadena, CA: William Carey Library, 2009.

Al-Ali, Nadje and Khalid Koser, eds. New Approaches to Migration? Transnational Communities and the Transformation of Home (New York: Rouledge, 2002).

Alliance News & Stories, The. Oct. 4, 2007. Accessed August 22, 2011. Available at http://www.cmalliance.org/news/?s=Dr.+Nghia+Pham%2C+Mongolia.

Anderson, Wanni W. and Robert Lee. *The Vietnamese in Canada as in Displacements and Diasporas, Asians in the Americas.* New Jersey: Rutgers University Press, 2005.

Andres, Thomas D. *Understanding Values.* Quezon City, Philippines: New Day Publishers, 1980.

_____. *Managing People by Filipino Values.* Quezon City, Philippines: Publishers Press, 1988.

Applebaum, S. "The Social and Economic Status of Jews in the Diaspora." In *The Jewish People in the First Century.* Edited by S. Safrai and M. Stern. CRINT 1.2. Assen: Van Gorcum; Philadelphia: Fortress, 1976.

Appleby, Jerry L. *Missions Have Come Home to America: The Church's Cross-Cultural Ministry to Ethnics.* Kansas City, MO: Beacon Hill, 1986.

Aragon, Averell, ed. *Phronesis: A Journal of Asian Theological Seminary and Alliance Graduate School*, vol 12 no.2 (2007).

Archer, Gleason L., Jr. *A Survey of Old Testament Introduction.* Chicago: Moody, 1974.

Ariel, Yaakov. *Evangelizing the Chosen People: Missions to the Jews in America*, 1880-2000. Chapel Hill: University of North Carolina Press, 2000.

Asamoah-Gyadu, Kwabena. "African-led Christianity In Europe: Migration And Diaspora Evangelism." *Lausanne World Pulse*. Accessed October 29, 2009; available at www.lausanneworldpulse.com/themearticles.php/973?pg=all/

"Attention, les Chinois débarquent!" *Aujourd'hui Le Maroc* (15 September 2004).

Ault, James. "Christianity in Africa." Footage of Film Documentary on Christianity in Ghana, 2008.

Australian Bureau of Statistics. Accessed August 22, 2011; available at http://www.censusdata.abs.gov.au/ABSNavigation/prenav/ViewData?breadcrumb=POLTD&method=Place%20of%20Usual%20Residence&subaction=-1&issue=2006&producttype=Census%20T.

Aviv, Caryn and David Shneer. *New Jews: The end of the Jewish Diaspora.* New York: New York University Press, 2005.

Aynte, Abdirahman. "Missing Youth Still Haunt Minnesota Somalis." (May 13, 2009); available at www.mshale.com/

Baeq, D. S., M. Lee, S. Hong, and J. Ro. "Mission from migrant church to ethnic minorities: A brief assessment of the Korean American Church in mission." *Missiology: An International Review,* (2011): 25-37.

Bakker, Janel Dragt. 2014. *Sister Churches: American Congregations and Their Partners Abroad*. Oxford Press.

Barboza, David. "China tells U.S. 'It must cure its addiction to debt.'" *New York Times*, August 6, 2011; available at http://www.nytimes.com/2011/08/07/business/global/china-a-big-creditor-says-us-has-only-itself-to-blame.html

Baldoz, Rosalinda. "The Overseas Filipino Workers (OFW) Phenomenon." In *Scattered: The Filipino Global Presence.* Edited by L. Pantoja Jr., S. Tira, and E. Wan. Manila, Philippines: LifeChange Publishing, 2004.

Bammel, Ernst. "Jewish activity against Christians in Palestine According to Acts." In *The Book of Acts in Its First Century Setting,* vol. 4, 357-364. Edited by Richard Bauckham. Grand Rapids: Eerdmans, 1995.

Banerjee, Biswajit "Social Networks in the Migration Process: Empirical Evidence on Chain Migration in India," *The Journal of Developing Areas*, Vol. 17, No. 2 (Jan.,

BIBLIOGRAPHY

1983)Barclay, John M. G. *Jews in the Mediterranean Diaspora: From Alexander to Trajan (323 BCE–117 CE)*. Los Angeles, CA: University of California Press, 1996.

Baron, Salo Wittmayer. *A Social and Religious History of the Jews*. New York: Columbia University, 1937.

Barr, Finn. "The New Age and Similar Movements in Israel." *MISHKAN* 38 (Jerusalem 2003): 16-23.

Barrett, David B. and Todd M. Johnson. *World Christian Trends, AD 30–2200: Interpreting the Annual Christian Megacensus*. Pasadena: William Carey Library, 2001.

Bartholomew, Timothy S. and Tim Huyen. *Ngaoundere News*, Volume 5 Issue 1 (April 2011). Accessed August 22, 2011; available at http://whchurch.org/files/missionaries/ Bartholomew.pdf.

Battenfield, James R. "A Consideration of the Identity of the Pharaoh of Genesis 47." *Journal of the Evangelical Theological Society* 15 (1972).

Bediako, Kwame. "The Doctrine of Christ and the significance of vernacular terminology." *International Bulletin of Missionary Research*, 22 no. 3 (1998):110-111.

Ben-David, Esther. "Europe's Shifting Immigration Dynamic. *Middle East Quarterly*, Vol XVI no. 2 (2009).

Beltran, Ruby P. and Gloria F. Rodriguez, eds. *Filipino Women Migrant Workers: At the Crossroads and Beyond Beijing*. Quezon City, Philippines: Giraffe Books, 1996.

Ben-Sasson, H.H., ed. *A History of the Jewish People*. Cambridge, MA: Harvard University Press, 1976.

Bernard, H. R. *Social Research Methods: Qualitative and Quantitative Approaches*. Thousand Oaks: Sage Publications Inc. 2000.

Blaiklock, E. M. "Tarsus." In *The Zondervan Pictoral Encyclopedia of the Bible*, Vol. V, 598-603. Edited by Merril C. Tenney. Grand Rapids: Zondervan, 1975.

Bock, Darrrell. *Acts*. Grand Rapids: Baker, 2007.

Bommes, Michael and Ewa T. Morawska, eds. *International Migration Research: Constructions, Omissions, and the Promises*. Vermont: Ashgate Publishing, 2005.

Boosahda, Elizabeth. Arab-American Faces and Voices: The Origins of an Immigrant Community. Austin: The University of Texas Press, 2003.

Borman, Lukas. *Philippi: Stadt und Christengemeinde zur Zeit des Paulus*. Leiden: Brill, 1995.

Boundary 2: An International Journal of Literature and Culture, Duke University, 37(1) Spring 2010.

Boyarin J. *Powers of Diaspora*. Paper presented to a panel on diaspora at the International Congress of the Historical Sciences, Montreal (1995).

Boyarin, Daniel and Jonathon Boyarin. "Generation and the Ground of Diaspora." In *Theorizing Diaspora: A Reader*. Edited by Jana E Braziel and Anita Mannur. Malden, MA: Blackwell Publishing, 2003.

Boyd, M. (1989) 'Family and personal networks in international migration: Recent developments and new agendas,' *International Migration Review* 23(3): 638-70.

Brah, A. *Cartographies of Diaspora: Contesting Identities*. London: Routledge, 1996.

Brändle, Rudolf and Ekkehard W. Stegemann. "The formation of the first 'Christian congregations' in Rome." In *Judaism and Christianity in Rome in the First Century*. Edited by Karl P. Donfried and Peter Richardson. Grand Rapids: Eerdmans, 1998.

Brautigam, Deborah. *The Dragon's Gift: The Real Story of China in Africa*. New York: Oxford University Press, 2009.

Braziel, Jana Evans, and Anita Mannur, eds. *Theorizing Diaspora: A Reader*. Oxford: Blackwell. 2003.

Brettell, Caroline and James F. Hollifield. *Migration Theory: Talking Across Disciplines*. London: Routledge, 2007.

Brewer, John and Albert Hunter. *Multi-method Research: A Synthesis of Styles*. Newbury Park, California: Sage Library of Social Research, 1989.

Bright, John. *A History of Israel*. Philadelphia: Westminster Press, 1981.

Brown, Colin, ed. *New International Dictionary of New Testament Theology*, Vol. 1. Grand Rapids: Zondervan, 1967.

Bruce, F. F. *The Book of Acts*. Grand Rapids, MI: Eerdmans, 1988.

_____. *Commentary on the Book of Acts*. Grand Rapids: Eerdmans, 1974.

Buhlman, Walbert, *The Church of the Future*. (Orbis) 1986:6.

Bui, Kim Ngoc. "Project Love Your Neighbor Ministry." *Newsletter*, Seam Reap and TonLe Sap Lake: Cambodia (December, 2010).

Bustamante, Jorge A. B. Guillermina Jasso, J. Edward Taylor & Paz Trigueros Legarreta, "The Selectivity of International Labor Migration and Characteristics of Mexico-to-U.S. Migrants: Theoretical Considerations," USCIR - Binational Research Papers http://www.utexas.edu/lbj/uscir/binpap-v.html Accessed Dec. 20, 2013. *"Characteristics of Migrants: Mexicans in the United States,"* Jorge A. Bustamante, Guillermina Jasso, J.Edward Taylor and Paz Trigueros Legarreta

Butler, Trent C., ed. *Holman Bible Dictionary*. Nashville, TN: Holman Bible Publishers, 1991.

Buttrick, George A., ed. *Interpreter's Dictionary of the Bible*. Vol. III. Nashville, TN: Abingdon Press, 1962.

Byrne, Michelle. "Ethnography As A Qualitative Research Method." *Aorn Journal* (July, 2001). Accessed June 1, 2010; available at http://www.findarticles.com/p/articles/mi_m0SFL/is_1_74/ai_76653445

Business Professional Network (April 23, 2011). Available at http://www.bpn.org

Camarota, Steven A. Immigrants from the Middle East: A Profile of the Foreign-born Population from Pakistan to Morocco . Washington D. C.: Center for Immigration Studies, 2002.

BIBLIOGRAPHY

Campese, Gioacchino and Pietro Ciallella. *Migration, religious experience, and globalization.* New York: Center for Migration Studies, 2003.

Cape Town 2010. "Cape Town 2010 Schedule." Accessed February 3, 2011; available at http://www.lausanne.org/cape-town-2010/schedule.html

Carmichael, A. "No Scar?" in *A. Carmichael, Toward Jerusalem.* London: Holy Trinity Church, 1936.

Casino, Tereso. "Global Diaspora: Basic Framework for theological construction." Global Diasporas Missiology Consultation, Taylor University College and Seminary, Edmonton (October 15-18, 2006).

Casino, T. C. "Why people move: A prolegomenon to diaspora missiology." In *Korean Diaspora and Christian Mission* (pre-publication version). Edited by S. H. Kim and W. Ma. Oxford: Regnum Books, 2011.

Castles, Stephen and Mark J. Miller. *The Age of Migration: International Population Movements in the Modern World.* New York: Guildford Press, 1998.

Chan, Kim-kwong. "Wenzhou Christians in Qinghai Province." In *Holistic Entrepreneurship in China.* Edited by Tetsunio Yamamori. Pasadena, California: William Carey International University Press, 2002.

_____. "The Back-To-Jerusalem Movement in Mainland China." In *Emerging Mission Movements: Voices of Asia.* Edited by Bambang Budijanto. Colorado: Compassion International/Asian Evangelical Alliance, 2010.

Chant, Sylvia and Cathy McIlwaine. *Women of a Lesser Cost: Female Labor: Foreign Exchange & Philippine Development.* Quezon City, Philippines: Ateneo de Manila University Press, 1995.

Charles, J. Daryl. "Engaging the (Neo)Pagan Mind: Paul's Encounter with Athenian Culture as a Model for Cultural Apologetics." *Trinity Journal* 16 (Spring 1995): 47-62.

Chavez, Leo R. *Shadowed Lives: Undocumented Immigrants in American Society.* Orlando, FL: Holt, Rinehart and Winston Inc., 1992.

Chen, Jia. "Over 23 Millions Christians in Country." *China Daily* August 2010. Available at http://www.chinadaily.com.cn/us/2010-08/12/content_11144948.htm

Chen, Yu. "Reports on the Situation of Chinese Merchants in Far East Siberia." Accessed November 11, 2004; available at http://peacehall.com/news/gb/chinese/2004/11/200411111357.shtml

"Chinese Consul Investigates Protest." *Vladivostok News* (April 23 2002); available at http://vn.vladnews.ru/arch/2002/iss306/News/upd23_3.HTM/

Choi, S. "Identity Crisis for Diaspora Community." In *Korean Diaspora and Christian Mission* (pre-publication version ed.) Edited by S. H. Kim and W. Ma. Oxford: Regnum Books, 2011.

Chun, D. M. "Kingdom-centered identity: The case of bicultural Korea-Brazilians." In *Korean Diaspora and Christian Mission* (pre-publication version). Edited by S. H. Kim and W. Ma. Oxford: Regnum Books, 2011.

Claro, Robert. *A Higher Purpose: For Your Overseas Job*. Makati City, Philippines: CrossOver Books, 2003.

Claydon, David. *Moving Europeans: Migration in Western Europe since 1650,* 2nd ed. Indianapolis, IN: Indiana University Press. 2003.

Claydon, David. "The Uniqueness of Christ in a Postmodern World and the Challenge of World Religions." *LausanneOccasional Paper* No. 31 (2005).

Clifford, James. "Diasporas." *Current Anthropology* 9 (3) (1994): 303.

Cohen, Robin. *The Cambridge survey of world migration*. Cambridge: University of Cambridge, 1995.

_____. *Global Diasporas: An Introduction*. Seattle, WA: University of Washington Press, 1997.

Collins, John J. *Between Athens and Jerusalem: Jewish Identity in the Hellenistic Diaspora*. Grand Rapids, MI: Eerdmans, 2000.

Collymore, Yvette. "Rapid Population Growth, Crowded Cities Present Challenges in the Philippines." Population Reference Bureau, June 2003. Accessed 27 September 2007; available at http://www.prb.org/Articles/2003/RapidPopulationGrowthCrowdedCitiesPresentChallengesinthePhilippines.aspx/

Commission on Filipinos Overseas (COF). *Annual Report 2001*. Manila, Philippines: Department of Foreign Affairs, 2001.

_____. "Stock Estimate of Overseas Filipinos As of December 2007." *Commission on Filipinos Overseas* (21 September 2008). Available at http://www.cfo.gov.ph/statistics.htm

_____. "Number of Filipino Fiancé(e)s and Other Partners of Foreign Nationals By Major Country of Destination:1989-2007." *Commission on Filipinos Overseas*. Available at http://www.cfo.gov.ph/statistics.htm

_____. "Stock Estimate Of Overseas Filipinos." *Philippine Overseas Employment Agency* (December, 2009). Accessed March 2, 2011; available at http://www.poea.gov.ph/stats/stock estmate 2009.pdf

Commission on World Mission and Evangelism. "Mission spirituality and discipleship: Beyond and through contemporary boundaries." *International Review of Mission*, (2010): 106-124.

Connor, P. *A Biblical Missiology for North American People Groups*. Accessed Feb 16, 2011; available at http://staging.namb.net/nambpb.aspx?pageid=8589967111

Constable, Nicole. *Maid to Order in Hong Kong: Stories of Filipina Workers*. Ithaca, New York: Cornell University Press, 1997.

Constable, Nicole. "Changing Filipina Identities and Ambivalent Returns." In *Coming Home?: Refugees, Migrants, and Those Who Stayed Behind*. Edited by L. D. Long and E. Oxfeld. Philadelphia, PA: University of Pennsylvania Press, 2004.

Cooke, Miriam and Bruce B Lawrence, *Muslim Networks: from Hajj to Hip Hop*. Chapel Hill: The University of North Carolina Press, 2005.Cooper, Harris M. *Synthesizing Research: A Guide for Literature Reviews*. Sage, 1998.

BIBLIOGRAPHY

Coote, Robert B. *Early Israel: A New Horizo*. Minneapolis: Fortress, 1990.

Corkin, Lucy. "Chinese Migrants to Africa: A Historical Overview." *The China Monitor* (February 2008): 4-5.

Cotter, Wendy J. "Cornelius, the Roman Army and Religion." In *Religious Rivalries and the Struggle for Success in Caesarea Maritima*. Edited by Terence L. Donaldson. Waterloo, ON: Wilfrid Laurier University Press, 2000.

Covell, Ralph. *Confucius, the Buddha, and Christ*. Maryknoll, NY: Orbis Books, 1986.

Creswell, John W. *Qualitative Inquiry and Research Design: Choosing Among Five Traditions*. California: Sage Publications, 1998.

Creswell, John W. *Research Design: Qualitative, Quantitative, and Mixed Methods Approaches*, 2nd ed. CA: Thousand Oaks: Sage 2003.

Cronin, V. *A Pearl to India: The Life of Roberto de Nobili*. New York: E.P. Dutton & Co., 1959.

Cruz, Gemma Tulud. "Expanding the boundaries, turning borders into spaces." In *Mission after Christendom*. Edited by by Ogbu U. Kalu, Peter Vethanayagamony and Edmund Kee-Fook Chia. Louville: Westminster John Knox, 2010.

Davids, Peter. *The Epistle of James*. Grand Rapids, MI: Eerdmans, 1982.

_____. *The First Epistle of Peter*. Grand Rapids: Eerdman, 1990.

Davies, William D. *The Territorial Dimension of Judaism*. Minneapolis: Fortress Press, 1992.

DeCarvalho, Levi T. "What's Wrong with the label 'Managerial Missiology'" *Mission Frontiers*. July-August 2002, http://www.missionfrontiers.org/issue/article/whats-wrong-with-the-label-managerial-missiology (Accessed Dec. 20, 2013)

de Haan, Charlene. "A Canadian Case Study In Diaspora Missiology." *Lausanne World Pulse*. Accessed September 23, 2009; available at http://www.lausanneworldpulse.com/perspectives.php

DellaPergola, Sergio. *World Jewish Population, 2010*. Connecticut: Berman Institute – North American Jewish Data Bank, 2010 No. 2 (2010): 60-62.

DellaPergola, Sergio, Yehezkel Dror and Shalom S. Wald, Project Heads. *Jewish People Policy Planning Institute Annual Assessment 2005 Executive Report: Facing a rapidly changing world*. Jerusalem: Gefen Publishing House, 2005.

Denzin, Norman K. and Yvonna S. Lincoln. *Handbook of Qualitative Research*, 2nd ed. Thousand Oaks: Sage Publication, 2000.

De Ridder, Richard. *Discipling the Nations*. Baker Book House, Grand Rapids, 1971.

Dexinger, Ferdinand. "Samaritans" in *Theologische Realenzyklopädie*, vol 29, 750-756. Berlin: Walter de Gruyter, 1998.

Diamond, David. "One Nation, Overseas." *Wired*, issue 10.06. (June 2002).

Dibelius, M. *A Commentary on the Epistle of James*. Philadelphia: Fortress, 1976.

Dimangondayao, Lorajoy Tira. "All to All People: Samples of Diaspora Filipinos Making Kingdom Impact." In *Scattered: The Filipino Global Presence*. Edited by L. Pantoja Jr., S. Tira and E. Wan. Manila, Philippines: LifeChange Publishing, 2004.

Dimangondayao, Lorajoy. "The Filipino International Network: A Case Study of Diaspora Missiology in Action." In *Missions Practice in the 21st Century*. Edited by Sadiri Joy Tira and Enoch Wan. Pasadena: William Carey International University Press, 2009.

Dorais, Louis-Jacques. "From Refugees to Transmigrants: The Vietnamese inCanada." In *Displacements and Diasporas: Asians in the Americas*. Edited by Wanni W. Anderson and Robert Lee. New Jersey: Rutgers University Press, 2005.

Douglas, J. D., ed. *New Bible Dictionary*. Leicester, England: Inter-Varsity Press, 1962.

Downey, Glanville. *Ancient Antioch*. Princeton: Princeton University, 1963.

Drummond, Rich and Beth Drummond. "International Team: Drummond Update." (April 2008). Accessed August 22, 2011; available at http://cambodiadrummonds.blogspot.com.

Dumapias, Rodolfo I. "My Journey as a Christian Ambassador." In *Scattered: The Filipino Global Presence*. Edited by L. Pantoja Jr., S. Tira, and E. Wan. Manila, Philippines: LifeChange Publishing, 2004.

Du Toit, Andreas B. 2000. "A Tale of Two Cities : "Tarsus or Jerusalem Revisited." *New Testament Studies* 46, no. 3 (2000): 375-402.

Edu-Bekoe, Yaw Attah. *Ghanaian Diaspora: An Integrative Study of Presbyterian Church of Ghana Congregations in the United States of America*. A Dissertation Submitted to the Faculty of Western Seminary, Portland, OR, 2011.

Ember, Melvin, Carol R. Ember, and Ian Skoggard, eds. *Encyclopedia of Diasporas: Immigrant and Refugee Cultures Around the World*. New York, NY: Springer Science & Business Media Inc., 2005.

Elwell, Walter. *Evangelical Dictionary of Theology*. Grand Rapids, MI: Baker Books, 1996.

Encel, Sol and Leslie Stein, eds. *Continuity, Commitment and Survival: Jewish Communities in the Diaspora*. Westport, CT: Praeger Publishers, 2003.

Engel, James F. "Will the Great Commission Become the Great Ad Campaign?" *Christianity Today*, 2007:216, http://www.rebuildjournal.org/articles/cmsnorcmpgn.html Retrieved Feb. 20, 2014.

Ernest, G., David Freedman and David Noel Wright. *The Biblical Archaeologist Reader*, Vol 1:106-107. Garden City, NY: Doubleday, 1961.

Escobar, Samuel. "Migration, religious experience, and globalization." *Missiology* 32, no. 4 (2004): 515-516.

Escobor, Samuel E. The New Global Missio: The Gospel from Everywhere to Everyone. InterVasity Press 2003.

Evans, Craig and Stanley E. Porter. *Dictionary of New Testament Background*, The IVP Bible Dictionary Series. IVP Academic, 2000.

"Faith on the Move – The Religious Affiliation of International Migrants," Pew Research Religion & Public Life Project. http://www.pewforum.org/2012/03/08/religious-migration-exec/ accessed Dec. 20, 2013.

Fawcett, James T. "Networks, Linkages, and Migration Systems," *International Migration Review*. Vol. 23, No. 3   Special Silver Anniversary Issue: International Migration an Assessment for the 90's (Autumn, 1989), pp. 671-680.   Published by: The Center for Migration Studies of New York, Inc.

Fee, Gordon D. *The First Epistle to the Corinthians*. Grand Rapids: Eerdmans, 1987.

Feliciano, Evelyn. *All Things To All Men: An Introduction to Missions in Filipino Culture*. Quezon City, Philippines: New Day Publishers, 1988.

_____. *Filipino Values and Our Christian Faith*. Manila, Philippines: OMF Literature Inc., 1990.

_____. *Fellowship of Companies for Christ International*. Accessed April 23, 2011; available at http://www.fcci.org/

Fennelly, Katherine and Christopher M. Federico. "Rural Residence as a Determinant of Attitudes Toward U.S. Immigration Policy." *International Migration* (February 5, 2008): 46:1.

Fennelly, Katherine and Helga Leitner. *"How the Food Processing Industry is Diversifying Rural Minnesota."* JSRI Working Paper, Vol. WP-59: East Lansing: Michigan State University, 2002.

FIN. *The FIN News*. Edmonton, Alberta, 2007-2008.

Finn, T. M. "The God-Fearers Reconsidered." *CBQ* 47 (1985): 75-84.

Fitzmyer, Joseph A. *The Acts of the Apostles: A New Translation with Introduction* and Commentary. NY: Doubleday, 1998.

Fujino, Gary. "Using Gospel Choirs to Multiply Congregations: An ode to creativity and invention for effective church planting in today's Japan, Part One." *Japan Harvest* (Fall 2010):13-16.

Fujino, Gary. "Using Gospel Choirs to Multiply Congregations: An ode to creativity and invention for effective church planting in today's Japan, Part Two." *Japan Harvest* (Summer 2011): 21-25.

Galvez Tan, Jaime. Quoted by George Wehfritz & Marites Vitug. *Newsweek* (October 4, 2004).

Garrison, David.   *Church Planting Movements: How God is Redeeming a Lost World*, (Arkadelphia: WIGTake Resources, 2004:243-244)

George, S. "Diaspora: A hidden link to 'From everywhere to everywhere' missiology." *Missiology: An International Review*, (2011): 45-56.

Georgiou, Myria. "Thinking Diaspora: Why Diaspora is a Key Concept for Understanding Multicultural Europe." *More Colour in the Media: The multicultural skyscraper newsletter*,Vol. 1 No. 4. (Tuesday December 4, 2001).

GhaneaBassiri, Kambiz. *A History of Islam in America: From a New World to the New World Order*. New York, NY: Cambridge University Press 2010.

Glaser, Mitch. "Community Based evangelism – A Model for 21st Century Jewish evangelism." *LCJE BULLETIN* 84 (June 2006):13-16.

Glenn, Rogers. *Evangelizing Immigrants*. Estherville, IA: Mission and Ministry Resources, 2006.

Glick Schiller, Nina, Linda Basch, and Cristina Szanton Blanc. "From Immigrant to Transmigrant: Theorizing Transnational Migration." *Anthropological Quarterly*, Vol. 68 No. 1 (Jan 1995): 48-63.

Gliebe, Kirk. "Children's Outreach: Past, Present and Future." *LCJE Bulletin* 65 (September 2001):17-25.

The Global Religious Landscape, 2012 also produced by Pew Research Center, Pew Forum for Religion and Public Life available @ http://www.pewforum.org/global-religious-landscape-christians.aspx.

Glossary of Statistical Terms," OECD. http://stats.oecd.org/glossary/detail.asp?ID=1562 Accessed Dec. 20, 2013.

Gold, Steven. *The Israeli Diaspora*. Seattle: University of Washington Press, 2002.

Gorgonio, Luis. "More Pinays marrying foreigners – religious group." *GMA News*, TV. October 16, 2007. Available at GMAhttp://www.gmanews.tv/print/64697/

Grabbe, L. L. "Synagogues in Pre-70 Palestine: A Reassessment." *JTS* 39 (1988): 401-410.

Grabbe, Lester L. *Ancient Israel: What do we know and how do we know it*. New York: T&T Clark, 2007.

Grayzel, Solomon. *A History of the Jews*, 2nd ed. Philadelphia: Jewish Publication Society of America, 1968.

Greenberg, Moshe. *The Hab/piru*. New Haven: American Oriental Society, 1955.

Greenway, Roger S. "Goals of Urban Ethnic Evangelism." In *Cities: Mission New Frontiers*. Edited by Roger S. Greenway and Timothy M. Monsma. Grand Rapids, MI: Baker Book House. 1989.

Guralnik, David B., ed. *New World Dictionary of the American Language*, Second College Edition. World Publishing, 1978.

Guthrie, Stan. "Globalization." In *Evangelical Dictionary of World Missions*. Edited by A. Scott Moreau. Grand Rapids, MI: Baker Book House, 2000.

Haar, Gerrie ter. *Halfway to Paradise African Christians in Europe*. Cardiff: Cardiff Academic Press, 1998.

Haddad, Yvonne Yazbeck. *Muslims in the West: From Sojourners to Citizens*. New York: Oxford University Press, 2002.

Haddad, Yazbeck and Jane Idleman Smith. *Mission to America: Five Islamic Sectarian Communities in North America*. Gainesville, FL: University Press of Florida, 1993.

Hagan, Jacqueline and Helen R. Ebaugh. "Calling Upon the Sacred: Migrants: Use of Religion in the Migration Process." *International Migration Review* 37 no. 4 (2003): 1145-1162.

Hale, Chris. "Aradhna: From Comfort to Discomfort, from Church to Temple." Available at http://www.ijfm.org/PDFs_IJFM/24_3_PDFs/147-150Hale.pdf

Hanciles, Jehu. *Beyond Christendom: Globalization, African Migration and the Transformation of the West.* Maryknoll: Orbis, 2008.

_____. "Migrant and Mission: Some Implication for the Twenty-first Century Church." *International Bulletin of Missionary Research*, 27:4 (October 1, 2003): 146-153. Accessed January 27, 2010; available at www.internationalbulletin.org/system/files/2003-04-146-hanciles.pdf

_____. "Migration and mission: the religious significance of the North-South divide." In *Mission in the twenty-first century*. Edited by Andrew Walls and Cathy Ross. Maryknoll: Orbis, 2008.

Harley, David, ed. "Thailand Report – Christian Witness to the Jewish People." *Lausanne LOP 7*, 1980.

Harris, Gerald "Shining the Spotlight on the IMB's Church Planting Movement," The Christian Index May 24, 2007 http://www.christianindex.org/3270.article (Accessed Dec. 20, 2013)

Hartmut, Renz. "Annual Report for LCJE Europe 2002." *LCJE Bulletin* No. 71 (February 2003): 16.

Harvey, T. A. "Diaspora: A passage to mission." *Transformation: An International Journal of Holistic Mission Studies*, (2011): 42-50.

Hastings, James, ed. *Hastings Dictionary of the Bible.* Peabody MA: Hendrickson Publishers, 1989.

Hedlund, Roger. *God and the Nations: A Biblical Theology of Mission in the Asian Context.* Delhi: ISPCK, 1997.

Hengel, Martin. "Der vorchristliche Paulus." In *Paulus und das antike Judentum."* Edited by Martin Hengel and Ulrich Heckel. Tübingen: J.C.B. Mohr, 1991.

Hellerman, Joseph H. *Reconstructing honor in Roman Philippi.* New York: Cambridge University, 2005.

Hesselgrave, David J. and Ed Stetzer. *MissionShift: Global Mission Issues in the Third Millennium.* Nashville, TN: B & H Publishing Group, 2010.

Hesselgrave, David J. *Paradigms in Conflict: 10 Key Questions in Christian Missions Today.* Kregel 2005

Hesselgrave, David J. *Planting Churches Cross-Culturally: North America and Beyond*, 2nd ed. Grand Rapids, MI: Baker Academic, 2000.

Hiebert, Paul G. "Cultural Differences and the Communication of the Gospel." In *Perspectives of a World Christian Movement*, 3rd ed. Pasadena: William Carey Library.

_____. "Missionary as mediator of global theologizing." In *Globalizing Theology*. Edited by by Craig Ott and Harold A. Netland. Grand Rapids: Baker Academic, 2006.

Ho, Phu Xuan. *The 2006 Annual Report*. Vietnamese Ministries, Inc., Anaheim, CA, 2006.

Hock, Ronald F. "Paul and Greco-Roman education." in *Paul in the Greco-Roman world*. Edited by J. Paul Stanley. Harrisburg: Trinity Press International, 2003.

Hoerber, Robert George. "Decree of Claudius in Acts 18:2." *Concordia Theological Monthly*, 31, no. 11 (1960): 690-694.

Hoffmeir, James. *Israel in Egypt: The Evidence for the Authenticity of the Exodus Tradition*. New York: Oxford University Press, 1996.

Hopler, Thom and Marcia Hopler. *Reaching the World Next Door*. Downers Grove: IVP, 1993.

House, H. Wayne, ed. *Israel the Land and the People*. Grand Rapids: Kregel Publications, 1998.

Houston, Tom. "Global Clashes, Global Gospel." Unpublished paper presented at the LausanneInternational Leaders Conference. Toronto, Canada, March 1998.

Howell, B. M. "Multiculturalism, immigration and the North American Church: Rethinking Contextualization." *Missiology: An International Review*, (2011): 79-85.

Hull, William L. *The Fall and Rise of Israel: The Story of the Jewish People During the Time of their Dispersal and Regathering*. Grand Rapids, MI: Zondervan Publishing Company. 1954.

Humphreys, Kent. *Shepherding Horses: Understanding God's Plan for Transforming Leaders*. Oklahoma City, OK: Lifestyle Impact Ministries, 2010.

Hunter, Alan and Kim-Kwong Chan. *Protestantism in Contemporary China*. New York: Press Syndicate, 1993.

_____. "Immigration in Minnesota, Discovering Common Ground." The Minneapolis Foundation. Available at www.MinneapolisFoundation.org/

_____. "About Migration." International Organization for Migration. Accessed March 6, 2008; available at www.iomint/jahia/Jahia/en/pid/g/

_____. *World Migration: Costs and Benefits of International Migration*, vol. 3. Geneva, Switzerland: International Organization for Migration, 2005.

"International Migration and Human Rights: Challenges and Opportunities on the Threshold of the 60th Anniversary of the Universal Declaration of Human Rights," Global Migration Group. http://www.globalmigrationgroup.org/uploads/documents/Int_Migration_Human_Rights.pdf Accessed Dec. 20, 2013.

"International migration: 2013: Migrants by origin and destination," UN Dept. of Economic and Social Affairs, Population Divisin, No. 2013/3, Sept. 2013. http://filipspagnoli.wordpress.com/stats-on-human-rights/statistics-on-xenophobia-immigration-and-asylum/statistics-on-migration/ Accessed Dec. 20, 2013.

Jackson, D. "Europe and the migrant experience: Transforming integration." *Transformation: An International Journal of Holistic Mission Studies*, (2011): 14-28.

Jacob, J.R. and Todaro, M.P. "The North American back-to-the-land movement," *Community Development Journal.* 31:241-249, 1970. Jacob J., *New Pioneers: The Back-to-land Movement and the Search for a Sustainable Future.* University Park: Pennsylvania State University Press. Halfacree, K. Back-to-the-land in the twenty-first-century: Making connections with rurality. *Tijdschrift voor Economische en Sociatle Geografie* 98(1):3-8, 2007.

Jenkins, Philip. *The Next Christendom: The Coming of Global Christianity*. New York: Oxford University Press, 2002.

Jenni, Ernest and Claus Westermann. *Theological Lexicon of the Old Testament,* Vol 1. Peabody, MA: Hendrickson Publishers, 1997.

Jeong, M. "Korean Evangelicals' response toward Muslim neighbours." In *Korean Diaspora and ChristianMission* (pre-publication version ed.). Edited by S. H. Kim and W. Ma. Oxford: Regnum Books, 2011.

Jewish Encyclopedia. "The Babylonian Captivity." *Jewish Encyclopedia*, 2002. Accessed June 4; available at http://www.bible-history.com/map_babylonian_captivity/map_of_the_deportation_of_judah_jewish_encyclopedia.html/.

Jewish Voice Ministries International. Available at http://www.jewishvoice.org/about_jb.php

Jin, Wang and Xian Yuanhong. "Bitter Winters for Three Major Shoe Manufacture Capitals." January 16, 2005. Available at http://finance.sina.com.cn/chanjing/b/20050116/11501297523.shtml

Jocano, F. Landa. *Filipino Value System: A Cultural Definition*. Metro Manila, Philippines: Punlad, 1997.

Johnson, C. Neal and Steve Rundle. *Business as Mission: A Comprehensive Guide to Theory and Practice.* Downer Grove: InterVarsity Press: 2009.

Johnson, Paul. *A History of the Jews.* New York: Harper and Row Publishers, 1987.

Johnson, Sherman E. "Tarsus and the Apostle Paul." *Lexington Theological Quarterly* 15, no. 4 (1980.): 105-113.

Johnstone, Patrick and Jason Mandryk. *Operation World 21st Century Edition.* Giorgia, U.S.: Paternoster, 2001.

Joly, Daniele, ed. *International Migration in the New Millennium: Global movement and settlement.* London: Ashgate, 2004.

Jung, Min-young. "Diaspora and timely hit: Towards a diaspora missiology." In *Korean Diaspora and Christian Mission* (pre-publication version ed.). Edited by S. H. Kim and W. Ma. Oxford: Regnum Books, 2011.

Kalai, Zekharyah and Moshe Weinfeld, eds. *Studies in historical geography and biblicalhistoriography: Presented to Zechariah Kallai.* The Netherlands: Kominkijke Brill, 2000.

Kalaw-Tirol, Lorna, ed. *From America to Africa: Voices of Filipino Women Overseas.* Makati City, Philippines: FAI Resource Management Inc., 2000.

Kanbura, Ravi and Hillel Rapoport, "Migration Selectivity and The Evolution of Spatial Inequality," September 2003. http://www.arts.cornell.edu/poverty/kanbur/KanRap.pdf Accessed Dec. 20, 2013.

Kapur, Devesh and John McHale. *The Global Migration of Talent: What Does it Mean for Developing Countries?* Center For Global Development. Washington D.C. , 2005. Accessed August 20, 2011; available at http://ucatlas.cisr.ucsc.edu/blog/?p=46/

Kawthoolei Karen Baptist Bible School & College. *Brief history.* Accessed Feb 15, 2011; available at https://sites.google.com/site/kkbbsc/home/brief-history

Kee, H. C. "The Transformation of the Synagogue after 70 C.E.: Its Import for Early Christianity." *NTS* 36 (1990): 1-24.

Kent, Mary Mederios. "U.S. Fertility in Decline." February 2011. Accessed August 17, 2011; available at http://www.prb.org/Articles/2011/us-fertility-decline.aspx?p=1

Kim, H. "Receiving mission: Reflection on reversed phenomena in mission by migrant workers from global churches to Western society." *Transformation: An International Journal of Holistic MissionStudies*, (2011): 62-67.

Kim, S. "Migrant workers and 'Reverse Mission' in the West." In *Korean Diaspora and Christian Mission* (pre-publication version ed.). Edited by S. H. Kim and W. Ma. Oxford: Regnum Books, 2011.

Kim, S. Hun and Wonsuk Ma (eds.) *Korean Diaspora and Christian Mission.* Regnum Books International, 2011

Kim, Sam-Hwan. "Address." In *21C New Nomad Era and Migrant Mission.* Edited by Chan-Sik Park and Noah Jung. Seoul: Christianity and Industrial Society Research Institute, 2010.

Kim, Yeong Ae. "Ammi Mission Fellowship" in *21C New Nomad Era and Migrant Mission* Edited by Chan-Sik Park and Noah Jung. Seoul, Korea: Christianity and Industrial Society Research Institute, 2010.

Kirshenblatt-Gimblett B. "Spaces of Dispersal." *Journal of Asian and African Studies*, Vol 9, no 3 (1994): 339-344.

Kitchen, K.A. "Egypt, Egyptians." In *Dictionary of the Old Testament: Pentateuch.* Edited by T. Desmond Alexander and David Weston. Downers Grove, IL: Invarsity Press, 2003.

Kirshenblatt-Gimblett, B. "Spaces of Dispersal." *Cultural Anthropology*, 9 (3) (1994): 340.

Kraft, Charles H.. *Christianity in culture: a study in dynamic biblical theologizing in cross cultural perspective,* Orbis Books, 2005.

Kjær-Hansen, Kai and Bodil F. Skjott. "Facts and Myths about the Messianic Congregations in Israel." *MISHKAN* (Jerusalem 1999): 30-31.

Kuffour, John Agyekum (former President of Ghana). Accessed on September 15, 2007; available at http://www.ghanaweb.com/

Lake, K. "Proselytes and God-Fearers." *Beginnings*, 5 (1933): 74-96.

BIBLIOGRAPHY

Lampe, Peter. *From Paul to Valentinus: Christians in Rome in the First Two Centuries*. Minneapolis: Fortress, 2003.

Lamphere, Louise, Alex Stepick, and Guillermo Grenier, eds. *Newcomers in the Workplace: Immigrants and the Restructuring of the U.S. Economy*. Philadelphia: Temple University Press. 1994.

LausanneCommittee for World Evangelization Issue Group No. 11: Marketplace Ministry. "Lausanne Occasional Paper 40: Marketplace Ministry." In *Forum Occasional Papers*, September 29–October 5, 2004. Edited by D. Clayton. Delhi, India: Horizon Printers and Publishers, 2005.

LausanneCommittee for World Evangelization Issue Group No. 26 A and B: Diasporas and International Students. "Lausanne Occasional Paper 55: The New People Next Door." In 2004 *Forum Occasional Papers*, September 29–October 5, 2004. Edited by D. Clayton. Delhi, India: Horizon Printers and Publishers, 2005.

LausanneCommittee for World Evangelization Issue Group No. 30: Business as Mission. "Lausanne Occasional Paper 59: Business as Mission." In *Forum Occasional Papers*, September 29–October 5, 2004. Edited by D. Clayton. Delhi, India: Horizon Printers and Publishers, 2005.

LausanneDiaspora Leadership Team (LDLT). *Scattered to Gather: Embracing the Global Trend of Diaspora*. Manila, Philippines: LifeChange Publishing, Inc., 2010.

LausanneOccasional Paper 56. "The new people next door." Available at http://www.lausanne.org/documents/2004forum/LOP55_IG26.pdf. 2005.

Lawless, Robert. "Philippine Diaspora." In *Encyclopedia of Diasporas: Immigrant and Refugee Cultures Around the World,* vol. I. Edited by Melvin Ember, Carol R. Ember and Ian Skoggard. New York, NYC: Springer Science & Business Media Inc., 2005.

Laws, S. *A Commentary on the Epistle of James*. New York: Harper and Row, 1980.

Leatherman, Benjamin. "Rabbi, Evangelist Debate Jewish View of Messiah." *Jewish News of Greater Phoenix*, Vol. 57, No. 33 (April 15, 2005).

Le, Thanh Trung. *The Vietnamese Diaspora: From Tragedy to Ripened Harvest*. Unpublished Paper submitted to the Gobal Diaspora Missiology Consultation, Edmonton, Alberta, 2006.

LeCompte, Margaret Diane, and Judith Preissle, with Renata Tesch. *Ethnography and Qualitative Design in Educational Research*. San Diego: Academic Press, 1993.

Lee, Everett S.. "A Theory of Migration,' *Demography*, Vol. 3, No. 1. (1966), pp. 47-57

Lee, Samuel. *Blessed Migrants: God's Strategy for Global Revival*. The Netherlands: Ministry House, 2006.

Leedy, Paul D. and Ormrod Jeanne Ellis. *Practical Research: Planning and Design*. Upper Saddle River: Prentice-Hall, 2001.

Leitner, Helga and Katherine Fennelly. "Narratives of the Immigrant Other in Small Town America: Racialization and the Defence of the Identities, Privigleges, and Place." Paper presented at the Annual Meeting of Association of American Geographers, Los Angeles. March, 2002. [In JSRI working Paper, Vol. WP-59] 2002.

"Let the 21st Century be the Mission Era of the Chinese Church." Febrary 21, 2007. Available at http://www.Gospelherald.com.hk/news/mis_350.htm/

Levinskaya, Irina. *The Book of Acts in its First Century Setting: Diaspora Setting*. Grand Rapids, MI: Eerdmans, 1996.

Levitt, Peggy. "Transnational Migrants: When "Home" Means More Than One Country." Migration Policy Institute, Migration Information Source. Accessed August 20, 2011; available at http://www.migrationinformation.org/feature/display.cfm?ID=261

Lewy, Julius. "Origin and Significance of the biblicalterm 'Hebrew.'" *Hebrew Union College Annual* XXIV, 1957.

Liebman, Charles S. and Elihu Katz. *The Jewishness of Israelis: Responses to the Guttman Report*. Albany: SUNY Press, 1997.

Life of Chinese Merchants in Moscow, The. Available at http://blog.wsj.com/chinarealtime/2010/02/09/video-the-life-of-chinese-merchants-in-moscow/

Locke, Lawrence F., Waneen Wyrick Spirduso, and Stephen J. Silverman, eds. *Proposals that Work: A Guide for Planning Dissertations and Grant Proposals*. Thousand Oaks: Sage Publications Inc., 2000.

Loden, Lisa. "The New Age in Israel at the Beginning of the 21st Century." *MISHKAN* 38 (2003): 24-38.

Lohmeyer, Ernst. *Galiläa und Jerusalem*. Göttingen: Vandenkoeck und Ruprecht, 1936.

Longnecker, R. N. "Antioch of Syria." In *Major Cities of the Biblical World*. Edited by R. K. Harrison. Nashville: Thomas Nelson, 1985.

Lopez, Robert Ferdinand K. "The Philippine Missions Association (PMA) Tentmaking Agenda: Raising an Army of Outstanding Filipino Witnesses." In *Scattered: The Filipino Global Presence*. Edited by L. Pantoja Jr., S.J. Tira and E. Wan. Manila, Philippines: LifeChange, 2004.

Lopez, Robert F. K. "The Unfolding Story of the Filipino Tentmaking Movement." *Connections: The Journal of the WEA Mission Commission*, 5, no. 1: (2006): 15-16.

Lorance, C. C. *An Introduction to Contextualization Among Hindus*. Accessed Feb 14, 2011; available at http://conversation.lausanne.org/en/conversations/detail/10373

Lundy, David. *Borderless Church: Shaping the Church for the 21st Century*. UK: Authentic. 2005.

Ma, Hucheng. "An Analysis of the Reasons for Rapid Growth of the Protestant Church in Today's China." In *Studies in Religious and Minority Questions in Modern China*. Beijing: CASS, 2010.

Mahalingam M, *India's Diaspora Policy and Foreign Policy: an Overview*, Global Research Forum on Diaspora and Transformation, http://grfdt.com/PublicationDetails.aspx?Type=Articles&TabId=30 Accessed 12/31/2013.Mandryk, Jason. *Operation World*. Colorado Springs: Biblica Publishing, 2010.

BIBLIOGRAPHY

Mandel, Jonah. "Think of non-Jewish Immigrants as close kin." *Jerusalem Post*. Accessed April 27, 2011; available at http://www.jpost.com/JewishWorld/JewishNews/Article.aspx?id=218017

Mandryk, Jason, ed. *Operation World*. Pasadena, CA: William Carey Library, 2010.

Mendez, Jose Gonzalez. "La pesadilla China." *La Jornada*, October 11, 2004.

Manzano, Jojo and Joy C. Solina, eds. *Worker to Witness: Becoming an OFW Tentmaker*. Makati, Philippines: Church Strengthening Ministry Inc., 2007.

Maoz, Baruch. "Trends and Circumstances within the Hebrew speaking churches in Israel." *MISHKAN 28*. (Jerusalem,1998).

Marchant, Colin. "Take a Walk: Urban Mission in the United Kingdom." In *Serving the Urban Poor*. Edited by Tetsunao Yamamori, Bryant L. Myers and Kenneth L. Luscombe. Monrovia, CA: MARC. 1998.

Marfo, Tom. "Pastor to Migrants in Dutch Society." In *A New Day Dawning: African Christians Living the Gospel—Essays in Honour of Dr. J. J. (Hans) Visser*. Edited by Kwame Bediako, et. al. Zoetermeer, Uitgeverij Boekencentrum, 2004.

Marks, Stephen, ed. *African Perspectives on China in Africa*. Oxford, UK: Fahamu, 2007.

Massey, Douglas S. et. al. "Theories of Internal Migration: A Review and Appraisal." *Population and Development Review*, Vol. 19 No. 39 (September 1993): 431.

Mbiti, John S. *African Religions and Philosophy*. New York, NY: Praeger, 1969.

McGavran, Donald Anderson. Ethnic Realities and the Church: Lessons from India. William Carey Library, 1979 McGown, Rima Berns. *Muslims in the Diaspora: The Somali Communities of London and Toronto*. Toronto: Toronto University Press. 1999.

Mendez, Jose Gonzalez. "La pesadilla China." *La Jornada* 11 October 2004.

Mendoza, Susanah Lily L. "Between the homeland and the diaspora: the politics of theorizing Filipino." Accessed August 20, 2011; available at http://books.google.com/books?hl=en&lr=&id=cKlw1AlY9OYC&oi=fnd&pg=PA1&dq=theorizing+diaspora&ots=x_6uO8Raz5&sig=rL-SiO5KpDEODtYCU5CiDzIeHpk#v=onepage&q&f=false/

Mercado, Leonardo N. *Elements of Filipino Theology*. Philippines: Divine Word University Publication, 1975.

Merrill, Eugene H. *Kingdom of Priests: A History of Old Testament Israel*. Grand Rapids, Michigan: Baker Books, 1996.

"Mexican-American Boom: Birth overtakes immigration, The." Accessed August 17, 2011; available at http://pewhispanic.org/reports/report.php?ReportID=144

Michel, Serge and Michael Beuret. *China Safari: On the Trail of Beijing's Expansion in Africa*. New York, NY: Nations Books, 2009.

"Migration Conceptual Framework: Why do people move to work in another place or country?" AAG Center for Global Geography Education. http://cgge.aag.org/Migration1e/ConceptualFramework_Jan10/ConceptualFramework_Jan10_print.html Accessed Dec. 20, 2013.

"Migration: The Human Journey" – National Geography Action! http://www.nationalgeographic.com/xpeditions/activities/09/gapacket05.pdf Accessed Dec. 20, 2013

Mihindukulasuriya, Prabo and Ivor Poobalan. *A Cultured Faith*. Colombo: CTS Publishing, 2011.

Miller, Roland. "Understanding Muslim Dilemmas in North America." *Word and World*, vol XVI no 2 (1996).

Mishra, Vijay. "The diasporic imaginary: Theorizing the Indian diaspora." *Textual Practice*, Volume 10 Issue 3 (1996): 421-447.

The Missiological Implications of Epistemological Shifts: Affirming Truth in a Modern/Postmodern World, Bloomsbury Publishing USA, 1999

"Missiologists Affirm New Models," Press release October 17, 1999 issued by William D. Taylor of WEF.

Mittelman, James H. *The Globalization Syndrome: Transformation and Resistance*. Princeton: Princeton University Press, 2000.

Moch, Lesslie Page. *Moving Europeans: Migration in Western Europe since 1650*. Bloomington: Indiana University Press, 2003.

Moffatt, J. *The General Epistles of James, Peter and Jude*. London: Hodder and Stoughton, 1928.

Montero, Darrel. *Vietnamese Americans: Patterns of Resettlement and Socio-economic Adaptation in the United States*. Boulder, CO: Westview Press, 1979.

Moo, Douglas J. *The Letter of James*. Grand Rapids, MI: Eerdmans, 2000.

Morawska, Ewa. "Disciplinary Agendas and Analytic Strategies of Research on Immigrant Transnationalism: Challenges of Interdisciplinary Knowledge." *International Migration Review*, Volume 37 Issue 3 (September 2003): 611–640.

Moreau, Scot and Beth Snodderly, eds. *Reflecting God's Glory Together: Diversity in Evangelical Mission*. William Carey Library, 2011.

Mortensen, Jan. "Large-Scale Jesus Video Project in Jerusalem." *LCJE Bulletin*, Issue 69 (August 2002): 6-10.

Muck, Terry C., ed. "Missiology: An International Review." *Mission and Migration* 31.1 (2003).

Mugo, Frida. "Sampling In Research." *Social Research Methods*. Accessed March 23, 2011; available at www.socialresearchmethods.net/tutorial/mugo/tutorial.htm.

Na'aman, N. "*Habiru and Hebrews:* The Transfer of a Social Term to the Literary Sphere." *Journal of Near Eastern Studies*, 45 (1986).

National Bureau Of Statistics Of China. "National Bureau Of Statistics Of China: 2009 Migrant Worker Survey Statistical Report." Accessed July 1, 2010; available at www.stats.gov.cn:82/was40/gjtjj_detail.jsp?searchword=-ifbase4-base92-JUMzJUYx JU15JUE0JnByZXNIYXJjaHdvcmQ9JUMzJUYxJU15JUE0KzIwMDkmY2hhbm5lbG kPTY2hhbm5lbGkPTY2OTcmcmYjb3jkPTU~/

National Jewish Population Survey (NJPS). Available at www.ujc.org/content_display.html?ArticleID=60346/

Neill, Stephen. *A History of Christian Missions*. New York: Penguin Books, 1986.

Netanyahu, Binyamin. "No Future for the Jews in the Diaspora." *Arutz 7 – IsraelNationalNews.com/* (6 October, 2006).

Nett, David.   in Foz do Iguassu, Brazil reported in *Christianity Today* [posted 12/6/1999 12:00AM] http://www.christianitytoday.com/ct/1999/december6/9te028.html Accessed Dec. 20, 2013.

Neusner, Jacob and William Scot Green, eds. *Dictionary of Judaism in the Biblical Period*. Peabody, MA: Hendrickson Publishers, 1999.

"New People Next Door: A Call to Seize the Opportunities, The." *Occasional Paper No. 55*. Produced by the Issue Group on Diaspora and International Students at the 2004 Forum hosted by the LausanneCommittee for World Evangelization in Pattay, Thailand, Sept. 29 to Oct. 5, 2004.

Nghia, Pham Xuan. *Newsletter*. Accessed Augsut 22, 2011; available at http://www.northhollywoodchurch.org/Ministries/Mongolia/Truyen_Giao_Mong_Co_Thang_2_

Nguyen Van Hue. *Report of the Vietnamese Mission Board, 2006*. Huong Di, 2010.

Norwood, F.A. *Strangers and Exiles: A History of Religious Refugees*. New York: Abingdon Press, 1969.

Oakes, Peter. *Philippians: From People to Letter*. Cambridge: Cambridge University, 2001.

Oh, D. K. "History of the Korean Diaspora Movement." In *Korean Diaspora and Christian Mission* (pre-publication version ed.) Edited by S. H. Kim and W. Ma. Oxford: Regnum Books, 2011.

Otto, Marvin. *Church on the Oceans: A Missionary Vision for the 21st Century*. Carlisle, California: Piquant Editions, 2007.

Overberg, Paul. "Hispanics in America." Accessed August 17, 2011; available at http://www.pewtrusts.org/our_work_category.aspx?id=212

Overseas Compatriot Affairs Commission. "Overseas Chinese Population Count." Accessed February 2, 2011; available at http://www.ocac.gov.tw/english/public/public.asp?selno=8889&no=8889&level=B

Owen, Greg, Jessica Meyerson, and Christa Otteson. A *New Age of Immigrants—Making Immigration Work for Minnesota*. Saint Paul, MN: Wilder Research, 2010.

Özden, Çaglar and Maurice Schiff, *International Migration, Remittances, & the Brain Drain*. New York: Palgrave and Macmillan, 2006

Paguio, Wilfredo C. *Filipino Cultural Values for the Apostolate*. Makati, Philippines: St. Paul Publication, 1978.

Pantoja Jr., Luis, Sadiri Joy Tira, and Enoch Wan, eds. *Scattered: The Filipino Global Presence*. Manila, Philippines: LifeChange Publishing Inc., 2004.

Park, Chan-Sit and Noah Jung, eds. *21C New Nomad Era and Migrant Mission*. Seoul: Christianity and Industrial Society Research Institute, 2010.

Parshall, Phil. Muslim Evangelism: Contemporary Approaches to Contextualization. Rev. Ed. Colorado Spring: Biblica, 2003.

Passel, Jeffery S. "Hispanics Account for More than Half of Nation's growth in Past Decade."Accessed March 24, 2011; available at http://pewhispanic.org/reports/report.php?ReportID=140

Passel, Jeffery and D'Vera Cohn. "A Portrait of Unauthorized Immigrants in the United States." Accessed August 17, 2011; available at http://pewhispanic.org/reports/report.php?ReportID=107 /

Patai, Raphael. *The Arab Mind*. Rev. ed. Tucson: Recovery Resources Press, 2007.Pearson, Birger A. "Christians and Jews in first-century Alexandria." *Harvard Theological Review*, 79 no 1-3 (1986): 206-216.

Pedersen, Heinrich. "Hinjews, Jubus and New Age Judaism." *MISHKAN* 38 (Jerusalem: 2003): 39-46.

Peil, Margaret. "Ghanaians Abroad." *African Affairs*, 94.376 (1995): 345-368.

Pex, Joshua. "The 'Israeli' House in Cochebamba." *MISHKAN* 38 (Jerusalem 2003): 64-66.

Pfister, Stefanie. *Messianiashce Juden in Deutschland*. Berlin: Lit Verlag Dr. W. Hopf, 2008.

Phillips, Tom and Bob Norsworthy. *The World at Your Door: Reaching International Students in Your Home, Church, and School*. Minnesota: Bethany House, 1997.

Philo *Leg. Gai* 214, 281-83; *Flacc*. 43, 45-46; *Vit. Mos.* 2.232; *Legatio ad Gaium* 23.155.

Photo Voice: Bhutanese Refugee Support Group. *Introduction*. Accessed Feb 17, 2011; available at http://www.photovoice.org/bhutan/

Phu Xuan Ho. *The 2006 Annual Report*. Anaheim, CA: Vietnamese Ministries Inc., 2006.

Pike, Kenneth. *Talk, Thought, and Thing: The Emic Road Toward Conscious Knowledge*. Dallas: Summer Institute of Linguistics, 1993.

Pilchik, Ely Emanuel. *Judaism Outside the Holy Land: The Early Period*. New York: Block Publishing Company, 1964.

Piper, John. *Let the Nations be Glad!* Grand Rapids: Baker Books, 1993.

Pipes, Daniel and Khalid Durán. *Muslim Immigrants in the United States*. Washington D.C.: Center for Immigration Studies, 2002.

Pocock, M., G. Van Rheenen, and D. McConnell. *The Changing Face of World Missions: Engaging Contemporary Issues and Trends*. Grand Rapids, MI: Baker Academic, 2005.

POEA. *Annual Report 2007*. Philippines: POEA, 2007.

_____. *Overseas Employment Statistics*. Philippines: POEA, 2007.

_____. *Philippine Overseas Employment Agency – Department of Labor, Republic of the Philippines*. Accessed 21 September 2008; available at http://www.poea.gov.ph/

Posen, Felix. "Concluding Reflections." In *The 2001 American Jewish Identity Survey Report*. Edited by Kosmin Maye and Kesars, 2001.

Poston, Larry A. with Carl F. Ellis, Jr. *The Changing Face of Islam in America*. Camp Hill, PA: Horizon Books, 2000.

Rad, Gerhard von. *The Problem of the Hexateuch and Other Essays*. London: Oliver and Boyd, 1966. Rajamanickam, S. "The Goa Conference of 1619 (A letter of Fr Robert de Nobili to Pope Paul V)." *Indian Church History Review*, (1968): 85.

Rajamanickam, S. "The Goa Conference of 1619 (A letter of Fr Robert de Nobili to Pope Paul V)." *Indian Church History Review*, (1968): 85.

Recommendations on Statistics of International Migration, Statistical Papers Series M, No. 58, Rev. 1, United Nations, New York, 1998 http://unstats.un.org/unsd/publication/SeriesM/SeriesM_58rev1e.pdf Accessed Dec. 20, 2013.

"Reflection on the Elche Incident." Available at http://news.sina.com.cn/c/2004-10-07/11433847992s.shtml

Reicke, B. *The Epistles of James, Peter and Jude*. Garden City: Doubleday, 1964.

Reis, Michele. "Theorizing Diaspora: Perspectives on 'Classical' and 'Contemporary' Diaspora." *International Migration,* Volume 42 Issue 2 (June 2004): 41-60. Accessed August 1, 2011; available at http://onlinelibrary.wiley.com/doi/10.1111/j.0020-7985.2004.00280.x/abstract/

Remigio, Amador A., Jr. "A Demographic Survey of the Filipino Diaspora." In *Scattered: The Filipino Global Presence*. Edited by L. Pantoja Jr., S. Tira and E. Wan. Manila, Philippines: LifeChange Publishing Inc., 2004.

"Reverse Missions: African Churches in Europe" (Accessed Dec. 20, 2013) http://israelolofinjana.wordpress.com/2012/01/25/reverse-missions-african-churches-in-europe/

Rhodes, Stephen A. *Where the Nations Meet: The Church in a Multicultural World*. Downers Grove, IL: InterVarsity Press, 1998.

Ricciotti, Giuseppe. *History of Israel, 2nd ed.* 2 vols.Translated from Italian by Clement Della Ponta and Richard T. A. Murphy. Milwaukee: Bruce Publishing, 1958.

Richard, H. "Good news for Hindus in the neighborhood." *Rethinking Hindu Ministry II: Papers from the Rethinking Forum*, (2010): 32-35.

Riesner, Rainer. *Paul's Eearly Period: Chronology, Mission Strategy, Theology*. Grand Rapids: Eerdmans, 1998.

Roberts, Bob, Jr. *Transformation: How Glocal Churches Transform Lives and the World*. Zondervan, 2006.

Robinson, Rich. *LCJE Bulletin,* No. 71 (February 2003): 9-14.

Robinson, Rich, ed. *The Messianic Movement: A Field Guide for Evangelical Christians*. San Francisco: Purple Pomegranate Publications, 2005.

Roetzel, Calvin J. "Tarsus." In *The New Interpreter's Dictionary of the Bible,* vol. 5, 474-476. Nashville: Abingdon, 2009.

Rogers, Glenn. *Evangelizing Immigrants: Outreach and Ministry Among Immigrants and Their Children.* Estherville, IA: Mission and Ministry Resources, 2006.

Ropes, J. H. A. *Critical and Exegetical Commentary of the Epistle of St. James*. Edinburgh: T & T Clark, 1916.

Rowton, Michael B. "Dimorphic Structure and the Problem of the ʾapirû-ʿibrîm." *Journal of Near Eastern Studies*, Vol. 35 No.1 (January 1976).

Rubenstein, James M., *An Introduction to Human Geography: The Cultural Landscape* 9th Ed. (Upper Saddle River: Prentice Hall, 2008), 82-85.

Rubesh, Ted. "Foundations for the Nations: The Nations in Genesis 1-12." In *A Cultured Faith. Edited by* Prabo Mihindukulasuriya and Ivor Poobalan. Colombo: CTS Publishing, 2011.

Rubesh, Ted. "Wandering Jews and scattered Sri Lankans: viewing Sri Lankans of the G.C.C. through the lens of the Old Testament Jewish diaspora," February 7, 2014

Rutledge, Paul James. *The Vietnamese Experience in America*. Bloomington, IN: Indiana University Press. 1992.

Saenz, Rogelio. "Population Bulletin Update: Latinos in the United States 2010." December 2010. Accessed August 17, 2011; available at http://www.prb.org/Publications/PopulationBulletins/2010/latinosupdate1.aspx?p=1/

Safran, W. "Diasporas in Modern Societies: Myths of Homeland and Return." *Diaspora* 1, 1991.

Samkutty, V. J. *The Samaritan Mission in Acts*. New York: T&T Clark, 2006.

Sänger, D. "Verflucht ist jeder, der am Holze hangt." In *Exegetical Dictionary of the New Testament*. Edited by Horst Balz and Gerhard Scheider. Grand Rapids, MI: Eerdmans, 1990.

San Juan, E., Jr. *From Exile to Diaspora: Versions of the Filipino Experience in the United States*. Boulder, CO: Westview Press, 1998.

———. *Filipinos Everywhere: Displaced, Transported Overseas, Moving in the Diaspora*. Philippines: Ibon Books, 2006.

Santos, Narry F. "Diaspora in the New Testament and Its Impact on Christian Mission." *Torch Trinity Journal* 13.1 (2010).

———. "Survey of the Diaspora Occurrences in the Bible and of Their Contexts in Chrisitan Missions in the Bible." In *Scattered: The Filipino Global Presence. Edited by* Luis Pantoja Jr., Sidiri Joy Tira and Enoch Wan. Manila: LifeChange Publishing, 2004.

———. "Diaspora Occurrences." In *The Bible And Their Contexts In Missions*. LausanneCommittee for World Evangelization. Accessed October 29, 2009; available at www.lausanneworldpulse.com/themedarticles.php/1104?pg=all

Scattered to Gather: Embracing the Global Trend of Diaspora (Manila: LifeChange Publishing, 2010).

Schenk, Wilbert. Cited in A. Christopher Smith. "Mission Theory." In *Evangelical Dictionary of World Mission.* Edited by Scott A. Moreau. Grand Rapids, MI: Baker Books, 2000.

Schirrmacher, Christine. "Muslim Immigration to Europe – The Challenge for European Societies – Human Rights – Security Issues – Current Developments." *MBS Text* 106. Martin Bucer Seminar. 2008.

Schmelzer, Paul. "Al-Shabab, Minneapolis Somali Youth." September 10, 2010. Available at http://www.Minnesotaindependent.com

Schmidt, Garbi. *Islam in Urban America.* Philadelphia, PA: Temple University Press, 2004.

Schnabel, Ekhard J. *Early Christian Mission.* Downers Grove: Intervarsity, 2004.

_____, *Paul the Missionary.* Downers Grove: InterVarsity, 2008.

Schoville, Keith. "Canaanites and Amorites." In *Peoples of the Old Testament World.* Edited by Alfred J. Hoerth, Gerald L. Mattinly and Edwin M. Yamauchi. Grand Rapids: Baker Books, 1994.

Schwartz, Meir. "Israeli Festival Becomes Jewish Encounter." October 16, 2006. Arutz 7-IsraelNationalNews.com.

Schwei, Tamara Downs and Katherine Fennelly. "Diversity Coalitions in Rural Minnesota Communities." *CURA Reporter.* Center for Urban and Regional Affairs: University of Minnesota, Winter, 2007. Accessed January 15, 2008; available at www.SCFS.org.

Seim, Brian, ed. *Canada's New Harvest: Helping Churches Touch Newcomers.* Canada: SIM Canada, 1999.

Seoul Declaration On Diaspora Missiology, The. Accessed March 25, 2010; available at http://www.lausanne.org/documents/seoul-declaration-on-diaspora-missiology.html.

Seters, John Van. *The Hyksos.* New Haven: Yale University Press, 1966.

Shandy, Dianna J. and Katherine Fennelly. "A Comparison of the Integration Experiences of Two African Immigrant Populations in a Rural Community." *Social Thought,* 45 (1), 2006.

Sheleg, Yair. "World Jewish Population Drops by 300,000." *Judaism Online.* Available at http://www.simpletoremember.com/vitals/jewpopdrops.htm/

Shirazi, Muhammad. *War, Peace & Non-Violence: An Islamic Perspective.* London: Fountain Books, 2001.

Sidel, Mark. *Vietnam-America Diaspora Philanthropy to Vietnam.* Accessed August 22, 2011; available at http://www.tpi.org/downloads/pdfs/Vietnam_Diaspora_Philanthropy_Final.pdf.

Sills, M. David. Reaching and Teaching: A Call to Great Commission Obedience, (Chicago: Moody, 2010)

Skarsaune, Oskar. "We have found the Messiah! Jewish Believers in Jesus in Antiquity." *MISHKAN* no 45 (Jerusalem 2005):17-20.

Smith, Christopher. "Mission Theory." In *Evangelical Dictionary of World Missions*, 642-643. Edited by A. Scott Morgan. Grand Rapids, MI: Baker Books, 2000.

Smith, Donald K. *Creating Understanding: A Handbook for Christian Communication Across Cultural Landscapes*. Grand Rapids: Zondervan Publishing House, 1992.

Smith, Jane I. *Islam in America*. 2nd ed. New York, NY: Columbia University Press, 2010.

Somali Social Structure, The. Available at http://somaliaholland.free.fr/somali_social structure.htm

Song, M. "The diaspora experience for the Korean Church and its implications for world missions." In *Korean Diaspora and Christian Mission* (pre-publication version ed.). Edited by S. H. Kim and W. Ma. Oxford: Regnum Books, 2010.

Sookhdeo, Patrick. *Faith, Power and Territory*. McLean, VA: Isaac Publishing, 2008.

SOPEMI, "Trends in international migration." Continuous Reporting System on Migration. OECD. Available at www.SourceOECD.org.

Sperling, David. "Hyksos." In *Encyclopaedia Judaica* 2008. Jewish Virtual Library; accessed October 7, 2010; available at http://www.jewishvirtuallibrary.org/jsource/judaica/ejud_0002_0009_0_09361.html

Spradley, James P. *Participant Observation*. New York: Holt, Rinehart and Winston Inc., 1980.

_____. *The Ethnographic Interview*. New York: Holt, Rinehart and Winston, Inc., 1979.

Spradley, James P., David McCurdy, and Dianna J. Shandy. *The Cultural Expereince: Ethnography in complex society*. Prospect Heights: Waveland Press, 1972 (reissued 2005).

Spencer, Stephen. *Mission and migration*. Calver, Derbys: Cliff College Publishing, 2008.

Stake, Robert E. *The Art of Case Study Research*. Thousand Oaks: Sage, 1995.

Stamps, Donald D. *The Full Life Study Bible, NIV*. Colorado Springs, CO: International Bible Society, 1978.

Stark, Rodney. *The rise of Christianity*. San Francisco: Harper Collins, 1997.

Steffen, Tom and Mike Barnett, eds. *Business as Mission: From Impoverished to Empowered*. Pasadena: William Carey Library, 2006.

Steinhardt, Michael. "On the Question of Crisis." *The Journal of Jewish Life Network*, Vol. 5 No. 3 (Spring 2003): 8-9.

Stoller, Paul. "West Africans: Trading Places in New York." In *New Immigrants in New York*. Edited by Nancy Foner. New York, NY: Columbia University Press, 2001.

Suter, Heinz and Marco Gmur. *Business Power for God's Purpose: Partnership with the Unreached*. Greng-Murten, Switzerland: VKG, 1997.

Sydnor, P. N. "Understanding the forced displacement of refugees in terms of the person." *Transformation: An International Journal of Holistic Mission Studies*, (2011): 51-61.

Szakolczai, A. (2009) "Liminality and Experience: Structuring transitory situations and transformative events", in *International Political Anthropology* 2 (1): 141-172. www.politicalanthropology.org

BIBLIOGRAPHY

Tan, K.-S. "In search of contextualized training models for Chinese Christian diaspora in Britain." *Transformation: An International Journal of Holistic Mission Studies*, (2011): 29-41.

Tano, Roodrigo D. *Theology in the Philippine Setting*. Quezon City, Philippines: New Day Publishers, 1981.

Tcherikover, V. *Hellenistic Civilization and the Jews*. New York: Atheneum, 1970.

Tcherikover, V. and A. Fuks, eds. *Corpus Papyrorum Judaicarum*. Vol. 1. Cambridge, MA: Harvard University Press, 1957–1964.

Tendero, Efraim. *Report*. FIN Global Consultation, Singapore 20 July 2002.

ter Haar, Gerrie. *Halfway to Paradise African Christians in Europe*. Cardiff Academic Press, 1998.

Terrillion, Raymond. "Refugees of the World." In The Indochinese Refugee Movement, the Canadian Experience. Edited by Howard Adelman. Toronto: Operation Lifeline, 1980.

Terry, John Mark. *Missiology: An Introduction*. B&H Academic, 1998.

Terrazas, Aaron. "Central American Immigrants in the United States." January, 2011. Accessed August 17, 2011; available at http://www.migrationinformation.org/usaFocus/display.cfm?ID=821/

Tettey, Wisdom J. "Transnationalism, Religion, and the African Diaspora in Canada: An Examination of Ghanaians and Ghanaian Churches." In *African Immigrant Religions in America*. Edited by Jacob K. Olupona and Regina Gemignani. New York, NY: New York University Press, 2007.

The LausanneMovement. *The LausanneCovenant*. Accessed Feb 18, 2011; available at http://www.lausanne.org/covenant

Thomas, T.V. "Mobilizing the Diaspora in Canada for Mission." Unpublished paper presented at the Lausanne International Leadership Conference, at Tyndale College & Seminary, Toronto, Canada, March 1998.

Thomas, T.V. *"Ministering to Scattered Peoples: Global Phenomenon of Diaspora."* Accessed Feb 17, 2011; available at http://conversation.lausanne.org/en/conversations/detail/11660

Timmer, Jeffrey John. "Japanese Gospel Choirs: community, relationships and Celebration in the Hallelujah Gospel family." An unpublished MA Thesis. Bethel University, May 10, 2010.

Tiplady, Richard, ed. "One World or Many? The impact of globalization on mission." In *Globalization of Mission Series*. Pasadena, California: William Carey Library, 2003.

Tira, Sadiri Joy. "Filipino International Network: A Strategic Model for Filipino Diaspora Glocal® Missions." *Global Missiology* (October 2004). Available at www.GlobalMissiology.org/

_____. "Filipino Kingdom Workers: An Ethnographic Study in Diaspora Missiology." Doctor of Missiology Product. Western Seminary, Portland, OR, 2008.

_____. "Kangaroo Church Birthing & Reproduction Model: A Case Study of Diaspora Missiology in Action in Canada." In *Mission Practice in the 21st Century*. Edited by

Enoch Wan and Sadiri Joy Tira. Pasadena, CA: William Carey International University Press, 2009.

_____. "Scattered With a Divine Purpose: A Theological & Missiological Perspective on the Filipino Diaspora." Unpublished paper presented at the Asia Pacific Alliance (C&MA) Conference, Taipei, Taiwan, April, 1998.

Tira, Sadiri Joy.(ed.) *The Human Tidal Wave*. Manila: Lifechange Publishing, Inc., 2013.

Tira, Sadiri Joy and Enoch Wan. "Filipino experience in diaspora missions: a case study of Christian communities in contemporary contexts." *Commission VII: Christian Communities in Contemporary Contexts*, Edinburgh (June 12-13, 2009).

Trebilco, Paul. "Diaspora Judaism." In *Dictionary of New Testament Background*. Edited by Craig A. Evans and Stanley E. Porter. Downers Grove, IL: InterVarsity, 2000.

Trinity International Baptist Mission. *Our Story*. Accessed Feb 2 25, 2011; available at http://www.tibm.org/our-story.html

Thanh-Dam Truong and Des Gasper, eds. Transnational Migration and Human Security-the migration-development-security nexus (Springer: Berlin & Heidelberg, 2011).

Tsagarousiano, Roza. "Rethinking the concept of diaspora: mobility, connectivity and communication in a globalised world." Westminster Papers in Communication and Culture, Vol. 1.1 (2004): 52-65. University of Westminster, London. Accessed August 20, 2011; available at http://www.upf.edu/materials/fhuma/ minories/docs_diaspores/tsagarousianou.pdf

Torres-D'Mello, Arlene. *Being Filipino Abroad*. Quezon City, Philippines: Giraffe Books, 2001.

Tye, Larry. *Home Lands: Portraits of the New Jewish Diaspora*. New York: Henry Holt and Co., 2001.

UNHCR, Report of the Steering Committee of the International Conference on the Indo-Chinese Refugees, March 6,1996. Accessed August 22; available at http://www.unhcr.org/refworld/docid/3b00f4940.html.

United Nations Department of Economic and Social Affairs, Population Division. *International Migration Report*. New York, NY: United Nations, 2002.

_____. Population Division of the Department of Economic and Social Affairs. *World Migrant Stock: The 200 Revision Database*, 21 September 2008.

United Nations High Commissioner for Refugees, UNHCR Fact Sheet. February 1984 - No. 9. Accessed August 22, 2011; available at http://www.unhcr.org/refworld/docid/4794774d0.html.

United Nations. "International migration and development: Report of the Secretary-General, 2010." Accessed February 19, 2011; available at http://www.gfmd.org/documents/65th-UNGA_Report-of-UN-Sec-Gen.pdf

United Nations. "United Nations' Trends In Total Migrant Stock: The 2008 Revision." Accessed July 14, 2010; available at http://www.esa.un.org/migration/

USAID. "Global Partnerships, *Diaspora Engagement: Remittances and Beyond."* (June 23, 2010). Available at http://www.usaid.gov/our_work/global_partnerships/gda/remittances.html

U.S. Census Bureau, Profile America Facts for Feature. Accesible August 22, 2011; available at http://www.census.gov/newsroom/releases/archives/facts_for_features_special_editions/cb08-ff05.html.

Vanderwerf, Linda. "Refugees from Burma settling in for work at Jennie-O store." *West Central Tribune* November 13, 2010.

Van Dijk, Meine Pieter, ed. *New Presence of China in Africa*. Chicago, IL: University of Chicago Press, 2009.

Van Engen, Charles. "Constructing a Theology of Mission for the City." In *God So Loves the City*. Edited by Charles Van Engen and Jude Tiersma. Monrovia, CA: MARC, 1994.

_____. "Locality and Catholicity in a Globalizing World." In *Globalizing Theology*. Edited by C. Ott and H. Netland. Grand Rapids, MI: Baker Academic, 2006.

van Gennep, Arnold, The Rites of Passage. Chicago: University of Chicago, 1960 (*Rites de Passage*, 1908) See Rosemary Zumwalt, "Arnold van Gennep: The Hermit of Bourg-la-Reine" [originally published in *American Anthropologist*, 84:299-313, 1982] Accessed Dec. 20, 2013. http://www.aaanet.org/committees/commissions/centennial/history/090vangennep.pdf

Van Hue, Nguyen. Report of the Vietnamese Mission Board, 2006. Huong Di, Christmas 2010 edition.

van Kerkhoff, Lorrae. *Strategic Integration: The Practical Politics of Integrated Research in Context*, 2005.

Van Rheenen, Gailyn. *Communicating Christ in Animistic Contexts*. California: William Carey Library, 1996.

Van Seters. *The Hyksos*. New Haven: Yale University Press, 1966.

Van Unnik, W. C. *Tarsus or Jerusalem: The City of Paul's Youth*. London: Epworth, 1962.

Vertovec, Steven. "Three meanings of 'diaspora' exemplified among South Asian religion." *Diaspora*, 7 (2), (1999). Accessed August 29, 20011; available at www.transcomm.ox.ac.uk/working%20papers/diaspora.pdf

Vertovec, Steven. "Transnational Networks and Skilled Labour Migration,"   Paper presented at the conference: Ladenburger Diskurs "Migration" Gottlieb Daimler- und Karl Benz-Stiftung, Ladenburg, 14-15 February 2002.

Vilya Gelbras's interview. *Vladivostok News*, October 25 2001. Available at http://vn.vladnews.ru/arch/2001/iss280/News/upd25.HTM/

Vo, Linda Trinh. "Vietnamese American Trajectories: Dimension of Diaspora." *Amerasia Journal,v*ol. 29:1 (2003).

VWCF, *Yearbook of Vietnamese Pastors and Churches (Vietnamese and Overseas)*. Complied and edited by Vietnamese World Christian Fellowship, Westminster, CA, 2011.

Wagner, C. Peter. Strategies for Church Growth: Tools for Effective Mission and Evangelism, (Ventura: Regal Books, 1987).

Waltke, B. K. *Genesis: A Commentary*. Grand Rapids, MI: Zondervan, 2011.

Walls, Andrew. "Culture and Coherence in Christian History," *Evangelical Review of Theology*, 9, no. 3, 1984

Walls, Andrew F. "Old Athens and New Jerusalem: Some Signposts for Christian Scholarship in the Early History of Mission Studies." *International Bulletin of Missionary Research* 21 no. 4 (1997):146-150.

Wan, Enoch, ed. *Mission Within Reach: Intercultural Miniseries in Canada*. Edmonton, Alberta, Canada: China Alliance Press, Inc., 1995.

_____ "A critique of Charles Kraft's use / misuse of communication and social science in biblical interpretation and missiological formulation," In *Missiology and the social sciences: contributions, cautions and conclusions.* Edited by Edward Rommen and Gary Orwin, p.121-164, Pasadena: William Carey Library. (1996)

_____ "Practical contextualization: A case study of evangelizing contemporary Chinese." *Chinese Around the World.* March 2000:18-24.

_____. *Questions and Answers to Christian Marriage: Practical Guide to Christian Family*. Overseas Magazine (2000). (In Chinese).

_____. "Mission among the Chinese Diaspora: A Case Study of Migration and Mission." *Missiology* 31 no. 1 (2003a): 35.

_____. "Rethinking Missiological Research Methodology: Exploring a New Direction." *Global Missiology* (October 2003b); available at www.GlobalMissiology.org/)

_____. "The Phenomenon of the Diaspora: Missiological Implications for Christian Missions." In *Asian American Christianity: A Reader.* Edited by Viji Nakka-Cammauf and Timothy Tseng. The Pacific Asian American and Canadian Christian Education Project (PAACCE) and the Institute for the Study of Asian American Christianity (ISAAC), 2004.

_____. "The Paradigm and Pressing Issues of Inter-disciplinary Research Methodology." *Global Missiology* (January 2005a). Available at www.GlobalMissiology. Org/

_____. "Missionary strategy in Epistle to the Romans." *To the End of the Earth*, Hong Kong Association of Christian Missions Ltd. (July-Sept 2005b):1-2 (in Chinese).

_____. "The Paradigm of 'relational realism.'" EMS *Occasional Bulletin* 19:2 (Spring 2006): 1-4.

_____. "Diaspora Missiology." EMS *Occasional Bulletin*, 20 no. 2 (Spring 2007a): 3-7.

_____. "Expectation and Reflection." On the occasion of Paul Hiebert's Passing (April 2007b). Available at http://paul-timothy.net/pages/gm/wan_reflections_on_paul_hiebert_4_2007.pdf/

_____. "Relational Theology and Relational Missiology." EMS *Occasional Bulletin* 21:1 (Winter 2007c): 1-7.

BIBLIOGRAPHY

_____. "Diaspora Couple Priscilla and Aquila: A Model Family in Action for Mission." *Global Missiology* (April 2009a). Available at www.GlobalMissiology.org. Originally published in *Great Commission Bi-monthly* vol 79 (April 2009). (In Chinese).

_____. "Core Values of Mission Organization in the Cultural Context of the 21st Century." *Global Missiology* (Januaty 2009b). Available at www.GlobalMissiology.org/

_____. "Global People and Diaspora Missiology."In Toyko 2010 Global Mission Handbook. Edited by Yong J. Cho and David Taylor. Published by the Tokyo 2010 Global Mission Consulataion Planning Committee, 2010a. Available at http://www.tokyo2010.org/resources/Handbook.pdf

_____. "Global People and Diaspora Missiology." Tokyo 2010-Global Mission Consultation: Plenary Session. May 13 (2010b).

_____. "Rethinking Missiology in the context of the 21st Century: Global Demographic Trends and Diaspora Missiology." *Great Commission Research Journal*, Volume 2 Issue 1 (Summer 2010c). (In Chinese). Available at http://apps.biola.edu/gcr/volumes/2/issues/1/articles/7/

_____. "'Mission' and 'Missio Dei': Response to Charles Van Engen's 'Mission Defined and Described.'" In *MissionShift: Global Mission Issues in the Third Millennium. Edited by* David J. Hesselgrave and Ed Stetzer. Nashville: B & H Publishing Group, 2010d.

_____. "A Missio-Relational Reading of Romans: A Complementary Study to Current Approaches." EMS *Occasional Bulletin,* Vol. 23 No. 1 (Winter 2010e):1-8. Also in *Global Missiology* (April 1, 2010e). Available at www.GlobalMissiology.org/

_____. "Moving to Reach People on the Move." Multiplex Session, "Cape Town 2010" (October 20, 2010f).

_____. "Partnerships Should Mimic the Trinity, " *Faith Today, July/August* 2010:27

_____. "Moving to Reach People on the Move." Lausanneconversation (2010g). Available at http://conversation.lausanne.org/en/conversations/detail/11438/

_____. "Ministering to Scattered Peoples - Moving to Reach the People on the Move." LausanneGlobal Conversation (2010h). Accessed Feb 17, 2011; available at http://conversation.lausanne.org/en/resources/detail/11438

_____. "Diaspora Missiology and Missions in the Context of the 21st Century." *Torch Trinity Journal*, Volume 13 No.1 (May 30 2010i).

_____. "Korean Diaspora: From Hermit Kingdom to Kingdom Ministry." In *Korean Diaspora and Christian Mission*. Edited by Won Suk Ma and S. Hun Kim. Eugene, OR: Wipf and Stock Publishers, 2011j.

_____. "Diaspora Mission Strategy in the Context of the United Kingdom in the 21st Century." *Transformation: An International Journal of Holistic Mission Studies. OCMS* 28.1 (January 2011a): 3-13. Available at http://trn.sagpub.com/

_____. "Research Methodology for Diaspora Missiology and Diaspora Missions. " North Central Regional EMS Regional Conference, Trinity Evangelical Divinity School, Deerfield, IL: February 26, 2011b.

———. "Global Status of Diaspora Ministry." Webseminar, *The Mission Exchange*. Global Issues Update (February 2011). Available at http://www.themissionexchange.org/ (See www.enochwan.com).

Wan, Enoch and Tuvya Zaretsky. *Jewish-Gentile Couples: Trends, Challenges and Hopes*. Pasadena: William Carey Library, 2004.

Wan, Enoch and Mark Hedinger. "Understanding 'relationality' from a Trinitarian Perspective." *Global Missiology* (January 2006). Available at www.GlobalMissiology.org/

Wan, Enoch and Linda Gross. "Christian Missions to Diaspora Groups: A Diachronic General Overview and Synchronic Study of Contemporary U.S." *Global Missiology*, vol. 3 no. 2 (2008). Available at http://ojs.GlobalMissiology.org/index.php/english/issue/view/11/

Wan, Enoch and Michael Pocock, eds. *Missions in the Majority World*. Pasadena: William Carey Library, 2009.

Wan, Enoch and Sadiri Joy Tira, eds. *Mission Practice in the 21st Century* Pasadena, CA: William Carrey Inernational University Press, 2009.

Wan, Enoch and Geoff Baggett. "A Theology of Partnership: Implications for Implementation by a Local Church. *Global Missiology* (2010). Available at http://www.GlobalMissiology.org/

Wan, Enoch and Kevin P. Penman. "The 'Why,' 'How' and 'Who' of Partnership in Christian Missions." *Global Missiology* April 1, 2010. Available at http://www.GlobalMissiology.org/

Wan, Enoch and Sadiri Joy Tira. "Diaspora Missiology and Mission in the Context of the 21st Century." *Torch Trinity Journal* Vol 13 No.1 (2010). Also in *Global Missiology* 1 no. 8 (2010); available at http://www.ojs.GlobalMissiology.org/index.php/english/article/viewFile/383/994/

Wan, Enoch and Thanh Trung Le. *Mobilizing Vietnamese Diaspora for the Kingdom.* (forth coming, Spring 2014)

Wan, Enoch and Yaw Attah Edu-Bekoe. "Diversity of Ghanaian Diaspora in the U.S.: Ministering to the Ghanaian Communities through Ghanaian Congregation." Presentation at North West EMS Regional Meeting, Portland, OR (March 20, 2010a).

———. "Diversity of the Ghanaian Diaspora in the U.S.: Ministering to the Diverse Ghanaian Communities Through Ghanaian Congregations." Presentation at 2010 North American Mission Leaders' Conference (NAMLC) in Charlotte, NC, September 23-25, 2010b.

———. "Diversity of Ghanaian Diaspora in the U.S.: Ministering to the Diverse Ghanaian Communities Through Ghanaian Congregations." In *Mosaic: Engaging the Beauty of God's Kingdom Diversity*. Edited by Scott Moreau and Beth Snodderly. EMS: Evangelical Missiological Society Series no.19, 2011c.

BIBLIOGRAPHY

Wan, Enoch and Johnny Yee-chong Wan. "Partnership - a relational study of the Trinity and the Epistle to the Philippines." *Global Missiology* (April 1, 2010); available at www.GlobalMissiology.org/

Wan, Enoch and Nary Santos. "A Missio-relational Reading of Mark." EMS *Occasional Bulletin*, vol. 24 no. 2 (Spring 2011):1-26.

Wang, Jin and Xian Yuanhong, "Bitter Winters for three major Shoe Manufacture Capitals." Accessed January 16, 2005; available at http://finance.sina.com.cn/chanjing/b/20050116/11501297523.shtml.

Wang, Mary. "Recent Situation of Chinese Mission Work in Europe." *Great Commission Bi-Monthly*, no. 61 (April 2006): 3-13.

Ward, Peter. *Liquid Church*. Carlisle: Paternoster, 2002.

"A Warm, but Empty Voice? Reflections on Face-to-Face Interactions," Blog post *by Enoch Wan* at Evangel-Vision: http://www.evangel-vision.com/2013/12/a-warm-but-empty-voice-reflections-on.html Accessed Dec. 2, 2013

Warner; R. Stephen and Judith G. Wittner. *Gatherings In Diaspora: Religious Communities and the New Immigration* (Kindle Locations 211-214). Kindle Edition 1998.

Weiner, Myron and Michael S. Teitelbaum. *Political Demography, Demographic Engineering*. New York: Berghahn, 2001.

Wiefel, Wolfgang. "The Jewish community in ancient Rome and the origins of Roman Christianity." In *The Romans Debate*. Edited by Karl P. Donfried. Peabody, MA: Hendrickson, 1977.

Werblowsky, R. J. Zwi and Geoffrey Wigoder, eds. *The Encyclopedia of the Jewish Religion*. New York, New York: Adama Books, 1986.

Wilcox, M. "The God-Fearers in Acts – A Reconsideration." *JSNT* 13 (1981): 102-122.

Williams Margaret H. *The Jews among the Greeks and Romans: A Diaspora* Sourcebook. Baltimore, Maryland: John Hopkins University Press, 1998.

Williamson H. G. M. and C. A. Evans. "Samaritans." In *Dictionary of New Testament Backgrounds*, 1056-1061. Edited by Craig A. Evans and Stanley E. Porter. Downers Grove: InterVarsity, 2000.

Witherington, Ben III. *The Acts of the Apostles: A Socio-Rhetorical Commentary*. Grand Rapids: Eerdmans, 1998.

Wolfe, Robert. "From Habiru to Hebrews: The Roots of the Jewish Tradition." *New English Review*, Oct 2009. Accessed May 27, 2010; available at http://www.newenglishreview.org/custpage.cfm/frm/48464/sec_id/48464/

Wright, Christopher J.H. *Living As The People of God: The Relevance of Old Testament Ethics*. Leicester, England: Intervarsity Press,1992.

Wright, J. Stafford. "The Historicity of the Book of Esther." In *New Perspectives on the Old Testament*. Edited by J. Barton Payne. Waco: Word, 1970.

WVAC. *The Worldwide Association of Vietnamese Alliance Churches News Letter*. No.1, 2008

Wylens, Stephen. *Settings of Silver: An Introduction to Judaism*. New York: Paulist Press, 1989.

Yancey, Philip. S*oul Survivor*. London: Hodder & Stoughton, 2001.

Yang, Fenggang. *Chinese Christian in America*. University Park: Penn State U Press, 1999.

Yin, Robert K. *Case Study Research: Design and Methods*. Thousand Oaks: Sage, 1994.

Young-Sang Ro, The Ecclesiastical Approach for the Integration of Multicultural Society: Intercultural 'Unity in Diversity' in the Multiethnic Ministry, " in Chan-Sik Park and Noah Jung, 2010, 123-148.

Zaretsky, Tuvya. *Jewish-Gentile Couples: Trends, Challenges, and Hopes*. Pasadena, CA: William Carey Library, 2004. Zaretsky, Tuvya. "Relations and Tension: Research on Jewish-Gentile Couples." *LCJE Bulletin* No. 77 (September 2004): 9-14.

_____. "A new publication about Jewish evangelism." *Global Missiology*, July 2005. Availalble at www.GlobalMissiology. org/

_____, ed. "Jewish Evangelism: A call to the Church." Lausanne LOP 60. Committee for World Evangelization, 2005.

_____. "The Gospel and Jewish-Gentile Couples." *MISHKAN: A Forum on the Gospel and the Jewish People* 47 (June 2006): 6-18, 27-32, 54-57.

_____. "Diaspora Missiology Report." Lausanne Consultation on Jewish Evangelism, 2007. Accessed September 22, 2009; available at www.lcje.net/papers/2007/Zaretsky.doc/

Zax, David. "Whose Diaspora is it Anyway?" *Moment Magazine* (October/November 2007).

Zekharyah, Ḳalai and Moshe Weinfeld. *Studies in Historical Geography and biblicalHistoriography: Presented to Zechariah Kallai*. Edited by Gershon Galil and Moshe Weinfeld. The Netherlands: Kominkijke Brill, 2000.

Zhang, Benzi. "Beyond Border Politics: The Problematics of Identity." Accessed August 20, 2011; available at http://www.english.iup.edu/tslater/Studies/PDFs31_1/BeyondBorderPolitics.pdf

Zhou, Min and Carl L. Bankston, III. *The Experience of Vietnamese Refugee Children in the United States*. Available at http://www.tolerance.org/sites/default/files/kits/vac_brief_history.pdf.

Zwi Werblowsky, R. J. and Geoffrey Wigoder, eds. *The Encyclopedia of the Jewish Religion*. New York, New York: Adama Books, 1986.

Resources

Resources on Diaspora Missiology and Diaspora Missions

Selected web sites on international migration:

- http://www.gcim.org/en/
- http://www.ilo.org/
- http://www.imi.ox.ac.uk/
- http://www.iom.int/
- http://www.oecd.org/migration
- http://www.un.org/esa/population/migration/
- http://isim.georgetown.edu/
- http://www.sourceoecd.org/database/16081269/intmigration
- http://family.jrank.org/pages/1170/Migration-Theories-Migration.html
- http://www.jdpayne.org/wp-content/uploads/2010/10/Scattered-to-Gather.pdf
- http://www.lausanne.org/documents/seoul-declaration-on-diaspora-missiology.html

Abu-Laban, Yasmeen and Christine Gabriel. *Selling Diversity: Immigration, Multiculturalism, Employment Equity, and Globalization.* Orchard Park: Broadview Press, 2002.

Adebayo, Akanmu G. and Olutayo C Adesina, eds. *Globalization and Transnational Migrations: Africa and Africans in the Contemporary Global System.* Newcastle: Cambridge Scholars Publishing, 2009. Available at http://www.c-s-p.org/flyers/978-1-4438-0535-3-sample.pdf

Aghamka, Atu Y. "Partnership in Witnessing to the Hindu Diaspora in North America." *Journal of the Academy for Evangelism in Theological Education* Vol 22 (2006-2007): 23-48.

Al-Ali, Nadje, Richard Black, and Khalid Koser. "The Limits to 'Transnationalism': Bosnian and Eritrean Refugees in Europe as Emerging Transnational Communities." *Ethnic and Racial Studies* 24 no. 4 (2001): 578-600. Available at http://www.tandfonline.com/doi/pdf/10.1080/01419870120049798/

Al-Azmeh, Aziz and Effie Fokas, eds. *Islam in Europe: Diversity, Identity and Influence.* Cambridge: Cambridge University Press, 2007.

Alba, Richard and Victor Nee. *Remaking the American Mainstream: Assimilation and Contemporary Immigration.* Cambridge: Harvard University Press, 2003.

Aleinikoff, Alexander T. and Douglas Klausmeyer, eds. *From Migrants to Citizens: Membership in a Changing World.* Washington, D.C.: Carnegie Endowment for International Peace, 2000.

Allievi, Stefano and Joergen S. Nielsen, eds. *Muslim Networks and Transnational Communities in and Across Europe.* Leiden, the Netherland: Brill Academic Publishing, 2003.

American Society of Missiology. "Migration Challenge and Avenue for Christian Missions." Missiology XXXI, (January 2003).

Andrade-Eekhoff, Katharine and Claudia Marina Silva-Avalos. "Globalization of the Periphery: The Challenges of Transnational Migration for Local Development in Central America." FLACSO Programa El Salvador, April 2003. Available at http://www.enlacesamerica.org/Final%20document%20globalization%20of%20the%20periphery1.pdf

Antoun, Richard. *Documenting Transnational Migration: Jordanian Men Working and Studying in Europe, Asia and North America*. New York: Berghahn Books, 2009.

Asamoah-Gyadu, Kwabena. "African-led Christianity in Europe: Migration And Diaspora Evangelism." In *Lausanne World Pulse*. Available at http://www.lausanneworldpulse.com/themearticles.php/973?pg=all/

Bailey, Olga G., Myria Georgiou, and Ramaswami Harindranath. *Transnational Lives and the Media: Re-imagining Diaspora*. London: Palgrave Macmillan, 2007.

Bakerwell, Oliver. "South-South Migration and Human Development: Reflections on African Experiences." Working Paper 15, International Migration Institute, University of Oxford, April 2009. Available at http://www.imi.ox.ac.uk/pdfs/imi-working-papers/wp-15-oliver-bakewel-south-south-migration

Benhabib, Seyla. *The Rights of Others: Aliens, Residents and Citizens*. Cambridge, New York: Cambridge University Press, 2004.

------. "Twilight of Sovereignty or the Emergence of Cosmopolitan Norms? Rethinking Citizenship in Volatile Times." *Citizenship Studies* 11.1 (February 2007): 19-36.

Benton-Short, Lisa, Marie D. Price, and Samantha Friedman. "Globalization from Below: The Ranking of Global Immigrant Cities." *International Journal of Urban and Regional Research*, Vol 29 Issue 4 (December 2005): 945-959.

Brettell, C. B. and J.F. Hollifield, eds. *Migration Theory: Talking Across Disciplines*, 2nd Ed. New York and London: Routledge, 2007.

Boyd, Monica and Elizabeth Grieco. "Women and Migration: Incorporating Gender into International Migration Theory." *Migration Information Source,* March 2003. Available at http://www.migrationinformation.org/feature/display.cfm?ID=106

Brenner, Neil. *New State Spaces: Urban Governance and the Rescaling of Statehood*. Oxford and New York: Oxford University Press, 2004.

Brody, Betsy. *Opening the Doors: Immigration, Ethnicity, and Globalization in Japan*. New York: Routledge, 2002.

Brubaker, Rogers. "The Return of Assimilation: Changing Perspectives on Assimilation and Its Sequels." *Ethnic and Racial Studies* 24 (2001):531-548.

Caglar, Ayse. "Hometown Associations, Rescaling of State Spatiality and Migrant Grassroots Transnationalism." *Global Networks* 6.1 (January 2006): 1-22. Available at http://onlinelibrary.wiley.com/doi/10.1111/j.1471-0374.2006.00130.x/pdf

REFERENCES

_____. "Rescaling cities, cultural diversity and transnationalism: migrants of Mardin and Essen." *Ethnic and Racial Studies (Special issue: New Directions in the Anthropology of Migration Research)* Vol 30 (6) (2007): 1095, 2007.

Castles, Stephen. "Towards a Sociology of Forced Migration and Social Transformation." *Sociology* 37.1 (2003): 1-34.

Cheah, Pheng and Bruce Robbins, eds. *Cosmopolitics: Thinking and FeelingBeyond the Nation*. Minneapolis: University of Minnesota, 1998

Chen, Sylvia Xiaohua, Veronica Benet-Martinez, and Michael Harris Bond. "Bicultural Identity, Bilingualism, and Psychological Adjustment in Multicultural Societies: Immigration-Based and Globalization-Based Acculturation." *Journal of Personality*, Vol 76, Iss 4 (August 2008): 803-838.

Claro, Bert. *A Higher Purpose for Your Overseas Job*. CrossOver Books, 2007. Available at http://ojs.GlobalMissiology.org/index.php/english/article/viewFile/215/600

Cohen, Robin. *Global Diaspora: An Introduction*. Seattle: University of Washington Press, 1997.

Collinson, Sarah. "The Political Economy of Migration Processes: An Agenda for Migration Research and Analysis." Working Paper 12, International Migration Institute, University of Oxford, 2009. Available at http://www.imi.ox.ac.uk/pdfs/imi-working-papers/wp12-collinson/

De Haas, Hein. "Migration System Formation and Decline: A Theoretical Inquiry into the Self-perpetuation and Self-undermining Dynamics of Migration Process." Working Paper 19, International Migration Institute, University of Oxford, 2009. Available at http://www.imi.ox.ac.uk/pdfs/imi-working-papers/wp19-2009-de-haas-migration-systems-formation-and-decline/

_____. "Migration and Development: A Theoretical Perspective." Working Paper, Center on Migration, Citizenship and Development, University of Bielefeld: COMCAD, 2007. Available at http://www.scribd.com/doc/19260119/Migration-Theory.

_____. "Migration Transitions: A Theoretical and Empirical Inquiry into the Developmental Drives of International Migration." Working Paper 24, International Migration Institute, University of Oxford, 2010. Available at http://www.imi.ox.ac.uk/pdfs/imi-working-papers/wp24-migration-transitions-1

De Ridder, Richard . *Discipling the Nations.* Grand Rapids: Baker Book House, 1971.

Donkor, Martha. "Marching to the Tune: Colonization, Globalization, Immigration, and the Ghanaian Diaspora." *Africa Today*, Vol 52, No 1 (Fall 2005): 27-44.

Eriksen, Thomas Hylland. *Globalization: the Key Concepts*. New York: Berg, 2007.

Faist, Thomas and Peter Kivista, eds. *Dual Citizenship in a Global Perspective: From Unitary to Multiple Citizenship*. New York: Palgrave Macmillan, 2007.

Faist, Thomas. "Transnationalization in International Migration: Implications for the Study of Citizenship and Culture." *Ethnic and Racial Studies*, 23:2 (2000): 189-222, 2000. Available at http://www.tandfonline.com/doi/pdf/10.1080/014198700329024/

GhaneaBassiri, Kambiz. *A History of Islam in America: From a New World to the New World*. New York, NY: Cambridge University Press, 2010.

Gicquel, Francois-Xavier. "Transnational Migrations – The Growth of Informal Economy." *Le Post* (April 2011). Available at http://www.lepost.fr/article/2011/04/20/2472451_transnational-migrations-the-growth-of-informal-economy.html/

Glick-Schiller, Nina. "From Immigrant to Transmigrant: Theorizing Transnational Migration." *Anthropological Quarterly* 68 (January 1995):48-63.

Glick-Schiller, Nina and Ayse Cagas. "And Ye Shall Possess It, and Dwell Therein: Social Citizenship, Global Christianity, and Non-Ethnic Immigrant Incorporation." In *Immigrants and Citizenship in Europe and the United States: Anthropological Perspectives*. Edited by D. Reed-Danahay and C. Brettell. Rutgers UP, 2008.

Glick-Schiller, Nina and Peggy Levitt. "Haven't We Heard This Somewhere Before? A Substantive View of Transnational Migration Studies by Way of a Reply to Waldinger and Fitzgerald." The Center for Migration and Development, Working Paper Series, Princeton University CMD Working Paper #06-01, 2006.

Glick-Schiller, Nina, Ayse Caglar, and Thaddeus Guldbrandsen. "Beyond the Ethnic Lens: Locality, Globality, and Born-again Incorporation." *American Ethnologist*, 33 (4) (2006): 612-633.

Guernizo, Luis E., Alejandro Portes, and William Haller. "Assimilation and Transnationalism: Determinants of Transnational Political Action among Contemporary Immigrants." *American Journal of Sociology*,108 (6) (May 2003): 1211-1248. Available at http://hcd.ucdavis.edu/faculty/webpages/guarnizo/AssimTrans.pdf/

Haines, David W. et al. "Transnational Migration in East Asia: Japan in Comparative Focus." *International Migration Review*, Vol 4, No 4 (Winter 2007): 963-967. Available at http://gunston.gmu.edu/dhaines1/pubs/IMR_minpaku.pdf/

Hanciles, Jehu J. *Beyond Christendom: Globalization, African Migration and the Transformation of the West*. Orbis Books, New York, 2008.

_____. "Migration and Mission: Some Implications for the Twenty-first-Century Church." *International Bulletin of Missionary Research*, (October 2003): 146-153. Available at http://www.internationalbulletin.org/system/files/2003-04-146-hanciles.pdf

_____. "Migration, Diaspora Communities, and the New Missionary Encounter with Western Society." *Lausanne World Pulse*, (July 2008). Available at http://www.lausanneworldpulse.com/themedarticles.php/975

Hansen, Randall. "Globalization, Embedded Realism, and Path Dependence: The Other Immigrants to Europe." *Comparative Political Studies*, Vol 35, No 3 (April 2002): 259-283. Available at http://homes.chass.utoronto.ca/~rhansen/Articles_files/20021.pdf

Hewison, Kevin and Ken Young, eds. *Transnational Migration and Work in Asia*. New York: Routledge, 2006.

REFERENCES

Hirschman, Charles, Philip Kasinitz, and Josh DeWind Taylor. *The Handbook of International Migration: The American Experience*. New York: Russell Sage Foundation, 1999.

Hu-DeHart, Evelyn. *Across the Pacific: Asian Americans and Globalization*. Philadelphia: Temple University Press, 1999.

Inda, Jonathan Xavier and Renato Rosaldo. *The Anthropology of Globalization: A Reader*. Malden: Blackwell Publishing, 2008.

Indra, Doreen, ed. *Engendering Forced Migration: Theory and Practice*. New York: Berghahn Books, 1998.

Iosifides, Theodoros. "Generic Conceptual Model for Conducting Realist Qualitative Research: Examples from migration studies." Working Paper 43, International Migration Institute, University of Oxford, August 2011. Available at http://www.imi.ox.ac.uk/pdfs/imi-working-papers/wp-11-43-a-generic-concepul-model-for-conducting-realist-qualitative-research-examples-from-migration-studies

Jennissen, Roel. "Economic Theories of International Migration and the Role of Immigration Policy [extended provisional abstract]." Research and Documentation Centre of the Dutch Ministry of Justice and Netherlands Interdisciplinary Demographic Institute. Available at http://epc2006.princeton.edu/download.aspx?submissionId=60112

Jenkins, Philip. *The Next Christendom: The Coming of Global Christianity*. New York: Oxford University Press, 2002.

Jones, Terry-Ann. "Migration Theory in the Domestic Context: North-South Labor Movement in Brazil." *Human Architecture: Journal of the Sociology of Self-Knowledge*, VII, 4, (Fall 2009): 5-14. Available at http://www.okcir.com/Articles%20VII%204/Jones-FM.pdf

Joppke, Christian. *Citizenship and Immigration*. Cambridge: Polity Books, 2010.

Kastoryano, Riva. "Religion and Incorporation: Islam in France and Germany." *International Migration Review*, Volume 38, Issue 3 (September 2004): 1234–1255.

Kitchen, K.A. "Egypt, Egyptians." In *Dictionary of the Old Testament:Pentateuch*, Edited by T. Desmond Alexander and David W. Baker. Downers Grove, IL: InterVasity Press, 2003.

Kivisto, Peter. "Theorizing Transnational Immigration: A Critical Review of Current Efforts." *Ethnic and Racial Studies*, Vol 24, Issue 4 (2001): 549-577. Available at http://www.tandfonline.com/doi/pdf/10.1080/01419870120049789

Kloosterman, Robert and Jan Rath, eds. *Immigrant Entrepreneurs: Venturing abroad in the age of globalization*. Oxford: Berg, 2003.

Landolt, Patricia. "Salvadorian Economic Transnationalism: Embedded Strategies for Household Maintenance, Immigrant Incorporation, and Entrepreneurial Expansion." *Global Networks* 1 (3) (2001): 217-241.

———Lausanne Committee for World Evangelization Issue Group No. 26 A and B: Diasporas and International Students. Edited by D. Clayton. Lausanne Occasional Paper 55: The New People Next Door. 2004 Forum Occasional Papers, September 29–October 5, 2004. Delhi, India: Horizon Printers and Publishers, 2005.

Laws, Glenda. "Globalization, Immigration, and Changing Social Relations in U.S. Cities." *The Annals of the American Academy of Political and Social Sciences*, Vol 551, no. 1, (May 1997): 89-104.

Levitt, Peggy and Rafail de la Dehesa. "Transnational Migration and the Redefinition of the State: Variations and Explanations." *Ethnic and Racial Studies*, Vol. 26 (4) (2003): 587-611.

Levitt, Peggy and Sanjeev Khargarm. *The Transnational Studies Reader: Intersections and Innovations.* London: Routledge, 2007.

Levitt, Peggy and Nina Glick-Schiller. "Conceptualizing Simultaneity: A Transnational Social Field Perspective on Society." *International Migration Review*, vol.38, no. 3 (September 2004): 1002-1039.

Li, Peter S. "Immigration from China to Canada in the Age of Globalization: Issues of Brain Gain and Brain Loss." *Pacific Affairs*, Vol 81, No 2, (Summer 2008): 217-239.

Light, Ivan H. *Deflecting Immigration: Networks, Markets, and Regulation in Los Angeles.* New York: Russell Sage Foundation, 2006.

Lin, Jan. "Globalization and the Revalorizing of Ethnic Places in Immigration Gateway Cities." *Urban Affairs Review*, Vol 34, No. 2 (November 1998): 313-119.

_____ "The New People Next door. "Lausanne Occasional Paper No. 55, Produced by the Issue Group at the 2004 Forum, Lausanne Committee for World Evangelization, Pattaya, Thailand, September 29 to October 5, 2004. Available at http://www.lausanne.org/es/documents/all/173-lop/871-lop-55.html.

Macedo, Donald and Panayota Gounari. *The Globalization of Racism.* Herndon: Paradigm Publishers, 2005.

Mandryk, Jason. *Operation World.* Colorado Springs: Biblica Publishing, 2010.

McCarthy, Cameron et al. "Afterword: Contesting Culture: Identity and Curriculum Dilemmas in the Age of Globalization, Postcolonialism, and Multiplicity." *Harvard Educational Review*, Vol 73, No 3 (Fall 2003): 449-465.

Meyers, Eytan. "Theories of International Immigration Policy – A Comparative Analysis." *International Migration Review*, Vol 34, No. 4 (Winter 2000): 1245-1282. Available at http://www.cpcs.umb.edu/~uriarte/Courses/Practicum%2007-08/Resources/Immigrant%20Integration%20in%20Western%20Countries/Theories%20of%20International%20Immigration%20Policy.pdf

Morawska, Ewa and Christian Joppke, eds. *Toward Assimilation and Citizenship in Liberal Nation-States.* London: Palgrave Macmillian, 2003.

REFERENCES

Morawska, Ewa. "Studying International Migration in the long(er) and short(er) duree: Contesting some and reconciling other disagreements between the structuration and morphogenesis approaches." Working Paper 44, International Migration Institute, University of Oxford, August 2011. Available at http://www.imi.ox.ac.uk/pdfs/imi-working-papers/wp-11-44-studying-international-migration-in-the-long-er-and-short-er-duree-contesting-some-and-reconciling-other-disagreements-between-the-structuration-and-morphogenesis-approaches/

Munz, Reiner. "Migration, Labor Markets, and Integration of Migrants: An Overview for Europe." Social Protection & Labor, The World Bank, April 2008. Available at http://siteresources.worldbank.org/SOCIALPROTECTION/Resources/SP-Discussion-papers/Labor-Market-DP/0807.pdf

Nagel, Caroline and Lynn Staeheli. "Citizenship, Nation, and Transnational Migration: The case of Arab-American Activism." Paper presented at the Globalization and Democracy Conference, Boulder, Colorado, April 2002. Available at http://www.colorado.edu/ibs/pec/gadconf/papers/nagel.html

Nyers, Peter. *Rethinking Refugees: Beyond State of Emergency*. London: Routledge, 2006.

Ong, Aihwa. *Flexible Citizenship: The Cultural Logics of Transnationality*. Durham: Duke University Press, 1999.

O'Rourke, Kevin and Richard Sinnott. "The Determinants of Individual Attitudes Towards Immigration." *European Journal of Political EconoMy*, Vol 22 Issue 4 (December 2006): 838-861.

Orozco, Manuel. "Remittances and Markets: New Players and Practices." *Commission Paper for the Inter-American Dialogue and the Tomas Rivera Policy Institute*, June 2006. Available at https://www.thedialogue.org/PublicationFiles/Orozco%20marketplace.pdf/

Osili, Una Okonkwo. "Remittances and Savings from International Migration: Theory and Evidence Using a Matched Sample." *Journal of Development Economics*, 83 (2007): 446-465. Available at http://www.ssrc.org/workspace/images/crm/new_publication_3/%7B0a07472e-4255-de11-afac-001cc477ec70%7D.pdf/

Ostergaard-Nielsen, Eva. *Transnational Politics: Turks and Kurds in Germany*. London, Routledge, 2003.

Pantoja, Luis, Sadiri Joy Tira, and Enoch Wan, eds. *Scattered: Filipino Global Presence*. Manila: LifeChange Publishing, 2004.

Park, Chan-Sik and Noah Jung, eds. *21C New Nomad Era and Migrant Mission*. Seoul: Christianity and Industrial Society Research Institute, 2010.

Park, Yoon Jung. "The Chinese Diaspora in Africa: An Introduction." *The China Monitor* (July 2010): 9-13.

Peccod, Antoine. "Thinking and Rethinking Ethnic Economies." *Diaspora: A Journal of Transnational Studies*, 9.3 (Winter 2000): 439-462.

Pike, Frank N. "Chinese Globalization and Migration to Europe." Working Paper No. 94, Paper presented at the Research Seminar, Center for Comparative Immigration Studies, University of California at San Diego, 9 March, 2004. Available at http://escholarship.org/uc/item/3gv6w1bj;jsessionid=EAE6A108B2E1FA51109BCF45D4E7A5EB

Portes, Alejandro. "Conclusion: Towards a New Model: the Origins and Effects of Transnational Activities." Ethnic and Racial Studies 22.4 (March 1999): 463-477.

_____. "Introduction: The Debates and Significance of Immigrant Transnationalism." *Global Networks* 1.3 (July 2001):181-194.

Portes, Alejandro, William Haller, and Lius E. Guarnizo. "Transnational Entrepreneurs: An Alternative Form of Immigrant Economic Adaptation." *American Sociological Review* (April 2002): 67: 278-298. Available at http://www.jstor.org/pss/3088896/

Pries, Ludger, ed. *New Transnational Spaces: International Migration andTransnational Companies in the Early Twenty-First Century.* London: Routledge, 2001.

_____. *New Approaches to Migration? Transnational Communities and the Transformation of Home.* London: Routledge, 2002.

_____. *Rethinking Transnationalism: The Meso-link of Organizations.* New York: Routledge, 2008.

_____. "The Disruption of Social and Geographic Space. Mexican-U.S. Migration and the Emergence of Transnational Social Spaces." *International Sociology* 16 (1) (March 2001): 55-74.

Pyle, Jean, L. "Globalization, Transnational Migration, and Gendered Care Work: Introduction." *Globalization*s Vol 3, No 3 (September 2006): 283-295. Available at http://ritsumei-ssgp.jp/sansyagp/lecture/lecture-pdf/Kyoung-Hee/100628Globalization_Tansnational_%20Migration_%20and_%20Gendered_Care%20_Work.pdf

Rath Jan, ed. *Immigrant Businesses: The Economic, Political and Social Environment.* Basingstoke, Macmillan, 2000.

Robinson, William I. "Saskia Sassen and the Sociology of Globalization: A Critical Appraisal." *Sociological Analysis*, Vol 3, No. 1 (Spring 2009). Available at http://www.soc.ucsb.edu/faculty/robinson/Assets/pdf/Saskia%20Sassen.pdf

Rubesh, Ted. "Foundations for the Nations: The Nations in Genesis 1-12." *A Cultured Faith.* Edited by Prabo Mihindukulasuriya and Ivor Poobalan. Colombo: CTS Publishing, 2011.

Samers, Michael. "Immigration and the Global City Hypothesis: Towards an Alternative Research Agenda." *International Journal of Urban and Regional Research* vol. 26, no. 2 (June 2002): 389-402.

Santos, Narry. "Diaspora Occurrences In The Bible And Their Contexts In Missions. *Lausanne Committee for World Evangelization.* Available at http://www.lausanneworldpulse.com/themedarticles.php/1104?pg=all

Shafir, Gershon, ed. *The Citizenship Debates: A Reader.* Minneapolis: University of Minnesota Press, 1998.

Sheppard, Eric. "The Spaces and Times of Globalization: Place, Scale, Networks and Positionality." *Economic Geography* vol. 78, no. 3 (July 2002).

REFERENCES

Smith, Michael and Luis Guarnizo, eds. *Transnationalism from Below*. Piscataway: Transaction Publishers, 1998.

Smith, Michael P. *Transnational Urbanism: Locating Globalization*. Oxford: Blackwell Publishing, 2003.

Smith, Robert C. "Migrant Membership as an Instituted Process: Comparative Insights from the Mexican and Italian Cases." WPTC-01-23, Conference on Transnational Migration: Comparative Perspectives, Princeton University June 30-July 1, 2001. Available at http://www.ime.gob.mx/investigaciones/bibliografias/smith9.pdf

Somerville, Will and Madeleine Sumption. "Immigration and the Labour Market : Theory, Evidence and Policy." Equality and Human Rights Commission & Migration Policy Institute, March 2009. Available at http://www.migrationpolicy.org/pubs/Immigration-and-the-Labour-Market.pdf

Taylor, Matthew, Michelle Moran-Taylor, and Debra R. Ruiz. "Land, Ethnic and Gender Change: Transnational Migration and its Effects on Guatemalan Lives and Landscapes." *Geoforum*, 37 (2006): 41-67. Available at http://www.ssrc.org/workspace/images/crm/new_publication_3/%7Be625c1f4-8650-de11-afac-001cc477ec70%7D.pdf/

Thapan, Meenakshi. *Transnational Migration and the Politics of Identity*. New York: Sage Publications, 2005.

Tira, Sadiri Joy, *Filipino Kingdom Workers: An Ethnographic Study in Diaspora Missiology*. Doctor of Missiology Dissertation, Western Seminary, Portland, OR, 2008.

Tira, Sadiri Joy and Enoch Wan. "The Filipino Experience in Diasporamissions: A Case Study of Christian Communities in Contemporary Contexts." Commission VII: Christian Communities in Contemporary Contexts, Edinburgh, June 12-13, 2009.

Tobler, Waldo. *Migration: Ravenstein, Thornwaite, and Beyond*. University of California. Available at http://docs.google.com/viewer?a=v&q=cache:Y0BIVYdg77wJ:citeseerx.ist.psu.edu/viewdoc/download%3Fdoi%3D10.1.1.146.4337%26rep%3Drep1%26type%3Dpdf+migration+theory&hl=en&gl=us&pid=bl&srcid=ADGEEShYKT6p0Bn0e2HfUOAaAt3PrNin7uFFkKhm3P2WDnJeDIk1QW_nGDgbRvSTaEjfulFLXxVcuuCOZXPEXVptV7yAE6Xw5_GM5i9zh-GTcffcrcnkZx-J1a1o2QnF1UVSBp_Z3V_S&sig=AHIEtbRjPQ5bitAZh_wKPMVOuU9isQGDYw/

Truong, Thanh-Dam and Des Gasper, eds. *Transnational Migration: The Migration-Development-Security-Nexus*. Berlin: Springer, 2011.

Tsianos, Vassilis et al. "Theory and Method of an Ethnographic Analysis of Border Regimes." Working paper No. 55, University of Sussex, Sussex Centre for Migration Research, April 2009. Available at http://www.sussex.ac.uk/migration/documents/mwp55.pdf

Tsianos, Vassilis, Sabine Hess, and Serhat Karakayali. "Transnational Migration and the Emergence of the European Border Regime: An Ethnographic Analysis." *European Journal of Social Theory* Vol 13, no. 3 (August 2010): 373-387.

Vertovec, Steve. "Super-Diversity and Its Implications." *Ethnic and Racial Studies*, Vol 30, no 6 (November 2007): 1024-1054.

Vertovec, Steve. "Trends and Impacts of Migrant Transnationalism." Working Paper No. 3, Centre on Migration, Policy and Society, University of Oxford, 2004. Available at http://www.compas.ox.ac.uk/fileadmin/files/pdfs/WP0403.pdf/

Vertovec, Steven and Robin Cohen, eds. *Conceiving Cosmopolitanism: Theory, Context and Practice*. Oxford: Oxford University Press, 2003.

Waldinger, Roger and David Fitzgerald. "Transnationalism in Question." *American Journal of Sociology* 109 (2004):1177-95.

Watts, Julie René. *Immigration Policy and the Challenge of Globalization: Unions and Employers in Unlikely Alliance*. Ithaca: Cornell University Press, 2002.

Werbner, Pnina. "Global Pathways. Working Class Cosmopolitans and the Creation of Transnational Ethnic Worlds." *Social Anthropology* 7.1 (February 1999): 17-35.

Wimmer, Andreas and Nina Glick-Schiller. "Methodological Nationalism and Beyond: Nation-State Building, Migration and the Social Sciences." *Global Networks*, vol. 2, pp. 301–334, 2002. Available at http://www.public.asu.edu/~nornradd/documents/B52.pdf/

Wong, Lloyd L. "Globalization and Transnational Migration: A Study of Recent Chinese Capitalist Migration from the Asian Pacific to Canada." *International Sociology September 1997, 12: 329-351*. Available at http://iss.sagepub.com/content/12/3/329.abstract/

Zaretsky, Tuvya. "Diaspora Missiology Report." *Lausanne Consultation on Jewish Evangelism*, 2007. Available at www.lcje.net/papers/2007/Zaretsky.doc

Selected Publications & Presentations on "Diaspora Missiology" by Enoch Wan

PRESENTATIONS:

2003 Jun Wan, Enoch. "Mission among the Chinese Diaspora: A Case Study of Migration and Mission." American Society Missiology Techny Tower, IL.

2008 Apr "The Filipino Experience in Diaspora Missions: A Case Study of Mission Initiatives from the Majority World Churches." North West EMS Regional Meeting, Portland, OR.

2009 Jun "The Filipino Experience in Diaspora Missions: A Case Study of Christian Communities in Contemporary Contexts." Sadiri Joy Tira & Enoch Wan. Commission VII: Christian Communities in Contemporary Contexts, Edinburgh, June 12-13.

2010 May "Korean Diaspora: From Hermit Kingdom to Kingdom Ministry." Korean Diaspora Forum, Seoul, Korea.

2010 Apr "Rethinking Missiology in the Context of the 21st Century: Global Demographic Trends and Diaspora Missiology." Lausanne Diaspora Educators Consultation in Europe, OCMS, Oxford, UK, April 16.

2010 May "Relational Paradigm for Ministry in the Context of 21st Century." Special Lectureship, OCMS, Oxford, UK, May 20.

2010 May "Global People and Diaspora Missiology, From Edinburgh 2010 to Tokyo 2010." Plenary session at Tokyo 2010, May 11th-14th. Video clip available at http://www.ustream.tv/recorded/6897559/

2010 Sept With Yaw Attah Edu-Bekoe "Diversity of Ghanaian Diaspora in the U.S.: Ministering to the Diverse Ghanaian Communities through Ghanaian Congregations." 2010 North America Missions Leaders Conference.

2010 Oct "Ministering to Scattered Peoples – Moving to Reach the People on the Move." Cape Town 2010. Available at http://conversation.lausanne.org/en/conversations/detail/11438

2011 Jan "A Relational Perspective on the Root of Human Problems around the World." Commencement Address, William Carey International University, January 4.

2011 Jan "Research Methodology for Diaspora Missiology and Diaspora missions." North Central Regional EMS Conference , Trinity Evangelical Divinity School, Deerfield, February 26.

2011 Feb "Global Status of Diaspora Ministry." Webseminar, The Mission Exchange, Global Issues Update. Available at http://www.themissionexchange.org/

2011 Feb "Multitudes Reaching A People-group by Reconciliation." JEMA (Japan Evangelical Missionary Association) Annual Retreat, Feb14.

2011 Feb "The Practice of Diaspora missions Globally and in Japan locally." JEMA (Japan Evangelical Missionary Association) Annual Retreat, Feb 15.

2011 Feb "Relational Paradigm for Ministry in Japanese Context," JEMA (Japan Evangelical Missionary Association) Annual Retreat, Feb16.

2011 Feb "Research Methodology for Diaspora Missiology and Diaspora Missions. " Presentation at North Central Regional EMS Conference, Trinity Evangelical Divinity School, Deerfield, IL., February 26.

2011 Sept With Larry E. Caldwell. "Riots in the City: Replacing 19th Century Urban Training Models with Relevant 'Urbanized' Training Models for the 21st Century." Evangelical Missiological Society Annual Meeting, September 29-October 1, 2011.

PUBLICATIONS:

Wan, Enoch (Ed.). *Missions Within Reach: Intercultural Ministries in Canada*. Hong Kong: China Alliance Press, 1995.

Wan, Enoch. "Rethinking Missiological Research Methodology: Exploring a New Direction." *Global Missiology* (October 2003). Available at www.GlobalMissiology.org.

Wan, Enoch. "Mission among the Chinese Diaspora: A Case Study of Migration and Mission." *Missiology* 31 no. 1 (2003): 35.

Wan, Enoch. "The Phenomenon of the Diaspora: Missiological Implications for Christian Missions." In A*sian American Christianity: A Reader.* Edited by Viji Nakka-Cammauf and Timothy Tseng. The Pacific Asian American and Canadian Christian Education project (PAACCE) and the Institute for the Study of Asian American Christianity (ISAAC), 2004.

Wan, Enoch. "The Paradigm and Pressing Issues of Inter-disciplinary Research Methodology." *Global Missiology* (January 2005). Available at www.GlobalMissiology.org

Wan, Enoch. "Missionary Strategy in the Epistle to the Romans." *To the End of the Earth,* Hong Kong Association of Christian Missions Ltd. (July-Sept., 2005):1-2. (in Chinese)

Wan, Enoch. "The Paradigm and Pressing Issues of Inter-disciplinary Research Methodology." *Global Missiology* (January 2005a). Available at www.GlobalMissiology.Org/

Wan, Enoch and Mark Hedinger. "Understanding 'Relationality' from a Trinitarian Perspective." *Global Missiology* (January 2006). Available at www.GlobalMissiology.org/

Wan, Enoch. "The Paradigm of 'Relational Realism.'" *Occasional Bulletin* 19:2 (Spring 2006): 1-4.

REFERENCES

Wan, Enoch. "Expectation and Reflection." On the occasion of Paul Hiebert's Passing. April 2007. Available at http://paul-timothy.net/pages/gm/wan_reflections_on_paul_hiebert_4_2007.pdf/

Wan, Enoch. "Relational Theology and Relational Missiology." *Occasional Bulletin* 21:1 (Winter 2007): 1-7.

Wan, Enoch & Linda Gross. "Christian Missions to Diaspora Groups: A Diachronic General Overview and Synchronic Study of Contemporary U.S." *Global Missiology* vol. 3, no. 2 (2008). Available at www.GlobalMissiology.org

Wan, Enoch. "Core Values of Mission Organization in the Cultural Context of the 21st Century." *Global Missiology*, (January 2009). Available at www.GolbalMissiology.org

Wan, Enoch. "Diaspora Couple Priscilla and Aquila: A Model Family in Action for Mission." *Global Missiology*, April 2009. Available at www.GlobalMissiology.org (Originally published in Chinese, *Great Commission Bi-monthly*, vol. 79 (April 2009).

Wan, Enoch and Johnny Yee-chong Wan. "Relational Study of the Trinity and the Epistle to the Philippians." *Global Missiology* (April 2010). Available at www.GlobalMissiology.org/

Wan, Enoch and Kevin Penman. "The 'Why,' 'How' and 'Who' of Partnership in Christian Missions," *Global Missiology* April 2010. Available at www.GlobalMissiology.org/

Wan, Enoch and Jeff Bagget. "A Theology of Partnership: Implications for Implementation by a Local Church." *Global Missiology* (April, 2010). Available at www.GlobalMissiology.org

Wan, Enoch & Sadiri Joy Tira. "Diaspora Missiology and Mission in the Context of the 21st Century." *Torch Trinity Journal* Volume 13, No.1, 46-6 (May 30, 2010). Seoul, Korea.

Wan, Enoch. "Global People and Diaspora Missiology, From Edinburgh 2010 to Tokyo 2010." In *Handbook of Global Mission: Consultation, 92-106.Celebration*, May 11th-14th, 2010.

Wan, Enoch. "Rethinking Missiology in the context of the 21st Century: Global Demographic Trends and Diaspora Missiology." *Great Commission Research Journal*, Volume 2, Issue 1 (Summer 2010). Available at http://apps.biola.edu/gcr/volumes/2/issues/1/articles/7.

Wan, Enoch. "'Mission' and Missio Dei." In *Missionshift: Global Mission Issues in the Third Millenniom*. Edited by David J. Hesselgrave and Ed Stetzer. Nashville,TN: B&H Publishing Group, 2010.

Wan, Enoch. "Diaspora missions Strategy in the Context of the United Kingdom in the 21st Century." T*ransformation: An International Journal of Holistic Mission Studies.* OCMS 28.1 (January 2011):3-13. Available at http://trn.sagpub.com/

Wan, Enoch & Yaw Attah Edu-Bekoe. "Diversity of Ghanaian Diaspora in the U.S.: Ministering to the Diverse Ghanaian Communities Through Ghanaian Congregations." In *Mosaic: Engaging the Beauty of God's Kingdom Diversity*. Edited by

Scott Moreau and Beth Snodderly. Evangelical Missiological Society Series, no. 19 (2011c).

Wan, Enoch. "Celebration, Consultation and Congress: From Edinburg 2010 to Tokyo 2010." In *Evangelical and Frontier Mission Perspectives on the Global Progress of the Gospel.* Edited by Beth Snodderly and A.Scott Moreau. Oxford: Renum, 2011.

Strategies:

- ¹ >to< & ² >through< (129)
- ³ >by< & >beyond< (131) } 4 types of strategy (129-13
- ⁴ >with< (133)

Strategy in MMP (114)

! Strategy in JMP (124)

Models:

kangaroo model (136)

model over strategy → Jesus (119)

Printed in Germany
by Amazon Distribution
GmbH, Leipzig